FOUNDATIONS FOR EXCELLENCE

23 award-winning articles from *Hospital & Health Services Administration*

Commemorative Edition

Pluribus Press
DIVISION OF TEACH 'EM INC.

CHICAGO
1982

Library of Congress Catalog Card Number:
82-60398

International Standard Book Number:
0-931028-32-9

American College of Hospital Administrators
840 North Lake Shore Drive
Chicago, Illinois 60611

Pluribus Press, Division of Teach 'em, Inc.
160 East Illinois Street
Chicago, Illinois 60611

Printed in the United States of America

Contents

Foreword

Is it true, as the French have suggested in their popular adage, that "the more it changes, the more it is the same?"

If you translate "it" as "hospital and health services administration," and, as a corollary, the attendant forces which challenge our profession, you might find it interesting to assess the prize-winning articles in this compilation against that maxim.

What has happened to our profession since these articles first appeared in our journal? Have the encroachments on the practitioner lessened or increased? Has education for the profession changed? Are our management problems more complex?

To answer these and many other questions that may come to mind—in short, to compare Yesterday with Today—we recommend this collection to you. It contains twenty-three winners of the College's Edgar C. Hayhow Award.

This award was created by the Board of Regents, as it was then identified, of the American College of Hospital Administrators, and the first award was granted at the third Congress on Administration in 1960.

The award is a tribute to Edgar C. Hayhow, Ph.D., the fourteenth president of our professional society, and the director for many years of the East Orange General Hospital in New Jersey.

The Hayhow award is granted annually at the time of the mid-winter Congress on Administration, our management-oriented educational meeting, to the author of the article judged "outstanding" among those published in the previous year in *Hospital & Health Services Administration* (née *Hospital Administration*), the College's scholarly journal.

The selection of the prize-winning paper is made each year by a special Committee on the Article of the Year Award, appointed by the Board of Governors.

As readers of the ACHA's journal, you know that each issue contains a biographical sketch highlighting the professional careers of the author/contributors. In this special collection, we are pleased to include the positions each individual held at the time the article was written, as well as the current positions of all the award winners: from Oswald Hall, Ph.D., 1959, to Austin Ross, 1981.

It is a pleasure to share with you this collection of the articles assessed as the best published in the College's journal during the past two decades.

It is also gratifying to include this volume in the many significant events and publications which will showcase the celebration of the College's 50th Anniversary: 1933–1983. This anniversary is an important event, and the annual Edgar C. Hayhow Award is an important part of our society's professional activities.

Charles T. Wood, FACHA
Chairman, 1981–1982
American College of Hospital Administrators

August, 1982

Notes on Authors

Edgar C. Hayhow Award-winning Articles

1981* "Organizational Linkages: Management Issues and Implications." Austin Ross, FACHA, wrote this article while in his current position as vice president of the Virginia Mason Hospital and administrator of the Mason Clinic in Seattle. Mr. Ross was a Governor for District #7 in the College between 1979–1983. He also serves as clinical professor of the University of Washington's School of Public Health and Community Medicine.

1980 "What Motivates People To Work Effectively?" David Babnew, Jr., Ph.D., LL.D., and FACHA, wrote the 1980 Hayhow award-winning paper while in his present position as president and founding principal of Management and Planning Associates, Inc., Miami Lakes, FL.

1979 "The Management of Disruptive Conflicts." Robert Veninga, Ph.D., was associate professor and associate dean of the School of Public Health at the University of Minnesota in Minneapolis at the time he wrote this article. He continues to be associated with that school and that program, currently serving as an associate professor in the Department of Health Education of the School of Public Health.

1978 "Evaluating the Performance of the Chief Executive Officer" by James D. Harvey, FACHA, was written while he was president of the Hillcrest Medical Center, Tulsa, OK, his current position. Mr. Harvey was ACHA chairman in 1975–1976 and in 1972 received the College's Gold Medal Award for Excellence in Hospital Administration.

1977 "Old and New Thinking about Hospital Payments." Everett A. Johnson, Ph.D., FACHA, wrote this paper, his second Hay-

*Refers to the year the winning article was published.

how winner (see 1972), while he headed his own consulting service, The Dunes Group, in Chesterton, IN. FACHA Johnson is now the director of the Master of Health Administration Program in the Institute of Hospital Administration at Georgia State University, Atlanta.

1976 "Evaluation of Administrative and Organizational Effectiveness in Hospitals." This was the second Hayhow award-winning article written by Charles M. Ewell, Jr., Ph.D., FACHA (see 1973). When he wrote this paper he was directing health care consulting for Arthur Young & Company from the firm's Los Angeles office. Dr. Ewell is currently the national director of health care for Arthur Young & Company.

1975 "The Ashland Plan: An Ambulatory Care Outreach Alternative for a Community Hospital," was written by John N. Simpson, FACHA, while he was administrator of the Richmond Memorial Hospital in Virginia. He was a Regent of the College for the State of Virginia for two terms: 1976 to 1982. Mr. Simpson has remained at Richmond as the chief executive officer; he now has the title of president.

1974 "The Crisis in the Health Care System: A Contrary Opinion." S. David Pomrinse, M.D., FACHA, wrote his award-winning paper while he was the director of the Mount Sinai Hospital in New York City. Currently, Dr. Pomrinse is president of the Greater New York Hospital Association.

1973 "Conflict of Interest: Ethical Dilemma" was written by Charles M. Ewell, Jr., when he was a DHEW Fellow at the University of Wisconsin, Madison, and a member of the faculty in that university's Program in Health Services Administration. This was the first of two prize articles by Dr. Ewell (see 1976).

1972 "An Emerging Medical Staff Organization." Everett A. Johnson, Ph.D., FACHA, wrote this paper, the first of his two Hayhow award-winners (see 1977), when he was administrator of The Methodist Hospital of Gary, IN. He served as chairman of the ACHA in 1971–1972.

1971 "Conflicting Economic Pressures in Health Care." James R.

Jeffers, Ph.D., was the director of the Health Economics Research Center at the University of Iowa, Iowa City, when he wrote his prize-winning article. At present, Dr. Jeffers is a professor in the Department of Economics at Iowa.

1970 "Professional Development Needs in Hospital Administration." This paper was written by Louis E. Davis, Ph.D., when he was professor of Organizational Sciences in the Graduate School of Business Administration at the University of California, Los Angeles. At present, Dr. Davis is chairman of the Center for Quality of Work in Life and a professor in the School of Business Administration at UCLA.

1969 "The Social Responsibility of General Hospitals" was written by Bright M. Dornblaser, FACHA, while he was the director of the Graduate Program in Hospital and Health Care Administration at the University of Minnesota, Minneapolis. He currently is professor and division head in that same program at Minnesota.

1968 "Applying Economic Concepts to Hospital Care." This article was written by Paul J. Feldstein, Ph.D., while he was an associate professor and director, Health Economics Group, Program in Hospital Administration, School of Public Health, University of Michigan, Ann Arbor. Dr. Feldstein currently holds two professorships at the University of Michigan: one in the Department of Hospital Administration, the other in the Department of Economics.

1967 "When Occupations Meet: Professions in Trouble" was written by Edward Gross, Ph.D., when he was professor of Sociology and Industrial Relations at the University of Minnesota, Minneapolis. At present, he is professor of Sociology at the University of Washington in Seattle.

1966 "A Philosophical Dimension of Administration." Leonard A. Duce, Ph.D., HFACHA, was dean of the Graduate School and professor of Philosophy at Trinity University, San Antonio, TX, when he wrote his award-winning paper. Following his retirement from Trinity in 1974, he served for a number of years as president of the Texas Military Institute, also in San Antonio. The ACHA granted him Honorary Fellowship in 1972. At the time of his death on June 9, 1979, Dr. Duce was serving as director of the Interagency Institute for Federal Health Care Executives.

1965 "The Administrator and Policy Processes." This article was written by John W. Hennessey, Jr., Ph.D., while he was professor of Business Administration and associate dean at the Amos Tuck School of Business Administration at Dartmouth College, Hanover, NH. Dr. Hennessey is the current Charles H. Jones Professor of Policy Studies at Dartmouth.

1964 "The Impact of the Hospital on the Physician, the Patient and the Community" by George Rosen, M.D., Ph.D., was written while he was professor of Health Education in the School of Public Health and Administrative Medicine at Columbia University, New York City. He served many years as the editor of the *Journal of Public Health*. Dr. Rosen was a professor and a scholar of the History of Science and Medicine at Yale University, New Haven, CT, at the time of his death at age sixty-six on July 27, 1977.

1963 "The Spontaneous Development of Informal Organization." E. Jackson Baur, Ph.D., was a professor of Sociology and Anthropology at the University of Kansas, Lawrence, at the time his paper was published. Now nearing retirement, Dr. Baur has continued his affiliation with Kansas as a professor of Sociology.

1962 "The Dynamics of Professionalism: The Case of Hospital Administration" was written by Harold L. Wilensky, Ph.D., while he was on the faculty of the Department of Sociology at the University of Michigan, Ann Arbor. He is currently a professor in the Department of Sociology at the University of California in Berkeley.

1961 "The Qualities of an Administrator" was written by Ralph N. Traxler, Jr., Ph.D., while he was an associate professor of Business Administration at Emory University in Atlanta. He is currently a professor in the Breech School of Business Administration at Drury College in Springfield, MO.

1960 "Problem-oriented Administration." At the time he wrote this article, Warren G. Bennis, Ph.D., was an associate professor in the School of Industrial Management at the Massachusetts Institute of Technology, Cambridge. For a number of years he served as president of the University of Cincinnati. He is currently a professor in the Department of Management and Policy Science in the School of Business Administration at the University of Southern California in Los Angeles.

1959 "Motivation and Morale." The first Edgar C. Hayhow Award-winning article was written by Oswald Hall, Ph.D., professor of Sociology at the University of Toronto, a position he still retains. Dr. Hall also contributed in 1956 to the first edition of the ACHA's journal, then a quarterly titled, *Hospital Administration.*

American College of Hospital Administrators Chairmen Officers/President 1981–1982

American College of Hospital Administrators
Board of Governors
1981–1982

Organizational Linkages: Management Issues and Implications

Austin Ross

The linking of complex health organizations into models is a critical and timely topic as these relationships have tremendous potential for affecting both quality and cost of health care. This is not to say that these models necessarily always improve quality or reduce costs, but the potential to accomplish these goals is there. In recent times, the rate of growth of linked arrangements might be compared with the Oklahoma land rush. Linking seems to be popular with almost everyone.

It also is fascinating to observe so many hybrid models. The corporate model is substantially different from more modest shared services consortium programs. Today, organizations concentrate on linkages between hospitals; but in the years ahead, relationships will be prospering between hospitals and related group practices, between nursing homes and home care agencies, and other varieties of health service facilities. A number of these relationships are developing because of the reintroduction of marketing and competition onto the health scene. Evidence of these new marketing forces may be found, for example, in the growth of privately sponsored health maintenance organizations in such cities as Minneapolis, Minnesota.[1] While the marketing implications may be more visible in health maintenance organization programs, marketing plays a much greater role in the more traditional health service field. A healthy dose of free enterprise appears to be surfacing in a field which has been virtually written off by health economists as one dominated by isolated units, providing inefficient services, enveloped in medical politics, and operating in an environment where traditional principles of supply and demand were inapplicable.

[1]Jon B. Christianson, Ph.D., and Walter McClure, Ph.D., "Competition in the Delivery of Medical Care." *New England Journal of Medicine,* October 11, 1979, pp. 812–818.

The more visible models appear to be unique and are headed by innovative leaders. Successful models seem to develop somewhat independently of each other, almost as if a germ of the idea was planted in different areas of the country and adapted to local conditions.

A rich mixture of incentives contributes to the growth of these linked organizations. There is a financial incentive to increase profitability by increasing volume in order to improve the economy of scale. There is the age-old need to market services to protect and/or improve patient referrals. Survival incentives are popular particularly with centrally-located urban hospitals which face competition from suburban medical facility growth. Some institutions respond to an incentive to serve rural populations, which, in turn, stimulates growth and linkages between urban and rural physicians. A common thread evident in most of these successful models is the matching of executive leadership in an environment of institutional expansion and solvency. This combination of leadership and available resources caters, to a degree, to the institutional and personal ego. In other words, linked programs develop because of *many* complex reasons rather than just a few.

Serious students of health systems may be frustrated somewhat because, oftentimes, these organizational relationships do not develop according to any carefully-prepared long range plan. Indeed, many seem to grow in response to short range concerns coupled with the ability of those involved to recognize opportunities. A common organizational characteristic seems to be that, at each critical point in the model's development, leaders were present who understood the need to take risks.

Herein, a vertically- or horizontally-integrated organization is defined as a group of institutions with a common set of goals; some sharing of resources and management; and service to a specific population, one not necessarily limited or defined by geography. These organizations need not be under common ownership, although the more highly integrated, the more the system will include characteristics of single ownership, integrated management, and a common medical staff. Absence of more than one of these characteristics makes it more difficult to achieve the necessary critical mass sufficient to control and manage change.

Vertical vs. Horizontal

The difference between the vertically-integrated structure and a horizontally-integrated structure has to do with the service mix. In a vertically-integrated structure something happens to the product—in this case, the patient. The patient in a rural hospital, for example, who requires specialty services is transferred to a central institution. In turn, the patient is returned to a community hospital or a community home care agency for continuing services, all services being linked within one organizational framework.

In a horizontally-integrated organization, the patient tends to be stationary and the organizational units tend to duplicate or complement services. These linked organizations will tend to relate closer to sharing of administrative services than medical services.

The relationship between two hospitals can begin with a horizontal organization where both belong to a shared service program and then change to a vertical arrangement when referral patterns are affected and a two-way flow of patients begins to take place. The sharing of administrative services is much simpler than the sharing of medical services.

Within a single hospital, activities are usually highly specialized, interdependent, and interrelated, so when multiple hospitals are linked with other types of health service units, the implications to the management processes can be significant. The intent here is to explore a few of these management implications associated with linkage.

Management Scale

The administrator of a 400-bed specialty/tertiary hospital operates with clearly-defined levels of authority and responsibility, and a staff including associate and assistant administrators. He or she is responsible for providing leadership and direction. By sheer physical proximity to a single institution's problems, the administrator can help associates and assistants mature and cope with change. The management processes can be nurtured daily.

If the scene shifts and this chief executive officer provides management for units geographically separated by distance or organizational characteristics (i.e., group practice), additional challenges will be encountered. Under this set of circumstances, the chief executive officer has to cope with the frustrations of directing from a distance, without the luxury of day-to-day contact. This can be quite frustrating to the traditionally trained executive, used to operating a closely-knit team. In establishing linkages, the chief executive officer experiences a greater margin for error in the process of selecting a manager for an outlying unit who will accept centralized management while still providing on-the-spot decision-making capabilities.

One problem is the difficulty of achieving an economy of scale through centralized control when more autonomy is provided the remote unit manager.[2] As the number of units increases, pressure grows to create a corporate structure. Controls are achieved through development of specialized management and reporting services. Visits to the remote units are made by financial officers, purchasing agents, or other staff specialists. Centralized management services, in turn, if not sensitive to the process, can detract from the autonomy of the local unit manager, which may have an adverse affect on managerial growth and create local vulnerability.

It is necessary to discover the appropriate balance. This is one of the challenges facing newly-linked organizations. In fact, the achievement of economy of scale may be less important over the long run than the need to initiate strong, effective local management, such as administrators who can function without a high degree of over-the-shoulder advice and control from a central office.

In terms of internal operation, the destruction of barriers between departments in a single institution frequently is complicated by the manager's understandable need to maintain control of the decision-making process affecting his or her department. In complex linked structures with more vested interests, these problems increase.

Management Philosophy

One element of the solution to this management dichotomy rests with the ability of the organization to articulate its managerial philosophy. It may be helpful to describe a few simple principles which, if genuinely applied, may reduce the level of friction and frustration associated with multiple unit operation:

First, linked institutions should operate with a single set of written objectives relating to patient care and administration. These objectives should be reviewed annually and serve as visible symbols of common purpose;

Second, administrators of the organizations must be selected to identify with broader group missions;

Third, department heads within individual units must be discouraged from playing one unit off another. For example, usually there are a number of shared services found in these organizations.

[2]R. Toomey, "Vertically Integrated Hospital System." In: Proceedings of the First National Forum on Hospital and Health Affairs, Durham, N.C., Duke University, 1965.

A hospital, for example, may furnish engineering services to an adjoining group practice. A request from the group practice administration for engineering services should receive the same service priority as one from a hospital department, even though the engineers are hospital-based. This is a very important aspect of management philosophy which must be supported by those in an integrated operation;

Fourth, if possible, administrators, from time to time, should be rotated from one unit to another and transfer preferences should be given to those who most closely identify with central mission statements. The movement of managers will reinforce the importance of understanding the overall program. All should be charged with maintaining system-wide discipline; and

Fifth, adequate overlap should be developed in board, medical staff, and administrative assignments. Top executives should be vested with more than one responsibility; for example, an administrator of an adjacent group practice could function as a board member of the hospital. Chief executive officers, in particular, must place a high priority on maintaining organizational surveillance relative to integration.

Allocating Management Time

Today, hospitals and other health institutions still appear to be under-managed. There seem to be too many administrators still unwilling to bite the bullet to allocate more dollars for enhancing the management processes. If one accepts this statement, multi-organizational arrangements must be approached with great caution. It is one matter to "close the deal" regarding a service relationship with a second institution, yet quite another to produce an end result which will ensure that the relationship is a building block for future arrangements rather than the weight that sinks the ship.

In an expanding multi-unit program, the issue of centralization versus decentralization must be addressed. Should a corporate headquarters, staffed with individuals who function as system specialty managers, be developed or does one create a management process where a local unit manager is linked with an existing associate or assistant administrator in the larger urban center?

One advantage of developing the core corporate staff is the creation of a structure with precise assignments and priorities. Those who operate as members of this core are not unduly confused by having to deal with as wide a spectrum of detail as those saddled with internal operating responsibilities.

On the other hand, creating a separate core staff can detract from the unit administrator's opportunities to participate fully in developing internal systems and managing the total process. As a result, the unit manager may have more difficulty in developing enthusiasm for the total management process.

While the more traditional approach in multi-institutional organizations is to develop a core staff of specialists to manage the process, there are variations which can work very effectively. One variation is found in an urban/rural network system where the rural hospital administrator is matched with one of the administrative officers in the larger urban hospital. Thus each of the four or five local unit administrators can have an inhouse "preceptor." This has the advantage of being able to mobilize shared core staff people more rapidly because of the vested interest that the urban hospital staff administrator develops in the remote or related unit.

Organizational Arrogance

Success in building relationships with other institutions and health facilities depends on support and endorsement from the top. The chief executive officer does not develop a program by dispatching an assistant administrator into the field to make an arrangement. The appearance of organizational arrogance must be avoided, meaning chief executive officers of larger institutions must recognize that they may be out of touch with the complexities of operating smaller hospitals or health units. The executives of larger hospitals have backup and expertise available, while the administrator of a smaller hospital operates as a generalist and without this staff redundancy. It is very important for the relationship between two units to be enriched by active participation and involvement between the chief executive officers, regardless of the size of the units involved.

In an urban/rural linkage, it is critically important that each refrain from imposing its own set of values on his new colleagues in the alternate setting. A sixteen-bed coronary care unit in a large hospital does not operate with the same set of problems found in a combined two-bed surgical special care and coronary care unit in a 25-bed hospital in rural America. Relationships between institutions prosper when institutions and their leaders recognize their role of responding to needs rather than creating them. A strong case can be made for the fact that the urban center is not necessarily competent to make all judgmental decisions on the needs of smaller units.

Another challenge to be faced relates to the matter of executive power.[3] The application and use of power varies with circumstances and style, but one payoff associated with the larger, more complex structure does relate to the simple acquisition of power by individuals. Organizations grow as a result of strong leadership, and the chief executive officer is in a position to acquire a power base. On occasion, some executives lose sight of the mission of the organization and begin to build an unhealthy personal power base.

Trappings of power, including exotic suites, limousines, and even private airplanes have been known to appear from time to time. These trappings reinforce the power-hungry individual. Sometimes this "aura" stimulates organizational growth and prosperity. But such power, if not used with caution, can become destructive. More than one organization has fallen on hard times because of the failure of the executive or the institution to recognize the pitfalls of power and the need for balance. Executive humility is a valuable commodity and a particularly useful characteristic in multi-institutional arrangements.

Building the Team

The success of integrated/linked organizations depends on how successfully the organization develops the management team. The building of a management team usually relates to individual management style. It could be dangerous for the team to vest too much decision-making in a few individuals at the top. Most decisions ought to be made at lower levels. A valuable lesson can be learned from the Japanese where decision ratification seems to take place at each organizational level. By the time the issue reaches upper executive officers, often times the decision has already been "made" and the chief executive officer completes the process by simply "signing off" on the decision.

Separate units in a multi-unit system should be encouraged to exchange information horizontally and should operate as task-oriented teams. Members of such teams should even try to forget they are associated more with one unit than another. If this philosophy is successful-

[3]Terrence Moore and Duane Wood, "Power and the Hospital Executive." *Hospital & Health Services Administration,* Spring 1979, pp. 30–41.

ly applied from the top down, the process will build strong management teams.

The egocentric chief executive officer who stresses a top-heavy vertical structure runs a risk of depriving the organization of its full potential.

Staff "Burn-Out"

Another challenge facing executive officers in linked organizations relates to an issue of executive burn-out. The pressures are severe in linked structures. Fail-safe systems should be created to prevent depleting the energies of these individuals. The cumulative effect of pressure can force executives to the outer reaches of ability and endurance.

The individual officer ultimately must be responsible for identifying limits of personal endurance, but the system has a responsibility to avoid overstressing any individual for a prolonged period. Second level executives, medical staff colleagues, and board members should be mindful of the fact that natural leaders often operate with a disproportionate amount of missionary zeal and will often expend more physical and mental energy than is desirable. The chief executive officer has a responsibility to protect the organization and should select subordinates who are willing and capable of sharing these high energy loads. Too much reliance on a single individual is an invitation to disaster. Some superb executives have been lost to the field because they failed to recognize that their energy is not a limitless commodity. The career paths of some of these individuals could be compared with the flight of a meteor or the return of the sky lab!

Coping with Growth

Adapting administrative style to a rapidly changing system is an important challenge. The urban center acquiring management interests in nursing homes, group practices, or home care health agencies needs to address this issue carefully. Here the chief executive officer faces the dilemma of having to modify his management style. An individual who performs well as an assistant administrator in a large unit may be a poor director of a smaller self-contained unit one hundred miles or one hundred yards away.

There are significant differences in management styles required to function effectively in administration within a group practice setting as contrasted with a hospital. Nursing home administration demands a different approach from that of managing an acute hospital facility. Relatively little "career crossover" takes place, so the pool of administrators trained in two or three different types of institutions is limited. A solution to this problem is not intended here; the point being that managing different types of units creates a new dimension which must be recognized by the chief executive officer in coping with growth.

Nurturing is another factor. Lack of contact between chief executive officers and second or third levels of management will foster turnover in a single unit. When a goal is to develop successfully a multi-unit program, it becomes even more important to remember continuity and contact. Young administrators need role models and, ideally, more than one. Maintaining contact with chief operating executives helps to retain good young executives and provides the chief executive with a means of selecting future leaders.

Planning

The sequence of planning for growth in linked organizations is another issue. Long-range planning is an over-worked phrase, and while few will quibble with the desirability of creating a ten-year plan, most multi-institutional system executives will perhaps remember that growth frequently resulted from the ability of someone in the organization to recognize and take advantage of opportunities. Long-range planning is essential in order to identify an overall direction and to establish guideposts along the trail, but high priority must always be placed on developing short term flexibility. Managers should be oriented toward recognizing opportunities. Management support systems should respect and nourish those individuals who have that invaluable quality of being able to leap to a proper conclusion without being encumbered with all of the facts.

Some of the finer achievements in organizational growth develop from a response to contingencies, around which plans are developed, as opposed to developing programs around long-range plans.

Summary

While a number of the inventives to create linked systems are based on self-preservation, integrated multi-unit organizations can provide better patient care at lower costs. Appropriately linked systems produce better care because the units use an approach to the patient which is based on a broader, less fragmented perspective. Many linked organizations specialize in administrative or management services because these are easier to develop than the sharing of medical services. Multi-unit managers should not be satisfied with growth based on exchange of administrative services, even though these are easier to justify on a cost basis. Instead, they need to turn their attention to establishing shared medical systems. Better coordination of care beyond the hospital walls can make the difference between a patient's rapid recovery or a slower, more prolonged recovery situation. Anything that can be done to nudge the patient gently from level to level of care and avoid the toboggan ride that results once the patient has left the traditional hospital base should be pursued. Linking of resources narrows these differences in care.

Five Success Factors

In conclusion, one needs to ask the question: Why does one linked system prosper while another fails? The answer may lie in part in these five factors:

> First, successful ventures operate within an organizational framework characterized by track records of financial growth, stability, and innovative leadership;
>
> Second, successful ventures are found in organizations outwardly driven by virtue of the need to develop a broader service market for long-range survival;
>
> Third, successful ventures are characterized by the existence of a management team consisting of individuals who possess special doses of enthusiasm and missionary zeal, operating together with a synergistic output;
>
> Fourth, the successful ventures are those which operate with sufficient management reserves to cope with brushfires and still manage the future; and
>
> Fifth, successful ventures are found where leaders are perceptive to new trends. While emphasis in the past has often been placed on multi-hospital organizations, the future calls for linking with different types of health institutions, including group practices, nursing homes, and home care services.

This is an era where there is magic associated with linking. While these efforts are universally supported, a final note of caution is worth repeating. Executives in multi-institutional units should always reflect carefully on the management implications associated with expansion. Success depends on the ability to change management style, to accept new commitments, and finally, to recognize the possibility of personal and organizational vulnerability.

What Motivates People To Work Effectively?

David Babnew, Jr., Ph.D., LL.D.

Rapidly changing technology and activity in the health care field no longer affords time for the young executive to develop competence through an extended and sometimes haphazard trial-and-error apprenticeship. In view of today's increasing technological orientation to business activity, the young executive is often selected because of his professional competence in the specialized areas of accounting, purchasing, personnel, public relations, or machinery. Yet, such practices only increase the need for a simple and practical theory of management that will accelerate his acquisition of administrative capability.

The aspect of motivation over which most health care organizations can exercise the greatest control, yet which is frequently left to chance, is the selection of people. Even though the selection process is written about, discussed, advertised, maligned and generally worried over far more than any other single aspect of personnel management, it generally is not understood.

Possibly more executives are concerned than is necessary with the techniques of selecting people. From a realistic and practical viewpoint, it is more important to understand the logic of the selection process, and the context within which selection occurs, than it is to know just how one ought to decide whom to hire, promote, or reassign to different positions. Only when the logic and the context are understood do the various techniques of selection make sufficient sense to be used—and, for that matter, chosen—intelligently.

Why does selection have such a pronounced effect upon motivation? The extent to which a person commits his abilities to the accomplishment of his work—that is, his motivation—is the end product of a process highly influenced by many factors. Several of these inputs would include supervisory styles, compensation, communication, etc. Even when each of these are being managed reasonably well, another factor always stands out as the main determinant of motivation—does the person like the job.

If the person finds his work reasonably dignified, interesting, and it provides him with a personal sense of accomplishment, the experiences inherent in the job itself will elicit his energies and talents. Contrariwise, if a person finds his work a bore, or degrading, or incapable of providing occasional ego fulfillment, no amount of supervisory artistry or anything else can sustain his devotion to it. He may perform minimally, doing only what must be done, but he can rarely be expected to devote any conscientiousness, ingenuity, or extra effort on it. The vital and crucial difference lies in how well the job is suited to the person.

This degree of "fit" or "misfit" between a person and the work he is assigned to do is the consequence of a chain of management decisions. Actually, the chain begins with the decision to hire the person in the first place, and it generally leads to the most recent decision to place him in his current job. All of these decisions were selection decisions—the man, or woman, who was assessed in comparison to other available candidates and in the light of the apparent probability that he could handle each assignment capably enough to satisfy management. Unquestionably, a considerable portion of every person's potential motivation is already inherent in him when he is hired, or even before that, and is certainly a part of him at the time he is given a specific job.

Thus, motivation, in a sense, can be hired; and indeed, the same can be said for the lack of it. Perhaps, the quality of motivation that appears in a person's work is not so much instilled in him by managerial practices as *it is elicited from him by his job*. The individual is his own reservoir of whatever motivation he is capable of; he may draw upon it extravagantly or sparingly, but he derives it from himself and not necessarily from the people who pay his salary. Management can influence his willingness to draw from the reservoir, but they cannot, except at the time of selection, influence how much or what kind of motivation will be available to their health care facility through this person.

Potentialities for motivated action—that is, these reservoirs—vary enormously among people. Some persons, at the peak of their form, can pour truly heroic efforts into their work; others achieve much lesser height; and even then, more rarely, some persons can tolerate, good-naturedly and with undiminished efficiency, stresses that would turn others into nervous ineffectuals. All of these differences are present, at least latently, at the time a person is the object of some official's selection decision. Precisely for this reason, considerable attention should be given to the selection of new personnel, for this process determines so much of the kind and caliber of motivations that will be available to the organization in the future.

Motivating to Work Effectively

Pausing, we might ask: What motivates people to work effectively? Perhaps, as previously suggested, a challenging job, one which allows a feeling of achievement, growth, advancement, responsibility, enjoyment of the work itself, and earned recognition. Today, money motivation realistically no longer has the capacity to make people work harder simply to retain their membership in an organization. Current income operates like a price mechanism to distribute the labor supply among employers, but it fails to affect the job performance in any lasting or significant way.

We can get an important clue to what must be done to make salary an effective motivator by examining the problem of wage-related turnover. An employer who is willing to raise the price he pays for labor (above prevailing rates) usually can attract a few employees to his staff from other health care facilities' payroll. This, in fact, is a fairly common practice, especially during periods of labor shortage or with some occupational groups, such as registered nurses, who chronically are in short supply. Needless to say, there is no foolproof defense against such recruitment piracy.

For instance, if an attempt were made to build a monetary wall around a few "exposed" employees, namely, those employees who are attractive to a competitive employer, equitability would eventually compel an exorbitant general increase. A more realistic defense might be based on the psychology of the exposed employee. Such strategy concedes some losses, but concentrates on raising the price that the competitor must pay to a level that minimizes the losses.

The more favorable the mix of satisfactions and dissatisfactions at a health care facility, the larger the gap must be before an employee will seriously consider leaving his current place of employment. An organization with a relatively unfavorable mix becomes an easy target for another organization tempted to woo to its staff a few experienced employees. An organization with a relatively favorable mix is reasonably well protected. To make the gap attractive to the employees of such an organization, the "raiding" firm is compelled to raise its bid (money or other fringe benefits) to levels that quickly become uneconomical. Wise management realizes it is unnecessary to match every offer in a tight labor market in order to succeed in containing a threat of turnover. What is necessary is a level of overall satisfaction high enough to make it uneconomical for another organization to offer enough inducements to be tempting.

What motivates the employee to stay or leave, when he finds himself in a seller's market, is the apparent relative increment in the mix of satisfaction and dissatisfaction between his present employer and the would-be employer.

Monetary Motivators

Money can motivate—that is, influence action—only when the increment that is in prospect is large enough relative to existing income. Most salary increases, bonuses, and profitsharing plans (and many commission and incentive pay plans) do not provide an increment that is sufficiently large to motivate any action other than the purely passive one of remaining in the organization. Usually these enticements are not large enough to motivate extra effort, extra creativity, or any other kind of non-routine performance. Motivation of that nature demands increments of a considerably greater order of magnitude than are usually available.

What dissatisfies workers? Quite frequently, those sources of dissatisfaction are factors which are peripheral to the job: coffee breaks, titles, work regulations, fringe benefits, seniority rights, holidays, etc. At what stage do workers become dissatisfied? Perhaps, employees become most dissatisfied when opportunities for meaningful achievement are eliminated, and they become sensitized to their environment and begin to find fault with it. Management has attempted for years to resolve the problems created by dissatisfaction.

Yet, highly motivated employees and executives might find it easy during the growth years of an organization to overlook or take in stride existing and latent problems associated with supervisory ineptness and communication breakdowns. But, in an organization when growth decelerates, motivation ceases to be self-generating and becomes increasingly dependent on the skill of good supervision.

However, before we proceed, let's consider two sets of factors; namely (a) dissatisfiers and (b) motivators:

(a) **Dissatisfiers** are made up essentially of such matters as salary, supplemental benefits, company policy and administration, behavior of supervision, working conditions, and several other factors somewhat peripheral to the task. Though traditionally perceived by management as motivators of people, these factors were found—or can be found—in some instances to be more potent as dissatisfiers. High motivation does not necessarily result from their improvement, but dissatisfaction does result from their deterioration. Negative motivators can be dissatisfiers, too, but not as frequently as some of these factors cited. For example, while achievement is considered a motivator, the *failure* to achieve can, of course, be a dissatisfier.

(b) **Motivators,** for the most part, are factors of achievement, recognition, responsibility, growth, advancement, and other matters associated with self-actualization of the individual on the job. Job satisfaction and high production normally are associated with motivators, while disappointment and ineffectiveness are usually associated with dissatisfiers. For years, the executive has been instructed on methods for motivating his subordinates so that they would work harder, improve their efficiency, and be more productive. However, there is a dearth of information to assist the man who motivates others in the most essential task of all: motivating himself! Everyone in his career has had the experience of being associated with a person who strives diligently for years to achieve success. Finally, he achieves the top executive role. What happens? Within a short time, he proves unsuccessful in his new position. He may even lose his job and be replaced by another candidate. He continues to ask himself, ''Why?''.

The answer is obvious: the individual mistook the beginning of achievement for the end! He may have been an expert in motivating other persons, but he was unable to motivate himself; and as a result he made the biggest mistake of his life when he concluded that the goal he had been working toward was already an accomplished fact. In his new position, his zest and enthusiasm dissolved. He ceased working hard and aggressively, not because of laziness but because he lacked the all important incentive of a goal. He no longer made careful plans in the essential areas that in the past had spiraled him onward and upward towards success.

All of us know this man is not alone, this situation not unique. Many administrators, executives and supervisors have made the same mistake. They spend years working long hours to achieve a planned goal. Once they achieve the goal, all the drive that brought them to the coveted position fades. They run out of steam. They relax in a comfortable chair, gaze smugly at their new realm, and let their dreamworld slip from under them. Any experienced, successful executive will tell you that he has yet to see an organization where a title on the door opened to a life of ease. Experience indicates, to the contrary, that the successful executive has to work twice as hard as ever before. He must continue to be creative or he will wither. When his enthusiasm atrophies, his domain will fold beneath him. If he doesn't continue to distinguish himself by competent performance, he will soon find that another man with the qualities he once possessed will take over as his successor.

Occasionally, the fruits of our efforts—status, title, authority—deceive us into thinking we no longer need to motivate ourselves. We ignore or lay aside tools of achievement: our minds, our hands, our spirits. We lose drive and momentum. We permit our humility to fade and the human touch to diminish. Sometimes a superior we used to rely on for assistance and guidance is gone and with him our inspiration and motivation. In such circumstances we find that we must stand more on our own two feet; now we are really alone. This is not accidental. The effective, efficient executive is expected to stand alone. Which takes us back to reflect on the basic question posed earlier: Who motivates the motivator? Who provides the drive for the manager to whom the others must turn for their inspiration and leadership? There is only one answer: He must motivate himself! No longer can this person look to his superior for periodical booster shots. Now *he* is the superior! Once he realizes that motivation for his continued success must come from within, he can proceed with the proper steps to achieve it. He can and must build a comprehensive program of personal motivation that will keep him steadily moving forward. He must press on. By standing still, he actually shifts into reverse. The executive who fails to motivate himself to higher goals is in trouble or, at the very least, is on the road to trouble.

Let's pause a moment to consider the symptoms. Generally, there are a number of danger signals to alert us when our self motivation is on the wane. These symptoms of "Executive Hari-Kari" can manifest themselves in the form of:

(1) *Lost Purpose*. There is abandonment of a concrete plan which earlier has been carefully developed to provide for achievement through progressive forward movement on a career objective. The objective already achieved is regarded as the wind up—the finale—instead of a new beginning of his career.

(2) *Doubt*. He may have doubts about his ability to perform the new job to which he has been advanced. Self-confidence is shaken; worry and confusion follow.

(3) *Self-Satisfaction*. He may have the tendency or desire to relax and take things easy. He is willing to settle for what is good

instead of what should be excellent. Such performance and attitude go hand-in-hand with a failure to encourage initiative in subordinates, and the false notion that entrenching mediocre employees in the next lower level insures one's own security.

(4) *Delay and Procrastination*. He permits the "mañana" philosophy to become dominant. He procrastinates, postponing decisions which should be made today for tomorrow. He steers clear of considered calculated risks and deludes himself into thinking that the problems ultimately will resolve themselves.

(5) *Symbol Worship*. He may have the tendency to surrender to egoism and status seeking, savoring the job's title instead of a sense of pride in taking advantage of his new power to better methods and refreshingly new ideas. Furthermore, he may prefer praise even more than specific achievements.

Any administrator, executive, or a supervisor who exhibits one or more of these danger signals is suffering from lost or faded motivation. He is adrift. And what's most important, his plan, his purpose, his pattern of life is in jeopardy. Many administrators or executives bind motivation with a subconscious personal career schedule for success. Simply stated, they say, "When I reach the age of 30, I will be administrator." This concept is not new. It is the subconscious application of the first step in a basic success formula that will help you achieve positions of executive, comptroller, assistant administrator, or virtually anything you desire. The following is the proved five-step formula:

1. *Clearly crystallize your thinking*. Establish a definite goal or objective for yourself with a definite time limit for its achievement. Nebulous generalities such as "wealthy by middle-age" will not suffice. Be precise. For example, establish a goal to earn a specific salary by a certain time. Follow your destination to the letter—if you really hope to get there.
2. *Prepare a plan*. Carefully develop a plan for the attainment of your goals and objectives. Such a blueprint will quickly convert you from a wandering generality to a meaningful specific. Write down your concrete plan. Use an outline format with various steps that can be checked off from time to time and that will reveal your progress or lack of progress. Don't cheat by checking off a step as being completed until you've already begun on the next step. This will insure against stopping short of your goal.
3. *Develop drive and desire*. Develop the initiative and desire to reach your goal through the use of your written plan. Make an exhaustive list of every possible benefit to be derived from reach-

ing this objective. Include all the advantages it will have for you, your financial position, your personality, your abilities. In addition, enumerate the ways achieving your goal will benefit your family, associates, friends, and even indirectly, your community and society at large. Compile this list and keep it with you. You might add to it each time you recognize new advantages. Delete items only as your sense of values change (and be prepared for this to happen).

4. *Have faith.* You must maintain an unshakable faith in yourself and your ability to accomplish your purpose. Brush aside modesty and list every positive attribute you possess. Make the list as long as you truthfully can. Then, study men and women who have already achieved success, whom you'd be willing to emulate. Note in particular the qualities that made them successful. List their attributes and compare them with your own. You might be surprised at the similarities! You then will realize that you, indeed, already possess many of the basic qualities you need. Have confidence in them and use them. But most of all, don't lose faith.
5. *Remain determined.* Develop a force of ironwilled determination that will surmount all obstacles in your path. If the benefits to be derived from achieving your objectives are worthwhile, any person or situation obstructing your progress should be considered as stealing from your future success. Any obstacle conceived by any man can be overcome by another driven by the passing desire and determination. Be so determined that it will eliminate any situation or circumstances standing in the way of attaining your objectives and goals.

The only motivational value of equitability, despite all the difficulties of attaining it, is that it motivates persons not to leave, strike, complain, waste material, or restrict production. For most people, effective motivation rests primarily in non-financial rewards. Understanding how these rewards operate requires a comprehensive view of the way in which organization, communication, and leadership interrelate with one another.

Future Readings Suggested by the Author

Rate Setting: Topics in Health Care Financing, Lemer, Robert S. and Willman, David D. (Germantown, MD: Aspen Systems, Inc. 1974)

Health Care Cost Containment and Other Proposals, Prepared by the Staff of the Committee on Finance, United States Senate, CP 96–9, Washington, D.C., 1979.

"Can We Control Health Care Costs?" Herzlinger, Regina, *Harvard Business Review* (March-April, 1978), p. 102–10.

"What's Good For General Motors." Cunningham, Robert M., *Hospitals* (August 16, 1978), p. 75, 80.

"The Case For Negotiated Rates." Sommers, Ann R., *Hospitals* (February 1, 1978), p. 49–52.

"Cost Containment: What the States Are Doing." Holcomb, B., *Health Care Week* (June 12, 1978).

A number of articles in *Review-Federation of American Hospitals* (December, 1978), p. 11–13.

"State Rate Controls: Documentation of the Bureaucracy's Imperfect Plan." *Review-Federation of American Hospitals* (December, 1978), p. 11–13.

"How One Hospital Broke Its Inflation Fever." Solomon, S., *Fortune,* (June 18, 1979), p. 148–154.

References

BOOKS

American Management Association, *Motivating the Employee on Today's Production Front*. (New York: American Management Association, 1952).

John L. Fuller, *Motivation, A Biological Perspective* (New York: Random House, 1962).

Robert Ferber, *Motivation and Market Behavior*. (Homewood, IL: Richard D. Irwin, 1958).

Abraham Maslow, *Motivation and Personality* (New York: Harper & Row, 1954).

Abraham Zaleznick, *Motivation, Productivity and Satisfaction of Workers* (Boston: Harvard University Press).

Justus George Frederich, *Motivational Research* (New York: Business Course, 1957).

American Management Association, *Motivation—The Core of Management* (New York: American Management Association, 1953).

Saul W. Gellerman, *Management by Motivation* (New York: American Management Association, 1968).

Alfred J. Marrow, David G. Bowers and Stanley E. Seashore, *Management by Participation* (New York: Harper & Row, 1967).

Lester R. Bittel, *Management by Exception,* (New York: McGraw-Hill Book Co., 1964).

ARTICLES

P. J. Meyer, "How an Executive Achieves and Keeps Self-Motivation," *Commercial and Financial Chronicle* (July 28, 1966).

W. J. Bowles, "Management of Motivation—A Company-Wide Program," *Personnel* (July, 1966).

The Management of Disruptive Conflicts

Robert Veninga, Ph.D.

It has been suggested that all social structures have elements of conflict as members compete for scarce resources, prestige, and power positions.[1] While all organizations have internal disagreements, the hospital exists in an environment which is particularly conducive to misinformation, misunderstanding, and disagreement.

Issues which often lead to conflict situations within hospitals are: unionization of personnel and the resulting negotiation process; the introduction of new methods of control, such as the Professional Standards Review Organization and/or the Occupational Safety Health Act; legal challenges including costly court cases; the emerging militancy of various professional and consumer groups; disagreements over authority and power between the professional staff and administration; requests to shift resources to new technologies, often at the expense of existing departments; and changing federal and state priorities which result in rapid expansion and equally rapid retrenchment.

The list could continue; the forces of change impinging upon hospitals is intense. Consequently, with the diversity of groups within the hopsital, it is understandable that the contemporary hospital is constantly confronted with the challenge of resolving tension, conflict, and friction.

Therefore, one of the most important skills which a hospital administrator, department head, or staff supervisor can develop is the ability to successfully resolve disruptive interpersonal and interdepartmental conflict. Whether staff members will be able to give effective care; whether departments will be able to work jointly on important issues; whether the administration is able to successfully cope with the changing environment will be dependent, in part, upon whether disruptive disagreements can be successfully negotiated.

[1]Lewis A. Coser, "Functions of Social Conflict" as found in *Sociological Theory: A Book of Readings,* Edited by Coser et al. (New York: Macmillan Co., 1969) p. 218.

Creating an Environment for Conflict Resolution

There are various strategies for dealing with disruptive situations in organizations. Alan C. Filley refers to three such strategies, one of which is appropriate for creating an environment in which disruptive forces can be successfully managed.[2]

Win-Lose Strategy

The first approach which Filley defines is a "win-lose" orientation exemplified by autocratic administrative practices in which the administrator feels that any conflict situation is ultimately a personal threat. Because the disagreements are seen as a personal threat, the basic objective of the win-lose administrator will be to keep the upper hand in negotiations. Perceived threats to the administrator's authority will often be confronted with forceful and essentially one-way communication patterns.

Staff members who work with a win-lose administrator often develop, over a period of time, rather intense frustrations. Inordinate amounts of energy can be spent by the staff in determining various strategies for coping with the administrator's style. The strategies often have rather serious and negative effects upon the organization. One strategy is to "communicate only what the boss wants to hear." By so doing, the staff members hope to avoid direct confrontation. When this happens everyone eventually loses. The administrator loses because accurate information is not conveyed; the staff lose because the administrator inevitably blames them for the problems once they emerge; the organization loses because energy that would normally be available for constructive problem solving is dissipated in the confrontations between the administrator and the staff.

Lose-Lose Approach

A second strategy for dealing with conflict is what Filley terms "lose-lose," so named because neither side really accomplishes what it wants, or alternatively, each side only gets part of what it wants. Lose-lose methods are based on the assumptions that half a loaf is better than none and avoidance of conflict is preferable to personal

[2]Alan C. Filley, *Interpersonal Conflict Resolution* (Glenview, IL: Scott, Foresman and Co., 1975) pp. 21–30.

confrontation on issues.[3] For example, the administrator and the nursing director discuss a mutually shared problem. From the administrator's perspective one solution is clearly the best and would, if implemented, strengthen the organization. The administrator projects, however, that the nursing director would never accept the solution and might create considerable difficulty if the decision were to be implemented. Therefore, the lose-lose administration reasons that it's necessary to back off from the most desired solution. A simpler approach might be taken by the nursing director who also has a specific solution to the problem but projects that the administrator would not agree to it. Therefore, both come to a conference not to find the best possible solution to a problem, but a solution which will not offend either party. The compromise generates little enthusiasm, there often is little commitment to it, and thus it often fails to be effective. In that sense everybody loses.

Filley notes that there are some characteristics common to the two strategies. There is very clear distinction between the parties, rather than a we-versus-the-problem orientation. Personalities become the center of attention rather than definitions of ways in which the problem can be approached and resolved. Under both strategies the respective parties approach the problem from their limited perspective rather than looking at the problem from the point of view of the organization. Both the win-lose and the lose-lose strategies accentuate interpersonal conflicts. The conflicts are often personalized and the defenses emerge to protect each party. In short, neither strategy is effective in solving organizational problems.

Win-Win Tactic

The primary goal of a win-win strategy is to find solutions to organizational problems which will have high quality and high acceptance. To realize this goal several values need to be integrated into the administrative patterns of the organization. The first value is related to the administrator's belief that it is possible to find solutions that will, in fact, have high quality and high acceptance. This value implies that the administrator is willing to look at the goals, motivations, and needs which others bring to the conflict situation. It implies a willingness to determine how the other individual perceives the problem and why that problem is seen from that perspective. It also implies a realization that

[3]Ibid., pp. 23–24.

whether a defined solution satisfactorily resolves a given problem will be determined by the commitment each party feels toward the solution. Therefore, the ability to find solutions which will obtain a high degree of commitment is a necessary prerequisite if the solution is to be maximally effective.

The second value which a win-win administrator must communicate is related to one's willingness to foster honest communication. The administrator who has this value is saying, "It is our collective responsibility to be open and honest about facts, opinions, and feelings."[4] If individuals believe that they are only receiving partial information concerning a problem, they become defensive. When someone is evasive about the reason a position is so strongly advocated, distrust tends to arise. Conversely, honestly begets honesty. When an individual can verbalize feelings, motivations, and perceptions, others in the group generally follow that norm. The result is that the problems can often be more sharply defined and the critical issues openly delineated. It is immensely difficult to find solutions to problems unless one has adequate information. As Norbert Wiener has stated: "The process of receiving and using information is the process of our adjusting to the contingencies of the outer environment, and of our living effectively within that environment."[5] An administrative pattern which accentuates open communication can provide vital information which is needed to adequately confront the problem.

A third value basic to win-win approaches is rooted in a conviction that serious problems are best resolved when well defined process-oriented decision making methods are used. To begin discussions of a serious problem without a method through which defensiveness can be diminished often results in heightened anxiety and hostility. The administrator who has this value is saying in effect: "I will control the process by which we arrive at agreement, but I will not dictate the content of our meetings." A problem solving methodology which is defined, agreed to, and practically implemented increases the probability that defensiveness can be diminished and that creative solutions can emerge.

How should the above values be reflected in an administrator's style? If win-win orientations are to become integrated into the daily patterns of administration, three competencies need to be developed

[4]Ibid., p. 29.

[5]Wiener Norbert, *The Human Use of Human Beings* (New York: Avon Books, 1950) p. 27.

and applied to organizational problems: the willingness to adopt and practice a confrontive style of approaching and managing conflict; a willingness to invest effort in helping others clarify the meaning of messages; and a willingness to follow systematic processes to arrive at high quality solutions which bring about high acceptance.

Competency One

A win-win orientation is facilitated when a confrontive approach is utilized. Every administrator has a style in approaching—or avoiding —conflict producing situations. There are five basic approaches: withdrawing, smoothing, compromising, forcing, and confronting.[6] For an administrator to be effective it is imperative that each style be understood and an effort made to integrate a confrontive method into one's management practices.

Withdrawal Approach

The first style is to withdraw from conflict producing situations by not initiating action unless it is absolutely necessary. When a disturbing memo is received, the answer is deferred or filed and forgotten. If someone raises a question about the memo the individual may reply that "it is being studied" or "I haven't had a chance to get at it." Robert Blake and Jane Mouton suggest that when the administrator cannot withdraw, the approach often taken is to maintain strict neutrality by not voicing any personal opinion.[7] Many problems can be deferred by such a strategy. Unfortunately, the acuteness of the problem remains and disruptive symptoms will subsequently emerge.

Smoothing Approach

An administrator who wishes to avoid disagreement, negative emotions, rejection, and frustration will often adopt a smoothing approach to conflict management. The emphasis is to accentuate the positive: "Well, I know that we have our difficulties, but look at all the good things we are doing" or "Let us not argue in our department—if we start disagreeing with each other we won't be able to stand up to anybody else around here." The individual who smooths over conflict

[6]R. J. Burke, "Methods of Resolving Interpersonal Conflict," *Personnel Administrator* 32 (1960): 48.

[7]Robert Blake and Jane Mouton, *The Managerial Grid* (Houston, TX: Golf Publishing Co., 1975) p. 94.

situations has a low tolerance for disagreements and the expression of negative emotions. Conflicts, they reason, hurt individuals and therefore should be avoided. No situation is so bad that it should cause differences of opinion that are hurtful.

The "look on the bright side" approach to conflict management does not necessarily result in a happy, cohesive department that the administrator would like to have. Employees become frustrated because issues are not confronted. The administrator is generally "such a nice person" that it becomes difficult to become angry with him or her. Because issues are not confronted a win-win environment does not emerge.

Compromising Approach

The basis of the compromise approach to conflict is the belief that administration essentially is the art of compromise. The compromiser finds a middle position where all parties feel relatively comfortable. Allan Filley describes this style as follows:

> The (compromise) person enjoys the maneuvering required to resolve conflict and will actively seek to find some strong middle ground between two extreme positions. He may vacillate between expressing anger and then trying to smooth things over and may seek to use voting or rules as a way of avoiding direct confrontation on the issues. If he is confronted with a serious disagreement, he will suggest some mechanism for finding a "workable" solution (such as voting) rather than working out the disagreement to find the best solution.[8]

When this approach is used, multiple problems emerge for staff members who are direct and confrontive. The subordinate who likes to deal with conflict situations by defining the best possible solution will find that such an orientation will not be favored by the compromise supervisor. The solutions that are stated by the subordinate may seem "too far out," "not realistic," "will never work around here." Consequently, the subordinate receives very little positive reinforcement for creativity. The internal frustration can either drive the employee out of the organization, or in time, force the individual to adopt a more compromising approach to conflict situations. The net result will be that the solutions which the subordinate subsequently states will not creatively solve the complex problems facing the unit and will generate little internal reward for the subordinate. The supervisor may

[8]Filley, *Interpersonal Conflict,* p. 52.

be pleased with the "realistic solution" but the organization may lose the one solution which could have creatively and competently resolved the problem.

When a subordinate practices a compromise orientation toward conflict, supervisors who are direct and confrontive tend to discount the subordinates' opinions. A subordinate who routinely compromises is perceived as being rather tentative and the supervisor comes to see the subordinate as lacking character, integrity, and internal strength.[9]

The most basic limitation of a compromise approach, however, is related to the intent of finding equitable solutions as opposed to determining the best possible solution for the problem. Since the emphasis is on compromise, effort is usually not expended in examining the quality of the solution but rather on how individuals will accept it. Creative solutions, which may in themselves generate conflict, are often eliminated in favor of less sound solutions which are perceived to be politically viable.

Forcing Approach

The forcing style of managing conflict is that in which the administrator seeks to meet his or her own goals at all costs, without concern for the needs or the acceptance of others.[10] For such an administrator, losing is perceived as reduced status, weakness, and the loss of self-image. Winning, on the other hand, gives a sense of exhilaration and achievement. The forcer has no doubt about the correctness of the position. Because there is no doubt, anger and frustration are expressed towards others who disagree. The main purpose of any resulting argument is to win.

This approach to conflict management can create immense problems for an organization over time. Since conflict is suppressed, issues which need thorough discussion are generally not raised. When they are raised, defenses will be heightened due to the fear among coworkers that "once we get into it we really will be in for a fight." Since conflict is personalized, the issues are seldom dealt with objectively. There will be a winner and a loser, and since the administrator can use the authority and power that goes with the position, subordinates generally lose their case. After subsequent losses, subordinates will begin to feel their efforts are fruitless. Subsequently, a superficial tran-

[9]Blake, *Managerial Grid,* p. 125.
[10]Filley, *Interpersonal Conflict,* p. 51.

quility may permeate the atmosphere of the office, while underneath hostility abounds.

Confrontive Approach

The confrontive problem-solving approach begins with a philosophical perspective: conflict is an inherent part of organizational life. Because of this, ongoing conflict resolution processes must be developed, implemented, and periodically evaluated. The confrontive problem solver not only believes that conflict is inevitable, but that it can be a creative force in surfacing issues and bringing about constructive change in the organization.

According to Filley, individuals with a confrontive problem-solving approach to conflict will actively seek to satisfy their own goals as well as those of others. The confrontive problem solver

> (1) sees conflict as natural and helpful, even leading to a more creative solution if handled properly; (2) evidences trust and candidness with others and recognizes the legitimacy of feelings in arriving at decisions; (3) feels that everyone's attitudes and positions need to be aired and recognizes that when conflict is resolved to the satisfaction of all, commitment to the solution is likely; (4) sees everyone as having an equal role in resolving conflict, views the opinions of everyone as equally legitimate; and (5) does not sacrifice anyone simply for the good of the group.[11]

The net result is that problems are constructively dealt with. Information is not hoarded by one party and used at strategic moments to advance a parochial point of view; rather, information is shared because members of the working unit recognize their interdependence if the goals of the unit are to be realized. Because conflict producing problems are seen as legitimate and normal occurrences, a sense of openness and support for one another emerges. The elusive concept of the management team begins to become a reality because of the mutual commitment of achieving agreed-upon goals, and being able to work in an environment in which collaboration rather than competition is rewarded.

Confrontation the Most Effective

As might be anticipated from the above description, the confrontation problem-solving approach generally is the most effective in

[11]Ibid., p. 52.

managing conflict situations. Lawrence and Lorsch (1967) investigated six organizations in determining the effects of confrontation (win-win methods), forcing (resorting to authority or coercion), and smoothing (agreeing on an intellectual or a nonthreatening level). On the basis of their research, they concluded that the two highest performing organizations used confrontation to a more extensive degree than the other four and that the next two organizations, in order of performance, used confrontation more than the lowest two. In 1970 Burke asked 74 managers to describe the way they and their immediate supervisors dealt with conflicts. His research used the five descriptive categories delineated.

> Comparing results relating to the variable of constructive use of conflict, the more effective supervisors used the methods in the following order: (1) confrontation, (2) smoothing, (3) compromise, (4) forcing, and (5) withdrawal. The least effective supervisors used instead: (1) confrontation, (2) forcing, (3) withdrawal, (4) smoothing, and (5) compromise. While it is surprising that confrontation is reported most frequently in the less effective group as well as the more effective group, the frequent use of forcing is not.[12]

One qualification should be made concerning the use of confrontation as a basic managerial method. There are instances where, because of the nature of the situation, a different method might be consciously chosen. It might be helpful to temporarily withdraw if an employee's anger precludes an ability to listen. If the causes of a problem appear to be a lack of recognition and/or support, smoothing might be the most appropriate method. If the immediate reduction of defensiveness is a basic objective, a compromising approach might be the most viable method. Generally, however, consistent use of a confrontive method, coupled with a conscious desire to minimize those instances where forcing is used, will create an environment where problem solving can be systematically undertaken.

Competency Two

A win-win orientation is facilitated when an effort is made to clarify the meaning of messages. One of the most important characteristics of individuals who are effective at resolving interpersonal conflict is that they have the interest and the ability to clarify the meanings behind words. This is neither a small talent nor an insignificant task. Because efforts are not often given to clarify the meaning of words, multiple

[12]Ibid., p. 31.

misunderstandings resulting in decreased productivity and morale abound in many organizations. The often heard statement: "But, I thought I told them . . ." is symbolic that the meanings behind the words were not understood.

Individuals bring a set of attitudes, beliefs, and values to any given communication situation. A single event, particularly if it is conflict producing, will be seen from multiple perspectives by individuals who view the same situation. Our construction of reality is highly personal and is unique to our own attitudes, beliefs, and values.

To illustrate the importance of how attitudes shape our perceptions, one might focus on a well-known case study surrounding a highly competitive football game between Dartmouth and Princeton.[13] After the game, Hastorf and Cantril determined the perceptions of the respective sides with a questionnaire and a film of the game which was shown to 100 students. The results were very divergent; it appeared that each side witnessed separate events. For example, the Princeton students "saw" the Dartmouth team commit more than twice the number of infractions reported by the Dartmouth students. Spectators from the respective teams "saw" more than twice the number of "flagrant" violations made by the members of the opposing team. Hastorf and Cantril concluded: "The same sensory impingements emanating from the football field, transmitted through the visual mechanism to the brain, obviously gave rise to different experiences in different people. The significances assumed by different happenings for different people depend in large part on the purposes people bring to the occasion and the assumptions they have of the purposes and probably behavior of other people involved. . . ."

Based upon this study as well as other research it can be concluded that:

> It is inaccurate and misleading to say that different people have different "attitudes" concerning the same "thing." For the "thing" simply is not the same for different people whether the "thing" is a football game, a presidential candidate, communism, or spinach. We do not simply "react to" a happening or to some impingement from the environment in a determined way (except in a behavior that has become reflecting or habitual). We behave according to what we bring to the occasion, and what each of us brings to the occasion is more or less unique.[14]

[13]A. H. Hastorf and H. Cantril, "They Saw A Game: A Case Study," *Journal of Abnormal and Social Psychology* 49 (1954): 129–134.

[14]Ibid., p. 133.

An administrator who starts with the belief that an event seen by two or more people will be seen basically the same way will ultimately become frustrated in communication situations. Such congruity in perceptions seldom takes place. What we see and what we hear is greatly influenced by our emotional state, past experiences, and the expectations we bring to a given situation. Because of this, individuals involved in a conflict must try to understand one another's point of view.

How does one determine the other individual's perspective on a problem? "Reflecting the *content* of a message," states R. Wayne Payce, "represents the interpreter's attempt to clarify by repeating to the source the same statement (the same literal meaning) uttered by the latter. This type of response permits the source to hear and mull over what he or she has just said. Hearing the utterance from a different source often provides sufficient motivation to think through the validity of the comment."[15]

For example, if the personnel director says to the administrator: "I think everyone in the hospital should have a 5% raise for this next year," the administrator may respond by saying: "You would say then that all employees, regardless of their classification, should have basically the same raise?" or "You believe then that the 5% figure is the appropriate figure for us to be considering. Is that correct?" Such a clarification can help both individuals' perceptions regarding the implications of what is being stated.

The reflection of *feelings* consists of expressing back to the source latent meanings, connotative meanings, and vocal tones that seemed to imply feelings of which the source may not be entirely conscious.[16] If you heard the above statement concerning the 5% raise you may well wish to feed back perceptions such as: "You seem comfortable with the 5% figure. Are you?" or "You seem to feel rather strongly that raises should be uniform for this next year. Is that correct?" Once again, by reflection, what it is that one is hearing there is the possibility of uncovering the latent meanings of the messages which may be very important in resolving tensions.

Research has demonstrated that "feeding" back to an individual what he or she has stated will elicit statements of the kind being reflected. William Verplank discovered "that both reflecting and agreeing with statements influenced the rate at which speakers stated

[15]Wayne Pace and Robert Boven, *The Human Transaction* (Glenview, IL; Scott, Foresman and Co., 1973).

[16]Ibid., p. 191.

opinions; the subjects increased the number of opinion statements they made when reinforced by statements of reflection and agreement.''[17] The ability to feed back what one is hearing provides avenues for clarifying because the other person will make additional statements.

Not only is it important to reflect what it is one is hearing to help ensure congruity in thinking, but it is essential that at the conclusion of each interview there is a summary statement. A concluding statement, such as the following one, can help to ensure that the conclusions arrived at are mutually shared: ''I will talk to Mrs. Smit and obtain her opinions about what to do concerning the problems of the new charting system. In the meantime, you are going to call Mr. Pierson at Shalom Hospital to see how they managed their new system. We will then meet at the beginning of next week and see what we might recommend in resolving those charting difficulties. Is that agreeable with you?''

The techniques of restating and summarizing may seem simple. In many respects such techniques are easy to implement providing that there is a highly conscious desire to use clarification procedures in interview situations. When such techniques are implemented, the rewards are immediate. The quantity and quality of that information improves. Agreements arrived at are more than affirmative nods of the head for there is a mutual understanding of the meanings of the agreements as they are perceived by the parties involved. Finally, communication misunderstandings are pinpointed in the early phases of discussion rather than emerging later.

Competency Three

A win-win orientation is facilitated by a problem-solving method. If a decision is made to work through a conflict situation it is important to use a method which will maximize the probability that decisions will have both high quality and high acceptance. Problem-solving methods are of immense value in building rationality into a discussion. Problem-solving methods help in pinpointing the precise cause of the difficulties and, if properly used, can be of assistance in finding creative solutions which would otherwise go undefined. The more complex the difficulty, the greater the need to use a problem-solving method. I would suggest that many interviews are not successful because a problem-solving method was not systematically followed.

[17]Ibid., p. 191.

A six-step process can assist in arriving at solutions which have high quality and high acceptance.

Step One: Timing

The first step is to determine whether it is possible to arrive at solutions which will have high quality and high acceptance. The timing factor in conflict resolution appears to be a critical variable which will affect negotiated outcomes. Individuals who have the greatest success in resolving staff dilemmas are those who understand how important timing is to the entire process of conflict resolution. The assumption here is that there are specific time intervals in which both parties would be most amenable to discussing the problem and there are time sequences in which both parties, because of their attitudes, beliefs, and perceptions about the problem, would not be able to competently and creatively solve the problem.

How does one know whether a particular time is right for resolving interpersonal problems? Individuals will want to resolve difficulties if they are sufficiently motivated to do so. If one is heavily invested in a problem he or she will welcome initiatives which seek to resolve dissonance and discomfort. Therefore, when the grapevine—which interestingly is usually quite accurate—indicates that a department head only talks about the "lack of fairness of an administrative decision," the time might be right for a meeting.

Individuals will also want to resolve the difficulties when they perceive that a discussion might result in each side winning. Therefore, if you sense that the outcome of a discussion could result in benefits to all parties, the timing is right for a meeting.

And, it is essential to confront a problem if it is seriously eroding the organization's effectiveness. Some problems, if left unattended, will only compound into greater difficulties. Such problems must be dealt with openly and directly even if the timing is not very conducive.

Step Two: Place

Attention should be given to the place the meeting is held. This is not an insignificant factor. While discussions of routine day-by-day problems can effectively take place in either the supervisor's or the subordinate's office, critical issues are discussed better in a neutral setting. A supervisor's office can intimidate employees to the point where they may not be willing to share their feelings about the conflict.

And getting away from distractions such as telephone calls or visitors is important.

It is also important to budget adequate time for any problem-solving process, particularly if the conflict is perceived as serious and there is a heavy personal investment. To allot 30 minutes to an employee who has been living with a difficult situation for months is an injustice to both the employee and the problem. Conflict resolution takes an immense amount of time and energy, and any brief conference to deal with the problem will result in more frustration. It is sometimes helpful to budget three or four meetings for the discussion of a problem, the first one only to verbalize varying perceptions of the difficulty. This way the administrator clearly signals his or her perceptions concerning the importance of the problem and a willingness to take the time to resolve tensions.

Step Three: Definition

Careful attention should be given to whether you are dealing with the covert or the overt problem. The overt problem represents the symptoms of the problem. The verbalizations of the overt problem are often those which are psychologically "safe" to talk about. We often spend a relatively small amount of time on problem definition and then rush to the solution phase without clearly delineating the causative factors.

For example, a dispute between the director of the patient education program in the hospital and the nursing director may appear to revolve under what are appropriate educational programs which should be planned for the coming year. In reality the dispute over the educational program (the overt problem) may be masking the most basic issue (the covert problem)—who has control over the educational programs. In this instance a great deal of time could be spent discussing the symptoms (Should we offer diabetes education or parent effectiveness classes?). Trying to determine which educational programs are appropriate would only delay the next confrontation. Only when the substantive issue is addressed—who has control over the educational programs—can meaningful strides be made at resolving the interpersonal conflicts.

Step Four: List Possible Solutions

Often referred to as the "brainstorming phase," in this stage individuals list possible solutions to the identified problem. The verbalization of creative solutions should be encouraged, even if the solution does not initially seem practical. All solutions should be placed in writing.

This process takes time and effort. You will be fortunate if, at the initial meeting, you are able to precisely identify the problem and list potential solutions. Do not be discouraged; defining the problem and listing possible solutions represents formidable progress towards the ultimate resolution. You may also find that the process is facilitated by pausing between steps four and five. Expectations and positive feelings are generally quite high after the completion of step four. It is not uncommon for people to leave the meeting saying: ''You know, I think we are beginning to get somewhere.'' Comments such as these mean that defensives are being lowered and individuals are becoming optimistic that, in fact, resolution of the complex problems will be found.

Step Five: Evaluate Solutions

This should be done systematically, first evaluating the strengths and then the weaknesses of each solution. Sometimes it is helpful to write each solution on a flip chart with its strengths and the limitations. When one of the solutions emerges as the most desirable, a sigh of relief and a feeling of accomplishment is felt by each member of the group. Because a carefully followed process was followed in which all members could share perceptions, a feeling of individual and group ownership of the solution becomes apparent.

At times, however, the best solution does not become apparent. When this happens it is best to evaluate and define the strengths and weaknesses of each of the solutions again. The group should then be asked to agree on those solutions which are clearly unsatisfactory. After discarding the unsatisfactory ones, two or three solutions will remain. After further discussion a vote should be taken.

Step Six: Implementation

The sixth step is to determine what must be done to implement the solution and who will be responsible for evaluating whether or not it is effective. Written agreements should be made to ensure that there is a common understanding about what is to be done to resolve the problem. The agreement should be clear (understandable to all; no vague words), scheduled (date stipulated as to when the solution will be implemented), measurable (everyone should be able to determine whether the solution has been effective), and the end result specified. For example:

> By November 30th, the patient education department will have written a five-page document explaining to parents of cleft children the following: a) nutritional problems associated with cleft anomalities, b) feeding procedures prior to surgery, and c) resources available to assist the parents. Mrs. Mary Peterson, Director of Patient Education, and Dr. Michael Broson, Chief of Pediatrics, will have responsibility for writing this pamphlet. The pamphlet will be given to parents within the first week of the child's birth to assist the parents in managing the child's dietary patterns.

By stipulating who is responsible for what and by what date, expectations are understood. Carefully written solutions increase the likelihood that the solutions will, in fact, resolve the problem.

In dealing with a complex problem, particularly if there have been strong feelings about it, it is wise to periodically check that the agreed-upon solution is adequately resolving the problem. One of the interesting aspects of conflict resolution is that new solutions designed to alleviate old problems usually create new problems. By recognizing that new solutions may cause organizational disruptions and by dealing with the emerging problems as they arise, the probability increases that the resulting conflicts can be successfully managed. Table I summarizes the above problem-solving methodology.

The above process represents a systematic method for problem identification and problem resolution. If systematically followed, it can build rationality into discussions. However, in addition to emphasizing the need to follow a process in resolving complex issues, it is important that there is a keen understanding that successful outcomes will evolve only if the basic human needs of those participating in the process are satisfactorily realized. It is possible to have a highly efficient problem solving process and to follow it to the letter of the law and yet fail. Often times that failure occurs because of personalities. From a behavioral perspective, failures occur because the psychological needs of individuals are not being satisfactorily realized.

There are three psychological needs which should be met when negotiating the terrain of a complex problem:

1. The need for security (Is my job in jeopardy?)
2. The need to belong (Am I still part of the team?)
3. The need for respect (In spite of the problem, am I still respected for what I can do?)

TABLE I: A Process for Resolving Interpersonal Conflict

Step One:	Is conciliation at this time really possible? — What is the level of discontent? — Can all parties "win"? — Is the problem eroding the effectiveness of the organization?
Step Two:	Where is the most appropriate place where a confrontation meeting can be held?
Step Three:	What is the problem? — Are we dealing with symptoms of the problem?
Step Four:	What potential solutions are there to the identified problem?
Step Five:	What are the strengths and limitations of each solution?
Step Six:	How will we implement the solution? Who will evaluate whether it has been effective? — Is the solution clear, scheduled, measurable, with an end result specified?

The sooner one is able to meet these needs, the better the individual will be able to enthusiastically commit oneself to implementing a solution. Statements such as the following, if genuinely made, represent one attempt to strengthen a person's self-respect.

> Well, I think that the procedures we have just outlined should help to solve the problems we have been having. Before you go, I do want you to know, Jane, that while we may occasionally differ, I am still very glad that we are working together.
>
> Mark, when problems have come up on our floor, I have often asked for your advice and suggestions. I appreciate the help you gave in finding the solution to this problem.

In the first example, the supervisor, in the concluding remarks, is seeking to affirm that while they may disagree with one another, the supervisor is indeed appreciative that they are "on the same team." In the second example, the supervisor is seeking to meet the subordinate's need for self-respect by affirming the value of the subordinate's advice and suggestions. The type of sensitivity reflected in the above statements cannot help but create a climate for good interpersonal relationships.

Finally, any emotional encounter between two persons generally results in a period of introspective analysis by those involved. "Did I say too much?" "Did he really mean that he appreciated my criticism of his leadership?" "Will she really follow through on what we decided?" Such anxieties can be allayed by the administrator by following through on whatever outcomes may have resulted. An effective administrator is one who tries to keep the staff informed about changes and developments which result from a problem-solving session. This is particularly true when the outcomes of an interview mean that the administrator will be taking responsibility to implement a decision. If for some reason or another the outcomes of a meeting cannot be implemented as readily as possible, a simple note or comment to the involved staff member is appropriate and will help to ensure continual support.

In summary, the goal of successful conflict management should be to find solutions to complex issues which have high quality and high acceptance. To accomplish this goal, careful attention should be given to one's personal approach to conflict situations. Avoiding, forcing, compromising and smoothing are generally not as effective at satisfactorily resolving conflict as is a direct, confrontive style. An important characteristic of the confrontive style is to be able to clarify the meaning of the messages which one is hearing. Such clarification procedures are of immense assistance in identifying the causes of the problem and finding creative solutions. Finally, when systematic problem-solving procedures are used, the probability increases that the conflict can be rationally approached and that high quality decisions generating high acceptance can be found.

Additional Readings Suggested by the Author

Alan C. Filley. *Interpersonal Conflict Resolution*. Glenview, IL: Scott, Foresman and Co., 1975.

Fred E. Jandt. *Conflict Resolution through Communication*. New York: Harper and Row Publishers, 1973.

Paul G. Swingle. *The Management of Power*. New York: John Wiley & Sons, Inc., 1976.

Evaluating the Performance of the Chief Executive Officer

James D. Harvey

In 1973, the American College of Hospital Administrators published a very important and potentially valuable task force report entitled *Principles of Appointment and Tenure of the Executive Officer*. Added to its usefulness as elicited in the document's title, it avers that:

> . . . . formal performance review of the chief executive officer should be done annually. . . . Evaluation is a major responsibility of the board of trustees, not to be delegated by them to anyone, regardless of the resources the board may choose to employ in this process. . . . Often, it isn't done well. Experience of consulting firms called into hospitals in which the chief executive has been terminated or is under board pressure indicates that, in a high percentage of these situations, routine formal evaluation is missing entirely, or the process lacks frankness or lacks criteria to which both parties would agree.

The task force report goes on to say that the evaluation should be carried out at four levels:

1. Areawide health care status
2. Institutional success
3. Role of the chief executive officer
4. Management skills

The report points out that while evaluation of the health status of the population served by the hospital might well be related to the effectiveness of the hospital itself, it is not fair to hold the chief executive officer (CEO) responsible for this aspect. It should always be considered, however, because this is the outcome sought by the individual hospital.

The institutional success level, the role of the CEO level, and the management skills level are all within the realm of chief executive evaluation, the document points out. It asserts that there are probably many ways for this process to be accomplished. It contains this one qualification: "However it is to be done, evaluating the CEO requires pre-agreement on what is to be evaluated and standards for measuring if evaluation is to be meaningful and equitable." Embodied in this mild statement are two word groups, the lack of which are the major obstacles to achieving effective evaluation. They are "pre-agreement" and "standards for measuring." Precious few hospital boards evaluate performance of the CEO by pre-agreed standards.

The ACHA, as if noting this deficiency, produced a report in October, 1976, on a pilot study on executive compensation entitled *The Position of the Hospital Chief Executive*. This document sharpened the CEO's accountabilities, e.g., those results expected of a chief executive officer in the performance of his or her duties.

Using the tenets contained in the *Principles of Appointment and Tenure of Executive Officers* and the accountabilities of the CEO as listed in *The Position of the Hospital Chief Executive,* a model emerges which can be used to develop an effective performance evaluation process.

The Position of the Hospital Chief Executive study suggests that the CEO has seven accountabilities. They fall within the following areas of activity:

1. Planning and organizing
2. Achieving hospital objectives
3. Quality of medical services
4. Allocation of resources
5. Crisis resolution
6. Compliance with regulation
7. Promotion of the hospital

Chief Executive Levels

Each accountability is written in one or two sentences. Each points out that the CEO may act within an accountability at one of three levels:

1. Chief administrative officer
2. Chief executive, tactical
3. Chief executive, strategic

This differentiation recognizes the fact that a CEO operates differently from institution to institution and implies that the governing board involves itself in the hospital in different ways. Rather than speculate as to which level a particular CEO may be involved, this article will demonstrate how measures and standards can be developed for each accountability. The type of standard used to gauge performance in fulfilling an accountability would naturally be derived from the level at which the CEO operates.

Accountability Statements

Following is a listing of each accountability statement taken from *The Position of the Hospital Chief Executive*. (The ultimate result of each statement is underlined.)

Accountability I. Planning and Organizing: Participates with the board in charting the course the hospital is to take in response to the developing needs of the community for formulating and recommending sound strategies and plans.
Comment: "Participates" and "formulating and recommending" are key words leading to "charting the course."

Accountability II. Achieving Hospital Objectives: Ensures the attainment of hospital objectives through the effective administration of the operation. This is accomplished chiefly through the selection, development and motivation of hospital personnel and the continuous review and control of their efforts.
Comment: This accountability emphasizes getting things done through people. The words "selection, development and motivation" stress this.

Accountability III. Quality of Medical Services: Responds to the community's need for quality health care services by monitoring the adequacy of the hospital's medical activities, and closely coordinating with the board and medical staff in achieving and maintaining the required standards of medical performance.
Comment: Key verbs in achieving this end result are "monitoring" and "coordinating."

Accountability IV. Allocation of Resources: Ensures the provision of health care services at prices the community can afford by the acquisition and utilization of available resources and the development of improved techniques and practices.
Comment: The action words deal with marshalling appropriate resources and operating efficiently.

Accountability V. Crisis Resolution: Fosters a smoothly functioning, efficient operation through timely and effective resolution of disturbances as they occur.
Comment: This is self-explanatory.

Accountability VI. Compliance with Regulation: Ensures compliance with all regulations governing health care delivery and the rules of accrediting bodies by continually monitoring the operation and its programs, and initiating changes where required.
Comment: The key action words are "monitoring" and "initiating changes."

Accountability VII. Promotion of the Hospital: Encourages the integration of the hospital with the community and a favorable attitude among its various publics by establishing and maintaining effective communication and public relations programs.
Comment: This emphasizes the use of communications to achieve the end result, presumably through means beyond conventional PR efforts.

The fulfillment of each of these accountabilities could never be verified if measures reflecting achievement were not articulated. This a step where the evaluation process could easily stall. Measures should be identified and agreed upon by the CEO and the governing board. Only after this has been done should standards be attached to the measures. Measures are the yardsticks to be used in determining accomplishment of accountabilities.

As an example, the measure for the high-jump is inches/feet or meters; for the 100-yard dash the measure would be hundredths of a second. The standard for the world record holder in the high-jump is 7′7¼″, while the standard for the world record holder of the 100-yard dash is 0:09.1 seconds. The standard for qualifying for the Olympics in the high-jump is something less than the world record. As a matter of fact, each high jumper has a different standard.

There may be measures that are applicable to one CEO's accountability and not to another's. Also, there are vast differences between institutions which would dictate that the standards for a CEO's job in one hospital would differ markedly in another hospital. This is why it is so important for a governing board and its incumbent chief executive officer to agree in advance about the latter's accountabilities.

Assigning Measures to Accountabilities

In developing the evaluative process, the major initiative normally should come from the incumbent CEO. If, however, a governing board is looking for a CEO and wishes to draft measures on its own to enhance its recruiting effort, consultative help probably should be sought. This will clarify the mutual expectations of the governing board and the prospective chief executive officer and can, in the future, be used as an objective means of appraising the CEO's performance.

Examples of measures which represent areas of activity in which standards could be established for the previously listed accountabilities are:

Accountability I. Planning and Organization

Possible areas of measurement:

- *Effectiveness of the planning process*
- *CEO's input to board decision-making*
- *Community's perception of needs being met*

Accountability II. Achieving Hospital Objectives

Possible area of measurement:

- *Institutional goal achievement record*

Accountability III. Quality of Medical Services

Possible areas of measurement:

- *Quality care reports and followup activity*
- *Development of new/improved patient care programs*
- *Mix of physicians by age, clinical background, etc.*
- *Effectiveness of medical staff organization*

Accountability IV. Allocation of Resources

Possible areas of measurement:

- *Cost containment effectiveness*
- *Budget performance*
- *HAS reports, comparison with other institutions*
- *Paid liability claims against the institution*
- *New/expanded revenue sources developed*

Accountability V. Crisis Resolution

Possible areas of measurement:

- *Number of problems*
- *Number of problems resolved effectively*
- *Review of systems developed as a result of conflict*

Accountability VI. Compliance with Regulations

Possible area of measurement:

- *Regulations not complied with*

Accountability VII. Promotion of the Hospital

Possible areas of measurement:
- *Public exposure*
- *Public relations*
- *Communication efforts/effectiveness*

A Personal Accountability

The CEO should add self-accountability assuring career-long competence. If he/she does not, the governing board might impose such an accountability as protection for the institution. Such an accountability might read:

Takes a leadership role in educational programs, including participation both as a teacher and as a student, to promote career-long competence in professional pursuits.

Possible areas of measurement:
- *Extent of teaching responsibilities*
- *Useful educational meetings attended*
- *ACHA advancement/recertification*

One might react to such a list of measurement areas by saying, "So what?" Certainly, one can't gauge achievement of these measures any better than the accountability itself. The point is that the measures should be developed as representing the areas of activity through which the CEO successfully accomplishes the specific end result. Only then should explicit standards be developed. It is important that the standards define and clarify the extent and direction in which the chief executive should be channeling efforts. The board/CEO agreement will stipulate that through these standards the end result will be achieved. It is impossible to set standards for every ounce of energy a CEO expends. This should not be the objective. The governing board and the CEO will agree that the negotiated standards, if accomplished as agreed, would signify that the job is being done.

Setting Standards

It is desirable to settle on a standard which, in the board's and incumbent CEO's opinion, would represent fully adequate performance. This is a level of performance which reflects that the job is being done in a way the governing board wants it to be done and in the way the institution needs it to be done. At performance evaluation time, bad marks or "brownie points" can be calculated in degrees of deviation from the fully adequate performance standard.

For the seven accountabilities for which measures have previously been suggested, standards can now be developed. It must be emphasized that the standards listed below are examples only. They are written to stimulate development of appropriate standards in specific situations. Areas of measurement, likewise, are only examples.

Accountability I. Planning and Organizing

1. Measure: Effectiveness of the Planning Process
   Suggested Fully Adequate Standard:
   - *The established planning process, including long-range plan, development of program elements, institutional management and departmental goals, and budgeting is carried out in a one-year continuing cycle, which includes annual review and endorsement by the medical staff and approval of the governing board*
2. Measure: Input to Board Decision-Making
   Suggested Fully Adequate Standards:
   - *The board is not forced by external pressure to initiate or disband any program, or conversely, all new programs approved by the board are generated through the planning process*
   - *Annual private poll of trustees concerning their confidence in making policy decisions is conducted, revealing 80% of the board is satisfied*
3. Measure: Community's Perception of Needs Being Met
   Suggested Fully Adequate Standards:
   - *Routine contributions to the hospital (provided it is a tax-exempt organization) exceed the previous year's level of contributions*
   - *Impressions of the institution's response to community needs by local and state health department officials plus local and state health planners is generally positive. This feedback should be solicited by the chairman of the governing board*

Comment: Overt responses from community service agencies and city-county governments might also be appropriate to obtain. The acceptable level of positive reactions from these individuals might be measured as a percentage of total reactions if the governing board and chief executive officer desire to go that far.

Accountability II. Achieving Hospital Objectives

1. Measure: Institutional Goal Achievement Record
   Suggested Fully Adequate Standards:
   - *Achievement of 80% of institutional and management goals set each year*
   - *Achievement of 80% of all departmental goals*

Comment: The assumption is that the goals mentioned are attached to organization subdivisions, while the program elements in the first accountability standard above deal with clinical services and programs cutting across organizational lines. A third standard might be:

- *Year-round planning cycle is adhered to by the administration*

Comment: This differs from the first standard above which emphasizes medical staff and governing board approval. This standard deals with process.

Accountability III. Quality of Medical Services

1. Measure: Quality Care Reports
   Suggested Fully Adequate Standards:
   - *A medical staff quality care report is rendered at each board meeting and each executive committee meeting*
   - *Decisions made in response to problem areas identified in quality care reports are implemented within the time frame designated 80% of the time*
2. Measure: Development of New/Improved Patient Care Programs
   Suggested Fully Adequate Standard:
   - *Achievement of 70% of the program elements contained in the long-range plan within designated time frame*
3. Measure: Physician Mix
   Suggested Fully Adequate Standards:
   - *As part of the continuing planning process, a study of the mix of physicians by age, clinical background, etc., is carried out annually with specific recruitment and retention goals set as a result*
   - *Goals established for recruitment and retention are accomplished in 80% of the instances within the established time frames*
4. Measure: Medical Staff Organization
   Suggested Fully Adequate Standards:
   - *A composite average attendance percentage of all physicians in all committees connected with medical staff activities is 60%*

Comment: This standard does not necessarily reflect effectiveness—it assumes that the more participation by physicians, the better the medical staff operates—and could be fallacious. However, it is better than nothing.

- *75% of the actions taken by the medical executive committee relate to major policy determination or changes in regulations and/or are reportable as such to the governing board*

Comment: Here, the function of the medical executive committee as a policy body as opposed to a "chowder and marching society" is emphasized. It is also good for the medical staff to understand such standards—but it's the CEO who must be facilitative.

Accountability IV. Allocation of Resources

1. Measure: Cost Containment
   Suggested Fully Adequate Standards:
   - *Cost containment goals are set for each department in the institution and are met 80% of the time*
   - *Aggregate cost containment results equal $100,000 (example only) each year*
2. Measure: Budget Performance
   Suggested Fully Adequate Standards:
   - *Budget is approved by the governing board prior to the beginning of the fiscal year*
   - *Expenses do not deviate from budget by more than 2% when adjusted for occupancy fluctuation*

Comment: Some boards may wish to establish a bottom line standard.

3. Measure: HAS Report
   Suggested Fully Adequate Standards:
   - *A comparison with HAS reports is revealed to the board on a semi-annual basis, together with appropriate analysis*
   - *By mutual consent, goals for improved performance in HAS indicators are negotiated annually by the governing board and the chief executive officer; achievement of 80% of the goals is expected*
4. Measure: New/Expanded Revenue Sources Developed
   Suggested Fully Adequate Standard:
   - *At least one new source of revenue (more than $10,000) is generated annually which does not affect the cost of patient care, but rather is recoverable from non-inpatient sources*

Comment: This kind of standard, of course, could vary considerably depending on individual circumstances.

5. Measure: Liability Claims
   Suggested Fully Adequate Standard:
   - *Claims experience for period under review is less than previous period*

Accountability V. Crisis Resolution

1. Measure: Number of Problems
   Suggested Fully Adequate Standard:
   - *No more than three internally generated problems requiring board action occur each year*

Comment: Examples are strikes, disciplinary actions on groups of employees or physicians, etc., serious problems in accounts payable in which creditors' lawsuits are brought against the institution, etc.

2. Measure: Number of Problems Resolved Effectively
   Suggested Fully Adequate Standard:
   - *A specific section of the CEO's annual report to the board deals with the CEO's impressions on problems facing the institution (not necessarily internally generated) which were solved effectively*
3. Measure: Review of Systems Developed to Resolve Conflict
   Suggested Fully Adequate Standard:
   - *In the annual report to the board, the chief executive officer reviews systems in place to resolve conflict, reports on the activities within those previously defined systems and makes comments as to their relative effectiveness by comparing statistics against previously agreed upon numbers*

Comment: Examples are grievance procedures, union contract negotiations, EEOC actions, unemployment compensation claims, worker's compensation, OSHA penalties, counseling activities, boiler inspection reports, malpractice record, physicians' due process appeals, etc.

Accountability VI. Compliance with Regulation

1. Measure: Regulations Complied With
   Suggested Fully Adequate Standards:
   - *Full licensure 100% of the time*
   - *JCAH accreditation maintained*
   - *CEO reports to board on all inspection/accreditation reports, submits plan for followup and reports followup on a routine basis.*

Comment: A fully adequate performance standard should normally require no less than full accreditation by the JCAH. There are institutions, however, where this might be impossible and a different standard would be appropriate.

Accountability VII. Promotion of the Hospital

1. Measure: Public Exposure
   Suggested Fully Adequate Standards:
   - *Twelve local speeches delivered by the CEO to an aggregate crowd of 1,000*
   - *Six appearances by the CEO on television and radio programs*

Comment: This kind of standard, since it deals with public exposure, does not deal with the quality of exposure. Another standard might involve public exposure by other members of the hospital family. Again, the numbers are negotiable.

2. Measure: Public Reaction
   Suggested Fully Adequate Standards:
   - *Answers to patient questionnaires meet predetermined percentage standards*
   - *Specific feedback from consumer groups and consumer surrogates with whom the hospital deals (HEW, Medicare and Medicaid, Blue Cross, etc.) indicates general satisfaction with institutional performance in specific relationships with the groups*

Comment: The governing board and the chief executive might establish actual numbers here. It should be noted that when accountabilities are subdivided into measures and standards, subjective opinions can be made more confidently because of the narrow range covered by the standard. There's nothing wrong with someone else's opinion being used in a performance evaluation so long as it relates to a specfic standard. The way someone feels is a fact, after all. A "feeling" on a narrowly framed standard is much more likely to be objective than a scatter shot opinion of a person in toto.

3. Measure: Communications Efforts and Effectiveness
   Suggested Fully Adequate Standards:
   - *A subjective review of internal and external communications by the development committee of the governing board is made and compared to previously established goals on written communications*
   - *Response from the reader population is ascertained by:*
     a. spontaneous feedback
     b. opinion poll which indicates level of satisfaction equal to a predetermined percentage

Comment: After one or two attempts, acceptable parameters could be established. Public relations prizes awarded for the hospital's publications would be another way of measuring effectiveness, though certainly not the only, or best, way.

In connection with the author's added accountability on assuring lifelong competence, the emphasis rests on the effectiveness of the educational process undertaken in the self-development of the CEO.

Measures:

- Performance as preceptor to students
- Performance in lectures to groups
- Participation in journal clubs and other in-house education activities
- Speeches to hospital-related groups
- Services on commissions and committees with health services and planning objectives

Standards should be as follows:

1. Measure: Performance as Preceptor
   Suggested Fully Adequate Standard:
   - *CEO is acceptable to a recognized graduate program to serve as preceptor*
2. Measure: Performance in Lectures
   Suggested Fully Adequate Standard:
   - *Group feedback—anonymous poll indicates 75% of the attendees are satisfied*
3. Measure: Participation in Journal Club and Other In-house Educational Activities
   Suggested Fully Adequate Standards:
   - *Regular participation—attends 60% of the designated meetings*
   - *Participates in six employee orientation meetings a year. Teaches hospital supervisors one six-hour course on leadership with no attendance requirements—75% of enrollees attend 50% of the lectures*
4. Measure: Speeches to Hospital-related Groups
   Suggested Fully Adequate Standard:
   - *CEO is invited to speak to one health-related group external to own hospital during a year's time*
5. Measure: Services on Commissions and Committees
   Suggested Fully Adequate Standard:
   - *Serves on at least one such group at all times*

A Word About Goals . . .

It should be noted that achieving the end results of accountabilities meets the continuing expectations placed upon the job holder by the governing board. Implicit in all jobs is the need to improve.

Improvement in performance of a job is accomplished through achieving goals which should not be interpreted in the same context as achievement of accountabilities. Thus, standards for specific accountabilities may well include establishment of a specific goal. For instance, if a standard stipulates that the number of days revenue in accounts receivable is 75, and the governing board and the chief executive arrive at an understanding that this could and should be improved, a specific goal to reduce that number to 60 days may be in order. Achievement of this goal would impact positively on the individual's performance for that period of time—thus more brownie points.

It should be pointed out that achievement of a goal tends to raise the standard of performance for a given accountability. This phenomenon is exemplified by athletes who are performing against standards today which, in some instances, were unattainable goals for their great grandfathers in the 19th century. The accepted standard today was an out-of-reach goal of yesterday. This is the nature of a system which emphasizes achievement of day-to-day end results plus goals, the latter serving to elevate the day-to-day standards in the long run.

The Process

Obviously, the entire governing board should not engage in negotiations to establish a CEO's accountabilities, measures and standards. The task should be assigned to no more than a three-person group, the chairman of the board being one. An understanding of the process is important for all involved. The same individuals should participate in the performance evaluation itself. An accounting of the process should be made to the full governing body periodically.

These guidelines are not intended to be prescriptive. Expected performance can be defined within understandable limits so that an objective performance appraisal can later be carried out. Having negotiated standards in advance allows performance of the individual concerned to be measured with ease. In itself, this process tends to improve performance. This is the object of any sort of evaluation. As the parties to the evaluative process become more sophisticated, performance at other levels might be defined, clarifying the difference between marginal and superior performance.

A definite schedule for developing the job description, accountabilities, measures and standards should be established, the board being advised, through appropriate mechanisms, on the progress being made. A continuing cycle is established so that review and salary decisions are made at predetermined dates. There should also be a time set aside to evaluate and update the CEO's accountabilities, measures, and standards themselves, as distinct from the process heretofore described. This should be done separate from the evaluation.

The CEO should furnish written input concerning his or her performance to the chairman of the governing board. This would follow the format above, with the CEO simply giving the facts. Based on these facts, the evaluators on the governing board would make a determination. Misunderstandings, before and after the evaluation, can be almost totally eliminated this way. Uncertainties in the relationships between the governing board and the chief executive officer of the hospital will disappear, effectiveness will be enhanced, and mutual satisfaction will prevail.

In those rare instances where the process causes dissatisfaction, a well understood and amicable disassociation has a better chance of taking place. Whatever the outcome, understanding and acceptance based on objectivity will have resulted. The motivational rewards for all involved will be plentiful.

References

ACHA Task Force V, *Principles of Appointment and Tenure of Executive Officers*. Chicago: American College of Hospital Administrators, 1973.

The Position of the Hospital Chief Executive. Chicago: American College of Hospital Administrators, 1976.

Accountability Management Performance Appraisal Manual: Hillcrest Medical Center, April, 1970. Dallas: Edward N. Hay & Associates, 1970.

Old and New Thinking About Hospital Payments

Everett A. Johnson, Ph.D.

The present-day extensive regulation of hospitals through the Medicare program is based on an assertion that federal dollars not be wasted, that accountability for government dollar expenditures is of first concern. However, the unstated objective in manipulating hospital payments appears to be to limit federal spending to Social Security Administration funds and congressional appropriations. Consequently, the Department of Health, Education, and Welfare continually defines and redefines allowable costs for hospitals.

After eight years of being directed and controlled through Medicare regulations, private hospital corporations are now almost as tightly controlled as military, veteran, and public health hospitals. The only significant remaining difference is that HEW actions have not saved money, but have shifted unallowable costs to the total responsibility of non-Medicare patients. HEW has been practicing cost shifting, rather than cost saving.

Should the federal proportion of patients be further expanded beyond Medicare and Medicaid and encompass a national health insurance program, control will then be as strong as in government-owned hospitals. Currently, the result of having an average of 35% of total revenues coming from federal sources allows the federal government to escape responsibility for deficits in operations as well as the freedom to carp about the high cost of hospital care.

To continue a federal program of cost-based payments to hospitals is to keep the cart before the horse. The principle is the same as the local supermarket permitting the federal government to control their accounting systems, pricing policies, profit centers, depreciation, expansion, and inventories, simply because they accept federal food stamps from their customers.

The basis of the present dilemma arose in the original Medicare legislation. The American Hospital Association encouraged the use of "reasonable cost" as the criteria for determining hospital payment.

The AHA should have used the concept of "cost plus." Any large contractor of the Department of Defense in the preceding 20 years could have quickly explained the differences and the necessity for such language in the legislation.

With eight years experience with "reasonable cost," hospitals are still receiving less than total cost for caring for *the beneficiaries* of government programs. There is an expanding belief by bureaucrats and Blue Cross executives that cost-based payment formulas for hospitals must be abandoned. Medicare and Medicaid bureaucrats, as well as an increasing number of Blue Cross executives, are now espousing prospective payment methods.

Looking for a New Way

For the past several years, the federal government has encouraged experimentation with a variety of new payment approaches. They hope to find an effective way to slow the continual rise in hospital costs and payments. How realistic is this hope? Is it a good theory that works in the real world? What effect will recent federal planning legislation have on hospital costs and charges? Are there economic forces in hospital care that are beyond the scope of hospital control? Underlying their efforts is a hope that hospital rates are controllable by hospital administration, rather than by external economic forces.

In the late 1940s, when Blue Cross had an explosive growth, ratesetting was almost completely a private affair. A rate structure was established according to a hospital's own needs and goals. When hospital costs began to rise significantly in the early 1950s, cost-based methods increased in popularity. Even today a significant number of hospitals do not receive most of their reimbursement through cost-based formulas, despite Medicare and Medicaid programs cost formulas. Such systems require an audit and a post-audit settlement when hospital revenues exceed a specific definition of cost.

Yet hospital costs have continued to increase as rapidly, or more rapidly, in those parts of the country where there is heaviest reliance on cost-based systems. Obviously, cost systems have gradually become ineffective, or at least do not now make a significant difference for cost containment purposes.

With national health insurance likely, it is worthwhile for future goals to review the rationale for prospective payment, since this will probably be the most seriously considered method of paying for hospital services.

Physicians and Community Reinforce Monopoly

In the hospital industry, market forces are typically inelastic because hospitals are a series of mini-monopolies. Why is this so?

In a community, two major forces tend to reinforce monopoly conditions. The first is the physician. Today, a majority of patients in hospitals are attended by specialists, since 82% of all physicians restrict their practice to a specialty. When a patient has more than one disability, is older, or is admitted for trauma, several physicians may be involved in his or her care. Hospital care is now practiced by a series of related specialists who may be involved with one patient supplementing the work of the attending physician. They are selected by the attending physician using personal knowledge of their abilities, judgments, and skills.

This kind of knowledge about a colleague's abilities is acquired over time, and is limited by the range of earlier experiences. Until a patient's problem is recognized as clearly beyond the capability of locally available physicians, the patient will not be transferred elsewhere. Patients obtain their medical care locally, except for that small proportion of patients who self-refer to a "super-clinic." In many communities less than 2% go elsewhere for care.

This is a reality of medical practice. It is reinforced by a public which selects, and prefers to remain with, one source of primary care. Economically, this practice tends toward a monopolistic hospital market condition, since a physician's knowledge of colleagues' competence is limited to those with whom he or she has frequent contact—typically to the hospital medical staff. Even if all physicians could attend their patients in all hospitals, this limitation would remain. The informal human restraint leads to referrals to local colleagues rather than distant medical centers.

The Community

Community attitudes are a second reinforcing element toward monopoly. Demographic studies on patient choice repeatedly report a preference for hospitalization near their place of residence. This should surprise no one, even though some patients occasionally bypass the nearest hospitals.

Most patients are part of a family and want them nearby in time of severe stress. The greater the distance to a hospital, the more difficult it becomes for a family to visit the hospital. Patients are also aware that in the local hospital their friends are on the hospital staff. This provides additional reassurance to them. Except for serious medical problems, patients do not readily accept distant hospitalization.

These two factors are sufficiently important to overcome any differences in hospital charges. Price variation does not effectively operate under these local monopoly conditions. In addition, third-party payments, government programs, insurance carriers, and the Blues provide coverage for more than 80% of hospitalizations. Consequently, price differentials are inconsequential for a substantial number of patients. The public is far more concerned with monthly insurance premiums than with the cost of a hospitalization.

In effect, hospital market behavior is what it is because physicians and patients make uneconomic decisions. Most people who have thought about these issues have therefore concluded that some type of price review and control is necessary for a hospital rate structure.

Most hospital administrators would not argue this conclusion. They would argue, however, for reasonableness in the use of any review mechanism, and for a need to allow surplus retention, or profit, for well-managed institutions.

Within this setting, the implications of a prospective payment system needs to be defined in terms of capital costs and operating costs of hospitals, as well as the effect of patient volume on hospital services.

The issues of capital cost have recently been faced by federal planning legislation. Because of local monopoly conditions in hospital markets, it is obvious that new services can be initiated, or existing ones expanded that are unneeded or uneconomic, such as the current excess of open-heart units. Planning agency approval must now be obtained for capital programs in excess of $100,000 if depreciation and interest costs are to be included in reimbursement from a federal program.

Solving the Problem of Excessive Development

The present thrust of mandated planning is to deter "excessive" hospital development. The implicit expectation is that somehow a process of attrition will gradually size hospitals to population needs. Unfortunately, mandated planning mechanisms still have to prove that this objective is achievable.

The real cure-all for over-expanded hospital facilities is a program which can use market forces to phase out institutions which have excessive charges for inferior services. As it is now, if planning agencies are responsible for this goal, they must face extremely sensitive issues because hospitals arouse local feelings of pride. In addition, planners are placed in the difficult position of making judgments on the competence of boards of trustees and hospital administrations, as well as levels of medical care for which no generally accepted criteria exist.

Market forces which operate in a competitive industry are ineffective in the hospital field, and excess capacity remains available at higher than needed market prices.

There are at least two ways to solve this problem. One is to limit the annual amount of payment-on-debt service that can be included in a hospital rate structure, and the other is to use rate ceilings to eliminate inefficient operations, i.e., hospitals that make poor capital investment decisions, in terms of financing instruments or estimating market demands.

At this time, planning agencies seldom consider the interrelationship between capital and operating costs. High construction cost often may mean lower than average operating cost; while lower initial capital cost may create higher operating cost. Life cycle costing is the only logical basis for determining the financial cost of a new project and it is rarely used.

The recently expanded, mandated planning process will substantially reduce future program flexibility and also delay the general use of new medical knowledge. The current situation of planning agencies is the fact that their planning has precedence over institutional planning.

In practice, the current $100,000 exemption on hospital projects means a detailed control of hospital capital costs since most significant improvements in medical instrumentation or programming exceed this amount. It is an example of unequal control because in a hospital with $1,000,000 a year revenue it is a 10% ceiling while in a $20,000,000 hospital it is 0.5%.

A planning agency, one step removed from the operating experience of hospitals, is more likely to attempt to plan future medical care schemes on the basis of "what ought to be," rather than "what the public will support," as outlined in PL 93-641 and PL 92-603. The efforts of the federal government to promote Health Maintenance Organizations (HMOs) is an example of encouraging a particular model of ambulatory medical care that has as yet to gain much public or medical support and is now caught in many bureaucratic entanglements.

While authority from planning agencies is a necessity, comprehensive, detailed control is a poor substitute for policy direction. The goal sought is a combination of concern for desired medical care programming and reasonable capital expenditures.

A major interest in medical programming is the administrator's concern about human behavior, particularly that of the physician. When a hospital does not go ahead and develop a new program, it may mean that some of the more competent and concerned physicians will shift their interests to another hospital where additional medical capability is available, depreciating the quality of care in their present hospital.

Rather than a nitty-gritty approach, it would be more sensible to set a sliding ceiling on capital costs to accommodate different volumes by size of hospital and inflation, and yet allow hospitals to proceed with plant expansion and new programs that are justifiable by market experience as reflected in hospital revenues.

Limiting Expenditures

There are two concepts that meet this criteria. One, a limit on total annual capital costs including leasing agreements to between 7–8% of total operating revenues. For example, an 8% ceiling for a $1,000,000 annual revenue hospital could have a total annual capital expenditure of $80,000, while a $20,000,000 annual revenue hospital would be authorized $1,600,000. Another is to set an indebtedness ceiling at one-and-one-half, or one times annual revenue. The total allowable long-term debt for a $1,000,000 hospital at one-and-a-half times annual gross revenue would be $1,500,000, and for a $20,000,000 hospital would be $30,000,000. Specific studies are needed to establish a reasonable range.

Reasonable ceilings for expenditures for annual capital equipment purchases and long-term needs are needed. Debt ceilings of these types would prevent gross over-expansion, and would eliminate capital cost mismanagement without undue and unnecessary interference with hospital operational autonomy. Under special conditions, an appeals process should be developed for unique situations.

These concepts do not imply an elimination of approving expansion plans of hospitals. However, rather than use a fixed amount of $100,000, no matter what the size of an institution's budget, a more reasonable approach could be to require planning agency approval for all building capital expenditures that exceed 10% of annual depreciation costs, or about one percent of revenue. This rule should apply no matter what the source of capital funds, operating surplus, mortgages, leasing or gifts. In addition, the required approach for "any substantial change in service" as included in PL 92-603, should be redefined to remove subjective interpretation.

Such changes in present planning legislation would eliminate a substantial amount of planning agency detail, allow an increase in hospital initiative, and permit time to be given to the serious, more meaningful areas for planning future developments of the health care system.

If a hospital program is demanded or required by a community and cannot be supported by patient revenues, special Hill-Burton type government grants might be considered. Alcohol and drug addiction treatment programs are examples. These grants should pay both capital and operating costs over a long period of time. In the past and present, government programs have provided only a partial subsidy of capital costs and a gradually decreasing support for operating expenses. It is time for government to consider once again the desirability for block grant funding, even though the present federal fiscal climate will not favor this mechanism.

A prospective payment program is a desirable vehicle for accomplishing change. It would eliminate a need for detailed planning reviews and allow time to identify serious unmet medical care needs, work out ways to meet them, and prevent unwise hospitals from acquiring excessive capital debt.

To facilitate competitive forces, well-managed profitable hospitals should be allowed to retain and spend their surpluses to increase working capital or one-time purchases of capital plant and equipment within these proposed guidelines. This would encourage the well-managed institutions to gradually improve their local market position by acquiring new, more sophisticated instrumentation or develop a stronger financial position. It would encourage rational hospital administrations to develop new programs of service which their markets would support, i.e., where new revenues exceed new costs. Unmet need would quickly become apparent to planners, who would have a well-defined mandate to lobby the development and funding of new programs to fill existing gaps in service. To perform at this level of sophistication will require more improved quality and expertise than current planning agencies demonstrate.

Operating costs are a second area of major concern in prospective payment. They are inevitably intertwined with the size and service volumes of a hospital, as well as its case mix of patients.

Within rather broad limits, a relationship exists between volume of service and cost per unit of service. This fact is often obscured by the use of gross measures of cost, such as patient day expense or case cost. At a department level, where individual cost data are maintained by test or procedure, a relationship to costs is much clearer. Gross statistics mask this relationship since it is generally true that the larger a hospital, the more comprehensive its medical care services and the greater its efforts to assure quality control.

For example, the larger the hospital, the greater the likelihood that there will be programs such as a social service department, a rehabilitation service, health education programs, and medical education. Each program adds to the total cost of hospitalizing a patient, but expands a physician's ability to cope with medical problems. Quality redundancy is increased by an organized infection control program, safety, fire, and disaster program, security efforts, and a multitude of management and operational procedures that insure hospital and medical staff performance.

Knowing the Case Mix of Patients

The case mix of patients affects a hospital's operating expenses. If there are many seriously ill patients with shortened lengths of stay who must use a high level of diagnostic and therapeutic services, costs are higher on a case-cost basis. A cancer patient treated by surgery, rehabilitative services, and radiation is a much more expensive case than a patient treated for an uncomplicated gall bladder removal, length of stay being equal. The proportions of each type of patient in a hospital population substantially changes operating costs. A hospital's case mix of patients will affect total costs, revenues, case costs, and per-patient day costs in a variety of ways.

Existing gross measures of overall measures of hospital costs and revenues are inadequate without a detailed knowledge of the case mix of patients.

At best, a community general hospital can control case mix only in a crude fashion. Three major ways are used by hospitals to exert a limited control and none are in a patient's best interest. The first is to block admission of patients who will probably have an expensive hospital stay; the second is to prevent the appointment of physicians to the medical staff who have a preponderance of expensive cases in their type of practice; and the third is to limit the types of equipment and trained personnel available, or as a variation, to restrict the number of beds in that clinical service. A hospital's control over case mix is therefore more fantasy than fact.

In the past, the costing of hospital care by disease entity has frequently been tried. Since indirect costs are generally between 30–40% of total expense, the results of disease costing have been ambiguous.

PSRO Programs

As a result of federal legislation, Professional Standards Review Organizations (PSROs) are responsible for admission, concurrent, and discharge reviews for each patient, for their length of stay and appropriateness of care. Useful disease-costing data can be accumulated through this program. Over time it is likely that the data will come to be used by PSRO programs to gradually encourage the standardizations of diagnostic procedures and treatment modalities. Its ultimate effect will tend to promote a lock-step method of treating patients. It is predictable that when physicians ultimately perceive this effect, their resistance to this program will and should substantially escalate. It is also likely that the federal government will attempt to apply disease costing to hospitals through the use of case cost ceilings. An embryonic effort in this direction was made under Phase IV of the Economic Stabilization Program in 1974.

If a market price is not achievable because of local monopoly positions of hospitals, and since cost-based payment provides no incentives for cost containment, what will? Some type of prospective payment is the probable future course of events. How realistic is this viewpoint?

Prospective payment can be designed in several different ways. No matter what the choice, *the desired goal is the maintenance of fiscally healthy hospitals needed to provide readily accessible services of a quality nature at a desired level of medical care, in a reasonably efficient manner*. At this time no federally-controlled payment program achieves this objective, nor recognizes the reality that a majority of hospitals will never achieve maximum dollar efficiency—just as in the case of all other industries.

A prospective payment system means that a hospital's rate structure is established prior to rendering patient care. It implies that no post-audit settlements are a part of the program, only that operating experience is considered when a new set of rate adjustments are requested. If a post-audit adjustment is involved, the system is again back to a form of a cost-based system, because cost caps are used. Further, prospective payment means that an external, more powerful agency reviews and approves or adjusts a proposed rate structure. In essence, a hospital proposes, and a more powerful agency takes action on, a rate structure.

Several schemes have been proposed that fly under the banner of prospective payment, but are, in fact, a camouflaged variation of cost-based payments. Line item budget review systems are an example. Here rates are established based on an analysis of the costs involved in each department. The Medicare method of apportioning departmental costs, based on the proportion of revenue from Medicare to total department revenue, is another. Target rates are also cost-based rather than prospective, because it is a system which uses group averages to arrive at approved rates. The systems are simply a bureaucratic rationale to justify cost-based payment systems.

Incentive rate systems which establish rates and then have the hospitals participate proportionately in profits or losses are also fundamentally cost systems. If the hospital kept all of the earned profits this would not be true. At the present time, hospital financial reserves have been so seriously reduced that the existing prospective system has in effect become cost-based because there is no absorption capability left.

To date, no system is in use that requires performance budgeting. This type of system requires that departmental statistics, as a ratio of inputs to outputs, be measured and paid. Many such ratios, using manhours per unit of output, are in regular internal use in hospitals. Unfortunately, certain areas of hospital operation can be calculated only in a gross fashion because they are variable as to meaning when quality control factors are considered.

Any sytem based on per-patient day, or case costs, or revenue, is not a prospective system. This is so because they are externally established and are based either on a hospital's cost of operation or some form of averaging a group of hospital changes. Such devices imply that all hospitals within a category can achieve the same level of efficiency.

The ultimate goal of prospective payment is to separate the efficient from the inefficient hospital, and reward efficient ones for superior performance or penalize the others for poor performance. The difficulty with this concept is that external forces determine a large part of the cost of operating a hospital. If a hospital is in a labor market where the minimum wage is $3 per hour, and another is in a $2 market, it does not necessarily mean that the higher cost hospital is more or less efficient. The higher labor market rates would raise the overall costs of operations approximately 19%. With between 58%–63% of hospital costs wrapped up in wage and fringe benefit costs, such differences have substantial impact.

Determining Efficiency

The size of a hospital usually correlates with the scope of medical services available. The larger the hospital, the greater the number of patient care services. It is therefore not logical to compare a 200-bed hospital to a 500-bed one. The smaller hospital is not necessarily more efficient because its average costs are lower. Marginal costs by service is a more meaningful way to analyze this issue.

Older hospital plants typically have higher operating expenses than newer ones. Generally an inner-city hospital is older and more expensive to operate, as well as to remodel, but has lower depreciation costs.

What is an efficient hospital? Even if performance budgeting were the basis of prospective payment, older physical plants, and out-of-date design will affect efficiency levels, as well as having their clientele determining the breadth of service demanded. Furthermore, the volume of service rendered by a particular hospital department is not within the control of the hospital administration. A small intensive care or coronary care unit may be essential, but if the need for it is sufficiently small so that a reasonable productivity level is unattainable, what then?

The total complexity and interweaving of these variables are incompletely understood. Any prospective system that attempts to categorize hospitals by these variables will produce inequities because the magnitude of the cumulative effects are unknown. At this time, it is impossible to easily separate the efficient from the inefficient hospitals.

Furthermore, at any point that a new payment system is introduced, hospitals will not all be equally situated. Any standardized approach will therefore fail to keep all needed hospitals fiscally sound, since efficiency in adversity will go unrecognized—and, some inefficient hospitals will need to be maintained because there are no reasonable alternatives for the populations they serve. Whatever the system, its goal should be to improve performance even in the needed, but inefficient hospital.

The problem of the efficient but unneeded hospital is a political dilemma. Realistically, the only acceptable decision is to allow it to continue to operate but to prevent its expansion. Over a long period of time, the establishment of more modern services in other hospitals will gradually increase their attractiveness to physicians and patients, and decrease that of the unneeded hospital. Eventually, the population base may increase sufficiently to justify expansion or it will collapse because of a decreasing or static population base.

In the past, the main focus of prospective systems has been to erect a logic based on consideration of a hospital's operating costs, or a limit of profits. Limitation on profits is an unwise policy when coupled with a rate reviewing process because it increases the penalty for increasing efficiency.

The public, however, needs protection from a hospital which sets its charges too high. Just because there may be a sufficient number of patients who will pay twice a reasonable charge for a service is no reason to ask them to do so when it is operating at 50% efficiency.

Buried in the problem of equitable hospital rates is the issue of payment to hospital-based physicians for their services. The majority of these physicians are on contracts that are a percentage of the gross or net revenue of a hospital department, so that an individual charge for service, such as $10 for an X-ray flat plate of the chest, includes a radiologist's fee for interpretation of the film. In other instances, such as laboratory tests, there is no direct involvement of the pathologist. When a hospital increases rates, additional income is added to the hospital-based specialist because of the percentage arrangement.

In federal medical programs, private practice physician fees are "usual and customary." To reduce the effect of hospital-based physician costs, federal programs should establish unit fees for these physicians so that they are treated like other physicians on a fee-for-service basis where standardized fees have been established. As it is now, if one radiologists receives 25% of the gross revenue for a $10 X-ray, he will receive $2.50, where another one at 33 1/3% would be paid $3.33.

National, regional, and local standardized hospital charges are an impossible dream because cost factors of production are significantly different between hospitals. Rates charged for services must reflect the uniqueness of a particular set of problems with which an individual hospital copes. To pay the same rates to two hospitals in entirely different circumstances may cause the efficiently managed one to go broke because it is attempting to play in a situation where community forces have stacked its deck. Equal rate structures imply equal community medical needs and support of hospitals. This is patently not the real world.

Prospective Rates Cannot Be Standard

Cost payment systems are bad, but the notion of changing from a cost-based to prospective payment mechanism, as presently understood, to escape the disincentives of a cost system is a myth.

The ultimate rationale of any price is justified by the costs incurred to produce goods or services. A market price is arrived at after considering its costs of production and marketing. If the price does not exceed its cost, no enterprise in any industry can produce a particular product—or service.

Hospital care is not divisible. If a service is essential, it must be provided. Albeit, a phasing-out of some services can be achieved if there is another alternative reasonably available, but where no alternative institutional option can be exercised, the only choice is to continue to operate an unprofitable service.

Prospective payment must therefore have a direct relationship to the costs of operating a particular hospital.

This fact does not mean that all prospective systems need to be scrapped. It does mean that standard prospective rates for all hospitals are unworkable. If a hospital is to be at risk for its pricing decisions, then post-audit adjustments for profits are completely illogical within an external rate review system.

The fundamental point in prospective payment is that it is a process by which a more powerful agency approves the rate structure of a hospital. There can be no mechanistic approach to rate-setting because of the many interrelated variables that affect hospital efficiency.

When management consultants judge the efficiency of hospitals, they work from a series of institutional performance indicators, and adjust it from its norm, either up or down, because of unusual circumstances. Through experience, the extent of the adjustment required to reflect earnest, competent administrative effort can be judged.

Using Prospective Payment

Before any form of prospective payment system can succeed, a large battery of performance indicators must be assembled and the conditions defined for approving variances for each indicator. Given the present state of knowledge about hospital operations, no other method can cope with hospital efficiency issues. All other schemes will eventually lead to gross inequities. Equitable treatment of hospitals is a necessity, if efficiently operated hospitals within their individual circumstances are to maintain financial health, and that is the most sensible of goals for any payment program. Inequitable systems pose the long-run threat that efficient, well-managed hospitals with unique sets of unfavorable circumstances may be forced into bankruptcy.

The use of well-defined performance indicators and approved variances will not completely separate the efficient from the inefficient institution. Assessment of quality of care levels is also an essential element to be measured and considered. Medical audit programs may ultimately fill this gap. They are now internally developed and monitored in hospitals, and ultimately must be externalized into a set of standardized parameters of medical care. Such an event will be a long time in coming, and will involve several basic issues in the philosophy of medical care.

The increasing scrutiny of quality of care has raised operating costs because new, detailed control measures, which require additional institutional procedures, are introduced as a response.

A successful prospective payment system must be an individualized institutional program. Any modification which attempts categorization of hospitals will be inequitable. The initial failure will be the downgrading of medical quality in high-cost but efficient hospitals, and ultimately substantial deterioration. A long-run failure will develop because hospitals will sooner or later actively oppose the continuation of inequitable treatment by a prospective payment system that is not based on performance indicators.

An individualized institutional payment system will require a large investment of research funds to develop meaningful performance indicators and quality assessment profiles. Several years of serious effort will be required.

Unfortunately, the imperatives of the American political process will probably ignore the need for this research. The present spate of legislative proposals for a national health insurance program with prospective payment requirements are global in their assumptions of practicality. It will most likely take the threatened collapse of several hospitals with national reputations before the reality of careful profile development is recognized as an imperative for an effective program.

A meat-ax approach by government should be immediately and intensively opposed by all non-government hospitals. If it does not succeed, then hospitals can look ahead to a piecemeal program of financial propping up of individual institutions through the use of special grants. Ultimately, the hospital field will come to see that government on a random, special need basis brought about governmental control of hospitals on a piecemeal basis. By then the final curtain will have been lowered and the struggle will be over without a shot being fired in anger.

These thoughts are not expressed as a plea for a return to the good old days of uncontrolled expansion and autonomous institutional rate setting. It is a statement reflecting on the glib use of the concept of prospective payments and suggesting a way of coping with the real world needs of financing hospital care.

In essence, what has been proposed is: a method for identifying efficient and inefficient institutions, even those in adverse circumstances, through the development of appropriate performance indicators; recognizing and controlling hospital expansion and development by relating reasonable need and financial responsibility; and establishing a way to reward superior financial performance and to place poor performance at risk.

The essential characteristics of a truly prospective payment are:

1. An established rate structure that has been reviewed by an outside authority and approved on the basis of acceptable standards of efficient operations that use performance indicators and case mix as the fundamental inputs;
2. The establishment of a reasonable relationship between total debt and annual capital expenditures by size of institution so that PL 92-603 Section 11-22 reviews are not more frequently required for larger hospitals;
3. A review of the results of hospital care by an external agency to determine that the quality of medical care meets minimally acceptable standards;
4. That where external reviews exist there are no post-audit adjustments that eliminate cost factors or limit net surplus.

The goal of any system of paying hospitals for services to government program beneficiaries must be the maintenance of fiscally healthy institutions that are needed to provide readily accessible care of a quality nature at a desired level of service in a reasonably efficient manner. It is in the public interest that hospitals never compromise this goal.

Evaluation of Administrative and Organizational Effectiveness in Hospitals

Charles M. Ewell, Jr., Ph.D.

How does one evaluate managerial and organizational performance in the field of health services administration? The development of approaches to this challenge is important, in fact, for administration of any organization. The need to measure organizational effectiveness stems from a desire to reach an ideal state: one in which management is able to exercise effective control so that objectives can be met. As suggested by Levey, this process requires that the administrator understand, and be able to use, such general management concepts and techniques as planning, resource allocation, scheduling, measurement, evaluation, feedback and control—and that particular skills in the evaluation process are necessary.[1]

Measuring management effectiveness is a function requiring value judgments. It also involves comparing plans against progress, and appraising the degree of achievement toward the attainment of organizational and individual goals. Although the early planning process is a key step in moving toward objectives, and should be included in any consideration of evaluation, the actual evaluation and control activities begin to occur after the plans are implemented. Generally, the process of measuring effectiveness involves all the steps taken to determine the extent to which predetermined plans and objectives are attained, and in this context evaluation can be viewed as the linking mechanism between plans and control. A major difficulty, as indicated by Hall, is that the measurement of effectiveness against goals may not recognize the presence of multiple, and frequently conflicting, goals within organizations.[2] Thus, effectiveness toward meeting one goal may, in fact, lead to ineffectiveness relative to other goals. This is more likely

[1]Samuel Levey and N. Paul Loomba, *Health Care Administration* (Philadelphia: J. B. Lippincott Co., 1973), p. 421.

[2]Richard H. Hall, *Organizations, Structure, and Process* (New York: John Wiley & Sons, 1972), p. 97.

to occur in organizations, such as hospitals, multi-purpose in orientation.

Presently, the literature on the subject of managerial evaluation and effectiveness is fragmented. Effectiveness is usually viewed as the variable to be measured in response to a variety of independent variables, although some suggest that effectiveness may be an independent variable which actually prescribes managerial approaches. The Ohio State Leadership Description studies offer one example of this, an illustration in which the manager's leadership orientation may be dependent upon his perception of worker effectiveness as being either high or low. In such a situation he may adopt a more "considerate" or "structural" leadership style dependent upon his appraisal of worker effectiveness.

Generally, however, effectiveness is viewed as dependent upon other variables. The problem of measuring effectiveness has been discussed in the management literature, with emphasis on several concepts which are hypothesized as related to it. Among the approaches that have been taken are these: leadership "traits" that are perceived as being causally related to performance; varying leadership "styles" that may affect performance outcomes; situational or contingency variables that are prescriptive of appropriate leadership styles; goal theory, such as MBO, which relates the establishment of measurable objectives with projected outcomes; the question of whether organizational leaders have *any* effect on organizational outcomes; and the value of pre-employment testing devices to obtain measurements of intelligence, abilities and attitudes on performance potential. Several of these theoretical perspectives will be examined later.

The Focus of Quality Appraisal

Study on effectiveness in the health services field has received a somewhat different emphasis than in general management sectors, due to the different nature of the product, the nonprofit orientation, and the difficulty of obtaining quantitative measures of performance. Predictiveness of managerial effectiveness, which has received considerable attention by psychologists in industry, has received less attention in the health field. This is in part due to the relative absence of easily quantifiable measures of performance, such as profits, return on investment, PE ratios, etc., and the presence of highly subjective interpretations of acceptable standards of professional performance related to the diagnosis and treatment of illness.

The emphasis on medical care quality appraisal has had two foci: the "process" of physician performance and the "outcome" of results of the performance. The question of which focus is more important has been raised in the literature; a clear answer does not appear. Brook and Appel suggest that efforts to assess medical care quality have generally examined physician performance.[3] It appears that few evaluative studies have used information about end results of care, although it seems reasonable to evaluate care in terms of how well objectives are achieved. Assessment of quality of care on the basis of physician performance (process) may not be appropriate insofar as many physician activities have not been systematically related to better health for patients. On the other hand, assessment of quality of care on the basis of results (outcome) also involves problems, since outcomes depend not only on physician effort but also upon other possible variables such as socio-economic status, demography, and available health services.

Health administration generally can be viewed as the planning, directing, and evaluation of the process and resources by which needs and demands for health care are converted to special services to individuals and communities. The process involves both internal organization and management of resources. Also of importance is external participation in community policy decisions that must be responsive to conditions of continuous change and increasing uncertainty in the social, economic, political, technological and professional environment.[4] The measurement of organizational effectiveness may involve a dual examination of internal and external performance. The Barr Commission Report on Hospital Effectiveness indicated that these two basic administrative areas of performance are viewed as counter-tensions operating simultaneously and involve internal processes of organization and allocation of resources, budgeting and financial control, and management and evaluation of organizational performance.[5] Externally, the primary function involves program planning and policy decisions, coordination of community health systems, and evaluation of impact on the community. The Barr

[3]R. H. Brack and F. A. Appel, "Quality of Care Assessment," *New England Journal of Medicine,* 288. no. 25: 1323.

[4]Anant P. Negandi, *Modern Organizational Theory: Context, Environment, Sociocultural Variables and Interdependency* (Kent, OH: Kent State University Press, 1973), p. 109.

[5]Barr Commission Report on Hospital Effectiveness.

Commission Report did little, however, to define outcome measures against which internal and external management effectiveness could be examined precisely.

An important internal characteristic of hospital operations which has not received adequate attention so far in the health research literature on measurement of effectiveness is the presence of what may be viewed as the professional versus the non-professional division of hospital activities. The preponderance of research on hospital effectiveness, as evidenced primarily in work by Donabedian and Roehmer, has focused on the development of professional performance measures related to changes in patient health status. The core of this work has been directed toward the value of peer-group performance standards in diagnosis and treatment situations and utilization of internal implementation devices to assure review.

The "medical audit" approach surfaced in recent years as the primary method available to review professional performance of physicians, based on retrospective work analysis of patient records. However, substantial weaknesses are evident in the record-review approach. Those include: incomplete and inaccurate records, hesitancy of peers to reprimand colleagues, absence of generally acceptable standards, fear of legal reprisal from peers and patients, and lack of adequate incentive among physicians to conduct the review. The problems, indeed, have been multiple. The primary weakness, however, is the lack of an acceptable understanding of what is "effective" in terms of output measures. Little research has been done in professional disciplines, other than medicine, to determine ways to measure effectiveness among groups such as nursing, pharmacy, physical therapy, and medical technology.

What has not been generally recognized in the literature, or at least what has received minimal attention, are measures of effectiveness in hospital departments which do not directly provide patient services. These would be admitting, laundry, credits and collections, housekeeping, engineering, etc., all of whom offer substantial opportunities for exploratory measurements of performance. Some degree of success has occurred with the Hospital Administrative Services (HAS) and the Commission for Administrative Services in Hospitals (CASH) multiple-hospital reporting comparisons of selected indicators, but that has been of marginal value since it emphasizes cross-institutional comparisons rather than measuring internal performance against internal objectives.

Hospitals should be paying increased attention to identifying measurable objectives non-professional departments which will provide less subjective bases for year-end appraisal of organizational effectiveness by trustees, administrators, and department heads, and can begin to provide answers to the question: "How did we do last year?" This area appears to offer more near-term potential for evaluation of the administrative function because of the quantitative measures which can be developed, unlike the professional areas, where indicators of performance frequently are highly subjective. It is more likely that an appraisal of non-professional performance, such as personnel turnover or percentage of uncollectable accounts will be more feasible than an attempt to determine if the institution produces high or low quality appendectomies or heart transplants. Measures of non-professional performance may also offer the advantage of providing the trustees of hospitals with more quantifiable data for use in evaluating administrative competence.

Complicating the difficulty of measuring managerial and organizational effectiveness in hospitals is the problem of multiple objectives reported by Hall. The typical general hospital states its broad goals in terms of patient care, education, and research outcomes; it is apparent that the primary concern to date has been patient care. Hospitals also must consider the measurement of performance in two other major areas, i.e., education and research, both of which have similar relationships to the patient care functions in hospitals, and an accompanying problem of identification of acceptable productivity measures.

Also contributing to the problem of evaluating administrative effectiveness in hospitals is the absence of a common understanding of the role of the chief executive officer and the major resources which must be managed in a hospital. Several researchers have sought to identify the role/task parameters of administrators in an effort to isolate the salient components of the job. Results have varied, dependent on two major variables: size of the administrative staff and levels of administration. In large hospitals with comprehensive programs and services, administrators take a more coordinative and consultative role, with greater emphasis on extended boundary-spanning functions. In hospitals with multiple levels of administration, duties of top level executives relate more to abstract planning and evaluation functions; lower level administrators are involved with detailed departmental operations.

An alternative approach to identifying the administrative role involves identifying the major problems which administrators confront on a day-to-day basis. This approach attempts to fix the role parameters of the administrator based on actual job requirements, rather than on subjective perceptions of trustees, physicians, administrators or educators. An obvious weakness of this conceptual approach is in its assumption that "what is" may also be "what should be," rather than critically analyzing the role without the "what is" bias.

The complexity of evaluating and measuring administrative and organizational effectiveness in hospitals stems from several sources: these include the nature of the "patient care" product; the difficulty in establishing professionally acceptable standards of care; failure to fully utilize non-professional, quantitative departmental performance indicators; absence of differentiated professional and nonprofessional goals; hesitancy to incorporate MBO-related research findings in the management process; dependence on extrinsic measures of performance by administrators; lack of initiative by trustees in promoting the use of systematic performance indicators; absence of substantive research in the health field to validate the theorized benefits of evaluative measures to the field; and, finally, the difficulty in clearly identifying role parameters for the chief executive officer of the hospitals.

Approaches to Appraise the Administrator

A number of different approaches and measures have been useful in administrative and organizational evaluation of effectiveness. For example, in the general management literature on effectiveness, several perspectives have been taken which suggest that the concept of "leadership" is a key variable highly correlated with effectiveness.

Although, as Filley and House suggest, the concept of leadership remains one of the least understood aspects of management, there has been substantial research done in an attempt to identify what kind of leadership is appropriate to improve organizational performance.[6] Prior study on leadership may be divided into four general categories: trait theory, task-oriented, person-oriented, and situational theory.

Trait Theory

The *trait theory* perspective of leadership suggests that there are a number of desirable managerial traits which, if they can be identified accurately, will serve as predictive mechanisms in determining who will and who will not be "successful." A list of all the traits which

[6]Alan C. Filley and Robert J. House, *Managerial Process and Organizational Behavior* (Glenview, IL. Scott, Foresman & Co., 1969), p. 416.

have been mentioned in the management literature as desirable for effective managers would include virtually every human characteristic. Included most frequently on the lists, to illustrate, are suggestions that effective managers must be decisive, aggressive, self-starting, productive, well-informed, determined, energetic, creative, etc., etc. Unhappily, these traits are not well-defined, are suggested by individuals in different job settings, and upon close examination, reflect characteristics which may not be longitudinally appropriate.

A promising research project by Ghiselli has uncovered a significant correlation between several traits and management performance in different organizations.[7] These traits were intelligence, supervisory ability, initiative, self-assurance, and individuality. However, research in trait theory has not generally been scientifically conducted and does not show much promise as a means of predicting management performance. The primary difficulty appears to be that the situational requirements for particular traits change as organizational settings change and, in fact, over time often change within individual organizations. The obvious problem is that trait theory suggests static formulae for changing conditions, whereas practicing management requires continued adjustment in response to changing conditions.

Task-Oriented Leadership

The *task-oriented* leadership theory uses as its theoretical base the notion that effective leaders use the classical management instruments of planning, organizing, coordinating, directing, and controlling the work of the organization in order to achieve goals. A major source of research done to examine the relative effectiveness of task-oriented leaders occurred at Ohio State University using the Leadership Behavior Description Questionnaire.[8] In that research, leaders with an "initiating structure" orientation were found to have a strong inclination toward plans, schedules, standards, procedures and a structural work environment. They were also found to rank higher in terms of their superior's evaluations of them; they scored higher on quantitative measures, such as productivity and costs. However, on the negative side, the task-oriented leader has been observed to generate minimal satisfaction among his subordinates (in terms of job

[7]E. E. Ghiselli, "Managerial Talent," *American Psychologist,* 18, no. 10 (October 1963): 631–641.

[8]A. K. Korman, "Consideration, Initiating Structure and Organizational Criteria—a Review," *Personnel Psychology,* 19, no. 4 (1960):349–361.

contentment). Also, the study suggests, he probably is best suited for assignments that are routine in nature and require little creative or analytic work.

Generally, it appears that the most effective leader will incorporate some of the aspects of task-orientation with an appropriate balance of person-orientation characteristics, dependent upon the administrative situation he is confronting.

Person-Oriented Leadership

Person-oriented, or behaviorial, leadership theory is based on the idea that the effective leader uses a supportive, considerate, democratic orientation in his relationships with subordinates. In this theoretical framework, the leader can be viewed as considerate of subordinate's needs, opinions and preferences, is not punitive, is participative concerning work problems, delegates authority, and permits a high level of on-the-job freedom. This perspective on leadership effectiveness is widely held among organizational sociologists and traces its origins to the seminal studies conducted at Western Electric's Hawthorne Plant.

The Ohio State studies again offer rich research findings on the "consideration" variable as an indicator of leadership effectiveness in organizations. The findings indicate that when subordinates ranked their leaders high in "consideration" there was less job stress, more group cooperation, higher subordinate satisfaction, and lower turnover rates. In addition to the attitude measures, it also appears that productivity is positively correlated with the "consideration" orientation. Generally, however, the evidence to support the suggestion of higher productivity by leaders who evidence supportive, person-oriented leadership styles has not been found to be consistent. Vroom's research indicates the reverse to be true when subordinates feel a high need for independence and direction, or when they are task-oriented themselves.[9] Thus, it appears that the individual expectations and needs of subordinates are paramount in any determination of an appropriate leadership style.

An additional element which complicates the issue of what constitutes effective leadership was identified by Berelson and Steiner, who found that superiors and subordinates tend to evaluate leaders differently, i.e., superiors tend to rate highly those leaders who are task-orient-

[9]V. Vroom and F. Mann, "Leader Authoritarianism and Employee Attitudes," *Personnel Psychology,* 13 (1960):125–139.

ed, while subordinates tend to rate highly those leaders who are person-oriented.[10] The obvious dilemma for the leader occurs in attempting to reconcile *his* style with both superordinate and subordinate personnel. The Ohio State studies suggest some help for leaders who must respond to pressure from above and below by implying that the "consideration"—oriented leader may augment his style to include an acceptable degree of "initiating structure" orientation without creating undue problems. While it suggests an impossible situation in which one could have his cake and eat it too, there is an intuitive appeal in the possibility of combining both the task-oriented and person-oriented styles of leadership, particularly if it can be viewed not as occurring simultaneously but rather as a decision choice situation calling for one or the other approach, depending upon situational variables.

Situational Leadership

The *situational* leadership theorists use as their base the belief that the effective leader utilizes a changing leadership style orientation dependent upon the changing organizational environment in which he works and the changing conditions of his particular job. This posture suggests that most managerial jobs have multiple dimensions and functions dependent upon a number of independent organizational variables. Some observations in the limited research in this area propose that the history of the organization, the style of the previous incumbent, and the leader's age may be prescriptive of an appropriate leadership style. It is particularly interesting to note that in explaining the theory the situational perspective seems to present the leadership style as both an independent and a dependent variable at different stages. It is dependent insofar as it is affected by the independent contingencies of the situation; it is independent insofar as it affects the dependent variable of effectiveness.

Feidler, in his work at the University of Illinois on leadership behavior,[11] takes a somewhat different view from the single situation researchers. He proposes that leadership attitudes affect group productivity to varying degrees dependent upon whether the leader, when evaluating subordinates, assumes a lenient or demanding

[10]B. Berelson and G. A. Steiner, *Human Behaviors: An Inventory of Scientific Findings* (New York: Harcourt, Brace and World 1964).

[11]F. E. Feidler, *A Theory of Leadership Effectiveness* (New York: McGraw-Hill 1972), Chapter 1.

orientation. Whether the leader should be more task-oriented or person-oriented is dependent upon what is referred to as "the favorableness of the situation." This, in turn, is determined by the leader's personal relationships with the group, his power and authority, and the degree of task structure. The leadership orientation called for in the highly favorable and highly unfavorable situations is more task-oriented ("discriminating," in Feidler's terminology) and more person-oriented when the situation is only moderately favorable or moderately unfavorable. In other words, the Feidler model suggests that a leader should be able to adjust his style dependent upon the favorableness of the situation, as described above. This may imply more attitudinal flexibility than many managers may be capable of accommodating, particularly in view of research on adult behavior modification, which indicates that basic personality orientations are only moderately changeable. It also implies that leaders have the cognitive abilities to appraise group situations accurately in terms of favorable versus unfavorable. Finally, it does not account for the differences in role perceptions among group members. These basic assumptions underlying Feidler's theory raise serious questions. Empirical evidence may indicate that leaders are neither as flexible in changing their leadership behaviors nor as astute in appraising group favorableness as Feidler hopes.

Management by Objectives

What about the use of the management technique referred to as MBO (management by objectives)? How may it be utilized appropriately in the framework of measuring administrative and organizational effectiveness?

The MBO notion is a theoretical outgrowth of the so-called behavioral school of socio-psychological researchers who suggest that participatory management styles are more likely to promote the desired effects of improved subordinate satisfaction and productivity. The basic attraction of this approach appears to be connected to its appeal to both traditionally-oriented managers and to the behaviorally-oriented managers. That is, the MBO approach, as viewed by the traditional leader, has value in that it may be related to higher productivity, profits and other quantitative measures of economic performance. On the other hand, it may be viewed by behaviorally-oriented managers as a real means to improve subordinate satisfaction, attending to individual needs and desires, and supporting the notion that organizations are made up of individual objectives as well as organizational objectives.

In hospitals, a basic difficulty with implementing MBO programs is that the emphasis only has been directed toward establishing moderately measurable objectives at the non-professional department level—with less concern for establishing management objectives at the institutional level (Parsons). The result has been a continuation of the tendency to measure hospital performance in terms of what Thompson refers to as extrinsic value, i.e., nonspecific, external benefits to the community served, which is, of course, not measurable in the comparative sense against past performance.

The entire notion that leadership has impact on individual or organizational performance has been questioned by some theorists and researchers (Gamson and Scotch), who suggest the possibility that managers do not make any difference in some situations![12] This line of reasoning may support the views of the contingency theorists insofar as it proposes that the effect of the leader may be dependent on his place in the organization, the organizational environment or standard characteristics, and that leaders may be more or less effective regardless of their personal leadership styles. Here, again, is the notion of leadership style as a dependent variable.

The development of a procedure for evaluating administrative effectiveness in a hospital requires that several general assumptions be made about the scope of hospital programs and activities. For the purpose of this illustration it will be assumed that the hospital is a "general" hospital, not a specialty facility; it is a voluntary hospital, not a government facility; and it does not have a formal performance evaluation program. It is further assumed that an evaluation of the administrative function addresses its primary attention to top management activities of interest to the institution's governing authority in its role as trustee, with responsibility for continued satisfactory organizational performance.

With these preliminary comments in mind, it is appropriate to examine the primary stated objectives of the hospital and the degree to which they may be specified, the perceived role and responsibilities of administration in attaining these objectives, and the multidimensional character of the hospital as a complex organization providing both professional and non-professional services which require different objectives. The general orientation will follow a hierarchical approach to the

[12]W. Gamson and N. Seaton, "Scapegoating in Baseball," *American Journal of Sociology*, 70, no. 1 (July 1964): 70.

development of objectives for the organization overall and a more participative approach for the development of specific objectives at operating levels below the top management level, i.e., key departmental objectives designed to support broad organizational goals. Both are assumed utilizable in the administrative evaluation process and are viewed as mutually contributory rather than exclusive.

Based on the author's perspective of measuring effectiveness in hospitals, there appear to be several reasons why many hospitals have not developed effective evaluation programs. One is the apparent difficulty in recognizing that the hospital is a complex organization that has, in effect, two major related dimensions: a professional dimension involving the provision of medical care services by highly trained individuals, and a non-professional dimension involving the provision of supportive services by individuals, such as engineers and dietitians. The professional dimension operates primarily in a *dynamic* task environment; the non-professional dimension operates in a relatively *stable* task environment reflecting the nature of its responsibilities. By not viewing the hospital with dual organizational functions, or units, there has been a lack of awareness in recognizing that different evaluative approaches are required of each dimension. As Thompson indicates, different organizations and organizational units facing different task environments seek to measure performance by utilizing appropriately different techniques.[13] For example, units facing relatively stable task environments seek to document fitness for future action by showing historical improvement, i.e., comparing their performance with that of the past to indicate satisfactory improvement. Hospital statistics on personnel turnover or financial results may be utilized in this manner. On the other hand, units in dynamic task environments seek to measure their performance against that of comparable institutions. Hospital statistics on surgical infection rates or infant mortality rates lend themselves to such comparisons. The point is that there has not been sufficient recognition that uni-dimensional approaches to the measurement of overall hospital performance is unrealistic because of the variation of task environment among organizational units.

A second difficulty, related to the first, is the tendency of hospital leadership to rely on qualitative measures of performance as a yardstick when the task environment elements do provide a quantitative basis for assessment of performance. While it may be assumed reasonable for extrinsic measures to be used on non-quantifiable programs

[13]T. D. Thompson, *Organization in Action* (McGraw-Hill) Chapter 7.

and services such as public relations, it is not reasonable for extrinsic measures to be utilized when quantifiable indicators of performance exist or may be developed. It appears that hospitals take the easy road in many cases involving appraisal of performance by stating accomplishments in general, qualitative terms rather than attempting to quantify performance.

A third problem area related to hospital evaluations is the apparent failure to carry the MBO notion beyond the departmental level in the hierarchy so that overall administrative performance, like individual departmental performance, can be measured against goals and objectives. There exist in hospitals a number of departments which operate in technological environments that are adequately stable and well-buffered to allow measurement, at least in terms of past efficiency comparisons. These are usually the so-called nonprofessional units. In the macro-sense the performance of these departmental units contains the potential for developing performance measures that can be related to overall management effectiveness of the organization's top level leaders against specific organizational objectives.

A fourth difficulty related to hospital managerial evaluations is political in nature and involves the role of the trustee in administrative evaluation. From a practical standpoint, hospital trustees, because of the nature of their part-time, voluntary role and lack of experience related to the health services field, are hesitant—or at least uninformed—about organizational goals and the need to square them against administrative performance. The board's traditional orientation is toward the financial and legal aspects of hospital operations. Beyond the areas where intrinsic measures of performance are available, they are inclined to rely on extrinsic measures, such as community attitudes toward the hospital, or the perceived value of the institution to the status of its general health. A basic difficulty appears to be that trustees are not inclined to feel accountable beyond their fiduciary role. If they should want to review additional yardsticks of performance, they may lack the technical knowledge to pose the right questions.

How can these recognizable constraints be neutralized? How can they be overcome to identify performance effectiveness indicators individually at both the nonprofessional and professional levels? The initial step in developing an evaluation program requires the formulation of goals and objectives, based on a formal, detailed assessment of needs, for both professional and nonprofessional programs in either intrinsic or extrinsic terms. In a practical sense, it appears that there may be varying degrees of both intrinsic and extrinsic goals for both components of the hospital; but it is likely that extrinsic goals will be more frequently utilized in measuring professional performance. The chart (Figure I) shows the differentiated perspective.

Evaluation of the non-professional aspects of administrative performance may be initiated by developing specific operational objectives for units of the organization where intrinsic measurements are available. Specifically, administrative performance in non-professional areas may be related to the following quantitative measures of performance against the suggested objectives:

Financial measures of internal performance, such as actual budgetary experience on income and expenses, against budgetary predictions and longitudinal appraisal of accounts receivable collection ratios.

Personnel management measures, such as turnover rates, rates of employee grievances, or percentages of board certified specialists employed.

Performance of support departments costs per unit of service delivered, such as laundry cost per pound, new food costs per meal, cost per prescription filled, or nursing unit cost per day. They can be used internally to measure historical performance against objectives within the institution, as well as for cross-hospital comparisons.

In addition to these examples of internal performance indicators, there are other indicators used in the HAS program which can be employed to develop internal operating objectives, and against which performance can be measured in individual hospitals, including macro-measures such as cost per day and average length of patient hospitalization.

Extrinsic measure can also be utilized to measure non-professional performance where quantitative measures are unavailable, such as the degree to which organizational units meet expectations of other units, the extent to which there is external recognition by professional associations, and the frequency and quality of publication associates in professional journals. Thompson refers to this type of appraisal as "open system logics" measurement, where more precise evidence of performance assessment may be unavailable.[14] Appraisal of administrative effectiveness may also incorporate a review of so-called "professional hospital activities," which are more directly related to patient care programs. Intrinsic goals and objectives can be established

[14]Ibid.

FIGURE 1

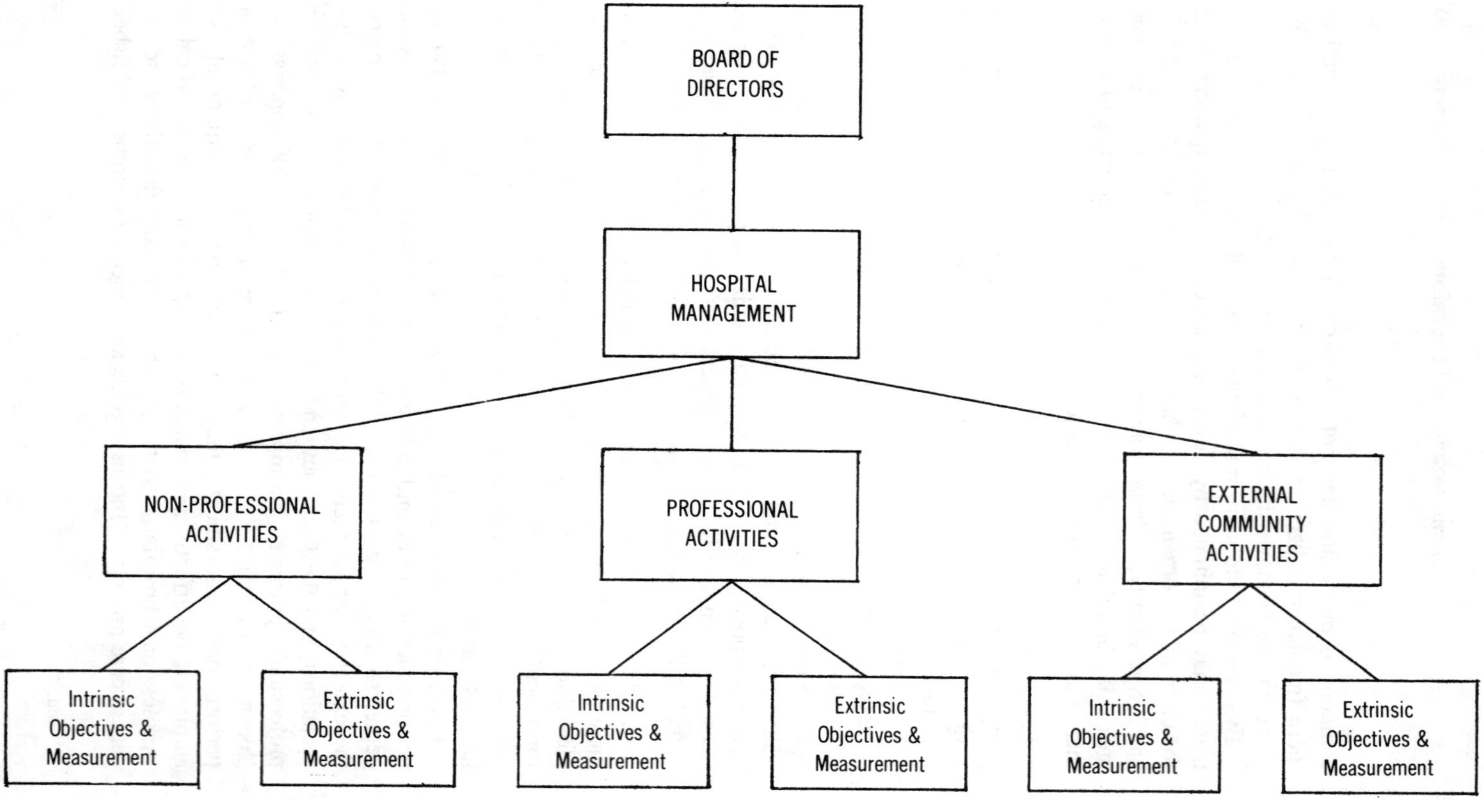
BOARD OF DIRECTORS
HOSPITAL MANAGEMENT
NON-PROFESSIONAL ACTIVITIES
PROFESSIONAL ACTIVITIES
EXTERNAL COMMUNITY ACTIVITIES
Intrinsic Objectives & Measurement
Extrinsic Objectives & Measurement
Intrinsic Objectives & Measurement
Extrinsic Objectives & Measurement
Intrinsic Objectives & Measurement
Extrinsic Objectives & Measurement

for some professional programs and, although acceptable standards of performance are more difficult to identify, some indices of performance are available. For example, it is possible to project desired levels of performance on infant mortality rates, surgical infection rates, autopsy rates, and occurrences of unneccessary surgery. Other measures of professional performance, more extrinsic in nature, are percentage of Board-certified physicians; presence of peer review mechanisms, such as medical audit committee; frequency of clinicopathological review conferences; changes in utilization review mechanisms; or credentials committee approval processes.

A third potential source of information the hospital may use to measure administrative effectiveness is results of an appraisal of external assessments of hospital performance, such as the health status of the community (intrinsic), and patient and community attitudes toward the hospital (extrinsic). Intrinsic measures of performance which may be incorporated in definable hospital objectives may include statistics on average hospital inpatient and outpatient visits per 1000 population, community mortality and morbidity rates, and rates of frequency for specific diseases, such as VD, alcoholism, psychiatric illness, and malnutrition.

Extrinsic measures of performance can be appraised with such instruments as community survey questionnaires. The use of the patient discharge questionnaire also can effectively identify consumer attitudes on selected hospital services, which can be charted statistically to provide guidelines for the improvement of services. In fact, some hospital boards of directors routinely review graphs and charts which indicate patient opinions on services such as dietary, admission and discharge procedures.

In summary, a hospital evaluation program can be effectively accomplished through the use of an approach which recognizes the internal differences between professional and non-professional hospital units, the need for formal and detailed assessment of needs, the requirement to measure on both intrinsic and extrinsic levels, the need to utilize measurable objectives at both the unit level and for the overall organization, recognition of community appraisal methods to measure institutional impact on the hospital's service areas, and the establishment of performance indicators which can be used for both inter- and intra-hospital evaluations.

The Ashland Plan: An Ambulatory Care Outreach Alternative for a Community Hospital

John N. Simpson

The Hill-Burton Law in the 1950s encouraged the establishment throughout the country of numerous metropolitan community hospitals. With the shifting of the populations in the 1960s and 1970s from the inner city to suburbia, many of the institutions today are discovering new challenges. Changing patient environment, newly constructed suburban hospitals, shifting physician loyalties, insufficient cash flow, personnel recruitment difficulties, are among the challenges which must be effectively met. The desirable location for a metropolitan hospital of the 1950s generally has become, in the 1970s, a socio-economic "grey area."

Some institutions anticipated these changes and challenges and established multi-hospital systems encompassing intercity and suburban hospitals. A few have discovered other methods to remain attractive in spite of the changing environment through comprehensive and complex specialized services unduplicated in their service areas. Then, there are those who are recently discovering the decaying situation and are searching for new alternatives. But past avenues are limited. High interest, tight money, uncertainty about future health care delivery methodologies and increasing governmental involvement have minimized these alternatives. One of the remaining alternatives which this article addresses has been recently developed by Richmond Memorial Hospital, a city community general hospital located in Richmond, Virginia. This alternative has been designated "The Ashland Plan."

Basics of the Plan

The Ashland Plan is an innovative ambulatory care outreach program sponsored by a community general hospital to minimize existing deficiencies in continuity of medical care within its primary service areas. This plan definition itself has numerous controversial points which must be analyzed before operational criteria can/could be discussed.

First, what is meant by "outreach?" Outreach is actually the hospital development or construction of medical facilities beyond the hospital grounds. The distance from the parent institution could be as far as 20 miles with good road arteries between the parent and outreach facility. Actually, there is nothing new about hospital outreach programs through a multi-hospital setup and satellite hospitals in rural and semi-rural areas. Generally, these outreach endeavors involve inpatient beds, but the definition refers to ambulatory care. The hospital in this alternative is developing off-premises physician office space and, at the same time, interweaving a relationship with the parent institution, hopefully assuring the patient continuity of care. Historically, a hospital's primary operational purpose may be inpatient care with limited commitment to ambulatory care, except in general referrals for utilization of specific diagnostic services. With the existence of an emergency room, the hospital may find itself in an unanticipated ambulatory maze, forced to provide weekend and evening coverage for episodic non-acute case loads.[1] Unable to assure continuity of care to the patient who may originate from a medically deficient area, the hospital faces the dilemma of providing less than desirable care. This patient continues to receive episodic care since the emergency room may offer him the only access to continued medical care. The hospital, at this point, must determine its responsibility for quality medical care to the community that it serves.

If this ambulatory maze exists and the development of these outreach ambulatory facilities is an acceptable alternative, how does one determine where the hospital should place the facility(ies)? It must be stressed at this point that the hospital, in establishing these outreach programs, is not practicing medicine, but is encouraging the ingress of physicians and allied personnel into underserved areas. The stresses placed on hospital emergency rooms are only symptoms of unmet consumer needs. The hospital's primary intent is to develop an attractive environment which should encourage the extension of the free practice of medicine into these medically deficient areas. In order to determine these areas, the hospital must define its primary service area and, utilizing acceptable statistical guidelines, survey and identify medically underserved areas through feasibility studies.[2]

[1]J. Wood, L. Prybil, and J. Simpson, "An Approach to Studying Emergency Department Utilization," *Virginia Medical Monthly* 101, no. 6 (June 1974): 458–464.

[2]Richmond Memorial Hospital has identified its primary service area through zip code analysis of home address on patients admitted and emergency room—outpatient service

Conceptual Criteria

In considering establishment of an ambulatory outreach program, specific conceptual criteria were formulated. The criteria selected are very similar to the basic requirements of a well-structured health care system as enumerated in the Regional Facilities Plan to the Capital Area Comprehensive Health Planning Council, Inc.[3]

First, the center must enhance the quality of health care delivered to the catchment area.[4] It is a basic prerequisite that mechanisms be established to allow consumer input, appeal and involvement. Valid medical audit programs with measurable criteria and appropriate action programs must be established.

Second, the center must be accessible to the catchment area that it serves. The consumers' needs will possibly require evening and weekend operational hours. Backup for the center by the parent institution for hours that the center is closed, as well as coordination of specialty services, is a must.

Third, the center itself must be attractive and functional. In other words, a place in which the professional is proud to work and which offers the consumer a pleasant environment.

Fourth, a system of care must be assured, guaranteeing the patient continuity of care. Well-coordinated planning should result in a competent organization that minimizes rigidity and is flexible to the changing consumer needs.

Finally, the center must be able to adapt to changing times and, in its future planning, must anticipate impact of federalization of health care delivery systems.

Feasibility Studies

The primary purpose for the existence of a center is to supplement medically deficient sectors within the hospital's service area. The hospital's service area can be determined through zip code analysis based on admission occurrences and emergency room and/or outpatient visits occurrences. Use of census tracts would offer a more definitive analysis, but requires more clerical hours in collection of this information.

[3] *Working Document to the Capital Area Comprehensive Health Planning Council, Inc.*, Gordon A. Friesen International, Inc., Washington, D.C., p. F 3/5.

[4] Catchment area is defined as the population sector which the primary care center will serve. A following section of the manuscript will outline how a catchment area is determined.

within a fiscal year from the specific zip code areas. With this identification, the service area can be further broken down into sectors, possibly by political subdivisions such as towns, counties, voting districts; by geographical features such as rivers, mountain ranges; or by socio-economic considerations.[5] Once these sectors are identified, their appropriateness should be given the following test:

(1) Does the population of the sector (catchment area) equal or exceed 12,000 individuals? If not, with anticipated growth figures, will it exceed 12,000 in the next two years?
(2) Is the driving time from the boundaries of the identified sector to the possible location of center less than 20 minutes?

If "yes" is the eventual answer to the above two questions, it is reasonable to complete a feasibility study in the sector.

The Ashland Plan, in determining need projections, incorporates two feasibility approaches. One is considerably simplified while the second contains other variables.

The simplified feasibility approach compiles from census figures the current population and applies a growth rate figure projecting the future annual population levels. Utilizing the guidelines established by the Emergency Manpower Act of 1972 which states there should be at least one primary physician for every 4,000 persons, this factor is divided into the projected population resulting in the needed number of practitioners. Subtracting the existing physicians in practice in the sectors from the number of needed practitioners, the resultant figure relates the unmet need. An example of this feasibility approach is offered in Table I on the following page.

It is generally felt that the simplified feasibility approach fails to consider other important variables, and there is some concern that one practitioner per 4,000 population is too conservative. The more sophisticated feasibility approach includes the variables of patient utilization, outward migration and physician work capabilities. Annual patient primary care needs (patient utilization factors) are projected at 3,058 medical, general practice and pediatric visits per 1,000 population. This figure accounts for both outpatient and inpatient utilization, as follows:

[5]Richmond Memorial has divided its service area into five sectors. One is separated by geographical features, two by townships and their adjoining area, another by accessible road arteries and another by economic considerations.

TABLE I
Service Population and Need Projection—Simplified Feasibility Approach

	Service Population	Divided by	Number of Needed Practi-tioners	Less Existing Practi-tioners	Less Primary Care Center*	Unmet Needs
1975....	30,800	4,000	7.7	4	0	3.7
1976....	31,800	4,000	8.0	4	3	1.0
1977....	32,800	4,000	8.2	4	4	.2
1978....	33,900	4,000	8.5	4	4	.5
1979....	34,900	4,000	8.7	4	4	.7
1980....	35,900	4,000	9.0	4	5	....

*Hospital sponsored center to be operational in 1976.

Primary Care Center by visits per year
per 1,000 of population 2,650
Inpatient visits per year per 1,000 population 408
Total annual visits per 1,000 population 3,058

The outward migration adjustment in the Ashland Plan has been set at 25 percent allowing for that certain percentage of patients who may seek care outside the designated sector.

Physician workload capabilities were studied in detail After much debate, the following annual workloads have been established:

Physician annual workloads currently
practicing in the sector .... 7,291[6]
Physician annual workload in center:
First year of practice 6,700
Succeeding years 7,766

The variation between the physician workload currently practicing in comparison to the center physician primarily is attributable to the center's anticipated utilization of nurse practitioners. Also, the workload capability of a physician in his first year in the center should be approximately 15 percent less than succeeding years, allowing for the

[6]American Medical Association, *Profile of Medical Practice*, 1973 Edition (1971 data), Chicago, Illinois.

gradual growth of the new practitioner's practice. The resultant feasibility approach is summarized in Table II on the following page.

Organizational Phase

At this point, the implementation or organizational phase of the Ashland Plan is totally dependent on the Plan's acceptability. Specific goals must have been accomplished in order to assure orderly and successful implementation of the Plan:

(1) Key members of the hospital's medical staff have accepted the leadership role in selling and implementing the plan.

(2) The Plan has been endorsed by the hospital's medical staff.

(3) Area medical societies have been informed and endorse the Plan.

(4) Community leaders, both political and non-political, who reside in the area where the center will be constructed have endorsed and encourage the development of the center.

(5) The Plan has been reviewed, discussed, and endorsed by physicians currently in practice in the area in which the center will be constructed.

To accomplish the above may be considered a momentous task, but a solid base of support must be established prior to commitment of capital funds for bricks and mortar and staff acquisition. The Plan for implementation does not necessitate 100 percent concurrence, but a careful evaluation of the significance of the dissenter(s) should be completed.

Functions of the Community Advisory Board

After commitment, key community leaders must become involved. The Ashland Plan incorporates this involvement through the establishment of a Community Advisory Board. The Community Board, as its name implies, acts in an advisory capacity to the Board of Trustees of the hospital in regard to the property, affairs and business of the center. Cross-sectional representation of the center's sector is most important, with terms of office established so that there is periodic rotation of the members. The Bylaws of the Community Advisory Board must allow for specific standing committees, of which the two most important are the Planning Committee and the Patient Grievance Committee. The Planning Committee, in its operation, will assist in the program devel-

TABLE II
Service Population and Need Projection—Sophisticated Feasibility Approach

	Service Population	Total Visit Needs[1]	Outward Migration[2]	Adjusted Visit Needs[3]	Existing Practitioners		Primary Care Center Practitioners		Unmet Pract.	Needs Visits[6]
					No.	Visits[4]	No.	Visits[5]		
1975	30,800	94,186	23,547	70,638	4	29,200	...	...	5.3	41,439
1976	31,800	97,244	24,311	72,933	4	29,200	3	20,100	3.0	23,633
1977	32,800	100,302	25,076	75,226	4	29,200	4	30,000	2.1	16,026
1978	33,900	103,666	25,917	77,749	4	29,200	5	38,800	1.3	9,749
1979	34,900	106,724	26,681	80,043	4	29,200	5	38,800	1.6	12,043
1980	35,900	109,782	27,446	82,336	4	29,200	5	38,800	1.9	14,336

[1]Service population divided by 1,000 x 3,058.
[2]25 percent of total Visit Needs.
[3]Total visit needs minus outward migration.
[4]Number of physicians x 7,291 annual visits.
[5]6,700 annual visits for initial year of practice and 7,776 annual visits for succeeding year of practice for hospital sponsored center to be in operation in 1976.
[6]Adjusted visit needs minus visits of existing practitioners and primary care center practitioners.

opment and recommend an operational master plan. The Patient Grievance Committee should offer a sampling of the community pulse beat as the consumers react to the services offered by the center. Specifically, the Grievance Committee should investigate complaints and submit recommendations to the Advisory Board.

Simultaneously with the establishment of the Community Advisory Board, a medical director of the center should be appointed. His role becomes one of medical leadership in establishing the operational concepts, assisting in recruitment of physicians, and consulting on the design of the facilities. His role is directly integrated within the Bylaws of the Community Advisory Board as an ex-officio member. He also serves in an ex-officio capacity as a member of the Planning Committee, and he may attend, or designate a physician representative to attend, the Patient Grievance Committee. For improved communications between the center and the hospital's medical staff, the center's medical director also serves in an ex-officio capacity at all meetings of the Executive Committee of the hospital medical staff. On a day-to-day basis, the center medical director has direct operational assistance from the hospital. Administratively, he can depend on the hospital administrative staff while medically, the hospital medical director and/or the President of the Medical Staff can act in a consultant capacity. Most important, though, is that his appointment as center medical director is made by the Board of Trustees of the hospital.

Operational Considerations

The center's operational concepts are designed to meet the unmet primary care needs of the sector it serves. The sophisticated feasibility study approach shown in Table II, as an example, demonstrates a need for 5.3 physicians in that specific sector. As indicated in the same table, the center, when opened, will offer a full-time compliment of three physicians, with planned expansion to five physicians in the following two years. These physicians in the Ashland Plan will develop their own patients in the community, enhancing the private practice of medicine through the operation of the center.

With a physician group, the center's hours of operation can be extended into evenings and weekends. Initially, the operational hours would not extend beyond 9:00 P.M. on several weekdays (such as Monday, Wednesday, and Friday) and would include several hours on Saturday and Sunday afternoons. As the center's professional staffing increased with consumer demand, the center's evening and weekend operation could be expanded. If the center were to strictly conform to the Monday through Friday, 9:00 A.M. to 5:00 P.M. syndrome, it is doubtful that the Ashland Plan could answer the problems of accessibility and continuity of care.

At the same time, the physicians will utilize the expertise of the nurse practitioner for roles which are proper and helpful in meeting needs, such as routine check-ups concerning catheter care or decubitus ulcer care, routine screening of simple respiratory infection or screening in epidemics. Home health visitation also can be performed by the nurse practitioner, if not met through other existing community services.

Basic X-ray and laboratory diagnostic services will be provided at the center. More complex studies would be referred to the hospital.

Since the center is designed for primary ambulatory care, arrangements would be made with local rescue squads for urgent referrals to the hospital. Inclusive with the center will be an emergency radio network connection and twenty-four hour telephone answering and physician paging services tied in with the parent institution.

The hospital, on the other hand, which may be plagued with the high demand for primary care in its emergency room can redirect consumers to the center, thereby offering something greater than episodic care. Eventually, with a network of centers, the demand for primary care in the hospital emergency room should decline, allowing the facility to return to its original operational purpose, while the consumer, hopefully, has an answer to his need for primary care within his own residential sector.[7] This is the operational goal of the Ashland Plan.

Professional Recruitment and Staffing

The success or failure of the Ashland Plan is totally dependent on the recruitment of physicians. Obviously, the sector, identified by the feasibility study, has had minimal success attracting physicians. Analyzing the reasons for the recruitment failure seemingly has centered around three basic problems: (1) capital risks on the part of the individual physician, (2) no income guarantees and related collection problems, and (3) excessive demands on the solo practitioners, thereby minimizing time off from the practice.

The Ashland Plan, as designed, attempts to eliminate these weak-

[7]Some studies are contraindicative; see G. T. Moore, R. Bersteen, and R. Bonanno, "Effect of a Neighborhood Health Center on Hospital Emergency Room Use," *Medical Care* 10 (May-June 1972): 240–247.

nesses for the sector which has unmet physician manpower needs. The hospital with its existing financial base, either through fund raising, endowments or other assets, provides the center's capital needs. Construction of a functional, attractive facility by the hospital offers the physician a base of operation with no personal capital risks. The hospital in its current operations, to be fiscally sound, must have established a fiscal expertise. This expertise with minimal changes can offer the center a collection capability which an individual practitioner cannot afford. Also, with the complexities of reimbursement, especially with increasing outpatient coverages, the individual physician cannot provide within his operation the software and hardware to satisfy these complexities. These complexities are nothing new to the already existing hospital's manpower and computer systems. The physician in the Ashland Plan is relieved of the direct concerns of cash flow. At the same time, the physician will be informed of the fiscal operation by being offered detailed reports and analyses. Even though he has been relieved of the petty details of fiscal affairs, he is still a manager of his practice and must be allowed his input into the fiscal operation of the facility. The hospital in its relationship with the physicians is not dictating fiscal policy but is offering its fiscal expertise in a supportive role.

It is felt, in order to offer a workable and attractive setting for the private practice of medicine, the Plan must guarantee the physician a minimum income based on a set number of office and hospital visits, which represents a break-even point for the center. If the center in a year sees fewer patients than budgeted, the hospital absorbs the loss. Should more patients be seen, the physician(s) would receive additional income per visit. The initial budget levels of visits are based objectively on national and regional averages of physician productivity. Table III offers an example of a center with a base of three physicians.

How the guaranteed $138,000 would be divided between the group of physicians is generally left to agreements among the physicians. As an example, one physician may limit his hours of availability while the other two may make up the deficiency. The division of this guarantee, therefore, might be divided on a 40-40-20 percent basis. The physicians also could form their own corporation and establish formal contractual agreements with each other. The Ashland Plan does not force the physician into an employment relationship; it only guarantees financial solvency for the participating physicians.

The Ashland Plan also incorporates a 10 percent provision for bad debts, allowances and charity. The responsibility for up to 10 percent bad debt rests entirely with the hospital. Should bad debts exceed this

TABLE III
Physician Remuneration—Volume Incentives

Annual Number of Visits Per Center[1]	Remuneration to Group of Three Physicians
1 – 23,298[2]	$138,000[3]
Each Visit Beyond 23,298	$5.92 per visit[4]

[1]Based on three physicians at 7,766 annual office and hospital visits per physician.
[2]Break-even point for operation of center.
[3]Based on average of $40,000 minimum guaranteed income, plus 15 percent fringe benefits
[4]Net reimbursement after overhead factor.

established level, the hospital will absorb the loss, but there also would be an adverse effect on the physician's potential income above the budgeted volume. Let's assume bad debts for a specific year were 12 percent, in the example offered in Table III. Financially, the hospital would absorb the 12 percent write-off, but the minimum number of visits to be reached per practitioner before receiving extra income would be raised 2 percent from 7,766 to 7,921, or, for the group, to 23,763 annual visits. With a 12 percent bad debt experience, Table III would be adjusted as follows (Table III-A):

TABLE III-A (Adjusted)
Physician Remuneration—Volume Incentives

Annual Number of Visits Per Center	Remuneration to Group of Three Physicians
1 – 23,763	$138,000
Each Visit Beyond 23,763	$5.92

As a member of a group, the participating physician is assured time off, sick time and vacation time. Also, should a crisis occur, the hospital, with physicians in the parent institution, could fill the void on a temporary basis.

The hospital will be financially responsible for the necessary supportive personnel. Based on national figures for allied health staffing for group practices, the hospital will supply the center with 2.2 full-time equivalent personnel per physician.[8] In addition, as stated before, a nurse practitioner will be provided at the rate of one per three or four physicians. The breakdown of ancillary personnel for a three-physician center is outlined in Table IV.

TABLE IV
Full-Time Equivalents
Allied Health Personnel Staffing

	Group of Three Practitioners
Registered Nurse	.999
Licensed Practical Nurse	.450
X-ray Technician	.786
Laboratory Technician	1.128
Medical Secretary	.762
Secretary-Receptionist	1.473
Other	1.059
	6.657

It is hopeful that as a consolidated package, the Ashland Plan will offer an attractive atmosphere for physicians and provide an incentive for quality care.

Land, Bricks and Mortar

There are many variables to consider in location and design of the center. Land has become an expensive entity. In considering the property, it should be strategically located, preferably in the center of the service sector with good ingress and egress to and from main road arteries. Therefore, property will undoubtedly be premium land especially if necessary utilities, such as water, sewer and power, are available. Also, care must be exercised not to buy too little or too much land.

The amount of land needed is directly related to the square footage of the building, future expansion considerations, and parking requirements/regulations. The Ashland Plan has two basic designs with square footage allocations as outlined in Table V.

[8]American Medical Association, *Profile of Medical Practice,* 1972 Edition, Chicago, Illinois.

TABLE V
Square Footage Allocation—Two Designs

	Design #1 (Gross Sq. Ft.)	Design #2 (Gross Sq. Ft.)
Physician offices (4)	400	400
Nurse Practitioner office (1)	100	
Examination room	700(7)	800(8)
Multi-purpose room (1)	350	
X-ray rooms—storage	1,500	1,000
Laboratory	620	600
Minor surgery (including toilet)	460	
Patient entrance—waiting room	1,000	1,000
Administrative area—patient files	670	600
Employee lounge	350	400
Storage	390	200
Janitor's closet	60	60
	6,600	5,060
Circulation and mechanical	2,300(35%)	1,530(30%)
Total square feet	8,900	6,590

The primary reasons for the variation in square feet of the two designs are two-fold:

(1) Anticipated need for expansion within the first two years of operation.

(2) Planned specialty programs and initial commitment to patient education.

If it is anticipated that consumer demand will necessitate expansion of the center within the first two years, the service core should be designed so that it can expand within the initially constructed structure. This is why there is more square footage allocated to X-ray, Laboratory, Administrative-patient file areas and Storage in Design #1. Therefore, future expansion would only necessitate the addition of more physician offices and examination rooms with minimal inconvenience to the service core. Design #1 also allows the luxury of an office for the nurse practitioner, but, if necessary, this could be converted into another physician's office. This flexibility would allow the acquisition of another physician while the center is in the expansion process.

Design #1 includes a large multi-purpose room which can be converted into two examination rooms or a large area for specialty care by affiliated specialists or an area for patient education. Examples of programs which could utilize this area might be a cardiac stress-exercise program, physical or occupational therapy rehabilitation sessions, emphysema training, medical and patient educational sessions, etc. This room could be an expensive luxury if not utilized effectively. The minor surgery room in Design #1 could allow affiliation with a specialist for handling of minor scheduled cases, while in Design #2, one of the eight examination rooms could be suitably equipped to serve a dual purpose. Again, anticipated utilization is a key factor.

Finally, how much land is necessary, especially since the Plan may require the purchase of premium land? Table VI offers a conservative breakdown.

TABLE VI
Land Site Considerations

Component	Gross Square Feet
Building	7,500
Parking	15,840
Landscaping	10,000
Sub-total	33,340 (approximately .75 acres)
Potential for expansion	98,010 (2.25 acres)
Total	131,350 (approximately 3.00 acres)

It is concluded that the center will necessitate a site of not less than one acre, if future expansion is not considered, but, preferably, three acres should be purchased initially.

Utilization and Financial Implication

Capital outlays and operational costs, anticipated revenues and cash flow all have significant implications for the successful implementation of the Ashland Plan. In order to offer an insight into these implications, it is necessary to expand on the example initially offered in Table II in which the sophisticated feasibility approach was demonstrated. In Table II, the number of practitioners and anticipated patient visits have been listed in column six. The center, in the example, was projected to begin operation in 1976 with three physicians resulting in 20,100 anticipated patient visits. Progressive growth in the following years was projected as follows:

Year	*Total Visits*	*No. of Center Physicians*
1977	30,000	4
1978	38,800	5
1979	38,800	5
1980	38,800	5

Utilization of center ancillary services also must be considered. After detailed research of local patterns, ancillary service utilization ratios per primary care center visit were developed and are outlined in Table VII.

TABLE VII
Ancillary Services:
Utilization Ratios Per Primary Care Center Visit

	Total	In House[1]	Referred[2]
Central Supply Units	.25	.25	...
Electrocardiology Procedures	.06	.06	...
Laboratory Examinations	1.00	.75	.25
Emergency Pharmacy Issues	.10	.10	...
X-ray Examinations	.13	.10	.03

[1] Procedures performed at center.
[2] Service need initiated at center but referred to hospital for outpatient work.

Applying these ratios to the anticipated patient visits, the demand for ancillary services in any of the projected years can be calculated as demonstrated in Table VIII. Total visits in Table VIII have been reduced from 20,100 to 17,425 since approximately 2,675 of the visits would represent visits by the primary care physician to inpatients.[9]

Before the financial solvency of the example can be studied further, capital outlays must be calculated. As enumerated in Table V, two plan prototypes have been developed; one with 8,900 square feet and the

[9] Please refer to section on Feasibility Studies and the breakdown between outpatient and inpatient visits per 1,000 population.

other with 6,590 square feet. Current calculations place the turn-key capital outlays, exclusive of land, for Design #1 between $630,000 and $650,000; while Design #2 is approximately $405,000 to $425,-000. Land costs, due to the desirability for premium land, are estimated between $20,000 and $30,000 per acre.[10]

In developing the projected financial statements for the center, other pertinent basic facts are reviewed or restated as follows:

Physician service revenue is based on an average center charge per visit of $11.50. Professional inpatient visit charges are $15.00 for the initial visit and $10.00 for subsequent visits.

Ancillary service revenue is based on the average charge for the service offered times the units of service as developed in Table VIII.

TABLE VIII
Projected Units of Service

		Total		In House		Referred	
	Center Visits	Factor	Units of Svc.	Factor	Units of Svc.	Factor	Units of Svc.
Central Supply Units	17,425	.25	4,356	.25	4,356	...	...
Electrocardiology Procedures	17,425	.06	1,045	.06	1,045	...	...
Laboratory Examinations	17,425	1.00	17,425	.75	13,069	.25	4,356
Emergency Pharmacy Issues	17,425	.10	1,743	.10	1,743	...	...
X-ray Examinations	17,425	.13	3,366	.10	1,743	.03	523

Referred ancillary service revenue is the accumulated charge for services provided referred cases in the base hospital. Table VIII includes the amount of anticipated referred ancillary service units.

As stated before, the center will provide a 10 percent bad debt or charity level. (Studies of local physician offices show that their current bad debt experience is around 5 percent.)

[10]Turn-key estimation includes construction costs, site development, movable equipment, contingency allowances, administrative costs and professional fees—based on 1974 Richmond Metropolitan construction and land dollar costs.

Professional and other personnel salaries are based on guarantees and incentives to the physicians, plus the complement of personnel multiplied by prevailing area wages.

The support component is the allocation of cost from the base hospital for administrative, medical and fiscal expertise.

With these understandings, a financial projection of the center can be developed, as listed in Table IX.

TABLE IX
Projected Revenues and Expenses

	1976	1977	1978	1979	1980
Operating Revenues:					
Physician Services	$225,400	$375,000	$518,500	$587,900	$ 646,700
Primary Care Center Ancillary Services.	127,400	209,500	287,000	325,100	357,500
Referred Ancillary Services	30,100	50,100	69,200	78,000	85,800
	$382,900	$634,600	$874,700	$991,000	$1,090,000
Less: Bad Debt & Adjustments	38,300	63,500	87,500	99,100	109,000
Net Operating Revenue	$344,600	$571,100	$787,200	$891,900	$ 981,000
Operating Expenses:					
Salaries, Wages and Fees .	$176,600	$298,800	$405,900	$446,500	$ 491,100
Supplies & Other Expenses	63,400	96,000	127,800	144,100	158,300
Referred Ancillary Services	20,200	33,700	46,400	52,300	57,500
Housekeeping & Maint . . .	36,600	40,200	44,200	49,200	54,100
Depreciation	36,100	36,100	36,100	36,100	36,100
Support Component	42,700	63,200	90,400	104,000	107,900
Total Operational Expenses . .	$375,600	$568,000	$750,800	$832,200	$ 905,000
Excess (Deficit)	$(31,000)	$ 3,100	$ 36,400	$ 59,700	$ 76,000

The first two years of operation, as indicated by Table IX, can have significant effect on the cash flow of the sponsoring hospital. From the financial statement, it is obvious that a positive cash flow from the operation of the center may not occur until the second year. Even though cash flow from depreciation will offset the operational loss, accumulation of approximately 45 days of accounts receivable will assure the negative cash flow status. The base hospital will have to be prepared to cover the projected deficit.

If bad debts are not maintained at 10 percent, referred services do not materialize, or the community acceptance is slower than anticipated, serious effects on fiscal solvency can result. The first two years of operation have minimal fiscal flexibility. Again, the base hospital must be prepared for the possibility of these negative variations, or the total outcome could be a fiscal fiasco.

It should be noted, on a positive note, that X-ray utilization figures are most conservative. One unit of service for every ten center visits may be too low. Therefore, increased revenue could be generated in this area. Also, depreciation figures in the example are based on an 8,900 square foot building, or Design #1. Annual depreciation expense on the 6,500 square foot building, or Design #2, would be approximately $13,000 less per year. Again, it must be emphasized that if expansion of the center is not anticipated within two years from its opening date, then it would be fiscally irresponsible to consider Design #1.

Medical Audit Program

One of the weaknesses of the Ashland Plan might prove to be its professional reimbursement formula. The formula as previously described encourages volume. Without a functional medical audit program, the Plan would only attempt to answer the problem of accessibility with "lip service" to the measurability of the quality of care delivered.

Professional Standards Review Organizations will undoubtedly be operational in 1976. It is only practical that the Ashland Plan have at its inception a functional medical audit program. Being affiliated with a base hospital, which under its hospital accreditation program is required to have a creditable audit program, should minimize the complexities of program development. The medical audit methodology recommended by the Joint Commission on Hospital Accreditation can easily be adapted to meet the medical audit needs of the Ashland Plan.[11] Even so, care must be exercised as to the methods of

[11]*TAP Institutes, Joint Commission on Accreditation of Hospitals,* 2nd Edition, February 1973.

implementation. The base hospital must assume an advisory role allowing the center physicians to implement and operate the medical audit program. In turn, the center physicians are responsible to the Community Advisory Board for medical audit accountability. The Community Advisory Board is accountable to the hospital's board of trustees, as well as to the sector's consumers whom they represent.

Justification of the Ashland Plan cannot be based on resultant inpatient utilization. Current studies relate that one center will generate approximately 312–488 admissions per year. Assuming an average length of stay of 8.5 patient days per hospital admission and a community hospital with an annual total of 140,000 patient days, the center's patient day contribution to the total would annually be only 1.8–3.0 percent. Even with four operational centers, the percent of the patient days would only be 7.2–12 percent. The purpose is to develop balanced hospital ambulatory and inpatient services while at the same time meeting a community need; not to stimulate inpatient utilization.

The Plan also must be integrated into existing services in the sector that it is serving. The center's ancillary services must be available to other sector physicians, and if specialty services are developed in the center, other physicians must be allowed to make referrals. An open, but controlled, staff atmosphere must exist in the center. Visiting nurse and public health associations must be included in the planning stages. Center services must complement and not duplicate health services.

The base hospital must also develop on-site ambulatory service expertise. With the development of outreach centers, the base hospital should develop a Department of Ambulatory Care, centralizing these activities under one administrative leadership. This development, therefore, is included as an integral part of the total master plan.

Governmental involvement in health care will have its effect on the Plan. A door must be left open for consideration of Health Maintenance Organizations, should a sector's consumer group feel that this is the best option. National Health Insurance, with its provisions, could necessitate Plan alterations. But, as stressed before, the Ashland Plan must be flexible to anticipated or unanticipated health field environmental changes.

The role of the center's nurse practitioner has not been developed in detail in this article. The nurse practitioner herself must help identify her role in concert with center physicians. Ideally, she should be hired at least six to nine months prior to the opening of the center so that her role and physician's relationship can be well integrated. Articles such as a recent one in the Wall Street Journal should dispel fears about consumer acceptance of the nurse practitioner.[12]

There are risks involved in the Ashland Plan, both in availability of physician manpower and financial considerations. The Plan does offer an alternative for the metropolitan community hospital which could serve both the institution's and community's needs. This is where Richmond Memorial Hospital stands today, at the threshold of implementation of the Ashland Plan. As the first two outreach centers become operational in the next two years, it will be most interesting to compare the operational realities with the Plan's projections.

[12]"Supernurses Provide Care for Thousands, Helping Doctors Cope," *The Wall Street Journal,* 3 July 1974, pg. 1.

The Crisis in the Health Care System: A Contrary Opinion

S. David Pomrinse, M.D.

When I was thinking about a title for this paper, I considered a number of possibilities. One thought recurred with great regularity, and I shall use it both as a subtitle and a continuing theme: "It ain't simple." Any discussion of health care in the United States must address itself to the intrinsic complexities involved or it will be caught in the trap (or should I say clap-trap) of over-simplification which one finds in most of what is written on this subject. The erroneous conclusions drawn from such over-simplification end up being included in many of the proposed solutions. I mistrust easy answers to complicated problems. If I leave you with nothing else, I trust you will at least be challenged to question glib, superficial solutions to the problems of a group of perhaps the most subtly interacting systems in our society. For we are dealing not with a single health care system, nor with the pejoratively titled "non-system," but with many systems. If we truly had a non-system, 3 million health workers would be unable to treat 200 million Americans with any effectiveness, death and morbidity rates would have skyrocketed and our institutions would not function at all.

Let me list some of the systems we do have. Among others, we have systems for private practice, for institutional care, for manpower development, for governmental service, for research, for special target population groups, for financing, for regulation, for the maintenance of professional values, for the protection of workers' rights, for the promotion of quality, etc. The surprising thing is not that the interplay among these systems doesn't work perfectly, but that the group of systems works as well as they do. I have yet to learn how perfection can be measured, and I have certainly not learned how it can be attained in all parameters at once, since one of the basic concepts of systems analysis is that of trade-offs: substituting all or part of one goal in favor of more complete attainment of another. We simply cannot have all the many health services instantly available to everybody, provided by expert practitioners at minimal cost.

A Rule to Apply

The title of this paper is "A Contrary Opinion." The term is used in the same sense that it is in stock-market forecasting where the presumption is that when everybody is thinking the same way, the smart trader acts in the opposite way. If everybody's buying, sell! At the moment, in the health field, everybody's buying "crisis," "inefficiency," "HMO," and "national health insurance." Contrary opinion would question whether there is a crisis, how efficient we are, what's good about fee-for-service and what's good about our present insurance arrangements. Obviously, I'm not suggesting that all is well and that we mustn't change a thing. My basic point is that we may be much better off as a nation by keeping what is good and adjusting those parts of the systems that appear to need it without destroying the fundamental ability of the system to function. Every physician is taught the fundamental rule of pharmacology: *primum non nocere*—above all, do no harm. Let's apply that rule to health care system planning.

Having introduced a medical concept, let's examine the problem the way a physician approaches his patient. First, he takes a history. Our patient, the health care system, appeared to be vigorous, growing in a healthy fashion, and well-loved (we mustn't forget his mental health) as long as his image was dominated by the friendly general practitioner who charged fees according to the patient's ability to pay, and by the relatively small voluntary hospital with a warm and involved community relationship, willing and able to support its modest deficits by fund-raising efforts. However, lest we forget, almost 40 years ago, in the midst of these halcyon days, the Commission on the Cost of Medical Care recommended many of the same organizational and financing changes which are widely touted today. This Commisson may have been exceedingly far-sighted or they may have been guilty of overprescribing.

But the picture I have painted of the family doctor and the protective hospital was slowly but inexorably changed by the accelerating pace of technology. The most able physicians were not satisfied passing out sugar pills and sugar-coated philosophy when more accurate methods of diagnosis and more effective modes of treatment became available. So the leaders of medicine became specialists and trained young doctors in their own image, and gradually a series of professional and academic rewards developed which, in turn, led to a financial reward system favoring the specialist over the generalist. The specialist, of course, needs more sophisticated equipment, and more and better prepared nurses and technicians, and he demanded that the hospital supply them. You're all familiar with what this has done to hospital costs, and since larger hospitals are better able to meet the needs of specialists and super-specialists it has led to increased hospital size. The need for around-the-clock medical coverage and the desire to train more young physicians had led to an enormous growth in the size of house staffs, another large component of cost.

Increase of Effective Demand

But what of more recent history? The nation decided that as a matter of public policy, health care was to be considered a right, and arranged for financial support for the aged and the poor through Medicare and Medicaid since these two groups were least able to pay for their own care. What happened? As the economists say, effective demand increased; the supply of doctors, nurses and beds was fixed, so, as could have been predicted, the price went up. The concept of donated services by volunteer physicians disappeared. Because of open-ended cost and reimbursement, hospital employees through their unions were able to demand and get sharply increased salaries. Hospitals were able to and did increase their programs and services in response to professional as well as community demands, thus adding to cost escalation. Predictably, governments reacted by reducing eligibility for their programs and restricting payment both to physicians and institutions. In other words, having whetted the appetite of the consumer for service, governments said: "Oh yes, health care is a right, but we didn't realize it would be so expensive so it must be the providers' fault." Unfortunately, the law of supply and demand has not been repealed and if demand is significantly increased and supply held constant, prices will rise and all the control technics can do is slow the rise, not stop it.

So much for our patient's history. The next step in the physician's problem-solving approach is to do a physical examination and to look at each of the patient's visible organs to see what he can find.

Cost inflation in hospitals is constantly identified as a particularly troubled part of the total health care system. We know that *per diem* costs have been rising at more than twice the rate of the total Consumer Price Index. The conclusion is then drawn that it must be because we are inefficient.

Use of Strike Threat

Salaries and fringe benefits constitute about 75 percent of total hospital costs and the rate of increase in salary levels has been far greater than that of the average worker. Unskilled hospital workers, with the effective assistance of their unions, have moved from being among the lowest paid service workers in this region to being the highest paid. And this increase has perforce rippled up through the skilled, technical and professional employees. A key reason for the inordinate rate of increase has been the use of the strike threat, a perfectly acceptable mechanism in industry where decisions can be made on purely economic grounds, but totally inappropriate in a hospital where the decision to take a strike is a decision to permit some patients to die. Interestingly enough, the cost of local city government has also been increasing at a rate similar to that of hospitals and for much the same reason: the city cannot tolerate a strike either.

The other reason for hospital inflation is a change in the mix of services. Ten years ago Mount Sinai had no intensive care units, no coronary care unit and essentially no cardiac surgery program. Each of these are vastly more expensive than the cost of an average patient day. Yet they are included in total hospital service costs, so the average cost of all patient days goes up. American industry has an historical increase in productivity of 3 percent per year. In hospitals, productivity is presently measured by considering how many man-hours it takes to produce a patient day or a clinic visit. This productivity figure has declined about 3 percent per year, reflecting these newer, more expensive services. Incidentally, the demands of governmental agencies for higher standards of patient care and more complex reporting systems has added significantly to the reduction in productivity.

Let's look at inefficiency—inefficient compared to what? Some months ago, we put together our costs for operating the Mount Sinai Hotel, including everything we would have to spend if all we took care of were healthy people. Our total expense, including room service from a selective menu three times a day, was about half what a guest would be charged in one of the better commercial-level hotels in New York. Yes, the hotel pays taxes and shows a profit, but still we must be doing something right! This doesn't mean we can't be more efficient, but the potential for major savings is small. Interestingly enough, our total hotel costs were only 20 percent of our total costs. In other words, 80 cents out of every dollar pays for patient care, professionally related costs which are much less amenable to comparison with the commercial world, and are generated and controlled more by the doctor than by the hospital manager.

High Rate of Inflation

Inflation of hospital costs is not just an American phenomenon. Average hospital costs in England, Sweden and Canada have been inflating at a slightly greater rate than ours and yet each of those countries have one or another form of governmental control of hospitals. The politicians like to say that if we don't control costs, they'll take us over. I say fine; if you do, the rate of inflation will quicken and God help the quality of care. It won't even be safe. The only two areas of the economy inflating at a higher rate than hospital costs are construction and the cost of local government, and for many of the same reasons.

This brings us to the physician. He initiates use of the hospital by having the patient admitted, he orders all those tests and procedures (X-ray use is increasing over 10 percent a year compounded), and he determines when to discharge the patient. In hospitals, we surround him with all sorts of bureaucratic controls which are being extended to his office practice in the hope of reducing expenditures. Payments to physicians constitute about 22 percent of the health care dollar and about one-third of that goes to pay his overhead. This net 15 percent of all health care expenditures, which is the doctor's income, is sufficient to develop an annual average income of just over $40,000 per year for America's practitioners, putting them in the highest income brackets in this country. By comparison with other countries, we treat our doctors well. Yet the potential for saving money by limiting his income is small—some percentage of the 15 percent. On the other hand, if he is motivated to use fewer hospital days, fewer nursing home beds, less expensive drugs, etc., the potential is enormous.

A Reorganization System

How about reorganization of doctors into group practice? According to *Medical Economics,* the average physician in a group practice nets a bit more than his solo practice colleague. He's also a bit more productive, but there's no magic in group practice, unless the financing mechanism and the incentive system are changed also. We presently reward doctors for over-utilizing—the more visits, the more hospital days, the more surgical procedures, the higher the individual doctor's income. One of the prime reasons for this reverse incentive system is, I believe, the split between Blue Cross and Blue Shield. The payment the doctor receives bears little relationship to the hospital bill and indeed most physicians have no idea of the size of the patient's hospital bill and, consequently, little reason to be concerned about it.

Possibly the most important organ of our medical care system is money. The importance of money is not its gross amount, but the way it flows and the actions this flow causes. It's impossible to argue that there's not enough money going into medical care in this country when we spend 7.4 percent of our Gross National Product and other industrialized countries spend around 5 percent. If we were spending less than 5 percent, mine would be one of the loudest voices calling for more total dollars. But there's enough money in the pot. So how about its flow?

What happened when the flow to hospitals was in the form of open-ended cost reimbursement is a matter of record. With no external reason to say no, salary levels soared, physicians' requests for staff were honored, new programs were started and hospitals reached out to their communities. Recent changes in reimbursement levels and techniques have put an abrupt halt to this approach.

The doctor has almost always been paid on a fee-for-service basis. This is both good and bad. It's good because it makes him clearly responsible to his patient. It's bad because it tends to encourage over-utilization. How about the alternatives to fee-for-service? There are really only two. The first is salary. If a doctor knows he won't profit from unnecessary care, he's less likely to provide it. The problem with salaried physicians is that they tend not to work as hard, as a carefully done study by Maloney of UCLA has shown. Unfortunately, doctors are not immune to the civil service mentality so that we must be concerned also with productivity. Consider what would happen if America's doctors who now work a 60-hour week were all to become salaried and work a 40-hour week; we'd need 50 percent more doctors!

A Monthly Payment Fee

The other alternative method to pay doctors is by having them share in the net proceeds of partnership income. If the partners charge on a fee-for-service basis, no special economies are likely to result. However, if the group collects prepayment on a monthly basis from subscribers, it is to their advantage to reduce expenditures, particularly if they share in any reduction of hospital use. Certainly the experience of the Kaiser plan must be noted where significantly fewer hospital days per thousand members are used than in the general population. Dr. Herbert Klarman has shown that when appropriate statistical corrections are made, the saving in hospital days is about 20 percent. One cannot help but wonder, however, how much undertreatment occurs in the Kaiser system, and whether adequate consideration is given to the 15 percent of care which their members buy in the fee-for-service market, even though they've already paid for total care under the prepayment mechanism. In summary, no technique for paying doctors is perfect since each method tends to encourage either over-utilization or under-utilization and the latter may be hazardous to health. Fortunately, the great bulk of physicians are basically honest and make their decisions on professional grounds. But as a former practitioner I can testify that economic considerations cannot help but sway marginal decisions on individual patients, and if we can structure payment mechanisms to encourage appropriate utilization of all health services, we will have made a most valuable contribution to the American health system.

Is there evidence that, properly organized and controlled, private practicing physicians will reduce hospital use and, therefore, cost? Let's look at GHI's experience. They provide fee-for-service medicine at a fixed fee schedule. About half of New York's doctors agree to accept the payment and make no additional charge. Payment for lab and X-ray is made. GHI competes with HIP and Blue Shield to cover New York City employees. They perform careful and effective claims review. Recently, New York City published data which showed that GHI subscribers used only 1 percent more hospital care than HIP and there was, of course, free choice of doctor and no prepaid group practice. Interestingly enough, Blue Shield subscribers used 35 percent more hospital care than HIP—an indication that to make fee-for-service work takes administrative know-how and good controls, but it can work and compete with prepaid group practice.

Another bit of evidence against swallowing the HMO concept whole: the Social Security Administration has published data showing that Medicare patients cared for by prepaid group practice in New York cost 11 percent more per person than those cared for in private practice.

One could examine many other organs of our system, but let us consider just one more: health manpower. I've concentrated on the doctor, but he represents less than 10 percent of all health workers. Largely in response to the growth of technology, we have seen an almost bewildering growth in varieties of personnel working in health, and, consequently, an increasing difficulty in relating them to each other in any rational way. Each group develops a self-protective definition of its functions and defies all others to trespass on its turf. So we have great rigidity in job function which leads to as many as 34 different types of people walking into a patient's hospital room to provide some part of his care. No wonder the patient gets confused and no wonder costs rise. Each group institutionalizes its job definition with credentials and laws and strives for professional status. In New York State, only a physician or a certified X-ray technician may take a chest film—a job that can be taught in a day or two. Yet to be certified as an X-ray technician, one needs two years of training. Nurses are trying to define a job function that has less and less to do with the physician's concept of what the patient needs; so a new group of people called physician's associates are being trained and will receive credentials in New York State. Right now the most careful hair-splitting of roles for physicians, nurses and physician's associates is underway. I can see two things happening; initially costs will rise since these new people will have to get paid. Later, if the associates work out as anticipated, we will have fewer nurses. In a sense the nurses will define themselves out of a job since their newer job expectations, no matter how desirable, are not critical to patient care. They may find they've won a battle and lost a war as we learn how to provide care at lower cost using a combination of physician associates and better-trained aides.

Public Acceptance of Basic Services

As the cost control pressures increase, consumers will have to accept only the more basic services and eliminate the more global efforts to consider total psychosocial and family needs, if they are not relevant to the medical problem at hand. In other words, if the patient sprained his ankle, we'll not be concerned if no member of the health team gets worried about whether his child is doing well in school. In a sense, some health personnel have gone looking for new business instead of just dealing expeditiously with what's at hand. We shall increasingly treat what the patient wants treated and not what the health professional thinks might be good for him, whether or not the extra service has any meaningful value to the patient. This is not to decry preventive medicine, but rather to expect that there will be enough public health education so that patients come to expect effective preventive services and don't consider them "unnecessary." This can work, as the experience with Pap smears has demonstrated.

In performing his work-up, following a physical examination, the physician turns next to the laboratory to gather objective data. Sometimes he over-utilizes the lab; I will try not to be guilty of that wasteful approach in continuing my diagnostic exploration.

Finding data accurate for comparison purposes among various health systems is not simple since the purposes for which the data are collected and, therefore, the format of how they are collected, vary so much. Hospital Administrative Services (HAS) has helped to begin the standardization of operating data, but still has a way to go. Utilization rates for a non-prepaid population can be obtained from special studies based on sampling. But our biggest problem is with output measurements—what did the care accomplish? Until we know definitively what we have done, we can't know how efficiently we've done it. Perhaps the greatest need in this entire field is to concentrate on disability rates, morbidity rates and mortality rates, rather than on inputs such as personnel and dollars.

More Medical Service?

Where outputs have been measured, the organization of care has been directly affected: it was the demonstration of a reduced mortality rate from coronary occlusion in coronary care units which led to the very rapid establishment of these units in almost all hospitals. Unfortunately, crude rates are less than useful. America's relatively high infant mortality rate is used to damn our health care system without considering the effects of the greater social pathology in the ghettoes of this country related to bad housing, and inadequate income for which medical care hardly appears to be the best method of therapy. Contrary opinion would question whether more medical service is a better investment than more food for pregnant women; or whether prepaid group practice would have more of an effect than a rat control program, better elementary education, more jobs or better housing.

Now, as a final diagnostic method, let's put the X-ray on hospital management itself and see whether my earlier comments regarding inefficiency can be supported. Voluntary hospital administrators are constantly accused of poor management because of the excessive rate of inflation, and urged to be businesslike. We're told that Kaiser is very efficient. I concur that as a system it is efficient because it provides only half as many hospital beds per thousand as is provided for the rest of the population in its areas. But as hospital managers, they do not do better than their colleagues. Moreover, do the vaunted techniques of business management actually work at Kaiser hospitals? With the help of statistical consultants, data from 17 Kaiser hospitals on *per diem* cost and length of stay from the guide issue of *Hospitals* were compared with comparable hospitals in the same geographic regions. In summary, there was *no* statistically significant difference either in *per diem* cost or in length of stay between the Kaiser hospitals and those hospitals serving the general community.

Commercial Hospital Chains

How about the commercial chains of hospitals? There is no doubt that they can run a hospital at less cost than the voluntary hospitals in the same areas. But they can only do it by eliminating programs which lose money such as education, or clinics, or by providing fewer hours of care per patient per day, assuming that pay scales are comparable. There's no magic involved: if you have as many hours of care multiplied by the same hourly rate, the personnel cost must be equal; personnel costs make up 75 percent of total hospital costs. Therefore, if you want to operate more cheaply you drop high cost programs and do only bread and butter care; you decide which programs you will operate only on the basis of the bottom line financial result and ignore the community needs for the service.

Voluntary hospitals have always taken the other approach: see what needs to be done and then figure out how to finance it. In the long run, some hospital will have to perform the necessary but money-losing functions, and the voluntary hospitals had better be kept viable so that they are around to pick up what the commercials reject.

One more point. The essence of good business management is an ability to make sensible long-range plans which lend themselves to necessary short-range modifications. How is one to plan when in the last four years we have had four different reimbursement schemes, some favoring one approach to cost management and some another. (The decision as to whether to lease or buy equipment is one example of this confusion.) Reimbursement controls are in the hands of the same state agency which is responsible for controlling Medicaid expenditures: can the judge be totally unbiased? At labor contract negotiation time, decisions on wages must be made if an unnecessary strike is to be avoided. Yet decisions on payment rates to cover the extra costs must come from three different agencies in normal times and four different agencies this year. At the critical hour, management doesn't know how much money it has. In capital planning we are controlled by an agency which is supposed to guide the hospitals into efficient use of community resources and rational organization of care facilities. Yet this very agency changes its basic policies almost cavalierly and ignores sizable capital expenditures made by individual hospitals in precise accord with its earlier position. I challenge any business executive to maximize efficiency when controlled by multiple, inefficient, poorly coordinated regulatory agencies.

Diagnosis and Treatment

We've completed the data gathering from and about our patient. Now let us proceed to diagnosis and treatment. We shall not use outdated methods of reporting our findings; we shall use the coming method called the "problem-oriented record" which takes each of the major identified problems, tries to establish a cause, recommends a treatment and follows it to cure. Obviously, today we will not be able to report on progress towards cure of any of the proposed solutions since it is not very likely that the patient will take his medicine!

Problem one: Excessive and improper demand. Fueled by money made available with little direct personal involvement, medical care is sought for trivia, for social reasons (clinics are good place to meet your friends), as a substitute for welfare services, for status purposes, and as a relief for psychological pressures. Just think of all the hours of doctor time which would be available if the uncomplicated common cold was barred from the doctor's office—he can't do anything for it anyway. Suppose everyone with a tension headache learned to talk it out with his spouse or his boss. What if lonely old people were really encouraged to visit day centers? These three moves alone would make a sizeable dent in the volume of visits patients make to doctors, reduce cost sharply and make it possible for doctors to have the time to spend with patients for whom they could so some good. If nothing else, clearing medical trivia out of the medical care flow would reduce physician boredom and would thus aid greatly in improving patient-physician relationships.

A major public health education campaign is recommended to try to get people to use doctors appropriately for prevention and early treatment but not for functions which non-physicians can perform better than physicians. But such a campaign needs to work and that means mobilizing the entertainment television programs, the comic books and similar behavior-modifying media, not the stultified approaches typical of professional health educators.

Problem two: Manpower. Conventional wisdom argues that since it's difficult to get a doctor to do things he doesn't want to do, like practice in a ghetto, make home calls or be available the moment a patient wants him, then there must be a shortage of physicians. Contrary opinion points out that demand is elastic and will expand to fit the available resources of physicians and dollars. Thus, the more doctors trained and the more money made available by government, the more demand there will be. The result is more money put into health services, not less.

A Sufficiency of Surgeons

There is little doubt that we have a sufficiency of many types of physicians such as surgeons, along with a shortage of specialists such as radiologists and, particularly, of generalists. To control the supply of the various specialists we need approval of training programs geared to the national need, not the educational interests of chiefs of services and their staffs. Let's stop creating so many surgeons and the rate of questionable surgical procedures will drop. It's just that simple. And this is the first time I've said anything in this field is simple.

The generalist question is more complex. Anyone trained for six to eight years after high school plus two years of family practice residency has a pretty impressive image of himself. Since he studied all those years to gain his union card as a family physician he must be pretty good and able to handle much of the illness he sees. He's taught to be a doctor, a curer. While he's also taught to refer, it's a challenge to his intellect and to his ego to go just a bit further than might be wise. He's taught to make a diagnosis and accept responsibility, and he will. Now what really should he be doing? Since over 80 percent of the conditions which bring people to doctors are self-curing, he must recognize them and treat symptomatically. Perhaps 8–10 percent are really too complicated for the generalist and should be referred, but he may be tempted to handle them himself. So we prepare fullfledged doctors who should intervene therapeutically and make it count in only 10–12 percent of the cases they see. What a waste. Think of the boredom facing a man with this much education who functions largely as a referral point. Remember these are highly intelligent people whom we're asking to function basically as technicians. In my opinion, which in all modesty is contrary to that of the United States Congress, most medical educators and leading professional societies, we don't need any more primary care generalist physicians. We need more primary care technicians who can do the sorting function and refer the 20 percent which require specific intervention to the appropriate specialists. The primary care technician is another name for the physician's associate. Having no more than four years of higher education, belonging to a group whose intelligence levels are a notch below that of the physician, presenting no self-image as a scientist and not trained to be the last word on anything, he is far less likely to exceed his proper bounds. If he's paid a salary rather than fees, he has no reason to. Will he make mistakes? Of course, but they will be a different quality than that of the generalist physician. He will get scared faster and get help sooner. I believe we should structure a primary care system based on technicians, closely related to those physicians who know them, who can supervise and control them and who will be legally responsible for them.

Within hospitals, I see a cadre of personnel trained as just described who will provide most of the ongoing care under the general orders of a physician. They will do many of the repetitive functions and, in smaller hospitals, will come to replace the foreign-trained house staffs. I see these people, many of them former nurses whose orientation has been changed, becoming the ward generalists. They will either provide or supervise all the care along with a cadre of aides. They will function as pharmacist aides and give medications, take an ECG, draw blood for the laboratory, write histories, do physicals, make observations of patient behavior, do procedures or help with them. Perhaps I've described a Renaissance person and am expecting too much from them. I don't think so. Such a person working with a small group of patients (six to eight) and doing everything for them would sharply reduce the over-all numbers of personnel needed in a hospital. It would stop the conflict of people from different departments competing for the patient in order to carry out separate functions and give the patient the security of a continuing relationship with one person. Can all this be taught in two to four years following high school? Of course it can. How many doctors have office assistants who do most of these functions and retain for themselves only the critical part of the procedures? How many public health nurses have functioned in patient's homes in this way and kept quiet about it because they're afraid of being accused of practicing medicine? Will it be done? That depends on whether the nurses associations decide to act like the dinosaur and not adapt to a changing world or seize the opportunity of redefining their role in a way that would be fulfilling for the nurses and useful for the nation.

Using the Nurse

In my contrary opinion, we need control of the numbers and types of specialists and the rapid development of large numbers of primary care technicians who function both in the hospital and out. The reservoir available, with little additional training, to fill this role is the nurse. Longer range, educational programs should be pointed directly at this newer job definition. Money redirected from creating new medical schools would more than suffice to support this education.

Problem three: Access. This refers to the difficulties people have in getting medical care when they think they need it. But this cannot be discussed without looking at organization. Medicine has been called a cottage industry. Some industries should continue to have a large number of small units rather than become totally centralized. On the other hand, doctors do not need to work entirely alone. To my mind, the small multi-specialty group practice of six to ten doctors in association with at least an equal number of primary care technicians is about right. The size permits coverage in the different specialties yet doesn't get so big that it becomes bureaucratic. The group needs and can afford X-ray and lab service, social work and a business manager. I would like to see these group practice units scattered throughout our cities and rural areas. And, if financing is available, they will be. Doctors don't practice in ghettoes because they can't make a living. Given some form of insurance covering the poor which pays at rates similar to that collected from the middle-class, doctors will move into ghettoes. They started to do this in New York when Medicaid was liberal and moved out again when it was cut back.

Growth of Private Practice Groups

In my opinion, it will be a rare doctor who chooses to work alone in the future, particularly since in a group he would have a pool of primary care technicians to draw on and would not have to be their personnel officer as well as their supervisor. More doctors are joining groups because it's easier on the doctors as well as being better for the patients. And the really rapid growth is not in prepaid groups but in fee-for-service, private practice groups.

Given large numbers of such groups with an on-call roster of physicians and primary care technicians, patients will be able to see someone whom they know is a member of the group and in whom they have confidence. Wouldn't this be better than the commercial home-call services using moonlighting residents which are now springing up in all our cities?

But let me be perfectly clear. I don't mean that such groups should be mandated, but that they will evolve because they tend to be the most satisfactory form of practice arrangement both for patients and for doctors. Government should not use its funds to push doctors into such groups, but rather it should subsidize groups to locate in economically unviable geographic areas if the general method of payment for services is inadequate.

Problem four: Quality. Needless to say, no organizational pattern will be worthwhile if the quality of the service is not at an acceptable level. The conventional jargon says excellence for all. Nonsense, all service cannot be excellent since some physicians are going to be better than others, better being defined in any way you wish. However, all service should be at levels defined from time to time by national bodies as attainable by the majority of practitioners.

Then it must be monitored. One of the most promising methods for such monitoring of care outside the hospital is the medical foundation which uses a claims review technique. My only concern is that the foundations will become so enamored of financial controls that they will forget to watch quality.

For in-hospital care, the organized medical staff now functions in this regard. It is not necessary to create a whole new organizational pattern, but rather to define accepted, objective standards for what is meant by adequate care. How high should the post-operative infection rate be before corrective action is required? What death rate from acute myocardial infarction is considered acceptable? These are value questions having immediate impact on the behavior of doctors, as well as on the cost of care. Until we are prepared to face up to them, discussions of quality have little meaning.

Approaches to Financing

Problem five: Money. There are many ramifications of this problem. The first is the source of the money to pay for care. As far as I'm concerned this is a political, rather than an economic or operational, question. There's only one source of money, and that's the production stream of the national economy. Whether medical care is paid directly by labor and management as a fringe benefit or whether taxes are paid and the government purchases the care is not as basic as how the care is provided. There's no question that some method of spreading the risk of illness is necessary. The number of organizations who handle the funds is related to administrative cost and should be decided on the basis of how it can be done most economically.

Second. What part of the bill most bothers people? For the young it is the grossly inadequate coverage provided by Blue Cross for obstetrical care; for the middle-aged, the threat of being wiped out by a major illness; and for the poor, the cost of any medical service. We have tried, it seems to me, to do too much for too many with single forms of coverage and, consequently, have not done enough for some and perhaps, too much for others. We need insurance (or payment) programs aimed at the major economical and medical threats. The alternative is to provide comprehensive coverage for all, medical and dental services to all, recognizing how this would increase effective demand even more, and would raise costs to levels which our political and business leadership would find unacceptable.

Third. How can we give physicians incentives to reduce the costs of hospital care, as well as ambulatory drugs, laboratories and X-rays? Our present Blue Cross/Blue Shield policies reward the doctor for over-utilization. I have two suggestions. One is to pay the under-utilizing physician at a higher fee schedule than the average and to pay the over-utilizing physician at a lower rate. He'll get the message quickly. The other idea is to award the physician a total amount, and let him pay the hospital bill, keeping the remainder for himself. Watch his length of stay and his unnecessary ordering of lab and X-ray drop! A working, rather than a theoretical model of cost control via physician activity is the medical foundation. By reviewing individual doctor's claims it can spot apparent excessive utilization, and by peer pressure it can help to reduce it. In some foundations there is a total pot of money, and each service is paid for at a percentage of the sum. Don't think there isn't careful scrutiny of claims and firm pressure on the high utilizers.

Looking at Hospital Costs

Fourth. How about hospital costs? Let's consider per diem costs first. They are made up basically of salary rates and levels of care or complexity of service. Until society finds a way to control salary rates in hospitals, costs will rise. And until society says, and means it, that it will settle for less than the best, the levels of care will rise and will increase costs. But let us consider community-wide hospital costs. Here the answer is clearer and simpler. If you want to reduce the cost of hospitalization, reduce the number of beds. This means strong regional planning and a willingness to accept long waiting lists. But if fewer beds are operating, the cost of hospital operation drops. The quickest and surest way to reduce hospital costs is to close one-fourth of the presently operating beds in a city, starting with the poorest physical plants. Many communities now have three beds for each 1000 potential users versus the national four per 1000. The pain in reorganizing medical staffs and trustee relationships will be great. But until it's done, I will not believe that we want to do something about the high cost of hospital care.

Fifth. What about alternatives to hospitalization? Ambulatory care, home care, extended care facilities and nursing homes are cheaper units of care, but they all add up as additional services which must be paid for. New services mean new costs. They may reduce the pressure for expansion of hospitals, but they won't save money.

Sixth. We need a national consensus on what we're willing to accept as a level of care. We can't have everything for everybody and expect it to be cheap. We can make the system run better, but we have to translate our value systems into quantifiable terms: How low should the infant mortality be? What percentage of cervix cancer patients should live? How much money are we prepared to spend? These questions are inseparable and must be faced for our solutions to be rational.

A National Health Insurance Scheme

Given all of the above, a source of funds, incentives for physicians, identification of special needs of different groups, a reduction of hospital beds and operational targets, we can devise a national health insurance scheme that will work. I don't mean it must be operated by the government; we could legislate mandatory coverage for the working, with payment by government for the indigent. This pragmatic, cautious approach of gradually adjusting components of the total system, while being sensitive to how each change affects the rest of the system, is contrary to the usual one of testing political waters and seeing what will fly. My approach may not garner votes, but it's more likely to work.

I've tried in this paper to cast light, rather than to quote dogma. I've tried to make you see that much of conventional wisdom in the medical care field is based on false assumptions and inadequate data. I've suggested an approach which might correct the present problems and ease the present concerns. But my major concern is that given the complex systems we have in this field, we should try new things carefully and with thorough documentation and study. Let us not force four million health workers and 200 million potential patients into operational modes which may not work. My proposed solutions to individual problems in the total system do not vitiate the basic proposal that we are dealing with extreme complexity. Each change will produce presently unknown results on other parts of the total system. Without change, we will finally have revolution. With careful change, we can have evolution.

I believe that in a pluralistic society there should be many approaches to health care organization and, given honestly free choice, the best overall system will evolve. It may or may not resemble what I've been describing, but I think these approaches should be tried.

We need diversity in this country. We have thrived so far because of it. We need experimentation. We need to make mistakes and to learn from them. We cannot afford to stop the present medical machinery while we attempt to create something perfect. No human endeavor is perfect, some are less imperfect than others. America now has a superb system of care by expert specialists. It needs to improve its primary care system and its financing mechanisms. Let's adjust our machine to strengthen its weak points and get on with the job of caring for the sick.

A quotation from Isaiah is very apt: "Where there is no vision, the people perish."

Conflict of Interest: Ethical Dilemma

Charles M. Ewell, Jr.

"In the modern social order the person is . . . exposed to relentless actions and reactions of conflicting interests and appetites. . . ."
—Jacques Maritain, *Three Reformers,* 1925

To many hospital administrators, conflict of interest has been a familiar and not unfriendly term. It has been easily used to determine whether a board member who owns a local business should also be a hospital vendor, or whether the board member-attorney should function as the hospital's legal counsel. More recently the term has often been used defensively in the controversy over an appropriate role for physicians in hospital governance. During the last two years, however, the familiar term has been applied to hospital administrators in less friendly forms. Some consumer groups, and public officials, have used it to support claims that hospital administrators are a major factor behind the striking rise in health care costs because of their conflicting roles as hospital executives on one hand, and their simultaneous roles as powerful members of Blue Cross rate-setting boards, health planning councils and other health policy-making groups.[1]

This particular interpretation of conflict of interest appears to stem from a feeling by consumer-oriented interests that they do not play a role in making key decisions on the kinds of health services they will receive, and worse, that the decisions are being made by people with special interests which are different from the general public's interests. The dissident voices are saying that just as military policy is too important to be left to the generals, so is health policy too important to be left to the health professionals.

An indication that the complaints are being heard is evident from the moving and shaking going on in the health field, particularly during the past year, such as the realignment between the American Hospital Association and Blue Cross, resignations of some hospital administrators

[1]*Chicago Tribune,* 8 November 1971.

from Blue Cross plan boards, and a new emphasis on consumer participation on planning councils and hospital boards.[2]

As with most emotional issues, however, the shrieks cloud the logic with the result that actions occur without the benefit of reasoned analysis and impartial evaluation of alternatives. The notion of conflict of interest is, for all its surface simplicity, fuzzy, complex and multidimensional. In approaching the problem in the general sense conflict of interest will refer to "participation through decision, approval, or recommendation in matters which may be inconsistent with a primary loyalty."

The Personal Dimension

To the man on the street conflict of interest implies a disloyalty which traces its origins from the Biblical maxim that a man cannot serve two masters. The interpretation has made its way into common law rules governing the relation of master and servant, principal and agent, fiduciary and beneficiary, and attorney and client.[3] It has at its core the idea of "personal" conflict of interest as it may be related to financial interests. In the hospital field it is manifest in a variety of ways including the American College of Hospital Administrators' *Code of Ethics* which refers to the administrator's holdings, interests and investments, and the possibility that they may constitute "a conflict of interest in the administration of his health service organization."[4] This dimension of conflict of interest which stresses the personal aspect is the most commonly referred to and most clearly understood. A second dimension, related to "system" aspects of conflict of interest, is less clearly understood and forms the core for much of the present controversy over conflict of interest in the health field.

Personal conflict of interest has a history as old as man's own history. Our participative, democratic form of government lends itself easily enough to the activity, and dark cases are available for view in the Library of Congress. Applied to federal government employment, conflict of interest expresses the widely acknowledged but ill-defined

[2]*Hospitals* 7, no. 44 (16 January 1971); and *Hospital Week* 7, no. 44 (29 October 1971).

[3]Dorothy C. Tompkins, *Conflict of Interest in the Federal Government* (Berkeley: University of California, Bureau of Public Administration, 1961).

[4]*Code of Ethics* (Chicago: American College of Hospital Administrators, 1972).

proposition that there are activities occupying an area between bribery and graft—and innocent association with suitors for government favor —which are "inconsistent with holding a government job and which employers of the United States must, in decency, forego.[5]

Conflict of Interest Statute

The basic conflict of interest statute applicable to federal employees is Title 18, Section 208, of the United States Code which prohibits an officer or employee of the executive branch from participating 'through decision, approval, disapproval, or recommendation, the rendering of advice, investigation, or otherwise in a matter in which he, his wife, or child has a financial interest," and was passed in the 1962 Congress.[6] The widely publicized Sherman Adams affair was one of the key factors that gave rise to a review by Sen. Emanuel Celler of legislation up to that time. Before the 1962 legislation there existed only eight ineffective statutes enacted prior to 1863 which addressed these issues: assistance to private parties; self-dealing; augmentation of income by private parties; and post-employment restrictions.[7]

Although the 1962 law was an improvement in the executive branch it did not affect the legislative branch at all, and there still remains to be passed in Congress a set of strong standards affecting the key areas of (1) outside communication on sensitive issues, (2) disclosure of personal income and (3) a meaningful code of ethics. The only two things which do exist at present are a weak code of ethics passed in 1958, and a weak Standards and Conduct Code passed by a Senate Select Committee. Apparently many suggestions have been made but all have died in committee or on the floor of the house or senate. The key to legislative conflict of interest appears to be public disclosure of personal finances, which is a "remedy the patient refuses to take."[8] The need surfaces occasionally by disclosure of conflicts by legislators in cases involving the intent to influence, such as the Bobby Baker, T.F.X. and Billy Sol Estes issues.

[5]U.S., Congress, Committee on the Judiciary, Antitrust Subcommittee, Washington, D.C., 1958.

[6]*House Reports* (1834).

[7]Robert S. Getz, *Congressional Ethics, the Conflict of Interest Issue* (Princeton, N.J.: D. Van Nostrand Co., 1966).

[8]*Ibid.*

Public Disclosure Laws

At the state government level, however, some recent stirring has occurred regarding public disclosure laws as a result of apparent misconduct by lawmakers. A large midwestern state recently was forced to face the issue when public ire was raised to the breaking point following news reports which indicated gross conflicts of interest between groups seeking special legislation and a sizeable number of legislators.[9]

The judiciary branch of government has not found itself completely removed from conflict of interest situations either as evidenced by the resignation of Justice Fortas, a few years ago due to his inappropriate relationship with the executive branch of the federal government. That relationship constituted a conflict of interest in terms of the original Constitutional concept of separation of the three branches of government. Most judiciary examples of conflict of interest, however, go a step beyond the strict interpretation of conflict and become criminal bribery, where intent to influence has progressed to the point where there is actual payment to perform in a certain way. A thin line appears to exist between the interpretation of conflict of interest and the more blatant bribery.

The notion of personal conflict of interest as it applies to hospitals is considerably less splashy than the examples from government, or examples from business and labor. In hospitals the possible applications relate to the three key elements of the organization; the board, the doctors, and the administration.

Personal conflict of interest, as it may be applied to hospital boards of directors, usually occurs when a board member seeks to gain personal, financial benefit by using his influence as a board member. The classic cases involve members who own or operate enterprises that market products or services which may be purchased by the hospital, such as building supplies, foodstuffs, insurance, or banking services. In large communities this problem can be completely avoided with an understanding that nothing will be purchased from a board member or his firm. In small communities where there are commercial monopolies the problem becomes more acute for the hospital.

Personal conflicts of interest, as they may be applied to practicing physicians, usually land in two areas of discussion. The first regards whether physicians should be appointed to hospital boards, and the

[9] "Scandal Prompts Ethics," *Wisconsin State Journal* 216, no. 128 (15 January 1972).

second whether they should own and operate their own health service enterprises.

The first issue—board membership—has stewed for many years as those who oppose the idea present the arguments of M. T. MacEachern, M.D. discouraging participation by doctors on the board.[10] The arguments stress that the doctor cannot be expected to carry on professional medical dealings with the hospital and at the same time function as a member of the primary policy-making body without perforce being in a conflict situation. However, the trend during the last few years has been clearly in the opposite direction as shown by an American Medical Association report in 1970 indicating that about 50 percent of short-term general hospitals in the United States now have members of the medical staff on their governing boards.[11] Statements by the A.M.A., the American Hospital Association and the Joint Commission on Accreditation of Hospitals range from strongly to mildly supportive of membership by doctors on the board.[12] The A.H.A. makes the important qualification that the board should select a physician for membership rather than his being selected by the medical staff or other special interest group, and that the physician-member should function as a community representative without special interest allegiance. The conflict of interest which may arise from physician membership on the board appears to have taken a back seat to the positive aspects of improved communication between the board, physicians, and administration.[13] Legal support for the doctors recently came from Florida where a circuit court judge ruled in favor of two physicians who were challenging a state law prohibiting board membership for physicians based on the conflict of interest notion.[14]

For-Profit, Doctor Owned Corporations

The second issue relating to physicians and conflict of interest developed over the years as physicians combined their medical roles with

[10] M. T. MacEachern, *Hospital Organization and Management* (Berwyn, Ill.: Physicians Record Co., 1946).

[11] L. O. Simenstad, ''Physicians on Hospital Governing Boards,'' *Nebraska S.M.J.* 56 (June 1971): 224–226.

[12] *Ibid.*

[13] A. J. J. Rourke, ''The Doctor in Hospital Governance,'' *Trustee* 24, no. 5 (May 1971): 1–9.

[14] *Hospital Week* 8, no. 1 (7 January 1972).

entrepreneurial ventures in the health system. The big impact has come, however, as a result of the rapid increase of for-profit, doctor-owned, corporations which operate chains of health facilities in many parts of the country. According to the A.M.A.'s *Code of Ethics* doctors may own shares in for-profit institutions so long as they place the welfare of their patients above their own financial interests. Quite obviously it is difficult to draw the line between patient and profit, and the general public's reaction seems to indicate more problems for the A.M.A.'s public relations staff. One recent example in Massachusetts resulted in the state medical society admitting that "It looks bad on the surface" that a for-profit medical conglomerate associated with a not-for-profit university hospital was doing enough business to provide a key physician/owner with $93,000 in annual income over and above his university salary.[15]

Personal conflict of interest by hospital administrators has recently become a controversial issue and, with the exception of a few owner/operators of for-profit institutions, has never been. Hospital administration has been a notably clean occupation with only an occasional smudge occurring in arrangements between vendors and purchasing agent/administrators; however, there are curious activities in which some hospital administrators are involved which provide for interesting discussion and may be interpreted as conflicts of interest in the strictest sense.

One of these activities is receiving compensation from corporations for participation in programs to test new medical products or ideas, which requires the use of hospital resources. This practice differs from the consultant/client relationship between an administrator and a corporation where a fee is paid to the administrator for expert advice given outside the hospital after regular working hours. The former practice appears to raise a very real question as to whether the participating administrator is functioning in such a way as to compromise his primary loyalty to his hospital, thus placing him in a conflict of interest position.

Soliciting the Administrator's Services

Another difficult problem occurs for administrators who are asked to become board members, principals, or act in an advisory capacity for a fee, for businesses which sell products or services that might be

[15] "Doctors in Business," *Newsweek*, 31 January 1972.

purchased by their own hospitals. It usually remains for the administrator to determine whether his services have been solicited by the business for his legitimate expertise, or whether he is expected to become a customer as well. The most reasonable reaction is for him to automatically exclude his institution as a customer of the firm's product or service. This may not completely solve the problem, however, because the firm's product or service may in fact be the best available and exclusion of it may work to his hospital's disadvantage; in which case he is in a reverse state of conflict of interest.

Other areas where hospital administrators may be subject to conflict of interest criticism involve: appointment to boards of other hospitals, acceptance of free goods or services from companies that may sell to their hospital; advertising their hospital's programs or services; free use of hospital services or equipment for non-hospital purposes; and employment of their relatives in the hospital. Still, with a handful of exceptions, these occurrences have not had the graft stigmas attached to them which have been given to counterpart chief executives in business and industry. These and related questions are presently being studied by an A.C.H.A. Special Task Force on Conflict of Interest which was established in 1972 and will be making recommendations later this year.

In summary, the personal dimension to conflict of interest is that side of the coin with which most are familiar. It relates to personal financial gain, and can be described as participation in an activity, whether it be by decision, approval, or recommendation in which an individual or his family has a personal financial interest.

The System Dimension

What will be referred to as the system dimension might also be called the "organizational" dimension, the "social" dimension, or the "consumer" dimension. By whatever label, it refers to the nonpersonal side of conflict of interest where the emphasis is not on financial gain to individuals but on the potential for larger conflicts of interest between hospitals and health insurers or between hospitals and health planning organizations. It is within this conflict of interest dimension that much dialogue is currently taking place in the health field, and it is within this dimension that hospital leaders have the least credibility with consumers and stand to lose the most public confidence.

It is also within this dimension that key health organizations such as the American College of Hospital Administrators must establish parameters to assist health professionals make decisions on the pressing question of system conflicts of interest. Questions such as "should administrators continue to serve on Blue Cross boards and areawide planning councils?" and "should hospital trustees continue to participate in those organizations?" If they should continue to serve, should it be on a non-voting basis; or should there be only a certain small percentage of "provider" representation on those boards? This last section addresses the concept of "system" conflicts of interest, and is followed by a look at some alternatives.

In the world beyond the health care industry, particularly the world of business and government, there does appear to exist the same phenomenon which has been referred to as system conflicts of interest, vis-à-vis the health system. A look at some examples outside our field may help us to see the problem more clearly.

Military and Defense Industry Alliance

A Pentagon report issued in January, 1972, and compiled at the insistence of Congress, indicates that during the prior 4½ years the defense industry recruited 1,101 high Pentagon civilian officials or retired and reserve officers holding the rank of major, lieutenant commander, or above; and that the Pentagon hired 232 executives from the defense industry or civil service ranks of GS-13 and above. To the Pentagon's critics, particularly Senator Proxmire (D-Wis.), the two-way traffic between the military and the defense industry has caused an alliance which violates existing conflict of interest laws. The report has produced new pressures for a stiffer conflict law on the basis that the titles uncovered suggest the possibility that informal favor-seeking goes on behind the scenes.

Present conflict of interest laws prohibit a retired officer from directly selling at all to the military service in which he served, although he may sell to other branches of the Defense Department after a three-year wait. Critics say that the retired officers work around the rules and engage in indirect selling with military friends.[16]

Another case of possible system conflict of interest which occurred recently involved the Atomic Energy Commission, which became impaled on the horns of the environmental protection movement. Several groups, including the American Public Health Association, made their dissatisfaction known regarding the A.E.C.'s dual (and allegedly conflicting) roles of promotion of nuclear energy and public protection

[16] "The Military-Industrial Job Hoppers," *Business Week,* 15 January 1972.

from radiation hazards. The groups recommended that all radiation protection activities of the federal government be brought together under one agency, stating that "the apparent conflict of interest at the A.E.C. had weakened the credibility of that agency in its responsibility for protection of the public."[17]

Both of these cases are good examples of how conflict of interest can exist even when there is little evidence of personal, financial interest, i.e., where there is a system conflict of interest.

The last area of examination relates to the most touchy and most interesting aspect of system conflict of interest—the dimension as it applies to hospitals and their relationships with Blue Cross and health planning groups, and other health-related organizations.

Relationship Between Blue Cross and Hospitals

To gain an understanding of the relationship between hospitals and the Blue Cross plans it is helpful to briefly review how it developed: Blue Cross was first established in the 1930's in order to make available a method for the community to prepay for guaranteed hospital care. It has always functioned as the financial arm of hospitals and even though many battles have been fought with hospitals, Blue Cross has always sought to strengthen the partnership. Even during periods when the distance between hospitals and Blue Cross was greatest, major efforts were taken to bring them close together and, in 1960, they agreed to swap board members and take other interlocking steps.[18]

However, the scene changed drastically with the passage of Medicare and the assumption by Blue Cross of the intermediary role for transfer of funds between the federal government and hospitals. The responsibility of Blue Cross quickly changed from one of hospital associate to public trustee, and as public trustee they were obligated to guard against questionable hospital management, inadequate facilities and improper staffing and costs. At about the same time, hospital costs were taking their highest leaps and Blue Cross was clearly caught in the middle with the public demanding less upward cost pressure, and the hospitals demanding more money to meet expenses.

Insofar as hospitals are basically private organizations providing a

[17]"Conflict of Interest in the Atomic Energy Commission," *Journal of the American Public Health Association* 16, no. 12: 2538.

[18]Robert E. Toomey, "Hospital-Blue Cross Relationships: The Scene Changers," *Hospitals* 40 (1 August 1966): 46–49; and "AHA and Blue Cross Split But Still a Twosome," *Medical World News* 12 (10 September 1971): 20–21.

public service it can only be expected that there must be public accountability. And who now finds itself in the position of assuming that the public weal is protected—Blue Cross!

It was unreasonable to expect that the historical relationship between Blue Cross and the nation's hospitals would escape the eyes of critics looking for reasons behind the rapid rise in hospital costs. They found it with a vengeance, and the resulting public criticism (the most popular cry had to do with the fox guarding the henhouse) has led to, among other things, the separation between the A.H.A. and the Blue Cross Association, and a new list within B.C.A. toward the angle of cost controls and better management within hospitals.[19]

Criticism of Relationship

The B.C.A. board also has begun to address the sensitive issue of conflict of interest by urging that plan boards exclude provider representation when negotiating reimbursement with providers. This recommended step, if followed, should help to quiet critics who insist that it is unjustifiable to have a provider representative participate in rate-setting on Monday and go back to his hospital on Tuesday to collect the rates that he set the day before.

Other recent B.C.A. board policies stress the need to broaden representation by consumers, and urge a consumer majority for each plan board, and the requirement that a conflict of interest policy be developed by each plan. Perhaps of greatest significance is a resolution that "the primary objective of Blue Cross is to provide the strongest possible community-oriented service instrument through which the public can prepay its health care expenditures. . . ."[20] While it may sound basically similar to the original purposes established by Blue Cross, it is unlikely that the public interest has received such attention in the past as it will be receiving in the future.

At the same time that Blue Cross has been altering its posture to provide more emphasis to its public trustee role, the A.H.A. has been laying some groundwork in its Council on Financing to provide for changes in makeup of local Blue Cross plan boards. Its Special Committee on Blue Cross Approval Standards developed recommendations that would require boards to have one-half public representation (pre-

[19]Robert E. Toomey, "Blue Cross and Hospitals Face the Future," *Hospitals* 43 (16 January 1969): 49.

[20]Minutes of the Blue Cross Association Governing Board (undated).

sently one-third) and one-quarter provider representation (presently one-third).[21]

It didn't take long for the national separation between the A.H.A and the Blue Cross Association to become known before the state ramifications were being felt. Already six administrators have resigned from the Nebraska Blue Cross board claiming conflict of interest, and several plan boards have special committees studying the alternatives for the future.[22]

Although one might criticize the need for such immediate reaction, it must be understood that some rather rank conflicts of interest have occurred. One example in the Midwest involved a hospital trustee who found himself serving as chairman, and Blue Cross representative, of a joint rate review study committee meeting with the state hospital association. The hospital association's chief delegate on the committee was the administrator from the same hospital as the trustee. A hot-blooded consumer advocate could hardly be convinced that the public's interest was being adequately served in that arrangement.

Serving on Health Planning Councils

Turning to the question of possible conflict where administrators serve on health planning councils, the issue has less immediate urgency simply because, unlike Blue Cross which has had a clear impact on the health scene, areawide planning councils have had only a modest and relatively undocumented impact due to the absence of legislative authority and adequate funding to support their activities.[23]

One nationally regarded hospital administrator gives an example of their lack of clout telling of an occasion when he was invited to address the annual meeting of the most successful health planning council in the country, only to find in the local newspaper that morning an article indicating that a hospital group had announced that it was going ahead with its construction plans even though the planning council had blackballed the project as unnecessary and wasteful. Nevertheless, the issue will become more pressing publicly as the states pass legislation which

[21]Personal communication with David F. Drake, Ph.D., Secretary, Council on Financing, American Hospital Association, Chicago, Illinois.

[22]*Hospital Week* 7, no. 44 (29 October 1971).

[23]Personal communication with Ray E. Brown, Executive Vice-President, Northwestern University—McGaw Medical Center, Chicago, Illinois; and Eugene D. Rosenfeld, "Areawide Planning Controls Costs," *Hospitals* 46 (1 February 1972): 36.

puts teeth in the planning groups' recommendations—about fifteen states have recently passed the needed legislation.

The issue of conflict of interest as it applies to health planning councils closely parallels the Blue Cross issue, and questions whether providers of services should pass judgment on plans for health programs which directly affect their own institutions. Critics point out that it is common for hospital administrator-members of areawide planning councils to engage in mutual back-scratching in order to have their construction projects, and other programs, approved by the councils.

Participation in Areawide Health Planning Decisions

The question of whether an administrator can, or indeed should attempt to, function as an impartial, unbiased participant in areawide health planning decisions has been challenged by some in the field who feel that a hospital administrator has a clear and unbending responsibility to represent only his own institution. They interpret any indication by an administrator that he is an unbiased community representative as evidence of less than acceptable allegiance to his own hospital. One planner admits and "when it comes down to the final points they must consider their own hospital before the community's interest."[24] The same argument could be made regarding participation on Blue Cross boards.

In summary, the system dimension of conflict of interest is that side of the coin which most health professionals have not sorted out clearly for themselves. It relates to system conflict of interest and involves "participation by an organization, or individual representatives of an organization with other individuals or organizations in decisions, approvals, or recommendations which may require actions that are inconsistent with a primary organizational loyalty."

Some Possible Alternatives

The following comments relate to the second dimension of conflict of interest.

Of course, the most extreme alternatives to the system dilemma come from two sides: those who would change nothing in the present

[24]Personal communication with Samuel S. Long, Past-President, Association of Areawide Health Planning Agencies, and Director, Health Planning Association of Northwest Ohio, Toledo, Ohio.

system arrangements and those who would turn the entire thing upside down. Between these two extremes are the more moderate possibilities that will probably serve as the basis for near-term modification. Included among the total are: (1) Provision for a limited, maximum percentage of health-provider representation on outside health-related boards and councils. Most common suggestions are that there be a maximum of 10–15 percent representation by providers. (2) Retention of the present percentage of representation by providers, but a restriction that would exclude providers from participation in certain decisions such as rate review on Blue Cross boards, or approval of their own projects when presented to planning councils. (3) Continued membership by providers, but on an ex-officio, no-vote basis, so as to retain the technical advantages of provider membership but eliminate the apparent conflict of interest. (4) Participation by providers through a general advisory committee mechanism, but without an actual membership provision. (5) (Similar to the foregoing)—Participation by providers on a number of appropriate committees and sub-committees, but without full membership. (6) Retention of present provider participation, but with providers selected by the board or council itself rather than by a state hospital association or state medical association as is presently done in many states. (7) Elimination of all provider representation, based on the belief that participation constitutes a potential for conflict of interest and is contrary to the public good.

It appears evident from a review of conflict of interest issues that there is a growing requirement to review the role, and in fact the appropriateness, of provider participation on health-related boards and councils. It is also apparent that some additional and perhaps more specific, guidelines need to be developed which will assist administrators when they must make decisions related to their own potential personal conflict of interest. Present public criticism, the possibility of declining consumer confidence, and the need to adjust to the changing roles and responsibilities of health-related organizations will require that health professionals be prepared to appraise the current issues with a logic that outweighs sentimentality, and reason that is equal to the demands.

Further Readings Suggested by the Author

Bajonski, Andrew. "The Blue Cross Double Cross." *Chicago Journalism Review,* February 1972.

Hedgepeth, Jay. "Hospital Trustees and Conflict of Interest." *Trustee* 26 (March 1973): 25.

''The Hospital Business.'' *Washington Post.* (Series) October 29—November 3.

Mattison, Berwyn. ''Community Health Planning and the Health Professionals.'' *American Journal of Public Health* 58 (June 1968).

''Opponents of A.H.A. Financing Policy Attack Control by Planning Agencies.'' *Modern Hospital* 110 (June 1968).

Prior, Faith. ''A Look at Consumer Skepticism About Health Care.'' *Trustee* (25 February 1972): 9.

An Emerging Medical Staff Organization

Everett A. Johnson, Ph.D.

By and large, during the past several decades, the hospital corporate structure, with its power separation between medical staff and administration, has remained unchanged. Existing divisions of authority have continued; their evolution into one common organization has been blocked by trustee isolation from current realities in hospital operation.

In the past two decades, the only major organizational innovation developed to coordinate these disjointed functions was the use of the Joint Conference Committee. Whatever effectiveness this committee had initially, it has gradually lessened, as one special committee after another was appointed to implement and direct new complex medical care activities. As time lags have shortened between the development of new medical technology and its every day use, the appointment of new, functionally-oriented committees has increased.

Objectives of Physician Appointments

Some hospitals perceived the organizational impact of these new medical care modalities and attempted to shore up the medical staff by making a few full-time physician appointments. This was mostly done through establishing positions in medical education activities. In a few instances, positions have been created for full-time, salaried chiefs of clinical services and, occasionally, for chief of staff positions.

Another strategy used to make the medical staff organization structure more responsive to increasing medical care complexity was recognizing the growth of specialized functions by modifying the number of clinical departments. Differentiation within major clinical services increasingly has taken place. Where one clinical department, such as surgery and all of its sub-specialities, existed twenty years ago in a single unit, it has not been separated into multiple clinical departments such as orthopedics, plastic, genito-urinary, thoracic, etc. Instead of six or seven major clinical divisions, a medical staff today may have twenty or more clinical services, some with only two or three members but with as much status as departments having thirty or more members.

As medicine's state-of-the-art rapidly increased at the local level, there was rapid expansion in the number of part and full-time physicians employed by a hospital for specific clinical responsibilities. Two decades ago, the only hospital-based physicians were pathologists, radiologists and anesthesiologists. Now this group includes neurologists, nephrologists, internists, psychiatrists, emergency room physicians, medical educators and others. They direct coronary care, intensive care, recovery rooms, and other, more specialized diagnostic and treatment programs. In large-sized medical staffs, during the past fifteen years, the ratio of part and full-time hospital-paid physicians to totally private practicing physicians shifted from 5 percent to 15 percent and, occasionally, to 20 percent. This figure excludes interns and residents.

The Attending Physician's Complex Role

In yesterday's medical world, each major clinical area was simple enough for one attending physician, with occasional help from one or two consulting physicians, to manage the total care of a complicated case. In today's world of complex medical functions, attending physicians must deal with seven or more specialized physicians when using sophisticated complex medical procedures.

The result of this piece-meal tinkering with medical staff organizations to accommodate new clinical services has been a jerry-built administrative structure. Although substantial changes have taken place in clinical services, traditional medical staff attitudes concerning administrative arrangements have blocked changes in this area. The outcome is a command system, based on unpaid physicians operating through a committee structure which stalls their decision-making processes in many areas. In a decade of major impending changes in medical care delivery, this attitude is unthoughtful and disadvantageous for physicians.

The major elements of a medical care system that will be operational by the decade of the eighties are identifiable as the decade of the seventies begins. As changes take place to implement an emerging system, a medical staff's organizational structure will be seriously affected.

The primary thrust of the coming change will be higher achievement levels of integration in a community's health care system. As greater unity is developed through greater systemization, several existing operation modes must change. This change process will affect traditional patterns and practices of medical staffs.

Five Forces Causing Changes

The specific forces which will cause changes and thereby attain a more integrated health system are: 1. The development of hospital and health facility chains within localized geographic areas; 2. An improvement in physician productivity by increasing efficiency in the use of medical manpower; 3. An increase in the hospital-based practice of medicine to provide an adequate economic base for developing super-clinical specialties to implement new medical knowledge outside university medical centers; 4. A modification in the concept of total, or private, medicine practice to accommodate the development of various government encouraged or sponsored group practice schemes; 5. Continued expansion of ambulatory medicine practices and associated technology.

These five specific outcomes will be rationalized and publicly promoted as palliatives for abating rising medical care costs. Even though available evidence cannot now substantiate such a conclusion, arguments for change will be based on a cost containment theme or its major variant, greater medical quality for the same cost. It will probably be impossible for any health group to divert pressures generated, and to a lesser or greater extent, each objective will be achieved.

Every major step toward improved health care integration will have an impact on traditional medical staff organization. Development of localized corporate health firms must be established on a *unified,* medical staff concept, for a continuum between levels of health care to exist. The existing health care system's best served components are physicians offices and the acute, general hospital. Other parts of the system, such as nursing homes, community-operated sheltered workshops, private laboratories and old folks homes, can be characterized as almost totally non-medically directed.

Putting these several types of health facilities together in one local organization, in most cases, will be unjustifiable on any non-medical cost reduction rationale. Cost savings from joint purchasing, laundry and other service functions of the health facilities will be insignificant to justify such mergers. What will occur, however, is a rapid increase in the quality of medicine practices in these peripheral-type medical institutions. As quality goes up, so will the use of diagnostic tests and the therapies ordered. A net outcome will be higher operating costs and much better medical care.

The real purpose for developing a local health chain will be to make medical manpower effectively useful at more levels of care than the two levels which now exist. During the decade of the seventies, the early years of merging pieces and parts of different health facilities will find medical staff organizations expanding in traditional ways to handle additional responsibilities.

Establishment of Community Medicine Departments

Probably, the first adjustment will see community medicine departments established as major clinical services in general hospitals. As various types of facilities are added to the chain, the end of the seventies will see medical staffs bending and buckling under their expanded bureaucratic over-structures. The solution will then be obvious to all participants: full-time chiefs of services to serve as administrators of their clinical areas for all institutions within the chain. Initially, to justify these new hospital costs, sub-specialties within each major clinical area will be brought back into larger specialty groupings.

In larger chains, chiefs of services will have administrative staffs responsible for major functional areas of responsibility. One position in each clinical division will obviously be an assistant director of medical education, to direct graduate and post-graduate educational activities for the clinical service. A second position will be filled by a non-physician, an administrative person to coordinate, schedule and act as secretariat for affairs of the clinical service.

Consolidation of sub-speciality areas into major services in a full service health corporation will result in eight administrative-clinical areas: surgery, medicine, obstetrics and gynecology, pediatrics, pathology, radiology, physical medicine and community medicine.

Such a move will mean the abandonment of the present two track medical staff chain of command. The operational or clinical decision-making process and the deliberative or committee-type decisions will be combined into one, full-time, chief of service position.

The current notion that clinical specialities will be reorganized into new speciality areas of the body organs, such as urologists and nephrologists combined into a renal department, will not occur as a possible reorganization combination within a medical staff structure.

The block to reorganizing clinical services on this basis will be the existence of large numbers of physicians already certified by the various American specialty boards. They will feel they are losing recognition earned through their residency years.

Dimensions of Hospital Relationships

What will take place, where additional emphasis on a particular, specialized clinical program is desired, is a more functional development of their hospital relationship. A director and staff members will receive special appointments in a specialized administrative department. For example, a cardiovascular unit will be established as a separate administrative unit and its physicians appointed from existing, clinical medical staff divisions. This is a current, typical practice in major medical centers and will be used as a model when highly specialized medical programs are initiated in community general hospitals.

The second postulated change of improving medical manpower efficiency will not be reflected in any medical staff's organization chart. Formal recorded relationships do not show informal relationships which develop to make organizations livable and flexible. In hospitals with predominantly private practice physicians, a substantial number of personal commitments are necessary to provide continuity of medical direction. As the only available solution many times, these commitments have been arranged inefficiently because of personalities and a physician's independent actions.

Provisions for alternate coverage, referral patterns, unbalanced small groups in speciality areas and unanticipated demands for medical services are all a part of the ebb and flow of a physician's daily activities that reduce efficiency. Each physician or joint-practice group caters to their individual idiosyncrasies, personal style, opinions of fellow practitioners, judgements about medical skills and quality of judgements used. He is least concerned about optimizing use of total medical manpower. Since only a hospital relates to all physicians, loss of individual physician efficiency is mostly unrecognized or believed to be uncontrollable from that perspective.

Development of physician assistants is not a useful approach in solving the need for increased medical manpower in urban areas of the country. Particularly in a corporate health system, nurses will continue as traditional extensions of physicians. In general, no adjustments in medical staff organization structure will occur to accommodate physician assistants.

Opportunities for Cost Containment

A lack of pre-planned coordination between physicians or between physician and hospital staff is a major cause of a physician's inefficient use of time. By remaining uncommitted in a work day, having no central scheduling mechanism for coordinating their individual activities, and an insistence on independently determining all medical care procedures for their patients, these groups create multiple slow downs daily, lowering their efficiency. Medical care's greatest opportunities for cost containment exist in articulating, predicting, standardizing, and scheduling physicians' work. It may be done within the present framework of the physician's concept of acceptable private practice activities. All this will probably not take place unless hospital administrators are capable of defining and arranging ways to help physicians understand these inherent advantages. They must gradually proceed to implement systems within hospitals to achieve integration of medical services.

As knowledge increases about treatment of specific diseases and the efficiency of treatments is more accurately measured, small changes in treatment techniques between physicians will be eliminated. A great deal of physician and hospital staff time would be saved by standardizing therapy procedures. As mathematics and computer analysis are increasingly used to measure parameters and characteristics of specific diseases, deeper understandings will permit greater standardization in treatment. Unfortunately, there is little sense of urgency to achieve medical care cost reduction through standardization. Yet in other parts of our society, this route to greater efficiency is arduously pursued.

Coordination of Standards

Until full-time combined administrative-clinical positions for service chiefs and their administrative-support positions are established, organized efforts, with sufficient thrust to improve physician productivity, will not take place. Even today, traditional medical staff decisions through committee processes are not capable of sufficient detailed study and planning to solve many operational problems. Prolonged, major emphasis will be required on cost issues before physicians will relinquish sufficient individual autonomy to allow an adequate degree of standardizations. It will probably be at least a decade before this level of concern will be widespread among physicians.

During the decade of the sixties, large building programs were carried out by community hospitals. They expanded to the same or even larger size than many university medical center hospitals. Sophisticated medical services development was also undertaken. As the number of complex diagnostic and therapy programs continue to expand, there will be an increasing number of private practice physicians on a hospital payroll, either on a partial or full-time basis.

As this trend continues, there will be piecemeal shift in the present meaning of private practice. Generally a physician whose major income is from billings to individual patients is perceived by his colleagues to be totally supportive of private practice concepts. However, currently there are many physicians receiving some of their income from hospital sources for part-time work in the hospital such as assistant medical education directors, emergency room service, employee health service and a variety of diagnostic and therapeutic activities.

Implications Toward Separate Billing

With increased super-specialization and involvement of several physicians in medical routines necessary for the care of a patient with a severe problem, individual physician's services will not be easily identifiable to patients. Opportunities to directly bill patients gradually will be more and more restricted. Undoubtedly, as new complex services are instituted in hospitals, these physicians will believe that they should have an equal right to bill patients. Confusion and antagonism over multiple physician bills will occur. Eventually, it will be decided jointly that a fee arrangement should be worked out between hospital and physician and their right to bill separately phased out and included in a combined hospital charge for specialized services.

A decade from now, probably thirty-five to forty percent of the medical staff will be on some type of contractual arrangement for half-time or more with a hospital. In addition, the practice of a patient directly paying an attending physician and other physicians for his care will probably wane. For example, the present practice is for a general practitioner or internist to admit a surgical case and then still serve as attending physician for the case, even though the surgeon also submits a bill. Probably this will shift to a practice of the surgeon functioning as both surgeon and attending physician. If nothing else, the continued rising costs of medical care will force most patients to give up their current practice of using two physicians, where one would be sufficient.

An Emerging Concept

As a result, broad generalizations about private practice definitions will be drawn more sharply in the future. The emerging concept will be a primary care physician and an attending hospital physician for typical kinds of medical care, as the primary remaining component of private practice.

A fourth predicted outcome also relates to a shift in concepts of private medicine practice. As the federal government continues to endorse, sponsor and support various group practice schemes, other adjustments in its meaning will take place.

During the next ten years, it is clear that the idea of per capitation methods of buying medical care will be expanded. In large urban areas, existing medical society mechanisms quickly will prove inadequate as a base for establishing and operating such systems. A medical society's structure basically is focused on representation functions and not on daily health care operations. With no significant experienced management capacity directing it, the structure will probably never be able to assume direction of HMO's or other similar programs. Physicians will seek to use a hospital's medical staff organization as a preferred way of organization for meeting the group-practice, per-capitation imperatives.

Major administrative and hospital difficulties will ensue. It will be a period of testing hospital administration leadership. If administrators are inflexible to physician interest, if they are incapable of defining alternatives and anticipated outcomes, a more central control from government sources will probably occur.

The Health Maintenance Organization

A current prototype useful in thinking about per-capitation group practice is that of the Health Maintenance Organization (HMO). Initially, this type of medical practice will be developed from existing physicians in a group practice. To succeed, the initial group will need to be one of the largest groups or semi-groups in a locale and predominately a general practice group, internal medicine group or surgical-obstetrical group. The initial medical group must be a major force in medical staff organization.

Few initial groups will have sufficient manpower and breadth of medical specialties to be a full service range group. To plug these gaps, part-time arangements will have to be made with physicians outside the existing group but who are members of the same medical staff. Except in the largest medical staffs, a majority of staff members will need to be included in the HMO group.

If these new groups succeed beyond two or three years, traditional medical staff organization may be completely changed. Short of such drastic steps, present trends in medical staff organization development will continue. HMO's will be seen as more superficial administrative-type arrangements superimposed on an existing organization, rather than as a fundamental reorganization.

Per-capitation Group Practice

Late in the decade of the seventies, per-capitation group practice will probably be different than it is conceived now. However, attempts to encourage this type of medical practice in the early seventies will permanently change existing medical staff structure. Medical staffs and hospital administration will be pulled much more closely together because their communality of interest will be demonstrated. By then, most medical staff members probably will have contracts for some service to a per-capitation group, and hospital administrators will be used as administrative agents for medical groups.

An example of one process may be useful to demonstrate some of its implications. Under existing Medicare requirements, utilization review of hospital services is mandated, and penalties are directed at individual patients and hospitals. However, malpractice liability questions directed at hospitals, attending physicians and utilization committees are inherent in these regulations, when opinions are divided between committee and attending physician.

Appropriate Utilization of Hospital Services

If a utilization committee orders a patient's dismissal over the objection of an attending physician, one must be freed from any additional judicial harm and the other protected for his medical judgments. Group practice cost benefits are hinged on appropriate hospital utilization, Gradual tightening of utilization review procedures in government-supported medical care programs will not be effective for per-capitation groups in situations where their numbers are a medical staff minority.

When the majority of a medical staff are in some way tied to a group, utilization control will be improved; where all staff members have such a commitment, it will be optimal. However, few hospitals will attempt to restrict their medical staff to only group members. Therefore, interests of non-group members will be protected. Administratively, a medical staff appointment must continue to be attractive to both group and private practice physicians. This can be achieved if a hospital and medical staff perceive each other as independent entities providing separate programs of care, but privately negotiating among themselves within the health corporation, as to who does what, for how much.

Increased Emphasis on Ambulatory Medicine

A fifth outcome of increased health care integration will be increased emphasis on ambulatory medicine. A major clinical division of community medicine will be added to existing divisions. It will serve as an operational manpower source for contracts entered into by a medical staff to provide medical services in areas distant from the hospital site and for ambulatory care programs.

By the nineteen eighties, medical staff organization structure will have evolved from the present form into a still unpredictable structure. If the dominant forces of the sixties had continued uninterrupted in the seventies, its structure in the eighties could be easily predicted. It is unrealistic, however, not to assume that some types of per-capitation group practices will be widespread within ten years. The issue then is to attempt to judge this effect, as well as existing trends now in process but not yet completely developed.

Characteristics of the Future Medical Staff

Even though a typical medical staff organization structure of the future cannot now be projected, influential characteristics are now definable:

1. Decision-making through a committee structure will be substantially reduced. Committee structure disadvantages for routine, non-policy type decisions are well known. Increasing complexity of medicine technology, its increasing dependency upon hospital personnel and a great increase in frequency for decisions will compel a transfer of decision-making authority from non-paid physician committee members to salaried positions. If one wanted to prove the present ineffectiveness of medical staff committees, records of inattendance, multiplicity of committees and apathy of physicians toward all issues except major organizational crises would easily make the point. In fact, by the eighties, the committee structure will be in a state of near total collapse.

2. A residual committee structure will still be around but will function as an advisory mechanism. Since rates of change between hospitals are uneven, a medical executive committee may be either a source of final decisions or an advisory committee to a salaried chief of staff.

Committees will become more ad hoc, brought together to establish or evaluate a diagnostic or therapeutic program, such as a diagnostics committee, rather than existing individual committees (ie. laboratory, nursing, etc.).

3. Most administrative decision-making will be placed in positions filled by part or full-time paid physicians. Functions, such as utilization review, medical records, pharmacy, education activities, etc., will be made routine job assignments, carried on within broad policy decisions as hospital administration now works.

4. Physicians and administrators routinely will be members of boards of trustees, with the chief executive officer as president. Policy making will be board work, with control, direction and coordination activities removed from trustees' hands and delegated to the hospital's chief officer. One present day medical staff committee will report directly to the board of trustees: the credentials and professional standards committee.

5. The traditional dual medical staff structure of handling administrative work by committees and clinical work by departments and divisions will be passé. One organization will result with key activities covered by salaried physicians. It will operate similarly to a corporation with one central chain of command.

6. Hospital administration will act as a bargaining agent in negotiating medical services delivery for both physician and hospital to large purchasers of medical care. Internally, consortiums between various physicians and the hospital will be negotiated to meet contract requirements for different medical care programs.

7. Non-physicians, such as clinical psychologists, bio-chemists, etc., will not make much progress in becoming members of medical staffs. A medical staff, when dealing on an organized basis to sell medical services, will quickly perceive their organization as a clinical and economic entity. Consequently, non-physician medical specialists will be positioned on the hospital side of the organization where their financial concerns are removed from medical staff affairs.

8. Role differentiation between nurse and physician will continue to increase. In this process, nurses will continue to substantially expand their therapeutic responsibilities so that physicians can be diagnosing patient illness and ordering therapy modalities. Nurses will then be totally responsible for directing, observing and evaluating responses. When patient response diverges from a usual path of recovery, a physician will reenter the situation. Nurses and other skilled hospital-based or trained personnel will care for normal people and the typical treat-

ment of illness that is responding as expected. Physicians will limit their activities almost totally to evaluating people with abnormal clinical pictures or difficult medical problems.

Diminishment of Economic Stronghold

Since organizations reflect both goals and personalities, the impact of these eight changes will evolve over the next decade into a variety of medical staff structures. In the process, one of the last economic strongholds of rugged individualism will diminish by the events of the seventies.

Conflicting Economic Pressures in Health Care

James R. Jeffers, Ph.D.

All Americans, health professionals, economists, and others of all professions and walks of life are becoming increasingly concerned with the *effectiveness, efficiency,* and *equity* of health care as it is being delivered in our country today. These three words, and how they are related to current problems of health care delivery, by an economist's way of thinking, constitute the focal point of this paper. Before discussing them, however, the paper addresses a few remarks about the concept of the "health care delivery system" as the framework within which health care delivery is usually conceptualized by health professionals. It also develops a view of health care delivery within the analytical perspective of the economist's concept of an industry. Once having sketched the outlines of the health care industry, the paper attempts to show the meaning of the concepts of effectiveness, efficiency, and equity within the context of such a perspective.

The Health Care Delivery System

It seems to be fashionable among economists and others who often are critical of the pattern and organization of health care delivery in the United States to deny that this nation enjoys what might be worthy of the label, a "system of health care delivery." The basis for this posture is that the concept of a system involves elements that are lacking in the case of health services as they are currently being delivered in this country.

By system, one generally thinks of an orderly flow of activity into a transformation process which results in the output of a well-defined product or service. In the case of a health care delivery system, what is implied is an orderly or systematic flow of patients through an integrated set of nodes or centers where health services are rendered or produced, with patients exited from the system, presumably with some improvement to their health status.

Essential Elements of an Ideal System

Certain elements essential to our ideal health system would include the following:

1. Numerous entry points freely available to medical patients.
2. An organized referral mechanism which assures that patients receive all the kinds and quantities of the health services that they need.
3. Numerous exit points involving uniform judgements concerning the patient's state of health, particularly as these relate to the conclusion that the patient can no longer benefit from receiving additional health services—death and complete cure being but two extreme cases where such uniformity of judgement is often achieved.

Surely, those who attempt to force the delivery of health services into a mold of this sort expect too much. The notion of a system in the sense described here is much too abstract, much too idealistic. Indeed, few of the major activities involving the production and distribution of goods and services in our society could measure up to these criteria.

Let me provide an example of one other area in our society that also fails to meet these criteria: higher education. Clearly not all young people have access to our "system of higher education." Not all of those who are fortunate enough to gain access have the opportunity to receive the best educational services available. And, once gained access, the process of education, as we all know, is extremely varied. The procedure, or steps, taken as students are advised or "referred" along the way varies enormously both within, as well as among, various educational institutions. Students are outputed or "graduated" from educational institutions with disparate educational attainments, stemming from wide differences in the period of study, the quality of faculty, and the content of course curricula.

The fact that we do not have a health care delivery system in the idealistic sense should be no more surprising than the fact that we do not have an educational system according to the same or analogous criteria. Moreover, a "systemic view" is not a very useful device for analyzing all health care delivery problems, however appealing the "system concept" may be to health professionals, those interested in merely describing the myriad of activities involved in health care delivery, and those who feel that our major health care delivery problems can be solved with changes in organizational arrangements. I have a strong feeling that Americans expect too much of their health system and fail to recognize that other major activities also fail to measure up to ideal standards.

We do have problems of health care delivery, of course. These range from blocked access to health services, loose referral mechanisms which interrupt the continuity of health care delivery, and non-uniform decisions (judgements) relating to when patients can no longer benefit from receiving medical services. But, the same is true of almost any other "system" of our society; and there are other problems as well.

The Health Services Industry

Rather than viewing the delivery of health services from an organizational perspective, economists prefer to view these activities somewhat differently. Before developing this analytical perspective, however, let me first make certain that we share a set of facts that reflect both the magnitude or volume of activities we are talking about and the significance of certain recent events.

In particular, and taking a broad view of health services activities in the United States, they include those involving professional, sub-professional, and ancillary personnel; hospitals, nursing homes, suppliers of equipment, and educational facilities; and research, legislative, and home care activities. A few statistics: almost 4,000,000 persons are employed in the health services industry. Of those, over 1,000,000 are professional or sub-professional workers. Outlays for health services have increased from approximately $13 billions in 1950 to nearly $60 billions in 1969. On a per capita basis, these outlays have increased from $84 in 1950 to approximately $300 in 1969. Over this same period, outlays on health as a percentage of Gross National Product (GNP) went from 4 percent in 1950 to nearly 7 percent in 1969.[1] (See Figure 1 on the following page.)

Howard R. Bowen has written:

> Together, these various activities may be regarded as a great "industry" analogous to the food industry or transportation industry—consisting of many specialized firms which employ varied kinds of capital and labor, organizes the

[1]Figures for 1950 were taken from Dorothy P. Rice and Barbara S. Cooper, "National Health Expenditures, 1950–67," *Social Security Bulletin*, January, 1969, pp. 12–13. The 1969 figures are extrapolations based on the 1967 figures provided in the document cited.

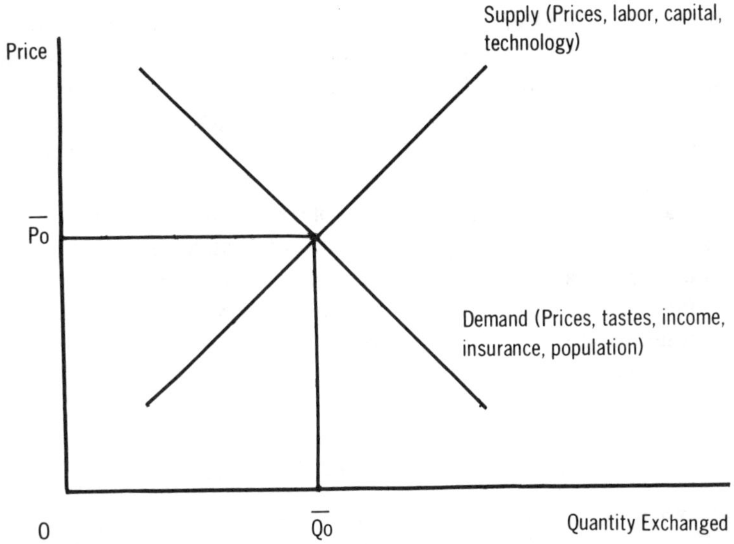

Figure 1. The Health Services Industry

"production" of many different services, and sells or otherwise dispense these services to consumers (sometimes via middleman). . . . One might, then, think of a great market for health services with the supply flowing from the industry, the demand flowing from the public, the prices determined by the interaction of demand and supply, the quantity and character of services responding to changes in pubic demand, to changes in the supply of labor and capital, and to changes in technology.[2]

Obviously, this view is broad and fails to reflect many of the peculiarities of the health industry as compared to other industries in the economy.

What are these peculiarities and what is their meaning?[3]

The first substantial difference between the health industry and other industries is the general lack of knowledge of its members in their roles as consumers of health services, particularly in comparison as consumers of other goods and services in our economy. Individual perception

[2]Howard R. Bowen, "The U.S. Health Services System: An Introduction to its Economic Aspects" (unpublished manuscript: processed September, 1969), p. 3.

[3]For a more extended discussion of aspects of the health services industry that are different from those of other industries, see Herbert E. Klarman, *The Economics of Health* (New York: Columbia University Press, 1965).

of needs is much different from medical judgments related to needs for medical services. The average consumer is virtually ignorant of his health needs even when he knows he is ill, and he has little or no knowledge of what therapy exists to relieve his illness. The absence of informational literature about medical problems; the reluctance of many physicians to describe conditions, therapy, and drugs in non-technical language; and the failure of other health professionals to inform the consumer, even under conditions of treatment, result in maintaining consumer ignorance at a high level. As a consequence, the consumer rarely can assess the quality of the services that he receives. The result is that the consumer is rarely in a position to make an intelligent consumption decision concerning the purchase of medical services.

The Problem of Market Imperfections

Another characteristic of the health services industry is the fact that market imperfections exist in a greater degree than in other industries. Monopolies over education, licensure, and certification serve to block or impede the flow of human resources into the industry. These same restrictions also serve to inhibit the mobility or resources within the industry. Restrictions on type of practice and patterns of organization prohibit the introduction of organizational and administrative arrangements permitting resources to be combined more optimally, thus contributing to inefficiency. A further result is that the industry has a difficult time adjusting to changes in demand, in expanding, and otherwise adjusting to the vicissitudes of a dynamic society.

A most obvious difference characterizing much of the health services industry in contrast to most other industries in the economy is the non-profit character of health services. Somehow, health professionals view the pursuit of profits as undesirable or unethical. How can this be when most of the rest of the private sector is profit-seeking? Is it, in fact, true that major portions of the health services industry are non-profit oriented? Or, is this an anachronism or illusion of the past? And, is it true that in the case of those so-called non-profit-seeking segments of the industry surpluses over costs are, in fact, generated, but are spent in a manner that results in a greater quality or quantity of services?

A Characteristic of Medical Services

In other industries that are profit-oriented, high profits (surpluses over costs) attract more resources into the industry. This growth takes the form of an expansion of the scale of operations of firms already in the industry and the entrance of new firms. If there exist appreciable economies of scale in production (lower per unit costs accompanying expansion in output), firms already in the industry have an advantage over new firms, since the former are likely to be able to expand output more rapidly because of scale economies. In the case of non-profit firms, surpluses over costs are seldom visible; therefore, additional firms are not attracted to the industry in response to the stimulus of prospective "profits." As a result, expansion tends to occur in firms already in the industry. It may be inefficient if scale economies do not exist. One further disadvantage: expansion of existing firms fails to increase consumer accessibility to health services in the same degree to which expansion of the number of firms in the industry accomplishes this goal.

An additional characteristic of medical services in many cases is that they are what economists call "public goods." The essence of a public good is that it is indivisible; once produced, it is impossible to restrict its consumption to a select few. For example, once knowledge is discovered, it soon is in the public domain and can be used over and over again. Public goods pose certain economic problems, since once such goods are produced and all enjoy them more or less equally, it is difficult to finance them. Persons are reluctant to pay, since, if they are somehow produced, there is no way to restrict any one individual from enjoying their benefits. Medical research is a commodity of this kind. Community hospitals, at least in the past, also have been treated in this way in cases where patient charges were not set at levels high enough to cover facility construction costs.

A related point is that medical services also exhibit externalities in consumption to a degree exceeding that of other goods and services. It is not necessary to immunize an entire population to eliminate a communicable disease. As soon as some are immunized, they cease to be carriers of the disease to the significant advantage of those not receiving the vaccine. This aspect of health, along with the public good nature, provides leverage, opening the door to government participation in the health industry.

The View of Health as Something "Sacred"

Another feature characterizing the medical services industry in contrast to other industries is that Americans attach a special emotional value to health. Health is viewed as something sacred. It is often argued that expenditures on medical services are a good investment.

Healthy people are more productive; they work more steadily, and without absenteeism. In addition, they generally live longer and thus can contribute more than those who are not healthy. There is also an equalitarian aspect of all of this; namely, that all people ought to have an equal opportunity to live (die) as a necessary requisite to the pursuit of happiness. Considerations that are often posed in opposition to this humanistic position are the following:

Man is mortal and must die sometime. Health, as an investment, has a finite life, and its costs and benefits should be calculated and compared to the returns from investments in other things, i.e., education and defense.

What is the connection between the delivery of medical services and health? We know very little about the comparative effects of environmental factors as opposed to medical services in terms of the impact of the former on health.

What do we know about the connection between style of living and other factors not affected by medical services and health?[4]

In short, what is the nature of the critical margin on which the consumption of medical services operates to improve the health status of our population in terms of a longer and more productive life? Purchases of medical services that do not accomplish these things must be viewed as consumption expenditures and not investment expenditures. As such, they contribute to consumers' satisfaction in much the same way that the consumption of other goods and services available in our economy contributes to consumer well-being and are not extra-ordinary. Medical services in this viewpoint, must compete with food, housing, recreation, and other ordinary services that yield satisfaction in the current period—in contrast to those of an investment character which yield a stream of benefits over extended periods in the future. Surely, a sizable portion of the 60-odd billion dollars being spent by Americans on medical services this year are of a consumption rather than of an investment nature.

Non-Economic Objectives of Health Professionals

Economists frequently point out many ways in which the health industry differs from others in the economy. However, they seldom indi-

[4]An interesting recently completed empirical study reveals that when medical care and education are controlled for, income and mortality are positively correlated. The authors suggest that unfavorable diets, lack of exercise, psychological tensions, etc., are positively associated with income, thus explaining the apparent inverse relationship between health and income. See Richard Auster, Irving Levinson, and Deborah Saracheck, *The Journal of Human Resources,* Volume IV, No. 4 (Fall, 1969).

cate an awareness of why such differences exist and what the consequences of these differences are in non-economic terms. It seems grotesquely unfair to simply point out the undesirable economic consequences of certain institutions, patterns, and ways of doing things. One must be aware of the benefits of these things as well as of their costs.

The public good aspect of many medical services and the phenomena of externalities in consumption and economies of scale are of natural origin; since they have no roots in man-made institutions, no one may be praised or blamed for their existence. However, many of the peculiarities of the medical industry have resulted from conscious efforts of health professionals to achieve various objectives, most of which are distinctly non-economic in nature. For example, the consumer is often purposely kept uninformed about the state of his health because of a fear that complete knowledge may engender undesirable stress and anxiety, which ultimately would be detrimental. Ethical standards against advertising were not reduced and designed to protect the consumer against medical quackery and fraud. They also serve to maintain the practice of medicine at an objective and scientific level, insulating it from emotional and promotional aspects.

Similarly, monopolies over education, certification, and licensure are designed to insure high quality of care in the delivery of health services. In the rendering of a personal service, quality is extremely difficult to judge or measure; quality control is partially (initially) maintained by controlling the quality of education, training, etc., of health professionals. The non-profit character of many segments of the medical industry stems from the ancient value judgment that no man should profit unduly from another's illness. In general, the same is true of our educational institutions, which are also non-profit oriented and, therefore, do not benefit materially from ignorance.

One Viewpoint: Health Is a Quasi-Public Utility

In short, many of the peculiarities of the health services industry which markedly distinguish it from other industries in the economy consist of measures undertaken more or less voluntarily by professionals in the interest of protecting the consumer. I do not think that it is far from the truth that health professionals view the health industry as a quasi-public utility. Furthermore, they have assumed an enormous burden of "public trust" in undertaking the responsibility for determining "what services will be produced," "how they will be produced," and "who will consume these services." These same decisions are made through the mechanism of the market in most other sectors of the economy. In this milieu, "consumer sovereignty" reigns, and producers ultimately must answer to the will of consumers if they are to survive.

In cases where suppliers make all or most of the important decisions for consumers, technological imperatives tend to prevail over almost all others, including those that are economic.[5] This is the case, for example, with national defense, particularly during a time of war. A major victory was claimed a few months ago when, for the first time in years, more than a perfunctory few hours were devoted to debate over the multi-billion dollar defense budget. The same kind of decision process is somewhat characteristic of our entire system of higher education in which suppliers (teachers) decide the content of courses, the methods of instruction, and the eligibility of students allowed to enroll in our nation's many colleges and universities. Health professionals may note with some weariness that in the case of higher education, the "patients" are unusually restive and, of late, are frequently inclined to revolt.

Effectivness, Efficiency, and Equity

Three criteria often advanced to evaluate the performance of the health services industry are effectiveness, efficiency, and equity.

Effectiveness means the extent to which the output of the health services industry maintains or advances the health of the population. Efficiency refers to the quantity or services obtained per dollar input of health resources. Equity refers to the accessibility of members of the population to health services. One should keep foremost in mind that in the rendering of a personal service, the production and distribution of a product occurs at the same point in time and at the same point in space. Health services, obviously are distributed at the point of production, contrary to the case with most other goods and services in our economy. Therefore, consumers must seek out the point of production, and accessibility to health services depends largely on the availability of production facilities.

Note that each of these criterion is related to one of the basic economic questions posed earlier. A general qualitative answer to the

[5]Victor R. Fuchs, "The Growing Demand for Medical Care," *New England Journal of Medicine* (July, 1968), p. 5.

question, "What services ought to be produced?" is that the most *effective* services should be produced. In responding to the question, "How should they be produced?" one is prompted to answer in the most *efficient* way possible. And finally, when asked, "Who should consume them?" the answer is likely to be that they should be distributed *equitably*.

It should also be pointed out that these criteria are inherently in conflict. Questions of effectiveness for example, are largely technical and, in this situation, can only be answered within the context of medical science. Effectiveness often conflicts with efficiency, since the latter involves economic considerations, i.e., the cost of medical resources. The most effective medical procedures may be the most expensive and frequently are prohibitive. Therefore, they are unfeasible. Effectiveness and efficiency, finally, are often in conflict with the criterion of equity. Accessibility to the most effective means of therapy is often lacking because of a scarcity in the means of delivering it. Since efficiency is often achieved by large-scale production units, the concentration of medical service capability in relatively few large centers reduces accessibility.

Conflicting Economic Pressures

In view of the fact that in matters of health, most basic decisions are made by suppliers, what are the implications for effectiveness, efficiency, and equity in the delivery of health services?

In cases of this sort, considerations of quality tend to predominate considerations of quantity and distribution. Since communication between the consumer and the professional traditionally, is rather minimal, the professional has little respect for the consumer's judgement about the quality of service he is rendering. Rather, the professional looks to his peers for approval or disapproval of the service he is rendering. Since the most substantive dialogue occurs among professionals where quality of individual skill and expertise tend to be the major standards of achievement, professionals tend to limit their output in order to achieve the highest possible quality care. In addition, there are strong incentives to specialize. Distribution of services tends to be limited in order to concentrate medical service capability and maintain or increase quality potential. This unfortunately, results in limiting accessibility. While the concentration of medical service capability within limited geographical areas may provide some potential gains in efficiency, these tend to be lost as the result of greater efforts to acquire more expensive equipment and trained personnel to deliver more effective and higher quality care. This is particularly true of hospitals where the prestige of the institution is measured more in terms of the range and complexity of services available and less in terms of the size and the number of patients treated. In effect, the continued emphasis on quality of medical care, resulting from the fact that suppliers of services dominate the decision-making process, tends to subordinate considerations of efficiency and equity to considerations of effectiveness.

Yet, because of the burden of "public trust" that health professionals have assumed for themselves, and because of their genuine concern for consumers who are subjected to random and unpredictable episodes of illness, traditionally, the determination of "who will consume products" has been this: *everyone* should be permitted to consume what they need. In other words, "Health is a right, not a privilege." Toward implementing this "right," sliding fee schedules, philanthropy, and charity have become important elements in the past and current history of the delivery of health services in this country.

Quality Over Quantity

However, this philosophical posture is in basic conflict with the way the health services industry currently is organized. Facilities and practices, for example, are arranged with quality and effectiveness of services more in mind than efficiency and accessibility or equity. The consumer has little competence to judge his needs. Furthermore, it is often suggested that even for the middle class, price serves as an effective barrier to acquiring health services. There has been a continual upgrading of quality and effectiveness of medical services which has led to higher medical prices with less emphasis on increasing the quantity of available services.

This latter point may be illustrated from data relating to physician and hospital services developed by Herbert Klarman for the period 1929–1967. Klarman calculated the average annual rates of change of total expenditures on physician and hospital services and fractioned them between price charges and an "all other" residual factor reflecting qualitative and quantitative or utilization elements.[6]

For the period studied, average annual expenditures on physician

[6]Herbert E. Klarman, "Increase in the Cost of Physician and Hospital Services," *Inquiry* (March, 1970).

services grew at the rate of 6.3 percent. Approximately 1.3 percent of this growth in expenditures is explained by growth in population, leaving roughly 5.0 percent to be explained by changes in prices and per capita utilization and quality. Fees increased at an average annual rate of 2.5 percent, and the "all other" category went up about the same, 2.5 percent.

Over the period for which data are available, average annual per capita expenditures on hospital services increased approximately 8.5 percent. Fragmenting this between price changes and "all other," and using the American Hospital Association's patient-day expense series as an index of price, we see that over this same period price increased at an average annual rate of 7.0 percent while the "all other" component went up at a rate roughly equal to 1.5 percent.

Since it is hazardous to interpret series of data over long periods of time during which many factors change—rendering things existing at the end of such periods not strictly comparable to things existing at the beginning of the period—let us look at two recent sub-periods, one for physician services and one for hospital services, for which Klarman also was able to provide data. The period in question, 1966–1967, reflects the impact of Title XVIII, Medicare, a program designed to remove substantially price as a barrier to accessibility to health services on the part of one segment of our population during this critical year.

An Industry Incapability

Over the studied period, per capita expenditures on physician services grew at an average annual rate of approximately 11.3 percent. This breaks down to 7.1 percent increase in fees and less than 5.0 percent increase in "all other." In the case of hospitals over the same period, per capita expenditures grew at an average annual rate of nearly 17.0 percent. However, over this period, prices show an almost 14.0 percent annual rate of increase, and "all other" grew an average annual rate of only roughly 3.0 percent.

Clearly, giving consumers more purchasing power is not the way to increase utilization of services. There is little *a priori* reason to believe that consumers can or will use it wisely; and more importantly, it is clear that the industry is not capable of responding to increased demands for increased quantities of services.

One thing is worth noting on this area of prices of health services. From 1950 to 1967, the consumer price index of medical care rose 86 percent (from 73.4 to 136.7) whereas the consumer price index for all items rose by 38 percent (from 83.8 to 116.3). Howard R. Bowen has written:

> Two major elements of medical care prices (1) prescriptions and drugs and (2) optometric examination and eyeglasses have behaved differently from the rest. Prior to 1960, the prices of prescriptions and drugs increased more slowly than the consumer price index for all items or for total medical care, and since 1960, have not advanced appreciably. The prices of optometric examination and eyeglasses increased more slowly than the general index until 1955 and since then has just about kept pace with the general index. It is possible that the behavior of these two elements is explained by the fact that both are primarily in the private profit-making sector of the economy operating under conditions of competition (though not perfect competition) and both have the ability—not shared by other elements—to expand production rapidly in response to increasing demand.[7]

Some Concluding Observations

Conflicting economic pressures in health care are of long origin. They primarily stem from a basic conflict of objectives and expectations between suppliers and consumers of these services. Public expectations are oriented toward a health care system that provides health services effectively, efficiently, and equitably to all consumers. Yet, health services delivery activities hardly measure up to the standard of a system as the term is usually understood. Few major activities in our society, in fact, could measure up to such criteria. While it is admirable for health professionals to strive for such a system, continued lip service toward that goal without substantial accomplishment widens the gulf between public expectations and its realization.

Health professionals have asserted an inordinate responsibility in shouldering the burden of "public trust" by making most of the basic decisions concerning health services delivery. Consumers who are unknowledgeable on health matters, as a consequence, know little about the quality of care they receive. Therefore, their expectations are largely formulated in terms of the availability and quantity of health services. They also expect services to be produced efficiently at prices they can afford. This is in basic conflict with the goals of health professionals striving for increased quality and effectiveness. Efficiency tends to be viewed more from a technological point of view and less from the point of view of economics.

Government programs which supplement the purchasing power of

[7]Howard R. Bowen, *op. cit.*, p. 8.

various health consumers without expanding the capacity of the industry to increase the supply of services tend to lead to increased prices. They also widen the gap between public expectations for increased quantities of medical services and actual increases in utilization. This gap will be further widened by the increase of private health insurance and the growth in personal incomes. Economists estimate that the income elasticity of demand for medical services is approximately unity, meaning that expenditures on health services grow proportionately with income.[8] Similar results may be expected to accompany growth in insurance coverage.

To Ameliorate the Mismatch

Physicians, hospital administrators, and other health professionals are "neither devils nor saints." Inexorable economic forces of growth of income and the shift of population from rural areas to cities will continue the mismatch between the availability of medical services and the public's desire to consume them. Ultimately, health professionals, at least temporarily, may have to abandon the pursuit of medical effectiveness and quality in the interests of achieving the more equitable distribution of efficiently produced services desired by our society.

Further Readings Suggested by the Author

Jeffers, James R. "The Economics of Health Services,"(co-author with Howard R. Bowen). An essay to be published by McCaleb-Seiler Publishing Company (Spring 1971).

Jeffers, James R., and Bognanno, Mario F. "Medical Economics: An Introduction," *Inquiry,* 7:4–14 (March 1970).

Jeffers, James R., Bognanno, Mario F., and Bartlett, John C. "On the Demand Versus Need for Medical Services and the Concept of Shortage," *American Journal of Public Health,* 61, 1 (January 1971), pp. 46–63.

[8]Victor R. Fuchs, *op. cit.,* p. 3.

Professional Development Needs in Hospital Administration

Louis E. Davis, Ph.D.

The environmental texture of health care systems, which so largely determines the objectives and roles of hospitals and the functions of its managers, has undergone a significant change. The change, influenced by a number of forces, began in the late 1950's and was identified in a study, undertaken in 1960, supported by a grant-in-aid from the Kellogg Foundation.[1] The report was not widely circulated.[2] The study sought to identify the state of the art in hospital administration, to determine its ability to respond to the evolving changes in health care systems as reflected in the functioning of hospitals, and to indicate the consequent professional development needs of its managers. The review revealed a number of needs that would have to have been met if hospital administrators were to develop capabilities adequate to strategically managing their changing institutions.

After Ten Years, What?

It would be comforting to look back after ten years and find that health care systems needs are being satisfied and its developing trends facilitated, the state of the art has significantly improved, and hospitals are significantly better managed. There is little to be gained by once again repeating that health care systems and their individual institutions are in a state of painful disarray and that the conventional wisdom handed on to its managers is increasingly less useful to present operations and emerging developments.

The purpose of this review is to re-examine past developments that contributed to the changed environment of health care systems, identify present developments and evolving trends, and, in the light of these, indicate continuing and new professional development needs of hospital administrators that will have to be provided.

[1]Professional Development Needs in Hospital Administration, Louis E. Davis, 1960.
[2]A copy of the report may be obtained from the author.

Past Causal Developments

Present developments and trends are an outgrowth of an evolving health systems context that began in the 1950's. In the 1960 report it was indicated that a variety of forces, different in origin, were operating to bring the previous era of hospital administration to a close. These forces were placing demands on hospital administrators for both sophisticated internal hospital management and strategic health systems management. There were those leading to demands for better utilization of community resources in meeting the community's obligations for the health of its citizens and for better interpretation of these needs in developing individual hospitals or health care institutions. These forces stemmed from rapid changes in medical practice and patient types resulting in increased costs (apparent or real) for growing segments of the population with low capacity to meet them.

It was held that if hospital administrators individually or hospitals collectively did not solve the problems of optimizing community resources, then pressures would generate movements in the direction of centralization. Hospital administrators were divided as to whether their responsibility extended beyond the hospital. Internally-oriented administrators saw themselves as obligated to do the best possible job within their hospitals whether expressed in form of lowest cost, best service, most equipment, etc. Community-oriented administrators saw themselves as managers of units of a community's total health care organization and saw their function as interpreting operations and administration within hospitals in terms of satisfying community needs and achieving optimum community resource utilization. Many university hospital administration programs supported the community-oriented view of administration.

Optimizing community resources to meet health needs would place demands on the administrator, taking him further away from internal operations without reducing the demand for effective operation. Administrators would be called upon to integrate and maximize existing community facilities and resources and to plan new facilities accordingly. At the same time, each would be called upon to develop effective performance in his own hospital, using all the means of modern management. Administrators who viewed these demands as being opposed to their internal responsibilities were overlooking their fundamental unity for community-oriented administration.

Given the growing need for community-oriented hospital administrators, how could they develop the capability to perform effectively both internally and community-wide? The only possible means for doing so lay in providing an organizational setting which relieved the administrator of direct management to a degree compatible with control and yet provided the means for effective internal operation. Some hospitals had succeeded in this. Future propects were not bright however, largely because of the industry's and university programs' singular concentration on preparing only hospital administrators and attempting to prepare them to satisfy both objectives simultaneously. Not recognized was the need to develop a supporting managerial infrastructure, nor that without it managers would continue to concentrate on internal operation to minimize risk of failure.

Third Party Representation

A second set of forces were generated by the growth of third party representation of patients, so that the power of the individual patient became immensely multiplied in the representative. Until then this power had been used sparingly, and, on the surface, there appeared to be cooperative relations between the representative and the hospitals. However, the interests of the third party representative lay in the domain of economy or value received. Hospital's continued inability to cope with costs would bring the representative's latent but very considerable power into use. With standards of care poorly defined and health care patterns changing rapidly, the key to continuing peaceful relationships was seen to be value received, which implied that hospital administration was taking all possible action to control costs of providing service at a standard of care chosen. However, this was far from the picture of what was generally going on in hospitals. Third party representation was seen to place demands on the administrator for more skillful internal management, more sophisticated methods of planning and control, and for development of measures of effectiveness that optimized the performance of the hospital given its assigned role and available resources.

Changing Knowledge and Technology

A third set of forces stemmed from the rapidly changing knowledge and technology underlying management decision-making, planning, and control including operations research, organization theory, electronic data processing, etc. These additions to knowledge, stemming from research in physical and social sciences as well as developments in mathematics, were moving management from art towards science.

They were changing the practice of management in business and industry, particularly in the analytic preparation of data for decision-making regarding choice of alternatives, utilization of organization's resources, planning and controlling operations, and organization design. The hospital administrator was seen to have little choice but to acquire and use these new analytic tools, for they seemed to be suitable for development of solutions to problems facing hospitals. In a few hospitals, the application of such sophisticated management analyses were providing the means for solving problems of staff assignment, personnel utilization, and facilities location previously thought to be insoluble. Not merely hospital administrators but all managers would be affected by these developments as was seen in the changes undertaken in university curricula in business administration.[3]

The fourth and last set of forces that were contributing to change in hospital administration were those stemming from research in general administration and hospital administration in particular. Administrative research was then particularly lacking in hospitals. However, research projects underway and anticipated heralded the closing of the era in hospital administration in which the practitioner was of cardinal importance and in which the consultant was venerated as a guiding light for his role as a transmission agent of the widest amount of existing practice. Hospital administrators with experience or training in research methods and conducting research in their hospitals would probably be the future innovators and leaders. Those who would develop the ability to identify the nature of system within which the hospital operates and control its environment rather than being controlled by the system's random forces would be making significant contributions.

Present Causal Developments

The developments of ten years ago are continuing and intensifying. It was noted then that the textural background of health care in hospitals had altered because of rapid changes in medical technology; rapid expansion of service through means of third party support; the presence of new concentrations of power in third party representatives; rapid development of science of planning, organizing and decision-making; and shift from a pragmatic practice basis to one of research and analy-

[3]See R. A. Gordon and J. E. Howell, *Higher Education for Business,* N.Y.: Columbia University Press, 1959, and F. Pierson et al., *The Education of American Businessmen,* N.Y., 1959.

sis in administration. Events of the past ten years indicate that present trends will continue and strengthen.

Intensified competition for available financial resources and the society's recognition of the problems of the central city and the disadvantaged have further accelerated the emphasis on health systems rather than individual programs, institutions or health care locations, such as hospitals. The next textural change will come when it is recognized that national resource optimization will occur when maintenance of health is seen in preventive terms. This will complete the change away from program and institution incrementalism to comprehensive and interrelated health systems. The role of hospitals in both the preventive and reparative aspects of health systems is still evolving and its final shape is uncertain. Internal orientation of hospital administrators will become an anachronism.

The continued growth of third party support for all socio-economic segments of the population is further changing relationships within hospitals and between them and their patients. The boundaries between different hospital systems and other health care systems are being blurred and will probably disappear. Again the focus will become integrated operational health systems. Surprisingly, over the past ten years the considerable power in the hands of third party representatives has been used very sparingly to require improvements in both internal hospital operations and community health systems organization. The structure for doing so has been developed. That interventions will take place is fairly certain; when cannot be predicted. Why they have not already taken place is a matter of history. They will take place because of market forces operating on third party organizations which go beyond present relationships between them and the industry.

Medical technology continues to develop intensively, maintaining the need for hospitals to be highly adaptive in organization and skills while changing the relationships between hospital and patient. Hospitals are having difficulties not only because of financial needs of medical technology innovation but because the industry has adopted a reactive stance in the face of the certainty of technological change, making changes into crises. Unlike other industries confronted by high rates of technological change, they have not undertaken systematic technological forecasting to aid in identifying the leading developments and what care systems will be involved, to prepare for future changes. The hospital industry appears to be overly oriented to past practice, locked into what may be obsolete systems of providing patient care. It approaches change in a piecemeal fashion responding to incremental pressures and may well be trying to make efficient care systems that should be set aside. In this context, innovations introduced by administrators may well increase the difficulties experienced by hospitals by disturbing existing systems. This is likely to persist until the central requirement of developing care systems that correlate with medical technology is satisfied.

Patients Now Asking Questions

In all cultures, the more science, the less protected is the witch doctor. Health care in the U.S. toward the close of the 20th century is no exception. The continued growth of medical science is changing the relationships among all those involved in health care—doctors, patients, nurses, technicians, administrators, and other health workers. Patients are and will continue to question all manner of formerly unquestioned arrangements. Third party representatives of patients will do so sooner and more vigorously. The same applies to the lesser orders working in health care institutions, its physicians' helpers, such as nurses, and technicians, and administrators' helpers. It is inevitable that both physicians and administrators will be challenged more and required to respond more rationally and openly.

Trend Toward Universalism

The developments of the various underlying sciences and technologies of planning, organizing, and decision-making have been vigorous and will continue to be. The consequences can be seen in the practices of leading industries, a very few hospitals, and in the programs of the outstanding graduate schools of business administration which have gone through a series of revisions to incorporate developments in decision theory, organization theory, behavioral theory, planning, and control. An accelerating trend which further departs from the basic premise of university hospital administration programs is the removal of specialization by types of industry or business from the programs of leading graduate schools of business administration. There is a strong trend at these schools, supported by developing science, toward universalism which has broken the boundaries between functional or disciplinary areas particularly when appropriate systems programs could be established. These developments provide a focus on the reality of complex interacting systems, bringing to problem solving interdisciplinary systems interaction approaches and evaluation of environment. Comparison with developments in university hospital administration programs raises the question of their suitability for the developing world of health systems. The best of the programs may be providing graduates who are only partially obsolete at the outset of their careers. What may be worse is that the best young minds will not be attracted to such programs. Outstanding students are attracted to challenges and to programs that prepare them to make contributions suitable to the level of complexity of the problems to be faced.

Expansion of services, new medical technology, large scale third party support, and changes in management on the one side and the growing turbulence of the social environment seeking to address itself to the urban crisis and the underprivileged on the other have in total made the world of hospital administration much less stable and brought latent problems to the point of action. The consequence is that hospitals are in a much worse state of internal disarray. The disarray will become worse, and if the industry cannot cope adequately in a reasonable time, a major system change can be expected. Hospitals are reaping the harvest of past poor "planning," i.e., disjointed incremental planning, in the misallocation of physical resources and intensified competition for available resources in an era of growing expectations.

Growing intensity of demand and medical technology are both contributing to the evolution of new and more health specialties in and out of the hospital. This movement will continue and presents urgent needs to develop new organizational arrangements. The drive toward further "professionalization" of various health specialities, led by nursing, will accelerate. This development is related partially to the growing base of science in health care and partially to a society-wide response on the part of those working in its institutions to enhance the quality of working life. In this instance, the fundamental issue is recognition of responsibility, not merely the more skilled conduct of tasks. Stated in other terms, it is the recognition, particularly relevant to the design of personal service organizations, that men in working systems are controllers and regulators of transformation processes and not merely performers of tasks. Present difficulties are further compounded by the attempts on the part of hospital employees to rectify long standing gross inequities in salary and other rewards. This raises for hospitals all of the issues, long present in other purposive institutions, of efficient utilization of scarce and costly manpower resources in ways that will enchance adaptation and response to change. The great difficulties in coping on part of hospitals may be a consequence of the isolation of hospital administration from developments in science of management and a lack of conceptual understanding of the history of other institutions as well as of the social, cultural and technological forces presently operating.

Residual Problems

In the context of hospital administration as a branch of the larger management family, a number of unsolved problems were identified in the 1960 study which bedeviled the practice of management in hospitals. Unfortunately these problems are largely still present as are the consequences of the failure to solve them. The problems stem from:

1. The failure to develop and secure wide enough acceptance of rules of behavior within the society of hospitals concerning the role of the hospital administrator as a custodian of a unit of community resources. The failure is manifested in a rugged individualism making for undue friction between administrators, in competition between hospitals frequently resulting in redundant or unnecessarily costly services and facilities, and in failure to undertake the concerted provision of common materials, equipment and services with its attendant economies of scale.

   To some extent these failures are being overcome. The continuing need exists to develop administrators having a community-wide orientation.
2. Failure to exercise organization skills to develop internal operational management support by developing competent internal operational managers. This leads to low effectiveness of hospital operation or to high demands on the administrator for supervision of detailed operations.

   The requirements for overcoming this failure are so onerous that they can be satisfied only by collective regional or national action undertaken by the operating and teaching segments of the industry.

   The acknowledged objective of practitioners and schools since professionalization began has been to improve the quality or competence of the hospital administrator. It has been intensively pursued by the university programs, the American Hospital Association (AHA) and the American College of Hospital Administrators (ACHA) through institutes and seminars. While proper for university programs, it is much too restricted an objective for the industry as a whole. The hospital industry has neglected to develop competent supportive operational management at the department level. The ability to continue to satisfy such a narrow objective appears to be coming to a close.

3. Failure by hospital administrators to provide for their hospitals needed technical management staff assistance to undertake internal consulting, evaluation, planning and control is a related organizational failure.
4. Failure on part of the industry collectively to either support research at universities or research centers, or to conduct research on administration within individual hospitals as an administrative function. This failure contributes to the view held by hospitals that their problems are unique when indeed they are common to the industry, leading to development of endless idiosyncratic solutions. Given the limited resources of individual hospitals many problems continue that could have been solved by studies undertaken collectively.
5. Related to research is the failure to develop measures of effectiveness and standards of performance, to identify controlling variables, and to evaluate standards, methods, equipment, procedures, etc.
6. Failure to disseminate and encourage more analytic and sophisticated methods of management. This failure may also account for the relatively passive caretaker role assumed by many administrators.
7. Failure of the hospital industry, its organized associations, and its educational programs to cope with the problems of managing small widely dispersed hospitals by providing professional counsel, common services, and training for administrators of small hospitals.
8. Failure to develop satisfactory tenure patterns for administrators and career patterns to suit different needs of the institutions as well as those entering the management of hospitals.

Professional Development Needs

To progress to the next stage in the advancement of hospital administration as a profession, and indeed if professional status is to be maintained in the long run, then the long-standing needs and new and evolving needs being generated by internal and external changes in values, environment, and expectations will have to be met. Satisfaction of needs of hospital administration requires the development of:

1. Skills and organization structures necessary to achieve effective interal operational management.

2. Orientation and skills to function effectively as a manager of a unit of the community's health-care resources.
3. Skills that are becoming basic to all management in its evolution toward a more analytic form. These are managerial skills in performing, directing, interpreting, and evaluating operations research, data processing, mathematical programming, forecasting, planning, etc.
4. Newly developed socio-technical systems theory and skills to analyze and design structure and relationships of the hospital organization and its extensions as well as the jobs of its members under requirements of adaptation to constant change.
5. Skills and orientation to organize, direct, and evaluate administrative research.

A review of these needs shows that they generate dual objectives and actions for the administrator to be both an effective manager of the internal operation of his own hospital and an active participant in planning and providing health care that optimizes community resources. On the surface it may appear that strengthening both internal management and integrative community-wide management are incompatible and therefore cannot be achieved jointly. Many leading practitioners and educators have taken this position. Acceptance of incompatibility as a fact seriously limits the development of constructive solutions. Competent administrators wish to acquire high level analytic skills to strengthen internal management. They would like to see preparation in these skills added to the university programs. Those administrators who are strongly oriented to solution of community health-care problems see this as urgent, as do many of the faculties of university programs. Although university programs are almost completely directed to the development of practitioners, which seems to be a narrow nonscholarly position for academicians, many of the faculties would like to move more strongly toward developing community-oriented administrators. The important and perhaps central consideration is that both developments have to be undertaken simultaneously, and that one depends on the other.

From Reacting to Assessing

The position of hospitals within a community as concerns both their control and the internal positions of administrators is such that there is little expectation that integrative community resource conservation behavior will be exhibited by the hospital administrator. This will be the case until administrators can develop effectively functioning hospitals and identify the variables affecting hospital performance so that these can be controlled. When this state is reached the individual administrator can assess the risks of managing by exception as a means of providing for himself the time needed for action in the community sphere. In effect this means that the administrator can change his stance from that of reacting to external forces (internal management) to assessing environmental forces acting on the hospital and attempting to regulate, control or modify the external forces.[4] In socio-technical systems terms, the primary role of the administrator is to manage the boundary conditions of the organization. Emery[5] defines boundaries of an organization as "those levels of exchange with the environment which allow it to survive and grow." They can be managed by regulating or co-managing the internal organization and its relevant environment. As Emery states it, "they can be managed only by managing the covariation of internal and external processes. In so far as a manager has to coordinate or otherwise resolve internal variances then he is distracted from his task."

When academic hospital administration programs accept this systems developed focus they will develop, in collaboration with other university departments, sophistication in managerial methods simultaneously with appreciative[6] and analytic skills to forecast and assess environmental forces to optimize community health care resources. For academic programs to develop a focus based on the exciting newly evolving social systems developments, they will have to shed their inward-looking focus and join other university departments concerned with the study of purposive organizations in their full environmental richness. It is predicted that, given limited available resources and talents, the forward-looking programs will become interdepartmental.[7] In the future the professional degree will very probably be given upon

[4]A number of useful programs are indicated for modifying the external environment. For example, based on commonly held objectives administrators may find strong support from third party representatives for changing the physical and operation care system to one based on time varying intensity of care. Such a change will address the pressures for internal efficiency and modify the constraint of resource availability. Appropriate appreciation studies will indicate others.

[5]Emery, F. E., ed., *Systems Thinking,* 1969, London: Penguin Books.

[6]Vickers, Sir Geoffrey, *The Art of Judgement,* 1965, N.Y.: Basic Books, *Value Systems and Social Process, 1968,* N.Y.: Basic Books.

[7]Based on the experience of the University of California, Los Angeles, professional degree program in Comprehensive Health Planning, an interdepartmental degree program given by the Graduate School of Business Administration, Graduate School of Public Health and Department of Political Science.

completion of a program jointly developed and supervised by university departments of public health, administration, political science, and urban planning, etc.

Providing for Professional Development

To provide for the professional development needs of all involved in hospital and health care, administration will require the development of a comprehensive program encompassing:

1. Integrated inter-disciplinary continuing education programs for all levels of management,
2. City or regional council or association-based technical management staff assistance, and
3. Research programs in administration.

Such an integrated program will require involvement on the part of the university programs, the AHA, ACHA, city state and regional hospital associations, and the support of foundations and the U.S. Department of Health, Education and Welfare. No specific program is being offered here. However, to be effective the program will have to address itself to:

1. Enhancing the competence of practicing administrators by providing organized comprehensive training programs designed to add newer analytical and planning skills and broader community orientation. Suitable training programs should be developed for administrators of larger and small hospitals. The training envisaged would be jointly planned and controlled by the university programs in hospital administration, business administration, political science, and urban planning, and local city, state, and regional hospital associations with AHA, ACHA and Association of University Programs in Hospital Administration (AUPHA) providing coordination and review. Such programs may be provided most effectively through extension or external departments of universities. Support from foundations and the Department of Health, Education and Welfare may well be sought for planning and trial installation. These programs and others indicated below call for strong and intensive roles to be taken by local hospital councils and associations in providing support and service to member hospitals.
2. Enhancing the competence of future administrators by strengthening university programs in hospital administration along gen-

eral lines indicated above to provide the needed analytic management skills. In addition to providing for internal management competence, the programs should provide needed preparation for community orientation. In general university programs need to move away from emphasis on descriptive study of current practice and the provincialism it engenders, and move toward grounding in the underlying technologies and systems as well as environments of hospital administration. Enhancing university programs will require modification and strengthening of faculties, formation of associations with other departments, and organization of related research programs.

3. Enlarging the roles of city and regional hospital councils and associations to: (*a*) support and participate in the training needs indicated above, (*b*) provide professional consulting staff for member hospitals, (*c*) undertake development of solutions to common problems and become a clearing house for dissemination of solutions developed in the industry, (*d*) provide integrated planning, (*e*) provide the means for conduct of administrative research, and (*f*) develop opportunities to provide common operational services and materials.
4. Providing supportive operational management for the administrator by enhancing the management skills of middle or department managers. It is frequently averred that the hospital administrator is a coordinator and integrator of professional departments, professionally managed. This extremely inaccurate statement is based on the most tenuous of assumptions regarding professional management of hospital departments. Criticism is not directed at department heads, many of whom are individually struggling to acquire the needed management skills. However, the fact is that neither administrators, hospital trade associations, nor the university programs have recognized the significance of building a supportive base of competent operational managers to support high level administration. As a consequence, much needed comprehensive operational management training programs have not been developed. Here again programs are envisaged that would be jointly planned and controlled by university programs in hospital administration and local city and regional hospital associations for which AHA can provide coordination and review. These training programs should also be provided through university extension or external departments.
5. Providing programatic means by which hospital administrators can both learn to properly use and secure supporting technical

management staff assistance who will aid in developing hospital organization structure, performance evaluation, planning and design of controls. Staff most needed at present are systems and organizational analysts, operations researchers, industrial engineers, etc.; all of these are also competent in computer application. Supplying this need calls for approaches different for large than for small hospitals. Large hospitals can profitably acquire their own technical management specialists while small hospitals will have to rely upon having such staff assistance provided by consultants on the staffs of regional and national hospital associations.

The technical management staff specialist brings with him the analytic skills needed to provide more sophisticated solutions. In using him the administrator may have these skills at hand considerably earlier than securing training for himself and his present assistants. There is some danger that the administrator may lack the ability to guide, evaluate, and interpret this work. The effective administrator will arrange to have his staff specialists provide him with training in the fundamentals upon which he can build his own competence.

Technical management specialists can provide the basis for management training of department heads and assist in developing local training programs. They can take the lead in organizing the problem solving projects among hospitals in the area providing the means for sharing in the development of solutions to common problems. Lastly, they can serve as a clearing house for developments elsewhere, providing modifications to suit local applicability.

6. Providing for the needs of enhancing the functioning of small hospitals which are also widely dispersed. In general, their needs are similar to those of large hospitals but the means of providing for them will have to be suited to managements and organizations that are isolated and have very limited financial and skill resources available. Training programs required are particularly the functions of regional and state associations assisted by extension programs of universities and AHA.

There is the need to provide large amounts of operational "how-to" information in the form of packaged data in operational handbooks. A large expansion of AHA's program will be required and perhaps the development of an agency within HEW to develop data and validate procedures.

Lastly there is the need to provide technical management staff assistance to help adapt packaged data to local needs. This need may be satisfied by having regional or state associations establish consulting services and acquire staffs of technical specialists. This would permit integrated programs to be developed and carried on with assurance of continuity. It would most efficiently provide for transfer of experience and solution of common problems in various functions.

7. Organizing research programs within hospitals, research institutes, and universities concerned with operational management and administration as well as planning and evaluation of health care systems. University programs and larger hospitals who are in leadership positions have responded very little to discharging their obligations of adding needed knowledge on operation and management of hospitals and the functioning of health care systems. Some may believe that considerable research is going on because of large numbers of case studies and comparative evaluations that are taking place. These descriptive studies, while very helpful in providing information on what constitutes present practice, provide too little insight as to the controlling variables. They yield little understanding of the operation of hospitals as systems and of the relationships of their component subsystems. Until the administrator knows which are the sensitive variables in his hospital system affecting its performance—i.e., until he can reliably predict the consequences of changes in variables, he cannot begin to control the operation of his institution.
8. Providing a basis by which administrators can enhance operational management by simply having fewer functions to manage and fewer services and personnel to coordinate. If this opportunity is further coupled with the prospects of having services performed more economically externally, then serious consideration should be given by administrators to divesting themselves of these services while having them performed locally under their partial control. This may well sound completely naive, for it asks that hospital administrators act contrary to Parkinson's Law, although the action is statesmanlike. What should be considered are experiments to provide a basis for deciding on whether and how to develop the means of jointly providing services and materials through local city councils or regional hospital associations.

At present there is need for a detailed study of how such divesting to a central service can take place, what functions and services to divest, the value to be derived in economic, service, and personnel terms, and the organizational needs of the local councils and associations in order to undertake these functions. It is realized that the changes suggested would modify the character of local councils changing their focus from information exchange to include providing service. The argument that each hospital is unique is too shopworn to be realistically considered as an inhibiting factor. Even granted this is so in a few cases, most hospitals can provide modifications to a common system to uniquely suit individual needs.

Threshold of Abrupt Changes

Hospital administration, in moving to enhance its professional capabilities, is on the threshold of great changes. These have already occurred in the management of business and industrial enterprises. Movements on a number of fronts are beginning to take place in developing quantitative analytic and decision skills, a technology of hospital operation and hospitals' roles in health care systems. The changing texture of the health care environment is such that the transition will not be leisurely. The pressures are great to develop adaptive hospitals capable of responding economically to: (1) increasing demands for services, (2) changing services, (3) professionalized and more independent staff, (4) use of community resources to meet health care obligations, and (5) demands for quality and individuality of care on the part of patients and their representatives. Administrators, in addition, are under pressure to follow the lead of business and industrial managers in utilizing the developments and specialists in planning, organizing and decision making, and to do so in the context of total health care systems. These different forces are joined in hastening the transition of hospital administration. Hopeful signs, already visible, are the increasing use of technical management staff specialists and development of training programs jointly with graduate schools of business administration and political sciences.

The role of administration statesman in the health community is the ultimate goal of many hospital administrators which places them in a risky position in their own hospitals. In satisfying his goal the administrator will continue to seek to minimize risk by developing adaptive capability of the organization which requires predictability for its operations plus operational objectives and controls.

The Social Responsibility of General Hospitals

Bright M. Dornblaser

The hospital field is under pressures from society to expand its missions, or to significantly alter how and where its missions are performed. What is the appropriate response?

Objectives

We recognize that the basic objective of the hospital as a social institution is to improve the quality of living—while working for life itself.

We further recognize that we can sharpen our ideas of ends of health care institutions from the honing action of experience in applying ideas within the context of the general hospital, its problems and realities. This is particularly so if cybernetics applies, if there is a feedback mechanism to the university or other sources of ideas which are being tested through application.

On the basis of experience, what should be the response to the question, "what is the mission of the hospital beyond beds and outpatient services?"

Thesis and Antithesis

One quick, if perhaps unpopular, answer to this question is "None!" The underlying rationale is that the hospital has more than enough to do to perform its medical care mission well, and "Whatever we undertake to do, we must do supremely well."

This position is, of course, the antithesis of a thesis with common currency today: That the quality of personal health care services for the middle class people now receiving such services is adequate; that the important unmet needs now are social; that hospitals have demonstrated a capacity to serve well; that they should expand their scope of service in response to social need; and that they are socially irresponsible if they do not. Is this thesis correct? Should the hospital become the hub rather than a medical care spoke of the health care wheel?

Medical Care Mission

Some traditionalists might respond by saying that to expand the general hospital's missions would jeopardize the quality of medical care. Our concentration, they believe, should continue on the quality of care provided to the individual patient who requests personal health services. The problems of continuing to provide care at the level of quality perceived possible by the producers of care are extensive, they are burdensome, and they are continuing. Subverting a specialized interest and skill to a more generalized concern, they feel, will exact too high a social price.

Proponents of this position suggest that the explosion of knowledge of the medical sciences and technology—with increased costs and shortages of dollars and competent manpower—can consume all the skilled health manpower and the fiscal, organizational, and managerial resources now available. These resources are subject to urgent demands today for improved efficiency, which suggests considerable change is manifest even within the medical model.

Wrestling with Social Assignments

Those pressing for increased efficiency state that quality of care to the individual is not enough, that medical care excellence is insufficient—the least hospital people must admit is their obligation also to serve the community with efficiency, so that the highest benefits can be obtained for the medical care dollars expended.

It is hard to deny the reasonableness of this position.

This argument will be reinforced by management incentives—a summarizing test of management.

By one means or another, hospital management will be stimulated to "reduce" cost by increasing efficiency:

Through higher productivity, e.g., through establishing group practice and use of full-time physicians;

Through trade-offs of less skilled health manpower for the more skilled;

Through trade-offs of less costly programs for the more costly;

Through control of the construction of facilities, costly to construct and still more costly to operate.

The hospital will be a key social control point, even if choosing to remain in the medical care mode. As such, it will receive inexorable pressure in the name of efficiency to make significant and traumatic changes in the ways in which the accepted medical model missions are executed. Wrestling with these socially loaded "bear-by-the-tail" social assignments is at first a full-time job. At this point we might identify with the farmer who protested to the Farm Bureau representative who wanted to instruct him on improved agriculture methods: "I ain't farming half as well as I know how yet!"

From these viewpoints we might well conclude that the hospital's first responsibility for service continues to be found in the medical model: Resources will be strained in order to continue executing these unique service responsibilities. Hospital representatives should be the leading advocates of continuing to perform them at a quality level. Furthermore, it is essential that hospital spokesmen not let others—who are clamoring for the general hospital to expand its mission—assume the continuance of past accomplishments, if added responsibilities are accepted.

Social Model vs. Medical Model

It is the view of the general hospital mission from the perspective of a social model which contributes to the demands for increased service. These accelerated demands, of course, reflect rising public expectations. They reflect a concern for the well, as well as the ill. Furthermore, they reflect a belief that the poor should have the opportunity and be encouraged to use the health care system. Drawing from the models of the past, the hospital is today expected to be more than the haven or *hospitia* for the wayfarers climbing over the snow-covered passes of life. In addition, it is expected to send out the human equivalent of the St. Bernard dogs, to seek actively those who may be in need. The president of the University of Minnesota has coined the word "communiversity" to express this sense of social responsibility in terms of the university.

Assuming hospital efficiency will be increased, how will the "saving" from increased efficiency be used? To reduce taxes, unlikely. To increase medical care benefits, perhaps. To increase social model benefits, more likely.

What are these social model benefits?

Fulfilling Social Demands

Basically, these benefits are intended to give substance to the accepted principle that health care is a right rather than a privilege.

We recognize this principle is more fiction than truth for perhaps 40 million Americans. We recognize, further, that those deprived of health services have advocates chanting, "we shall overcome."

The problems identified with our present health care non-system, which apply in varying degrees to all people presently served by our general hospitals, are familiar. They include:

1. Absence of program appropriateness, availability, accessibility, acceptability.
2. Absence of comprehensive care, of continuity of care.

From a social viewpoint, patient advocates state these deficits are intolerable, that they can be rectified if there is a will to do so, that they can be rectified without penalty if improvements in efficiency are made.

Patient advocates say, further, that the human costs gaps in health care services should be closed regardless of gains in efficiencies, despite the possible penalties of requiring a higher allocation of our gross national product, or of diminishing the quality of health care to our middle class society.

Patient advocates further assert that the general hospital has special capability to perform well the added health care missions of a social model, such as programs of "preventicare" and ghetto care. These characteristics and abilities include the needed philosophy of care, and the nucleus of the key health professionals needed to plan and execute such programs. It is natural that society, recognizing these strengths, and recognizing a heritage of a job well done, is asking hospitals to assume expanded missions of service to the community.

A second full-time job lies in fulfilling these social demands: To expand, relocate, and modify the manner of performance of general hospital missions.

Other Social Missions

There are still other social missions which hospitals are asked to undertake in serving the community. They should be assumed, if the hospital as a social institution is going to advance the society of which it is a part as fully as possible. Lists of these needs are readily available from numerous sources. However, the Commission on Civil Disorders provides a convenient catalogue. Such pressing needs as eliminating unemployment and underemployment, improving inadequate education, and reducing disrespectful white attitudes are examples of monumental problems which general hospitals genuinely interested in serving their communities can help resolve. The difficult social demands in these areas require not so much in the way of finances, knowledge, or skills, as in attitudes.

Concern for Human Values

Hospitals are being asked to provide their services in a human as well as humane fashion. While there are some penalties attendant in developing programs in response to social needs of this type—against only those which reflect the health needs of our medical model, the cost/benefit ratio is probably highly favorable.

Society needs individuals with a concern for human values, and for social health, which lie beyond a concern for individual personal health. It is to be hoped, at least, that the humanitarian-oriented health field will prove a repository for human beings interested in the human being. This is particularly requisite when this end requires primarily a change of attitude. This can be considered a third major job of hospitals today.

It would seem that a possible responsibility of the hospital is to serve as a hub of the health care wheel, and in addition, to form part of the axle joining the health care wheel to the social welfare wheel. Indeed we have come a long way from our mission of service to the community solely as a medical care spoke of the health care wheel.

Some hospitals are accepting these responsibilities today; others very likely will tomorrow. Many, if not most, however, without questioning the statements of unmet need, may well challenge the assumption that hospitals should meet them.

This position questions the timing and asks for a social cost/benefit study of alternatives. It recognizes the spirit of comprehensive health planning which pervades our land today asks, and even insists, that we examine alternatives in our planning process.

Health Care as a Right

Such study is needed. As one example, the costs of providing health care as a right to all, as some are privileged to know it today, is estimated as ranging on a gross basis as from $125 to $250 per person, for from 40 million to 200 million persons. Clearly, definitive study is needed of the economic consequences of implementing quickly and fully our stated natural health policy that health care is a right to all, rather than a privilege for the middle class of today. We should challenge the proclivity of some to promise benefits without resources to make them viable, except to ask those who have enjoyed benefits in the past to share them on the level of a greater common denominator. We should point out the problems of the "expectation gap" which are created by promises unfulfilled.

Clearly, the implications for health manpower requirements also need definition. The potential costs—or penalties, depending on our viewpoint—are also potentially large. Within this context, general hospitals can legitimately challenge the demands by public advocates by asking them to demonstrate the effective demand for health services from a large portion of the poor. For example, a stated need for improved health care service is conspicuously absent from the *Report of the National Commission on Civil Disorders,* which lists the twelve social problems identified as most important by the black community.

Further, it appears reasonable to challenge whether expenditure of funds to encourage effective demand for personal health services would provide the highest cost/benefit payoff. Environmental health expenditures, for example, might well have a higher payoff, socially and politically, as well as from a health viewpoint. So while allocation of savings from efficiencies to social model health programs is likely, the timing, appropriateness, and degree can be legitimately questioned.

We are entering an era when these now unanswered questions of cost/benefit relationships for personal health care services are of even greater importance. This is an era where personal health care services, or elements of such service, are increasingly going to be considered a responsibility rather than a right. A compelling case can be made for this principle. A proposal has been made that this principle be reflected in the health program in Minnesota's "Experimental City" by calling for compulsory annual multiphasic screening examinations. This requirement may well increase the consumers' effective demand upon providers of care to add or expand services, or both.

Synthesis

The demand upon the providers of care from the social model for increased quantity of care could be the straw that bends the quality care back of the medical model camel. Public advocates of the social model may prove stronger than the champions of the medical model. Selected health care providers should provide leadership, in a response to conflicting demands, by demonstration and research.

The general hospital is the health care cutting edge on the interface between social science and evolving technology. Society can expect hospitals to be vitally concerned with the development and use of the knowledge, one of the most fundamental of social commodities. It is only through the heuristic application of new knowledge that it gains ultimate social significance.

Selected general hospital leadership needs to demonstrate the equality of right to health care by finding ways to make it viable, while recognizing the penalties of broadly promulgating one alternative before planning others and examining them comprehensively. We do need, and should encourage and support, social model demonstrations such as may be found in Roxbury and Columbia Point in Boston, in the Grovenure program in New York City, in the Watts area of Los Angeles, and others. This is not the same, however, as asking all hospitals, as they are presently constituted, to do likewise.

The current focus of attention on the appropriate future mission of the general hospital is basically a matter of social organization. Demonstration and research into different organization models for the delivery of health care therefore is particularly pertinent. This approach offers hope for the development of an organizational base to mount programs which synthesize the conflicting demands of our medical and social health care models.

It is not a question of the appropriateness of goals and objectives—what the consumers or their advocates want, they will, like Lola, get. Consumer power as expressed through the political system does and will prevail. The question is the degree to which existing social organizations such as the general hospital will provide the means to the ends—to the evolving social objectives. It is a social organization question which asks:

1. Whether existing organizations, like the general hospital, will assume new program responsibilities, or whether new social organizations should be established which will be both more willing and able to do so.
2. Whether new organizations should be established to manage the health care system—removing and centralizing some decision-making authority now held by the service organizations, i.e., hospitals.
3. Whether new organizations should be established to perform existing programs to meet newly emphasized performance standards better than do existing organizations.

Hospitals, as we have seen, have a reasonable and perhaps even legitimate option of rejecting the social model to better serve the heavy demands of the medical model. Doing so efficiently releases resources to support other organizations endeavoring to meet the social model performance criteria for health care programs.

The general hospital has a further option within this context. It can choose to utilize programs developed by other community health care organizations, e.g., long term care, public health, Office of Economic Opportunity, model city organizations, rather than to plan and execute such programs within the general hospital organizational framework.

The Hospital's Option

If general hospitals individually or collectively provide leadership in the planning and organizing of health services, if not in the actual performance of them, they can in this organizational sense become the community health center which is the self-established model widely held by hospitals today. Whether other health service organizations would grant such authority to hospitals is of course a question.

Should general hospitals select these options, they should recognize they are accepting a mission as a medical care spoke, rather than the hub of the health care wheel. Other organizations will be needed to serve as other spokes of our health care wheel, and may have hub organizational responsibilities as well. Government has filled service, coordinative and directive needs of society in the past, when not provided by the private sector, and is one viable alternative for doing so again.

Hospitals should have no complaints if society forms other organizations to perform additional missions which hospitals elect to forego. Conversely, society should not be critical of hospitals for electing to be the public advocates of quality performance of certain health functions that have and will need considerable support if they are to continue to be provided on a quality basis.

Hospitals have still another option: To form vertically integrated "health utilities" in which they could perform their specialized function. Other organizational sub-units of the health utility could plan and execute the health missions demanded and needed by our social model. These missions possibly could include responsibility for selected environmental health or welfare programs. The utilities could well be responsible for developing or assembling associated prepayment programs.

This organizational alternative to planning and executing expanding health missions is to be preferred, in the author's judgement. It provides the scale to accomplish both medical and social missions, permits the advantages of specialization while reducing the organizational fragmentation of our health care non-system, and lowers the need for centralization of program planning and execution under governmental auspices.

These organizations could form the needed bridge between programs for the middle class and the urban and rural poor; permit a ''fresh start'' towards the changes needed for efficiency; and ease the pressure on the hospital to reduce quality in order to reduce high unit cost.

The health utility would provide an organizational symbol for the change of role of the central personal health care delivery organization. It could assist the assembly of managerial talent and staff resources needed for improvement in both efficiency and effectiveness. It would permit the continuance of specialized functional interest and expertise in humanly compatible organizational sub-units.

''Corner Grocery Store'' Orientation

The health utility with associated franchisement implies increased formal community responsibility and accountability, allocation of tax resources now reserved to governmental agencies, and centralization from a local perspective (but potential decentralization from regional and state governmental perspectives, and quasi-independence from their bureaucracies).

This organizational ''tool up'' may well be an essential foundation for the service and educational missions now being effectively demanded.

It is difficult to be sanguine that this organizational alternative will be adopted, except perhaps in such places as Minnesota's Experimental City, where it has been proposed. The existing hospital field still exhibits much of the ''corner grocery store'' orientation, in a chain store age. However, there are some hopeful signs. On this basis, as well as need, this alternative then is reasonable when endeavoring to define the general hospitals' future mission in service to the community.

Focal Point for Social Control

Regardless of the scope of the future mission, or the organizational context within which hospitals will operate, they will be a focal point for social control. The control will be concerned with both costs (efficiency) and benefits (effectiveness). The hospital's future missions will reflect judgments on costs and benefits, which in turn will reflect the criteria or standards used in making such judgments. The conclusions may well be expressed in franchisement of services. If hospital leadership wishes to have some control over the destiny of hospitals, for the quality and scope of hospital future missions, they need to be experts in the appropriateness of such standards.

This again will require a willingness to engage in collective effort. This could well be one of the most central and crucial missions of the general hospital in service to the community.

Conclusion

Society is demanding that further health missions be performed. Hospitals can legitimately consider their acceptance as alternatives, or their rejection so as to serve with excellence the continuing missions of the medical model. A preferred alternative is to develop health utilities. Such organizations could meet social needs for an expanded scope of service, while preserving the capability to perform on a quality, in-depth basis, the medical care functions which will need this concern in the future, as in the past.

Changes in the way existing health missions are performed, so as to increase efficiencies, can be anticipated. Allocation of the benefits of increased efficiency to expanded health/social missions can be expected. Both existing and expanded missions need to be performed with the social needs of minority groups in mind. Demonstration and research projects by selected general hospitals should show the way by synthesizing a response to the medical and social models. Translating the findings into standards of performance, for guidance of public expectations and decisions, is a basic mission.

Assiduous definition by public advocates of gaps in the meeting of health care needs should join with sedulous recognition of the ''tooling up'' effort needed to overcome these needs. The absence of qualified professional manpower is but one example of a long term obstacle even if organizational and financial problems can be overcome. Economic and social cures should be promised and delivered as carefully as medical cures. Full participation by the leadership of the hospital field can be vital to this end.

It is an endeavor worthy of the devotion of the talents and energies of the management of our nation's hospitals. Commitment of this capability with vision, imagination, drive, and resourcefulness will provide the managerial leadership demanded and needed by our times.

Applying Economic Concepts to Hospital Care

Paul J. Feldstein, Ph.D.

Can medical care be subject to economic analysis? Is the study of economics useful to a person such as a hospital administrator working in medical care? To say that economic analysis is useful for the study of medical care problems, one must first explain to the non-economist exactly what economic analysis is and then show how this analysis can be applied to the study of medical care problems. The rest of this paper will be addressed to this problem.[1]

Economics is concerned with the optimum use of resources, i.e., the best way to combine a given set of resources in order to achieve a certain purpose. Considered in this manner, it becomes apparent that economics can and should be applied to the study of medical care, for the resources devoted to medical care are scarce, and it is highly desirable to find the best of the many combinations of these resources that produce medical care—by using tools of economics. An economist can indicate how much of one resource should be used in producing medical care when compared to producing that same amount of care by use of other resources.

Another set of tools that the economist uses are the familiar terms—supply and demand; these tools usually are used for answering another set of questions. Supply and demand analysis is useful for explaining variations in prices and in utilization (or output) either over time or within a given time period. The price of medical care has gone up sharply in the last 15 to 20 years, and there are also great variations in the use of medical care services. Therefore, to have some understanding of future trends, it is important to understand why prices have gone up and why there are variations in utilization.

[1]Historically a large proportion of the work in ''medical economics'' has been descriptive rather than analytical. Much of the work which has been labeled ''medical economics'' has centered upon the study of trends in time series, such as medical care expenditures, and often such studies have employed neither the concepts nor the analytical tools of economic theory.

Two Applications of Economics

To summarize briefly, economic analysis can be useful to the study of medical care in two ways. First, a knowledge of the tools of economics will enable one to explain what has been occurring and what is likely to occur in the future. The ability to predict and anticipate changes that will occur in medical care and in the provision of care are important to health care administrators. Second, economic concepts are an aid in achieving an optimum use of medical care resources. A decision-maker, whether he is a hospital administrator, the executive director of a hospital planning association, or anyone working in medical care who is concerned with the use of resources and can change the combination in which these resources are used, should have an understanding of maximum efficiency, minimum cost, etc., in order to produce a given level of care (of a given quality) at minimum cost or, similarly, how to produce a maximum amount of patient care for a given budget. The use of the economist's tools can be helpful in deciding how the provision of care is to be organized.

We should start by describing what an economic problem is so that you will know when to apply the few economic concepts to be described. An economic problem exists whenever there are too few resources, that is, when there is too little time, people, dollars, etc., to do all that is desired. Since there are too few resources, all of which can be used for achieving other goals, it becomes necessary to allocate these scarce resources. For example, if there were an infinite amount of time available for studying, one would not have to allocate time to the various subjects he is studying. But since time is limited, and time spent studying for one course could be used in studying another, there is an economic problem—the available time must be allocated among the several courses to be studied. Defining economic problems in this manner—the allocation of scarce resources among alternative ends—enables us to see why economists are being used to analyze such diverse areas as water supply problems, the department of defense, natural resources, and, of course, health and medical care.

The problem of allocating scarce resources among alternative ends might be posed in another manner: For any given objective, what combination of resources should be used and in what proportions for achieving the objective at minimum cost? Or, alternatively, for any given budget, which resources and how much of each resource should be used in order to maximize the desired output from the given budget?

Developing Economic Concepts

As an aid in describing the concepts that an economist uses to analyze whether resources are combined in an optimum fashion, we will use a simple functional relation. Most economic concepts or tools of analysis may be developed by using a simple functional relation, such as the following: q = f (a, b, c). "Q" is a given level of output and is termed the dependent variable since its level of magnitude depends upon (f) the amounts of the inputs, (a, b, c) used.

Economic problems, hence economic anlaysis, can be described with reference to this simple functional relationship. If our concern is providing a given amount of hospital care at minimum cost, then "q" is the amount of care, while "a," "b," and "c" are the inputs for producing hospital care—such as the number of hospital beds, the number of physicians, and the number of nurses. The first step in an economic analysis, therefore, is to state what the output is and to specify the "inputs" used to produce that output. In this phase, therefore, it is necessary to define the dependent variable or output; in the above case, if our output were hospital care, the second part of the first step is to specify what the factors are that determine its level. This information usually comes from a knowledge and understanding of the field being studied. In medical care, for example, we would ask hospital administrators, doctors, and other knowledgeable persons what the various factors are that go into producing hospital care.

Answering Research Questions

However, the mere specification of the output and inputs used to produce hospital care does not enable us to determine the type and amount of each input to use in order to produce care at minimum cost. The second step, therefore, is to answer a research question—how does the level of output vary as each and every input is varied? For example: How much more hospital care is given by increasing the number of nurses while keeping the number of hospital beds and physicians constant? The last step in the problem of optimal allocation of scarce resources, then, is relating prices to the respective inputs to determine that combination of inputs that will minimize the cost of producing each level of output. For instance, while an increase in the number of doctors might result in a large increase in the amount of patient care, the cost of that increase in doctors may be much greater than the cost of a greater increase in the number of nurses. Therefore, the increase in patient care per dollar spent might be greater if we were to increase the number of nurses up to a certain point rather than spending all our money on increasing the number of doctors. These three steps then: The specification of the output and the inputs used to produce it, determination of how output varies with changes in each one of the inputs, and finally, the selection of the combination of inputs which, when used with the prices per input, results in the minimum cost for achieving any level of output, are the basis of any economic analysis. The rest of this paper, therefore, will be concerned with explaining what determines the combinations of inputs to be used when producing any level of output.

Before describing how prices are used with the functional relationship in decision-making to achieve an optimum combination of resources at any given level of output, it would be best at this point to describe further the nature of the functional relationship.

Assume the following functional relationship: q = f (a, b, c). The level of output depends upon the amounts of "a," "b," and "c" used. Let us assume that "a" is the size of a hospital, "b" is the number of services a hospital provides, and "c" is the number of nurses providing patient care; the dependent variable, "q," is the amount of patient care provided. The question is: How much of "a," "b," and "c" should the hospital administrator use to provide a given amount of patient care? If we were to assume that the administrator could vary all of the inputs, that is, "a," "b," and "c," then we are talking of a condition which is known as the "long run." The long run is a period of time in which all of the factors of production can be varied. The "short run" differs from the "long run" in that the administrator or the decision-maker is able to vary only some of his inputs. For example, perhaps he can vary only the number of nurses providing care, given the size of the hospital and the number of services that it has. If we assume a short-run situation, that is, the administrator is able to vary only the number of nurses in providing patient care, the question of interest becomes, "What is the point beyond which it is no longer worthwhile to increase the number of nurses?" Clearly, a hospital of a given size with given services and no nurses will have a large increase in its output, that is, patient care, when one nurse is added to the hospital.

The Incremental Effect

Assuming that a hospital of a given size with given services were full of patients and that adding one nurse to the staff resulted in a great increase in patient care, the question then is, "What would be the additional increase in patient care as the second and third and finally fiftieth nurse were hired?'' What we are interested in knowing is the incremental effect on patient care of adding each additional nurse. This incremental, or marginal, effect is not always constant, for as additional nurses are added, other things such as size of hospital and number of patients being constant, the resulting increase in patient care rendered is not proportional to or the same as when the previous nurse was added. This is because, after a point, as more and more nurses are hired, they will contribute less and less to patient care and more toward less important tasks. Therefore, the incremental increase in patient care falls after some point. The paradox that the increase in output resulting from an increase in one input, while the others are held constant, does not change in proportion to the increase in the input is known as the law of variable proportions or, more commonly, as the law of diminishing returns. This principle—that the marginal effect of an input changes as more of it is added—becomes important because it means that after some point it is not worthwhile to keep adding additional increments of the same input. It becomes important to understand the relationship between the change in output with the given change in input because, after a certain point, it may be possible to achieve greater increases in output by varying the quantities of another input rather than the present one being used.

Long- and Short-range Planning

If we assume a ''long-run'' situation, that is, we are now able to vary the size of the hospital and the number and type of services that the hospital can provide, as well as varying the number of nurses, then we will want to know the effect on patient care (which is our measure of output) as each and all of these inputs are varied. When we vary the hospital size while the other variables remain fixed, we find that we are able to increase the amount of patient care provided until the size of hospital increases to a certain point, but that after that point, continued increases in hospital size reduce the amount of patient care unless the other inputs are also increased.

For both long-range planning (the ''long run'') and for daily operations (the ''short run''), the administrator or the decision-maker should ask, ''What is the optimum combination of inputs to produce a given amount of patient care?'' In order to answer this question, it becomes necessary to introduce prices, for although the effects on patient care of an increase in any one input may be known, it is not possible to make a decision on which inputs should be increased on just this basis, since the cost of increasing any one input differs from the cost of increasing any other. For example, if we were producing patient care by using different types of nurses, we might achieve much larger increases in patient care by adding one registered nurse rather than by hiring two licensed practical nurses; however, the cost of adding one registered nurse might be much greater than the cost of two additional licensed practical nurses. Therefore, prices serve as a means of comparing the cost of increasing any one input with the others. Earlier we were able to establish what the marginal effect on output is when any one input has been increased. It was not possible, however, to judge which input should be increased, even though we knew the corresponding increase in output, because the cost of increasing any one input was different from the others. However, once we introduce prices, which gives us the cost of increasing an input by one increment to achieve an increase in output, we can then determine what the increase in output will be per dollar increase in inputs "a," "b," "c."

Assumption of Rationality

If the decision-maker then wishes to combine resources to minimize the costs of producing a given level of output (patient care); if he knows the resources (inputs) that can be used in producing patient care, and if he also knows the prices for increasing each input (and the increase in patient care that will result from each input increase), then the way to achieve minimum cost is as follows: *The decision-maker should use those resources in such a combination that the additional increment in patient care per dollar spent on each input is equal.*

As we see in the example above, prices are quite important. They indicate to the decision-maker which resources or inputs should be used for achieving a combination of inputs that will minimize the cost of producing any given level of output. Prices are thus used in the allocation of resources.

It should be mentioned at this point that we are making several assumptions about the decision-maker who allocates resources. First, we assume that the decision-maker knows about the effects on output when he increases any input. In other words, he knows the marginal effect of the change in input on output. Second, we assume that the decision-maker is rational in that he wishes to produce or provide a given amount of patient care at minimum cost. If these two assumptions are not met, it is useless to set up the decision-rule prescribing that the amounts of inputs used should be such that their marginal change in output per dollar is equal for all the inputs. If the decision-maker does not know the marginal effect per dollar of input spent, he can not approximate the optimum combination of inputs. In reality, the decision-maker rarely knows the exact marginal effects per dollar spent, but even if he has no information on marginal effects, marginal analysis would still be useful because it would force the decision-maker to think marginally. That is, the decision-maker would think in terms of "a little bit more or a little bit less," and he would carefully weigh the gains and losses of each action.

The more crucial assumption, therefore, is that the decision-maker acts rationally, and that he wishes to minimize the cost of producing any given level of output. If this assumption is not correct, it does not matter whether or not the decision-maker has knowledge on marginal effects. If he has the knowledge, he will not use it because he will have some objective function in mind other than minimum cost.

Minimum Cost Plus Quality

In the health field, therefore, we must determine how important the criterion of minimum cost is to decision-making. It should be emphasized here that the criterion of minimum cost does not mean sacrificing quality. The decision-rule of minimum cost means that resources should be used to produce a level of output that does not require more resources than are necessary in terms of amount, or that less costly resources will be used rather than more costly resources to achieve the same goal. For example, it is possible to provide patient care in the hospital, in a nursing home, at home, or at a doctor's office. Depending upon the illness, it is generally likely that several combinations of these inputs can be used to produce patient care for an illness. While it may be possible to provide all the patient care in the hospital, it is less expensive to provide some of the patient care in the hospital, part of it in a nursing home, part of it at home, and part of it in a doctor's office. The goal of minimum cost dictates that for a particular illness, less expensive care (with a given level of quality) should be provided when possible, i.e., nursing home for hospital, home care for nursing home care. This is the same thing as saying that the marginal effect on patient care of a dollar spent on hospital care should be equal to the marginal effect on patient care of a dollar spent on a nursing home, which should also be equal to the marginal effect on patient care of a dollar spent on home care, and so on for physician care, *ad nauseam!*

Prices Allocate Resources

To go back to the idea that prices allocate resources, let us use the example of different types of nurses providing patient care. Let us assume that there has been a change in the relative wage rate of one type of nurse. If, for example, there has been a rise in the wage rate of registered nurses relative to that of licensed practical nurses, then the optimum way for a decision-maker to combine his nursing personnel in providing patient care is to substitute licensed practical nurses for registered nurses. He will substitute until he reaches the point where the marginal effects on patient care per dollar spent on RN's and LPN's is again equal. The rise in the relative wage of RN's will increase the demand for licensed practical nurses while decreasing the demand for registered nurses. Prices, therefore, allocate resources in that they indicate how to achieve a minimum cost combination of inputs and indicate how much to substitute one input for another when there are changes in their relative prices.

It was stated earlier that almost all the economic concepts which will concern us can be expressed in terms of a functional relationship or are derived from the functional relation itself. To further demonstrate this, let us take two terms which are commonly used, "cost benefit analysis" and "opportunity cost," and show what they mean with reference to the functional relation. Cost-benefit analysis usually refers to the cost incurred from changing the inputs or, more likely, from increasing an input, and refers also to the benefits that result from an increase in the output which are occasioned by the increased input.

For example, let us assume the following functional relation: $x = f(a, b, c)$, where "x" refers to the mortality rate of a given illness; "a" refers to the treatment cost of caring for a person once he is discovered to have that illness; "b" refers to expenditures made on preventive care; and "c" refers to expenditures on medical research in order to find a cure for the illness being considered. Cost-benefit analysis, in this case, may be referred to as the value of a change in the mortality rate from a given change in one of the inputs, or the value of mortality-rate change from changing all the inputs. More specifically, there is a certain cost associated with increasing medical research, which is one of the inputs considered. This increased expenditure on medical research will have some effect on the change in mortality rate from that illness. We can translate the change in mortality rate into an economic return, for example, by estimating the increase in income from lives saved due to a reduced mortality rate. It is then possible to relate this change in income to the change in expenditures which are necessary to achieve it. Alternatively, we might relate the increase in income from a decrease in the mortality rate to the cost of changing each one of the inputs necessary to bring about this change in mortality rate. If our objective is then to minimize the income loss from this disease, we would then allocate our limited dollars to each of the inputs so that the increase in income per dollar spent on each input is equal.

Opportunity Cost

Cost-benefit analysis is actually more complicated than the above example, since the returns are over a number of years and the costs might also be for different periods of time. The example of cost-benefit analysis was used to demonstrate the applicability of using a functional relation and the value in using marginal analysis.

The other term frequently heard is "opportunity cost." Opportunity cost results when there is a scarcity of resources with alternative uses. In the above example of cost-benefit analysis, the opportunity cost of increasing expenditures on preventive care is seen when we consider that the same amount of money might have been used on medical research. The opportunity cost, therefore, of a dollar spent on preventive care is the return that the dollar would have achieved by being spent on medical research. What is clearly desired in this case is that the return per dollar spent should be in its highest use, that is, the change in mortality rate from a dollar spent on treatment costs should be equal to the change in mortality rate for a dollar spent on preventive care, which, in turn, should be equal to the change in mortality rate from a dollar spent on medical research. When these three returns are equal, we will then have achieved an optimum allocation of a given amount of dollars to be spent on reducing the mortality rate of this illness. As seen in this case, the economist must always consider alternative courses of action, and the selection of one alternative means that the foregone alternatives are the opportunity cost of his decision.

Series of Functional Relationships

Until now, we have been talking in terms of single functional relationships, and no effort has been made to relate different functional relationships to one another. In reality, the world in which we live is complex; functional relations rarely stand by themselves. Picture, if you can, a series of functional relations, the output of each one becoming inputs into a next higher functional relation, which in turn contributes its output together with the outputs of still other functional relations to form inputs of even higher functional relations. An example of such a series of functional relations in the health field could begin with the several different types of nursing personnel used to produce a given amount of nursing patient care. Nursing patient care in turn, which is the output of the functional relation just specified, is only one input which, when added to inputs such as drug therapy, physician care, and hospital care, produce patient care. Each of those other inputs are the outputs of lower functional relations. Patient care, which is the output of the second functional relation, is then just one input together with nutrition, proper shelter, clothing, etc., in producing another output of a higher functional relation, commonly called "good health." Again, each of the inputs of this higher functional relation, good health, has a series of lower functional relations whose outputs are inputs into this functional relation.

For proper understanding of health and medical care, therefore, we must be able to specify each functional relation and also be able to consider the outputs of different functional relations as inputs into higher functional relations. Once this is done, we then have what is known as a model of the medical care sector. This model will enable us to predict what will happen if we change an input in a functional relation, perhaps on the third or fifth level down, and what the ultimate effect of this change will be. For example, one functional relation in the system might relate to the production of nurses in society. In this relationship, how important is the recent legislation providing $300,000,000 for increasing the supply of nurses? The functional relation for producing nurses states that there are a number of factors that affect a girl's decision to become a nurse, only one of which might be the cost of training. An important question, then, is "What is the ultimate effect on patient care of this $300,000,000 compared to the opportunity cost of spending the $300,000,000 on other ways to improve patient care?" Only by specifying a complete set of functional relations and having an estimate of the magnitude of the effect of each functional relation's inputs will it be possible to make policy decisions and state what the effects of any changes will be throughout the whole system.

Effects of Price Changes

Let us now imagine that ideally each of these functional relations consists of inputs which are combined in the most efficient manner, that is, that the marginal effect on output per dollar of input is the same for all the inputs in a functional relation. Further, let us assume that this efficient combination of resources exists for each of the functional relations in our whole system. Let us then assume that there is a change in price of one of the factors, perhaps as a result of a change in insurance coverage. For example, formerly only hospital care was covered, and now outpatient care is also included. The question is, "What implications does a change in price of one of the inputs have on the whole system?"

First, let us take the functional relation in which the input's price change occurred, that is, a functional relation whose output was the provision of care for a particular diagnosis. Formerly, the physician in treating the illness combined the components of care, e.g., hospital care, physician care, home care, and outpatient care in a manner designed to minimize the cost to the patient for such care. If the patient had insurance coverage for hospital care, relatively more hospital care would have been used compared to less expensive forms of care. The change in insurance coverage, that is, outpatient care is now covered, would mean that the physician might now prescribe more outpatient care in the treatment of this illness than formerly. Therefore, within this functional relation, we would expect to observe a substitution of inputs, that is, outpatient care would be substituted for some hospital care so that the cost is again minimized for the patient as well as perhaps for the community.

Changes in Functional Relations

The analysis would not stop here, however. If we consider the lower functional relations leading up to this one, we would also expect to observe some changes. For example, in the functional relation whose output is hospital care, we would expect to observe a decrease in the demand for certain hospital inputs. Similarly, we would expect to observe a greater increase in the demand for inputs of outpatient care. We might also observe changes in higher functional relations. Since the change in insurance coverage resulted in the use of a less expensive form of care, the cost of providing this care was reduced. Patient care for an illness is, as we have said earlier, an input into a next higher functional relation which might consist of patient care, together with preventive care, and medical research as factors affecting the mortality rate from a given illness. Since the cost of one of the inputs (i.e., patient care) in this next higher functional relation has been decreased, this might result in the substitution of relatively more of this input for the others in order to reduce the mortality rate. Since, as we have said earlier, the marginal change in mortality rate for a given dollar spent on each input should be equal, and since the price of one input has been reduced, we would expect to see a relative shift in expenditures on these inputs, as well as a decrease in the cost of this functional relation for achieving the previous level of mortality.

The initial change in price will be reflected up to the higher functional relations. As the prices of certain inputs become reduced, there is substitution in the use of these inputs. Too, the cost of achieving the output level of that functional relation becomes less, and, therefore, the relative return from expenditures on this or similarly affected functional relations is increased. The same effects, however, may go in an opposite direction. For example, if the price of hospital care continues to rise, and if hospital care, as one component in a functional relation, increases in price, we then would expect to observe increases in expenditures on components other than hospital care, for substitution among inputs will occur. This shift in expenditures on different inputs would continue all the way up to higher functional relations, as well as being reflected in lower functional relations.

Thus, changes in prices affect the entire system. If, for example, there are controls on prices of some of the inputs of medical care or prices are set artificially on some inputs, this will reverberate throughout the entire system. The inputs whose price has been lowered will be substituted, in both demand and supply relations, for relatively more expensive inputs until "shortages" occur, since the price of the input will not increase to bring about an increase in supply. Higher and lower functional relations would be similarly affected.

How Prices are Determined

Prices are thus seen to be extremely important since they determine which inputs are to be used, i.e., the allocation of resources. The next step in economic analysis, therefore, is to find out how prices are determined. And this analysis leads us to the familiar concepts of "supply" and "demand."

Although we have introduced the terms "supply" and "demand," we will not abandon the idea of the functional relation, because supply and demand are terms used by the economist simply to classify functional relations. For example, a functional relationship between the amount of hospital care produced and the several inputs used to produce it is classified under the heading of supply. The relationship between the amount of hospital care purchased as determined by a series of factors, such as degree of illness, availability of hospital insurance, age, etc., is considered a demand relation.

Supply and Demand Relationships

Why is it necessary to classify these functional relations as being either demand or supply? Because a supply or demand relation by itself will not enable us to know the actual amount of hospital care produced and purchased. A supply relation is merely a schedule of how much can be produced at different prices and for different levels of the other factors (inputs) affecting supply. Notice, it does not say how much will be produced—just how much can be produced and the cost of producing that amount. Similarly, a demand relation shows what the demand for hospital care would be at different prices of hospital care and for different levels of the inputs (factors) affecting demand; hence, it is also merely a schedule. It is only through the interaction of supply and demand that the amount of hospital care produced and the price of that care is determined.

In the earlier discussion of functional relations, it was said that the decision-maker's objective in combining his resources must be specified. The objective which we believe should prevail in medical care, as in other areas, is that the resources should be combined to result in the minimum cost combination for producing a given level of output. In other words, for a given budget, as much output as possible should be produced. When demand functions are discussed, it is also necessary to specify the objective of the person whose demand function is being analyzed. Again, we are making the assumption of scarcity, that is, that a person has many wants on which he would like to spend his limited amount of income. He should, therefore, spend his income on those goods and services so as to maximize his total satisfaction from his expenditure. These assumptions and the objective are similar to what we have stated for the supply side. The question then becomes, "How should a person spend his limited dollars among goods and services in order to maximize his total satisfaction?"

The decision-rule here is the same as the decision-rule specified earlier—that is, he will allocate his dollars to those goods and services so that the marginal satisfaction per dollar spent on each good and service is equal. For example, if in an equilibrium situation there is a price change of goods and/or services that a person desires, the marginal satisfaction per dollar spent on the various goods and services would change. The person would have to change his expenditures slightly to re-create the desired situation in which marginal satisfaction per dollar spent on each good and service is equal to the marginal satisfaction of a dollar spent on every other good and service. Similarly, if a person were to receive an increase in his income and he could buy more of everything, the decision-rule to be used in allocating the increased income is the same; that is, he should still spend the additional money, and all his money, in such a way that the marginal satisfaction per dollar spent on each good and service is equal to the marginal satisfaction of a dollar spent on every other good and service.

Factors Influencing Demand

Therefore, if we wanted to specify a demand function for any one particular good and service, such as medical care or hospital care, we would say that the demand for hospital care, which is the dependent variable, is a function of the price of hospital care, the price of hospital care relative to the prices to other goods and services, a person's total income, and the person's tastes, which is a category that includes, in addition to his own preferences, a number of other social-demographic factors, that may affect the person's demand for the particular good of service. The expected relationship between the demand for hospital care and the price of hospital care is such that as the price of hospital care rises, less is demanded (this is the opposite of the supply relation). Why? Because if the prices of other goods and services and their marginal satisfaction are unchanged, and only the price of hospital care rises, to equate the marginal satisfaction of a dollar spent on hospital care with the marginal satisfaction of a dollar spent on all other goods and services, a person would demand less hospital care.

It is for this reason that we have included an additional variable—the price of hospital care relative to the prices of other goods and services. For example, if the price of nursing home care, which is one substitute for hospital care, were to decrease, this decrease would affect the demand for hospital care. The third economic variable included is "income," because in looking at the demand for an item, such as hospital care, we should hold constant or be able to allow for the effects of changes in income which would affect the person's ability to purchase all goods and services, including hospital care. If, for example, there were an increase in income, this might also result in an increase in hospital care, because with an increase in income a person might choose to spend additional money on hospital care.

Price and Income Elasticity

The technical term for describing the relationship between change in hospital care demand and a change in any one of the factors considered, such as price and income, is known as "elasticity." The "price elasticity" of hospital care is the per cent change in hospital care that would be demanded with a per cent change in price of hospital care. Similarly, the per cent change in hospital care with a per cent change in income is known as "income elasticity." Elasticity is a measure of responsiveness. For example, if, with a 10 per cent change in price of hospital care, the demand for hospital care, measured in patient days or admissions, changes by only 5 per cent, hospital care is considered to be "price inelastic." Similarly, if, with a 5 per cent change in income the demand for hospital care changes by 10 per cent, hospital care is considered to be "income elastic." The term "elasticity" is merely a means of expressing the responsiveness of the good and service demanded to the factors being considered. The term "elasticity" is also used with reference to supply relations.

Actually, a demand for any good and service is a little more complicated than the simple expression states above. In addition to prices and income factors mentioned, institutional characteristics of the market usually are included, as are a series of cultural and demographic factors that affect a person's demand for medical care. The point here is that prices are used again to allocate resources, by determining how funds should be spent in order to maximize one's satisfaction, given the prices of the goods and services to be purchased and given the marginal satisfaction obtainable from each good and service.

The Production Function

The supply relation, since it was discussed earlier, will be reviewed only briefly here. Underlying the supply relation is the production function. The production function states the relationship between the output of a good or service and the resources (inputs) used to produce it. For example, nursing patient care is the output of the number and type of nurses on the nursing unit. Once prices are used in conjunction with the production function (in this sense prices refer to the wage rate of the various nurses concerned), we can then develop a supply relation which will maximize the amount of output for a given cost at each level of output. This is done by employing the decision-rule of using resources to the point where the marginal effect of a dollar spent on each input, such as licensed practical nurses, is equal. Since for each given level of output we have a minimum cost combination, if we were to plot the minimum cost combination for each higher level of output on a chart, we would be plotting the supply relation—the amount of output that can be produced at different prices. The prices here refer to the minimum cost combination. For example, at a price of $10 per patient day, it is possible to provide ''x'' number of patient days. If we increase the price paid per patient day, then we can command many more resources for the provision of patient care. Usually supply schedules are rising; that is, as the price of the product or service rises, more can be produced, as in the above example. This is because in order to increase the provision of anything, more resources must be drawn to this area, and in order to do this, it is necessary to pay a higher wage or price for these resources in order to bid them away from their current use.

To briefly summarize the use of supply and demand analysis, we have classified functional relations which are parallel to one another on both the demand and the supply side, because only through the interaction of supply and demand relations can price and output be determined. The prices that result from the interaction of demand and supply are then used to indicate which inputs should be used to produce goods and services. Therefore, prices are determined by demand and supply and are in turn used to indicate which inputs should be used in production and also as to which goods and services should be purchased.

Restrictions on Production

It was stated earlier that supply and demand determine price. Price, in turn, determines the allocation of inputs to be used in producing a given product or service. Prices also influence the consumer's decision on what goods and services he should spend his money. The study of markets, or the market structure for different goods and services, is of interest to the economist because the structure of the market might have significant influence on which inputs can be combined with other inputs in producing patient care, as well as being influential in determining which goods and services the consumer could purchase. For example, if the hospital administrator is not able to combine patient care inputs as he would like in order to achieve a minimum cost combination because of restrictions on the use of certain inputs, then the extent of these restrictions will result in his having to use other inputs. The end result will be a combination of inputs at a cost higher than if the first selection of inputs could have been used. The restrictions would have forced him to use inputs that are either relatively more expensive or that are scarce. Therefore, the cost of producing a given level of output would presumably be higher than if there were no restrictions. The restrictions to which we are referring are a direct result of the "structure" of the market.

Restrictions can occur on both the supply and the demand side. On the supply side, examples of such restrictions might be very large economies of scale. For example, in some cases, in order to produce a given level of output at relatively low cost, a firm in an industry must be extremely large, i.e., the aluminum and automobile industry. It does not appear that industries in the health field are subject to such large economies of scale. There are, for example, many physicians in solo practice and also many small nursing homes; most hospitals are less than 150 beds, etc. A restriction on the supply side which is more relevant to medical care is "barriers to entry." "Barriers to entry" means that resources (health personnel included) are not free to move into uses or professions as the demand for them changes. For example, the licensing of physicians restricts the number of persons who can become physicians. Similarly, there are restrictions on the way in which a person might be used to perform certain tasks. For example, even if a licensed practical nurse were able to perform certain tasks that a registered nurse can perform, she is restricted from so doing. Substitution between these two inputs is limited.

Similarly, a registered nurse is not allowed to perform certain functions that only a doctor is "qualified" to perform. An example of this restriction on the demand side is in the purchase of close substitutes of one service for another. For example, if there are no close substitutes for physicians, in making a choice on his medical care expenditures, a patient is quite limited in how he can spend his funds. Restrictions affect demand and supply by limiting the way the producer or the consumer can spend his funds. The consumer is not able to equalize his expenditures at the margin; the marginal effect of a dollar spent on one input will not be equal to the marginal effect of a dollar spent on another good or input.

Effects of Market Structures

One type of market structure is that of competitive industries, which are characterized by many sellers of a good or service, each firm usually small in size. Another type is monopolistic industries, which are characterized by fewer (or one) sellers of a service. Different types of market structure have an important effect, for the price of a good in a competitive industry will be lower than if that industry were suddenly to become monopolized. Too, the output of a competitive industry is greater than it would be if that industry were to be monopolized. In medical care, segments of the industry become more monopolistic (e.g., physicians, specialists, hospitals, etc.) by placing restrictions on entry, for example, through licensing as a means of ensuring quality. Also, because knowledge is generally poor in the medical care market, as in most repair markets (e.g., auto repair), people are not able to judge the quality of the products produced, such as the quality of physician care. This lack of knowledge inhibits movement away from less efficient and low quality producers.

Evaluating Market Structures

The way in which market structures are generally evaluated, therefore, is by their effect on the price of the product being produced and on the quantity of the output produced. If the price is lower and the output is greater, this is, of course, preferable to an industry whose quality is the same but which has a higher price and restricts the output. Since it is difficult to evaluate whether prices could be lower and output greater if the market structure were changed, the industry's performance is generally inferred through an examination of the industry's structure. For example, if we observe a more competitive industry with fewer restrictions on the mobility of resources, we assume that the price is lower and the output greater than it would be if restrictions were added and the industry were to become monopolistic. Public policy, therefore, tends to influence an industry's performance by making changes in that industry's structure. Public policy measures are usually devoted to making an industry more competitive by taking away restrictions and by making resources more mobile, such as by increasing knowledge to workers, consumers, and producers.

It is therefore important to do separate industry analyses in medical care. For example, consider physicians as an industry, the drug industry, the insurance industry, the hospital industry, the nursing home industry. It is only by examining each industry separately and analyzing the restrictions that exist and their effect on the industry's price and output that it is possible to speculate whether the price could be lower, the output greater, or the quality higher, if changes were made in the industry's structure.

An analysis of the medical care market structure, hence its performance, should consider the effect that certain characteristics peculiar to segments of that industry will have on the provision of care and/or the price of that care (for example, the nonprofit nature of Blue Cross and voluntary nonprofit hospitals). In a profit-oriented industry, profits on the supply side are an incentive to increase supply when price rises; in this manner, prices are used to allocate inputs to achieve the minimum cost combination. In a nonprofit industry, what is the incentive to produce care at minimum cost? Is a person's desire to "do good" as strong an incentive to efficiency as a profit incentive? Are nonprofit hospitals as efficient as they might be? Or, is the objective in a nonprofit industry the maximization of an administrator's or other member's satisfaction? Most people in the health field have stated that competiton is not good, that it is harmful. Is this really true? In what situations is competition useful? Could it serve as a yardstick by which to judge nonprofit organizations?

To summarize briefly, then, we are interested in observing and analyzing market structure because it enables us to infer its performance, and performance is measured generally in terms of the price of the industry's output and the amount of output produced. If there are fewer restrictions in an industry, the price of the industry's output would be lower and the amount of output would be greater. The effect of restrictions with reference to our discussion of functional relations is that without such restrictions, we are able to combine inputs on the supply side at a lower cost, hence greater output, and we can then make choices on the demand side such that for any given dollar spent we will be able to receive more for our money. It will be possible to combine inputs more efficiently and at lower prices if there are no restrictions in the market in which these inputs are produced. Restrictions and the study of markets affect how we are able to combine inputs on the supply side, and how we can select goods and services on the demand side in order to achieve either maximum satisfaction or minimum cost for a given dollar amount to be spent.

When Occupations Meet: Professions in Trouble

Edward Gross, Ph.D.

Two major themes dominate recent discussions in the sociological literature on the professions: the great growth of the professions and the conflict between the needs and demands of professionals and the organizations that employ them. The numbers in the professions have increased from a scant 4 per cent of employed persons in 1900 to a point where they now make up something close to one in seven. This growth, as well as the emergence of new professions, is partly a reflection of growth in knowledge since the industrial revolution and of the growth in science. But that is not a sufficient explanation, at least not for professions like the ministry or law, which do not rest on a body of knowledge acquired through empirical scientific research, and only partly for such professions as social work or accountancy, in which professionalization takes the form of systematizing a body of practice which has grown up over a long period.

As important as growth of knowledge are the advantages of gaining recognition. If an occupation validates its right to call itself a profession, it becomes a monopoly in the public interest. The members of the occupation get the right to call others incompetents or quacks, and this enables the occupation to eliminate competition from outsiders and to validate its claim to be serving society in an honorable way. It can then insist on its mandate to do something important and claim the corresponding license[1] to do things differently from others. Further, since the work of a profession involves an essential service which no one else can perform, no one else can claim the right to tell the members of the profession how to do it or even how it should be evaluated. Consequently, professionals attain great autonomy and power. Still another advantage is that one can control entry, decide what the

[1]The concepts of "license" and "mandate" with reference to the professions were originally developed by Everett C. Hughes in "The Study of Occupations," in Robert K. Merton, Leonard Broom and Leonard S. Cottrell (eds.), *Sociology Today* (New York: Basic Books, 1959), Chap. 20.

qualifications of people who seek entry shall be, organize their training, and thus decide who one's colleagues are going to be. One gets to control the prices of one's services by the control of competition and influence on state and federal lawmakers, through professional associations and other pressure groups. One gets to control the behavior of the members of the occupation and hence is able to enforce standards and maintain whatever values the occupation thinks are desirable.

An Occupation by any Other Name . . .

So, we observe the tendency, described so well by Everett Hughes,[2] for the would-be professions to try to re-name themselves in the effort to upgrade their claims to professional rights. Commercial artists, appraisers, landscape planners, highway officers, morticians, photographers, piano teachers, radio and T.V. announcers, court reporters, travel agents, librarians, nurses, chiropractors, opticians, chemists, public-relations men, and even laborers, try to press their claim to be offering an honorable, self-sacrificing service to an otherwise deprived society which ought to reward them in the way that professionals deserve to be rewarded.

But as Harold Wilensky[3] has pointed out, although many seek professional recognition, only a small number succeed, and, perhaps, only a small number can. Evidence may be found in the observation that the attempts on the part of the would-be professions to make their case are often made in the context of public opposition, or opposition from the established professions. A librarian described her work as follows:

> The entire world's fund of information—now doubling in size every year—is our realm, and we must be able to call forth the most obscure fact rapidly and accurately, often with disaster simmering in the background. Recently, for example, in a Gulf coast town a volatile chemical broke loose from its container and flared up, threatening to destroy the dock area. The fire department put in an emergency call to the public library in order to find out the properties of the escaping liquid. With the information supplied by the library, the fire was quickly brought under control.
>
> In a large urban area . . . the library reference desks give out more than ten

[2]Everett C. Hughes, "Work and the Self," in J. H. Rohrer and Muzafer Sherif (eds.), *Social Psychology at the Crossroads* (New York: Harper, 1951).

[3]Harold L. Wilensky, "The Professionalization of Everyone?" *American Journal of Sociology,* 70, September, 1964, pp. 137–58.

million answers a year, answers that not only keep docks from burning, but bridges from collapsing, businesses from failing, and human beings from disintegrating.

The interesting point is that this justification was offered in an article entitled, "Don't Give Us Your Tired, Your Poor,"[4] The writer was protesting the tendency of vocational counselors and others to regard library work as a peaceful retreat for deadbeats and failures in other areas. So too, morticians have responded to the wholesale attack upon them in recent years by seeking to convince the public that they are "managers of grief."

Chiropractors have been driven, by opposition to what they call "the medical monopoly," into claiming that medical men really fear that chiropractors would put them out of business if given a fair chance. Hence, much of the case of the chiropractors is stated in ideological terms, appealing for simple justice for an oppressed minority, rather than trying to make their claim that they are a profession in scientific terms.

What seems to happen is that occupations that might otherwise, perhaps, be satisfied to stake out a limited claim, in which they would be prepared to compete with other occupations for an available market, find themselves pushed to extremes by the insistence of other professions that they are quacks and should be denied the right to compete at all. Their counter-defense becomes an exaggeration of their claims and often an argument on bases having little to do with any claim to specialized competence.

When the members of established professions deflate the pretensions of those who seek to share the professional stage with them, they see themselves as protecting the client from charlatans and insuring that the mandate to provide disinterested public service is not made a mockery of by these interlopers who desire to get on the gravy train. It is clear, however, that persons in the would-be professions do not see themselves in this light at all. They see the existing professions as holding an unwarranted monopoly which inevitably results in the public being more poorly served.

What is also clear is that the decision as to what shall be a profession and what shall not be takes the form of a political battle with appeals to legislatures to back up claims and to thrust down opposing claims. The decision will be made in terms of the balance of power rather than

[4]Margaret Bennett (pseud.), "Don't Give Us Your Tired, Your Poor," *Atlantic Monthly,* 215, May, 1965, p. 94.

in terms of a sober assessment of the ability of a particular group to provide the essential public services. At the very least it is not clear that the client will best be served by the outcome of such a battle.

Problems in Organization Practice

The established professions also have their troubles, mostly because they must practice in organizations. The physician in private practice, seeing one patient at a time, although providing us with one of the most appealing of models and one which has had an enormous amount of attention, was always and still is highly atypical. By contrast, social workers, accountants, airplane pilots, architects, clergymen, professors, dieticians, reporters, engineers, funeral directors, home economists, lawyers (in law offices or corporations), librarians, scientists, nurses, personnel workers, and teachers—all typically work for organizations, often for large ones.

Importing professionals into an organization means importing groups with a strong sense of identification. The members of the profession will have had a common educational experience. Whether this educational experience has been relevant or not, it has, at least, been a long one. In the process they will have been exposed to a set of values, which vary from profession to profession, but include a set of sensitivities and orientations to the client, to politics, and to other professions—particularly neighboring ones.

If a man has a graduate degree, then the value of the importance of pure research has certainly been transmitted to him. The graduate of a professional school (which includes graduate school) will also have a strong sense of his own competence, a feeling which will remain, whatever the evaluation of one's competence made by outsiders. For example, Kerckhoff[5] asked a sample of lawyers, clergymen, social workers and physicians to check which two professions, of nine listed, were best prepared to do marriage counseling today. The list included lawyers, clergymen, social workers, physicians and an occupation called "full-time counselor."

Strong Sense of Competence

He found that all four of the professions in the sample checked their own profession first, and all four checked full-time counselor second.

[5]Richard K. Kerckhoff, "Interest Group Reactions to the Profession of Marriage Counseling," *Sociology and Social Research,* 39, January-February, 1955, pp. 179–83.

In effect, they were saying the best qualified were obviously themselves in each case, and there really was no second choice, at least none of the other three professions constituted a genuine second choice. The lawyer, for example, implied that if you couldn't get to a lawyer, then you might as well go to a full-time counselor who would probably do you no harm. It was, at least, preferable to going to one of the other three.

A strong sense of competence is important because authority rests upon it. The professional in the last analysis has nothing else on which to base his authority. His authority is not charismatic, not based on tradition, nor on the occupancy, of a formal position. The strong sense of one's own competence will necessarily result in an unwillingness to accept orders or follow rules. Hence, the professional will insist that he knows best what is good for the client or patient and that the rules of the organization are just so much red tape that gets in the way of the attainment of professional goals.

Evaluation/Supervision Resisted

Nor is this the only type of conflict that professionals in organizations experience. They resist evaluation by anyone except their colleagues. Even then, the evaluation is likely to consist simply of an estimate of whether the person has followed "accepted professional practice," a standard which bears a suspicious resemblance to what in other contexts is called ritualism. Above all, professionals resist supervision, unless defined as professional supervision, as in the case of social work. Otherwise, supervisors are regarded as persons who have sold out, as in the case of nursing supervisors or academic administrators.

Professionals give further trouble in that they demand special rewards. They want money and power (to make all decisions about their own work), of course. In addition, they want the opportunity to gain professional recognition through attendance at professional meetings, memberships in their own organization, and the opportunity to do research, or to write and present papers. Doing these things requires time off from mundane labors. The loyalty to profession comes first. A chemist in a university feels the university to be little more than a set of facilities which he needs to carry on his work. In Alvin Gouldner's[6]

[6]Alvin W. Gouldner, "Cosmopolitans and Locals: Toward an Analysis of Latent Social Roles," *Administrative Science Quarterly*, 2, 1957–58, pp. 281–306 and 444–80.

words, he is a "cosmopolitan." Those who feel differently, for example, those who love old Siwash, are dubbed "locals."

The mood that animates most of the serious studies of professions can be clearly stated: professionalization is a good thing. The struggles on the part of occupations to develop a professional rationale, whether regarded with amusement, or even actively opposed, are certainly understood. Becoming a profession is, after all, simply one of the ways upward mobility takes place, and, in the United States, with the emphasis on success, one can hardly escape applauding the attempts of occupations to professionalize themselves.

In the process, they will surely examine themselves more carefully. Hence, little but good is likely to come of it, whether they succeed in the attempts or not. If they fail, it simply means that they are not ready yet. As public opinion polls show, the professions are highly respected and one can hardly criticize persons for seeking to be highly respected. In any case, it seems that a profession, by definition as a set of persons possessed of a large amount of knowledge and dedicated to public service, would be an ideal model for the organization of work.

So too, the literature on organizations, by its very emphasis on the conflict that the professionals face there, exhibits sympathy for the professional. It sees him as a disinterested craftsman, seeking to serve mankind in the face of opposition from organizations. The professional is shown to be interested in pure things—such as knowledge and the clients. On the other hand, organizations have only class interests, such as money. To that end, they do not stop at controlling and submerging the free flow of information, and limiting individual freedom and creativity. The professional is seen as a fighter for individual rights in the face of the giant octopus which seeks to destroy him. But there is another kind of conflict that professionals experience in organizations, which, when examined, suggests a revision of this positive view of professionalization. Perhaps conflict does professions some good, and when it does not, perhaps it is time to look for a different model for the organization of work.

Professional Monopoly Claims

Professions not only meet "the organization" in organizations, but also meet other professions. And here the claims of monopoly that a particular profession makes runs into stiff resistance from the counter-claims of other professions. For example, a study, by Zander[7] and others, of psychiatrists, clinical psychologists, and psychiatric social workers reported considerable conflict between them. Conflict was particularly likely when a clinical psychologist disputed the psychiatrist's claim to be the only person entitled to perform psychotherapy on the patient. He was happy to work with the clinical psychologist provided the latter would stay in his role as a person who performed tests. Conflict with the social worker was considerably less serious, partly because the division of labor was clearer. Nor did the social worker dispute either the psychologist's or the psychiatrist's claim to monopoly of psychotherapeutic competence.

Dying Patients: Nurses vs. Physicians

A study by Glaser and Strauss[8] of dying patients gives a picture of continuous conflict between nurses and physicians. Physicians avoid dealing with the dying patient for a variety of reasons, among which are the desire to avoid a nasty scene with relatives, and to avoid an affront to the physician's image of himself as a healer. They therefore relegate this piece of dirty work to the nurse, often without telling her. Nurses react with resentment and make use of the rationalization which many of the helping professions use when they describe themselves—they see themselves as saving the physician from his own mistakes and from his incompetence.

There is also conflict between professionals and the non-professional service staff. This is likely to be especially common in therapeutic institutions wherein a non-professional staff forms a part of the therapy, as in the case of the therapeutic community, or milieu therapy. One study[9] of five such treatment facilities for delinquent boys uncovered an almost continuous battle between the two groups. For

[7]Alvin Zander, Arthur Cohen, Ezra Stotland and Collaborators, "Average Attitudes of One Professional Group Toward Another," reprinted from a 1957 publication in Howard M. Vollmer and Donald L. Mills (eds.), *Professionalization* (Englewood Cliffs, N.J.: Prentice-Hall, 1966), pp. 237–43. See also Alvin Zander, Arthur R. Cohen and Ezra Stotland, "Power and the Relations Among Professions," in Dorwin Cartwright (ed.), *Studies in Social Power,* Ann Arbor: University of Michigan, 1959, Chap. 2.

[8]Barney G. Glaser and Anselm L. Strauss, *Awareness of Dying* (Chicago: Aldine Publishing Co., 1965).

[9]George H. Weber, "Conflicts between Professional and Nonprofessional Personnel in Institutional Delinquency Treatment," reprinted from a 1957 publication in Howard M. Vollmer and Donald L. Mills (eds.), *Professionalization, op. cit.*, pp. 251–61.

example, a psychiatrist discussed a cottage mother's management of a boy in the following terms,

Mrs. S. wants Bobby punished for his stealing, immediately, she isn't interested in studying it more thoroughly. She says that if he did it, he should be punished and then he has paid his debt. If anyone expresses any other ideas on it, she feels her position is seriously threatened. If pressed on the matter, she'll take her feelings out on the boy.

But a cottage parent, in turn said,

It's fine and easy for (those) people working up in the administration building to come at eight o'clock, leave at five and have a half-day off on Saturday, but we cottage parents are with the boys all the time.

Another cottage parent said,

That guy who calls himself a psychologist is so busy with what he calls psychopathology and working in therapy that he doesn't know the rest of the world the kid lives in . . . (He) only (has) to deal with one boy at a time and he is putting his best foot forward most of the time when he is up seeing them.

Yet another form of conflict which is often not recognized as one which professionals meet in organizations is created by a group who reject the professional model, but who do not see themselves as oriented to organizational goals, nor as non-professionals performing a service function. I refer here to those who adopt what Smith[10] names the "calling model." These are persons who are oriented to the client as a good in himself. Examples here are the social workers who reject the professional's model as being too much hung up on status, and who see the agency as just a lot of rules and red tape, but instead see themselves as "the only one around here who seems to be interested in the client." A similar orientation is provided by those who remind us that the term "principal" is, after all, short for "principal teacher." Other examples are the nurse who keeps reminding her colleagues how important it is to prescribe TLC, those that have ideological orientations, who are carrying on a special mission, or who represent ethnic groups or minority races.

Professionals do not enjoy these kinds of conflicts. It could hardly be otherwise. It is bad enough to have one's plans disputed by the organization itself, but there may be ways of fighting the organization. It is more difficult to battle other professions that are as established as

[10]Edmond A. Smith, *Social Welfare Principles and Concepts* (New York: Association Press, 1965).

yours is, and you have no alternative but to deal with non-professionals, whose services you must have. The physician may be annoyed by the persnickityness of the lab technician but he has no alternative but to make use of the hospital and the many non-professionals he finds there. The social work supervisor may be upset by the non-professional attitudes of the social workers whom he supervises, some of whom let their humanitarian impulses carry them away. But he is stuck with the galling fact that only about 30 per cent of the paid social workers in the U.S. belong to the National Association of Social Workers. It is estimated that only about 16 per cent have had the full graduate two-year curriculum and another 11 per cent have had some graduate training. Of the remainder, some 60 per cent have had no study at all in a graduate school of social work. Hence the supervisor had better use these persons whether he likes it or not.

Conflict Is Unavoidable

Nobody likes all this conflict, and everyone complains about it, or hides it from the outsider. But, a strong case can be made that this conflict is desirable both for the professions and for organizations. The literature in industrial sociology has documented extensively the danger of viewing manager-worker conflict, for example, as due to lack of mutual understanding. It has been shown that conflict is unavoidable in organizations because there are large differences of interests. There are only so many good hours, so many favorite locations, and so many desirable duties in an organization. There is only so much money, and so much prestige. When some get more, others get less. In organizations, it would be a safe conclusion that the administrator who insists he does not have conflict is simply not being told about it.

Conflict Can Be Functional

Lewis Coser, in his classic work on conflict,[11] makes the case that conflict can also be functional in providing boundary maintenance and in increasing group cohesiveness. It is possible to go further and point out that conflict can also be creative. It is not simply that conflict leads to problems being solved, as Coser (elaborating on Simmel), points out. For an open battle may simply be resolved by victory going to the stronger, not to the more deserving or the more correct. Conflict can be a way of creatively solving problems if it takes place in a context in

[11]Lewis Coser, *The Functions of Social Conflict* (Glencoe, Ill.: Free Press, 1956).

which it is institutionalized and in which the rules make certain the conflict is a fair one with the sides being permitted to make their case as strongly as possible.

The ideal situation, of course, is the courtroom in our society. It is not assumed that truth is obvious or that it lies wholly on one side or the other. The only way (it doesn't always work) of getting some idea of where truth lies is to provide a situation in which the two opponents each attempt to knock down the ideas of the other. A similar model is evident in science where it is assumed that the only way of testing an hypothesis, apart from gathering data for it, is to deliberately try to knock it down with contrary data. When many try and fail, the hypothesis is felt to have withstood the criticism test.

Conflict, when it takes the form of public criticism of the ideas of colleagues, will also serve the important function of drawing attention to these ideas. Alex Simirenko[12] calls this effect, in connection with Soviet criticisms of Western ideas in Soviet journals, "creative debunking." His point is that a device for channeling information from the outside world to the Soviet reader in a fashion that will not disturb the foundations of the Soviet system is to do so through a searing criticism of these foreign ideas. In order that the reader can understand what ideas are being criticized, it is clearly necessary to present the ideas first. If the foreign ideas are particularly important and therefore deserving of serious criticism, then it becomes all the more necessary to describe the foreign ideas in greater detail so that their many weaknesses can be gone into.

In a like manner, the criticism and the conflict which professionals experience in organizations, particularly from other professions (and from non-professionals as well as from others that we have described) may be of direct assistance to the professionals themselves, however unpleasant the professionals themselves may find it. It may also be of benefit to the organization. Often administrators, in their alarm about such conflict, express the wish that "professionals, non-professionals and all others will cooperate." And yet since the professions believe strongly in their own unique competence, their "cooperation" with other professions as well as with non-professions will often take the *form* of a battle. It is only through the results of such a battle that the real contribution that each profession can make may be discovered.

[12]In a paper delivered at meetings of the Pacific Sociological Society, April, 1966, Vancouver, B.C.

Administrators and Conflict Control

The important point is that the administrator cannot tell what the probable contribution of the nurse, the aide, the physiotherapist, the psychiatrist, the social worker or the dietician might be by asking them. If he should, they will assert the common professional claim of exclusive knowledge, and proceed to knock the others. How then is the administrator to discover just what the contributions of each might be? The most obvious answer is by letting them fight it out to prove what their contributions can be and ought to be. The administrator's task becomes that of controlling the terms of the conflict to be sure that the leading contenders' points of view and potential contribution are heard.

The same thing is true of research ideas in industry, whose value can only be discovered by providing an arena in which they can be criticized. In order to make sure that the criticism is a good one, it is necessary to have other professionals with different ideas and particularly those who dispute the research man's claim to exclusive competence. The social work administrator will similarly find that neither the social worker with a sense of calling, nor the fresh graduate out of social work school, necessarily have the full answer as to how the client ought to be treated. The client may well best be served by a temporary truce between these persons, the terms of which can hardly be settled by any other process than conflict between them. This is not to say that one or the other will be victorious for the conflict is continuous and will be represented, at any given time, by partial ascendancy of one or the other.

The Dangers of Exclusiveness

It is also possible that conflict, providing it is engineered and controlled, may be of assistance to the professions themselves for it may be that they are being hurt by the very autonomy and professionalism which is so dear to them. To begin with, there is their restrictiveness. In their claims of autonomy and monopoly, professions run into the criticism which many have made that they tend to adopt a craft-union restrictionism. Professions are not much disturbed at this criticism since it is simply another way of saying that they feel an exclusive competence. But the claim of exclusiveness may itself produce a dilemma, taking the following form.

On the one hand, the profession performs functions vital and essential to society. This is the basis for its mandate and for its claim that it deserves privileges. On the other hand, the profession also insists that it is the only agency which can perform the function—that all others are incompetent or quacks. Yet this very insistence on exclusiveness creates the danger that the essential, vital need which they are supposed to supply may not be best supplied by them. It may be supplied well at one time, but poorly handled at a different time. Yet the claim of monopolistic exclusiveness will remain, thus preventing the need from being met at all. In time, a process of deprofessionalization may set in through which the professional activity is broken up and assigned to other professionals or even to non-professionals.

Examples of Deprofessionalization

Something like this may be happening to counseling psychology. The Poverty Program created an enormous need for guidance counselors in the many centers created by that program. The Manpower Administration turned to counseling psychologists for assistance in meeting this need. The response, however, was that it would be difficult to meet the need because of the very extensive training which was necessary for a fully professional counselor—university graduation, a master's degree (preferably more), clinical training, and so forth. The government therefore set up its own program, known as CAUSE, through which counselors were produced in twelve weeks. There were two such programs, in successive summers, resulting in the training of a large number of counselors, who then went to work in Youth Opportunity Centers, as well as other places in which counselors were needed. The evidence so far is that they seem to be working out quite well. It would be hard to imagine anything more threatening to professional integrity. Of course the "counselors" are not fully professional, but they are doing some professional tasks. The case illustrates the possibility that a profession can be *too* vital to the point where the profession is no longer permitted the exclusive right to handle the activity.

Producing a Trained Incapacity to Act

Another example illustrates the possibility that a profession, in its very emphasis on a particular kind of professional training, may produce a trained incapacity to handle a need when it occurs. Social workers who have been trained in graduate schools of social work often discover they are called upon to perform activities which are "unprofessional." I refer, for example, to the clerical activities incidental to establishing eligibility for benefits, or the exploits of "night raiders'' (who spend their time seeing whether a male stranger shows up in the home of an AFDC recipient who claims that she has no husband). Since the professionally trained social worker refuses to do these things, they will be handled by others. The social worker, in turn, will try to move into situations in which she can practice the skills for which she has undergone such a long period of training, as in a family agency or a hospital where she can practice case-work.

In the Youth Opportunity Centers, counselors find that a high percentage of their clients are Negroes, Puerto Ricans, Indians, migrants and other such distinct groups. In general, the whole approach through bureaucratic government offices does not work very well with them. They are highly suspicious of such institutions and impatient at explanations in terms of ''Automation,'' regarding such explanations as a dodge, because they see that they are rejected for jobs that they know they are qualified for. They are distrustful of training programs since the payoff is in the future and they know that often these programs do not work for them because unions or others will simply not let them go to work even when they have the proper training.

Counselors in the Youth Opportunity Centers, as a consequence, often report that clients from these groups are passive, perceiving the counselor as simply another adult to be manipulated, and hence cooperating little—or no more than they feel is necessary. A common problem is the tendency of clients to refuse to show up for appointments or to come in late and then to feel rejected if they cannot be taken immediately on their arrival. Many clients perceive the counselor as a policeman, as ''Charley''—that is, the white man, who stands in the way, rather than the person who can be helpful. Counselors also raise the question of how they should handle the discovery of illegal activities. Of course, counselors in general are confronted with this problem but what is special about these populations is that the probability of discovering crime and other quasi-legal activities is considerably higher. A report from a group of counselors in New York City expressed particular alarm at the amount of narcotic-pushing which clients referred to. In view of the fact that the counselor's records can be subpoenaed by the courts, what should the counselor do in trying to provide assurances of confidence to the client? Another problem is that of getting to the clients themselves. The model of the client who refers himself to the counselor for assistance does not apply often to these underprivileged populations. Indeed, partly because they are suspicious of those in the program and their motives and partly because they simply may not care, it is often necessary for the counselor to assume an active role in soliciting the client and motivating him to come in to see him. The program known as Project Outreach in the Youth Opportunity Centers specifically provides that counselors shall make some attempt to move directly into the ethnic community and make themselves available or provide other motivations for persons to come forth.

Some of these problems may be handled through changes in the training of counselors. For example, special courses at universities might be offered dealing with the cultural characteristics of these groups or special lectures on the subject might be given in conjunction with regular courses which counselors in training take. A great deal of work needs to be done in the development of special tests which make little use of verbal materials and tests which do not require knowledge of English.

Untenable Assumptions

The Community Action Program approach under the Office of Economic Opportunity is a step in that direction. Through CAP, the attempt is made to involve the minority group itself in the direction of programs to serve that group. As is well known the approach has met strong opposition in local communities from other members of the local power structure. But what is needed is a direct recognition of the *organized character of the clients* with whom the Employment Service deals. When attempting to deal with these clients—according to traditional counseling conceptions, one at a time and assuming that the client voluntarily presents himself for a service which he desires, and presents himself to a professional whose authority he respects—*none of these assumptions is tenable*. A wholesale revision of the counseling approach so that it is adapted to the group character of the client would seem to be necessary. The leadership of these groups may have to be brought directly into the planning program as employment offices are set up. They may have to be involved directly in counseling itself, in the form of the use of counselors who are also members of the groups, in careful follow-ups of the experiences of placed clients with the help of the minority top leadership itself and other measures of this kind.

When we shift to the very top of the prestige scale, we see some big changes in the role of physicians. A number of studies have shown that the ratio between physicians and population (or potential patients) in the United States is declining, and that per capita service is low in comparison to other countries. And it can be fairly easily shown that there is a crisis in the availability of physicians. Confronted, then, with the classically insoluble problem of rapidly increasing the supply of professional labor in the short run, persons advocate crash programs to train physicans rapidly, meanwhile attacking the conservatism of the American Medical Association.

Social Organization Is Changing

There seems little question of the need to increase the supply of physicians, and rapidly. But estimates of the *numbers required* may be wide of the mark unless account is taken of the fact that the social organization of medical practice is changing. Physicians are simply not being used in the way they used to be. The "physician per population" ratios are the equivalent, at the statistics level, of the celebrated "physician-patient relationship." But what is clear is that the relationship is changing, to be replaced by the model of the health care team. This new social organization includes nurse, physiotherapist, diagnostician, surgeon, lab technician, social worker, psychologist, inhalation therapist, prosthetic technician, electronic data processing specialist, and, with the looming development of organ and mechanical transplants, engineer and mechanic.

Shortages or surpluses in any one of these occupations can be created not only by shifts in need but also by shifts in the way the health care team is organized. The shortage of doctors may be solved, then, in much the same way as the United States solved its "servant problem": we create a new way of organizing the activity which makes us less dependent on the occupation. Evidence from studies of who shows up at emergency admission offices in hospitals between the hours of five in the afternoon and eight in the morning indicates that a high proportion are simply persons seeking a doctor for conditions which are not acute or of an emergency character. Perhaps, then, it is not necessary to lament the decline of the general practitioner and to seek means to increase his number. Rather, we should ask how the hospital can do better, what it is beginning to do: serve as the center for general practice.

Forecasts Drop in Status for Doctors

It is not implied that the physician is about to be de-professionalized, but it is implied that changes in the status of the physician are quite likely. In addition to the phenomenon of over-exclusiveness that I have described, which has incapacitated the physician to meet the need, and which has led, partly, to a wholesale reorganization of the whole health care activity, other changes will affect the status of the physician. The patient himself is changing in status. Middle-class patients are better educated and in a better position to put pressure on physicians. Many working-class patients are able to coerce service through their unions and other group-sponsored organizations. In addition, the militancy of the poor and ethnic groups in recent years, developments such as Medicare and other group insurance arrangements further reduce the power of the physician. As physicians are forced to work with other professionals, especially in hospitals, they will come under the close scrutiny of other professionals. Then, as the physician takes his place as one of the elements in the division of labor we call ''medical care,'' a reasonable forecast is that he will drop from his position at the top of the prestige hierarchy.

Other Advantages of Conflict

There are other ways conflict will result in improvement in professional service. When professionals insist on the fight to evaluate themselves, there is the danger they will evaluate themselves too highly and therefore, many who need their service will be unable to afford it. By building in conflict, professionals will be forced to lower their fees or else competitors will take away their clients. There is evidence, for example, that chiropractors have taken away a good deal of the business which physicians used to have in small towns, mainly because physicians have left such towns. Or group practice may be organized in such a way as to lower the cost to the patients.

The claims to exclusive competence that professionals make may have to be revised when they are forced to associate with other professionals. Although the psychologist will resent working with the psychiatrist and vice versa, when they must work with each other, they may very well discover that they can be helpful to one another. A physician may find that a good hospital administrator, far from being a source of red tape, is a godsend that enables him to do his work much faster.

Competition with other professionals may lead to overcoming rigidities that professions seem to develop. In the Soviet Union, there are 332,440 women doctors and surgeons and 379,000 women engineers. In the United States, there are only 16,000 women doctors and a mere handful of engineers. When one profession meets another and discovers that its claim that only men can perform some activity is belied by the fact that a related activity is performed by women, these ideas may be revised. For example, the nursing profession is beginning to see the value of having male nurses, not simply to do the dirty work but also because men will act to raise the status of the profession. Men will not for long put up with low salaries and long hours. Social work agencies are slowly recognizing that being a male does not automatically assure one of competence as a supervisor. Partly this is due to the increased use by social work agencies of professionals other than psychiatrists. In the 1920's, when social workers looked around for a body of knowledge on which they could base their claim to be a profession, they took over psychological and psychoanalytic theory intact. It was often, therefore, felt appropriate that a man should be supervisor since he could serve for "transference" and as a father-figure. Contact with sociologists has led some administrators to the conclusion that it is possible that there are some organizational functions which an administrator can perform, and that women may be quite as good at these as men.

Competing professions in organizations provide each other with important sources of evaluation of competence. The professions, of course, insist that they can and must police their own deviants. The evidence we have, though, shows they seem to do a poor job of it.[13] The major technique for handling deviants is to stop referring clients to them and that is obviously a slow and inefficient way of doing it. When a professional meets other professionals or professionals who are his supervisors, or non-professionals with whom he must work, a much better job of evaluation and identification of incompetence will occur. Hospital administrators are now routinely requiring an examination of tissue removed by surgeons to estimate whether the tissue is normal or not and, therefore, whether the operation was actually necessary. Such evaluation will, of course, be resented by professions but it would seem to be in the long-run interests of professions to have inadequate competence taken care of, and rapidly. To do otherwise is to invite the possibility of more severe controls.

Conclusion

In the last analysis, these are the only ways of insuring high quality service to the client. The professional insists that his training and internalized service norms will make sure that the client is well served. It is

[13]See, for example, Eliot Freidson and Buford Rhea, "Knowledge and Judgment in Professional Evaluations," *Administrative Science Quarterly,* 10, June, 1965, 107–24.

sometimes hard to distinguish this claim from a mere self-serving attitude. One way to make sure that the client is well served is to subject the professional to the test of the organization, where he meets other professionals and where he must prove his competence, where he meets organization demands which provide standards of judgement, force him to ask himself whether he's doing the job as well as it can be done, and force him to see how valuable is the help that he receives from other professionals, non-professionals, and from the organization itself, with its richness of facilities and its legitimation in the community. So it may be that the conflict which the professionals lament so much may be the means whereby they can continue to maintain their professional rights.

A Philosophical Dimension of Administration

Leonard A. Duce, Ph.D.

The title of a recent book, *The Age of Analysis,*[1] seems to summarize fairly succinctly the dominant intellectual characteristic of our time. As never before, the human mind subjects everything, including itself, to scientific scrutiny, seeking, as it were, "to cut everything at the grain" so as to understand it better and to manipulate it more effectively. The various types of administration have not escaped the scalpel. They have been analyzed into many phases and stages. Out of the analysis have come such well-known terms as "communications," "human relations," "leadership," "operations research," "management engineering," "problem-solving," "organizational structure and function," *ad infinitum*. Not for a moment would I belittle the analysis or suggest that these terms do not refer to real and important factors of administration. They are significant results of the attempts to conceptualize a very complex process—and as such, need to be understood and taken seriously. However, these analytic terms do have their limitations.

First, there is the danger of seeing in one or two of them an ultimate description of administrative activity, to which all other concepts are secondary. It is easy, for example, to be so impressed by the importance of "human relations" that administration is reduced to a kind of sentimental attempt to keep everyone happy or to be so taken with "management engineering" that the administrator forgets that the medium in which he works is always human nature with its fallibility and unpredictability.

Second, there is the danger of conceptualizing the administrative process so analytically that the relation between the various concepts is overlooked. It is not enough to assimilate these concepts and to learn the procedures they entail. They must be organized into some mean-

[1]Morton White, Editor, *The Age of Analysis,* New York: Mentor Books, New American Library, 1955.

ingful whole. Otherwise the essential unity and simplicity of administration are destroyed. It is easy to lose sight of the forest because of the concern for the trees.

Semantic Trap

Third, descriptions of important aspects of administration are verbal and must not be identified with what they describe. This is a semantic trap peculiarly characteristic of our contemporary culture. In the intellectualizing of the administrative process for the purpose of understanding and teaching "principles of administration" we talk freely, and sometimes rather vaguely, of the "science" of administration. Likewise, in the discussion of the "activities of administration we refer honorifically to the "art" of administration. Since we have desired to give administration the status of a profession, it has been important to assure ourselves that there are a body of knowledge and a set of skills sufficiently well defined to warrant this status for administration. Moreover, "science" and "art" are laudatory words in the contemporary semantic situation and bestow a kind of prestige wherever they can be used with some relevance, however tenuous. Although they have validity as generalizations of different aspects of the administrative process, as exemplifications of its complexity, and as descriptions of its various strands of thought, decision, and action, their verbal acceptance does not make us successful administrators.

It is becoming increasingly apparent that these analyses must be related to a more comprehensive view of administration, in at least two ways. First, we must develop an understanding of the total process of administration, into which these various aspects may be fitted and which will give them a ground and a goal. Administration is an organic activity, in which the whole is always more than, and in some sense prior to, the parts. To have some grasp of that "wholeness" is as essential as knowing what to do in particular situations and mastering specific skills for distinguishable aspects of administration.

Second, underneath our specific knowledge and skill and their implementation, there are certain basic ideas and attitudes which only occasionally do we consciously relate to our administrative activity, but which, nevertheless, determine the success or failure of that activity perhaps more than our deliberate application of administrative science and art. I refer to our fundamental outlook upon and our basic ideas of, man, society, the institutions we administer, and ourselves as men and administrators.

Subtle Distinction

If it is examined carefully the phrase "the philosophy of administration" has another duality of meaning which must be recognized. It may refer to "the philosophical examination of administration" or to "the philosophical aspects of administrative activity." The former is an intellectual enterprise directed at administration, while the latter consists of intellectual activity within administration. The difference is a subtle one, and yet failure to recognize it is the source of much confusion in contemporary literature. Marshall Dimmock's *A Philosophy of Administration*[2] is illustrative of the way a writer can move from one meaning to the other, sometimes knowingly and sometimes unconsciously. At times his term "a philosophy of administration" refers to a way of thinking *about* administration and at other times to a level of thinking necessary within administration. The two interpretations are obviously related. It is doubtful whether one can think philosophically *as* an administrator unless he has thought philosophically *about* administration. On the other hand, the latter does not necessarily entail the former. One can think scientifically or philosophically *about* administration and still be very unscientific or unphilosophical *in* his administrative activity. There are emotional and existential dimensions of *thinking within,* which are not necessarily present in *thinking about*.

In our consideration the emphasis will be on thinking *within* administration but will also involve some necessary thinking *about* administration. We shall examine "a philosophical dimension of administration," with reference to both understanding what administration is and engaging effectively in it. The word "dimension" is used advisedly. A dimension is a level of expression or a frame of reference. It is not something added to whatever has it, but a pervasive quality which somehow determines the nature of its possessor. The term, "philosophical dimension of administration," refers to a specific level of thinking necessary to administrative effectiveness. Without it, administration is either a kind of intuitive, "seat-of-the-pants" activity or a prosaic, clerical subservience to rules and regulations. While the former may be occasionally successful, it usually makes for arbitrariness and unpredictability. The latter leads to dullness, monotony, and ultimate frustration. At this point I find myself in complete agreement

[2]Marshall E. Dimmock, *A Philosophy of Administration,* New York: Harper and Brothers, 1958.

with Dimmock when he writes concerning the activity of decision-making:

> If the decision cannot be related to a grand-strategy philosophy it will have to be related to something else.
>
> All too often the alternative is rules and procedures, which when not understood in their ultimate significance result in behavior by rote. . . . The rote person becomes dull and discouraged. The organization loses its zip and its spontaneity. Customers complain about rigid rules and unfeeling employees. . . .
>
> The only sure solution is to give people at all levels a sense of mission, an understanding of interrelations, and a compelling sense of overall objectives and values. If this means, as I think it does, that the only sure way of keeping an organization viable and progressive is to see that people at all levels are encouraged to develop a philosophy of administration, then the sensible thing to do is to institute measures which will bring about this desired result.[3]

Meaning of Philosophy

For the purpose of our discussion then, the word "philosophy" will be used to refer to that kind of thinking which is concerned with a fundamental understanding of human experience in general, or of some particular phase of it, and with the relation of that understanding to our own behavior. This meaning of philosophy goes back at least as far as Socrates. Plato has immortalized Socrates' defense of his philosophical activity in the Dialogue, *The Apology*. Among the words of the gadfly of Athens to his judges are these:

> Someone will say: Yes, Socrates, but cannot you hold your tongue, and then you may go into a foreign city, and no one will interfere with you? Now I have great difficulty in making you understand my answer to this. For I tell that to do as you say would be a disobedience to the God, and therefore, that I cannot hold my tongue, you will not believe that I am serious; and if I say again that daily to discourse about virtue, and of those other things about which you hear me examining myself and others, is the greatest good of men, and that the *unexamined life is not worth living,* you are still less likely to believe me. Yet what I say is true although a thing of which it is hard for me to persuade you.[4]

Socrates was driven by a need to get behind the superficial notions and the superstitious myths which went under the label of "knowledge" in his day. He was convinced that only truth can be the suffi-

[3] *Ibid.*, p. 6.

[4] Plato, "The Apology," *The Dialogues of Plato,* Great Books of the Western World, Chicago: Encyclopaedia Britannica, 1952, p. 210.

cient guide for effective personal and social living. For this reason he probed everything and everyone, perchance to glean a little knowledge here and a little understanding there, which when put together might make sense of human existence and its various activities.

In its essential expressions, philosophy still has this central *motif.* While it has developed many technical sidelines, such as the analysis of language and the construction of abstract metaphysical systems, its central effort has been to find in, or to give to, human experience and activity some kind of rational structure. Abraham Kaplan recently wrote,

> To describe a man's philosophy is to say how he orients himself to the world of his experience, what meaning he finds in events, what values he aspires to, what standards guide his choices and all he does.[5]

Through the centuries since Socrates, philosophical thinking has taken many forms, some of which have developed their own specific methodologies to the point where they have become separate disciplines. Thus, most of the sciences owe their existence to philosophical endeavor although, like many human children, they either repudiate their parentage or look upon it with condescension and scorn. Interestingly enough, the very scientific specialists who reveal this attitude do not hesitate to make assumptions about life in general and even about their own disciplines which could stand some of the philosophical thinking they shrug off so cavalierly. Like the Sophists of Socrates' day they seem to be unaware that their specialized knowledge, wonderful and practical as it is, does not safeguard them from uncriticized generalizations or contemporary myths.

Philosophy and Ideology

Perhaps we can get at the notion of philosophy if we remember another word which has great vogue today, "ideology." Often "philosophy" and "ideology" are used synonymously. While both of them signify some kind of basic and systematic understanding, when used precisely they are completely different, and this difference is central to our discussion.

An ideology is a system of ideas accepted without serious examination. It is not worked out critically and creatively by the individual or

[5]Abraham Kaplan, *The New World of Philosophy,* New York: Vintage Books, Random House, 1963, p. 4.

the group which gives it allegiance, but it is taken in an *a priori* fashion—as a set of axioms which *must not* be questioned and which must be *adhered to and obeyed,* no matter what.

There are many ideologies in our present world, but two kinds are peculiarly relevant to our discussion; first, the kind that is forced upon people by some authority, and second, the kind that insinuates itself, out of the general culture or the mood of the time, into the minds of individuals and into the thinking of groups. The most graphic illustration of the first kind is to be found in Communism today. The ideology of Karl Marx is taken as the absolute and only set of ideas to which all Communists must give complete allegiance. The other kind of ideology is illustrated by all sorts of ideas which come to us from the culture, the social milieu, and the prevailing thought-forms of our day. Ideas which are part of our common experience and training become ideological when they are accepted uncritically as authoritative and necessary ways of thought. When they are so accepted they become straight-jackets for our living, producing stereotypes in whatever area of activity we project them. In other words, there is within each one of us a set of basic ideas which has been developed from our cultural background, our educational experience, and our successes and failures in human relations of every sort. These are ideological if we do not examine them or if we allow ourselves to be governed by them uncritically and unthinkingly. Thus, even well-formulated interpretations of administration may become ideologies if we accept them as absolute or final without putting them through the mill of our own evaluative thinking.

Internal Vitality

Philosophy differs radically from ideology, for it is always the product of critical examination and creative thought. Ideology imposes itself upon our minds, while philosophy is the product of our minds. Ideology is not rational or deliberate; philosophy is deliberately rational. Ideology gets its power from sources external to the person accepting it; philosophy has its vitality from within the person creating it. From Socrates to the present, genuine philosophers have fought against ideology and against the ideological acceptance by others of their own philosophical creations. The Stoics said that every man should be a philosopher and went on to define the philosopher as one who should do his own thinking and do it as rationally as possible. Plato insisted that men should be governed by philosophers, that is, by men who developed a *techne,* a creative understanding of themselves, their society and their world. In a recent book, contemporary philosopher Henry Aiken writes, "Philosophy . . . [is] that primordial activity whereby self-respecting men seek to come to terms, not only with the ends of science or of art or of government, but with their own individual destinies."[6] Philosophy may be systematic or it may be unsystematic, but it is always the philosopher's own attempt to give to experience and reality some kind of rational meaning.

In the light of this definition of philosophy let us look first at what might be called "philosophy in general for hospital administration." Here we are concerned with certain philosophical possibilities in our thought of and attitude toward (a) society and its constituent structures; (b) man or human nature; (c) the hospital and the institution to which you are committed.

As an aid to our discussion, may I suggest that possible views of each of these areas of concern arrange themselves upon a scale, with extremes at each end and between them many intermediary positions. We can delineate only the extreme views and what seems to be the most creative position between them. Note that this third position always involves a kind of balance or "dynamic-tension" between whatever truth there is in the extreme views.

Society

By society I mean, in general, the totality of human relations in the midst of which we work, and, in particular, the organized patterns of social life which form the background of our work. Society itself is the sum of human relations and the complex of organizations by which these relations are expressed. How we look at society and how we relate ourselves to it are central determinants of our basic ideas and attitudes, that is, of our philosophy. The two extreme views of society and the intermediate positions are:

(1) *Collectivism,* the view according to which the totality of society rather than its members is the dominant reality. This is the philosophy espoused by communism and fascism. It is also the determinate ideology of "the organization man," where the totality is that of the particular organization rather than society at large. Collectivism may be

[6]Henry D. Aiken, "The Fate of Philosophy in the Twentieth Century," *Philosophy in the Twentieth Century,* William Barrett and Henry D. Aiken, editors, New York: Random House, 1962, Vol. 1, p. 17.

described in some such terms as, "the individual exists for society, not society for the individual;" "the state is more real and more important than the citizen;" "the organization must take precedence over its members," etc.

(2) *Individualism* is the philosophy that both the totality of society and its various organizations are subordinate in reality and value to the individuals within them. We have often called this attitude, "rugged individualism." It is best exemplified in modern France, although we have much vocal expression of it in our own country.

(3) *Democracy* is the philosophy that individuals, organizations, and the totality are equally important and must be kept in creative tension with each other. It recognizes that human life has ineradicable social and individual qualities, neither of which can be depreciated without serious consequences.

These are not merely theories of states, but basic interpretations of society. Whichever view we hold tends to determine our attitudes and activities not only toward society in general but also toward those organizations in which we participate administratively.

Man

By man, I am referring to human nature. We may not be aware of it, but we do have a fundamental view of man in terms of which we orientate ourselves to individual men. To make this view deliberate and thoughtful is an essential phase of the philosophical dimension of administration. It is undoubtedly this fact which has prompted so much emphasis on human relations in recent literature on administration—but unfortunately much of this literature has concentrated on the technique of human relations rather than on the concept of man which must underlie these techniques.

May I again suggest that our interpretations of human nature fall into three categories, two of which represent extremes and the third a creative and mediating view.

(1) *Cynicism* views man as undependable, perverse, irrational, selfish, and insignificant. Its essence has often been stated, "You must always expect the worst from men," or "never trust anyone but yourself," etc.

(2) *Idealism* interprets man as essentially honest, altruistic, reasonable, dependable, and therefore, perfectible. It sees human nature as good, that is, as either actually or potentially oriented more to virtue than to vice, more to value than to disvalue.

(3) *Realism* recognizes man as a complex being, a strange combination of the demonic and the divine, impelled by irrational and selfish drives but driven by impulses to reason and to nobility.

(Selekman has given us a suggestive treatment of the first two views, which he calls "cynicism" and "perfectionism" respectively.[7])

If we are fundamentally cynical about men, our cynicism will inevitably reveal itself in our administrative relationships, no matter what other superficial theory we may profess. Moreover, such belief about human nature usually results in an authoritarian type of administration, just as the collective view of society leads to some form of dictatorial administration. On the other hand, idealism eventuates in lack of leadership and disorganization, for there is a close correlation between idealism and individualism, just as there is between cynicism and collectivism. Genuine realism is a recognition in man of both the qualities which call for organization and control and the qualities which demand the delegation of authority and the encouragement of creative freedom. In other words, it is the correlative of the democratic view of society.

The Hospital

It would be presumptuous of me to dwell at length on the hospital. Certainly I shall not attempt to define it or its functions. Again, however, I should like to go behind the usual discussions of the institution to three possible evaluative attitudes toward it, the ideological or philosophical importance of which we do not normally recognize.

(1) *The hospital as an institution is an end in itself, more important than the patients who are served or the professional men who serve or the employees who help to keep it running effectively*. As in the collectivist view of society, so here, the strictly human is depreciated except as it contributes to the prestige or reputation of the institution. It may seem strange to say that this view, like the glorification of big business, represents a kind of cynicism, but if we examine it carefully we discover readily enough that it contradicts the humanistic motives which brought the hospital into existence and which have made it an essential arm of society.

(2) *The hospital is not an end in itself, but exists for the individuals who receive medical care and for the persons who find vocational*

[7]Benjamin Selekman, *A Moral Philosophy for Management*, New York: McGraw-Hill, 1959.

expression through it. Indeed, it is nothing more than these services to individuals; its importance as an institution is practically nil.

(3) *The hospital is an arm of society serving both individuals and society*. It is an institution which *cannot be reduced to the sum of the persons and things which make it up and yet which serves these persons both for their own sake and for the sake of society as a whole*. It is society at one place and in one form—a democratic expression of the mutual relation between society and man in the area of sickness and health.

Changing Social Interest

This third interpretation is tremendously relevant to what is happening in the whole health care field today. The human concern with health has always been a significant personal *motif,* but only recently has it become a predominant social interest. The causes of this change are too well known to recite here in detail. Three of them, however, are so important that they must be mentioned. The first cause is the rapid development of medical knowledge and skill, and the multiplication of technological and pharmaceutical aids to medical practice. The success in the diagnosis and treatment of disease, the effectiveness of preventative medicine, the lengthening of the life-span, and the extension of health services to a large part of our population have brought the whole matter of health to the forefront of our attention and concern as a society. In industry, in education, in business, and at all levels of government, the repercussions of this fact are apparent everywhere.

The second cause is the complex nature of health care today. What was once only a simple relation of doctor, patient, and family has become, in addition, a complicated interworking of institutions almost too numerous to mention. These institutions are themselves complexes of science, technology, manufacturing, finance, research, all kinds of professions, and just about every other work-activity we care to name. In a way, health care is a predominant social force in our society, partly because its implementation requires such a large and complicated social structure. Moreover, it has become so interrelated with the economic and political aspects of our culture that its essentially personal and human goal may be hidden.

The third cause is one which affects equally every other major concern of our lives, namely, the rapid and wide dissemination of information and misinformation today. The demand for health care is in proportion to the awareness of its possibility. Whether that awareness is based on information or misinformation seems irrelevant at times to the demand, but in the long run it has everything to do with the public attitude to the whole health care field. No health care administrator can afford to be ignorant of this fact; nor can anyone else involved in this field, for that matter. From the semantic point of view alone, we are bombarded from every side with the symbols of our social concern with health. And I am not thinking primarily of the strange gimmicks which Madison Avenue has confused with health care in its humorous T.V. commercials. The multiplicity of organizations, the interminable controversies about this or that aspect of medical care, and the ubiquitous appeals for money have made the social concern for health not only predominant but also terribly confusing in our culture.

A Social Necessity

A basic social imperative of our time is to extricate health concern from this morass of confusion and give it a structure and a rationale capable of bringing together our tremendous medical capacity in all of its ramifications and our many health needs. Obviously this imperative is too comprehensive to be dealt with here. It involves the whole spectrum of social philosophy and not just health care as such. However, since the hospital, with its various forms and functions, is at the very center of the picture, its administrator has a special responsibility for delineating and making clear what his institution contributes to the fulfilment of our personal and social concern for health.

The administrator must recognize that the hospital has both a social and a personal mission. While the latter has been stressed in the literature, the former has sometimes been depreciated or ignored. The hospital is one of the instruments by which society organizes itself to meet the health needs of the community. It is society at the cutting edge of its concern to maintain and improve the physical and mental condition of its members, just as the school is society at the cutting edge of its concern to perpetuate and improve its way of life. Therefore the hospital must be both responsible and responsive to the community it serves. One of the administrator's important tasks is to ensure that his institution takes its responsibility seriously and that it is intelligently sensitive to the community's needs and demands. The first part of this task is fulfilled by the simple effectiveness of his work. The second part represents the larger role he must play in relation to his community and the public.

Self

The other phase of our topic to which I would call your attention has to do with the administrator himself and his relation to his administrative activity or role. There is a "first-person-singular" quality of administration which is implied in what we have already said concerning the general philosophy and what we have heard concerning the ethical responsibility of hospital administration. Perhaps we can label it "administrator and/or administration," for it concerns the nature of the administrator's commitment to administration in general and to his specific job in particular.

Recently, I was involved in a study of a similar question about the philosopher and his philosophizing. The study revealed that there were two kinds of philosophical commitment, the "human" and the "professional." It also revealed that, for reasons too complicated to discuss here, these types of commitment had recently become almost violently opposed to each other. As might be expected, the conclusion of the study was that while they were clearly distinguishable, both of them were present in every great philosopher, without confusion yet without conflict.

It seems to me that, by analogy, we may think of the administrator's relation to administration as a dual one. Here too the "human commitment" and the "professional commitment" may be distinguished but they must be integrally related in any truly successful administrator. By "human commitment" is meant a dedication to the administative process as a way of life or, in Dubin's phrase, "a central life interest."[8] By "professional commitment" is meant a serious application of professional skills to a particular administrative task but *not necessarily* as "a way of life" or "a central life interest." There is plenty of empirical evidence to show that both commitments are made by administrators, sometimes separately and sometimes together.

During the past half-century many kinds of skilful activity have attained genuine professional status. Administration has been foremost among them, including administration of such services as health care and education. The development of a scientific background, a complex of necessary skills, a code of ethics, and a process of ensuring the continuation of the activity through formalized education are the marks of this attainment. Along with these very important ingredients of

[8]Robert Dubin, *Human Relations in Administration,* Englewood Cliffs, New Jersey: Prentice-Hall, Inc., p. 78.

professionalization have also come elements of prestige and a certain narrowing through the clarification of aims and limits. Administration has become a much more directed and purposeful activity and, therefore, much more effective in general. Without question, this has been largely beneficial to organizations and to the services performed through them.

The Human Commitment

On the other hand, the human commitment to administration has been less emphasized in recent years, except in certain books on "human relations," leadership," and "the psychology of administrative behavior." The reason is found in the ultimately indefinable character of this commitment. It cannot be completely structured by scientific formulae or assured through formal processes of education to the degree possible with the professional commitment. Too often the conclusion has been drawn that it is neither reasonable nor profitable to be concerned with it.

From the psychological point of view it can be argued that while administrative activity is genuinely professional and can be distinguished from the nonprofessional roles the administrator plays in his family, his clubs, his church, etc., its very nature is such that his essential ego-structure is involved in it. In ways perhaps not so characteristic of other professional activities, although a good case could be made out for most of them, administration requires a partial integration of the administrator's other roles into its functioning. For in one sense, administration is a way of living, as well as a kind of work. This truth, and not the superficial "how to win friends and influence people" techniques which fill many of its pages, constitutes the meaningful core of "human relations" literature.

Maintaining Perspective

Certain attitudes and qualities which are necessary to his other roles must carry over into the administrator's professional conduct, not alone for his own psychological integrity, but also for the effectiveness of his work. We often argue that this should not be, that the administrator has the same right as anyone else to live his own life, that he is under no obligation to be tyrannized by his responsibilities or by the institution in which he fulfils them. And our argument has a certain validity if we make clear what we usually mean by "live his own life" and "under no obligation to be tyrannized by his responsibilities or by the institution.'' For I suspect that in this argument most of us are reacting against the artificial demands which either society or tradition mistakenly imposes on the administrator rather than against the positive personal involvement it entails. Moreover, while administration demands this integration of roles and this personal involvement, it does not follow that it must supersede or dominate the non-professional roles which the administrator plays in the other equally important areas of his life. While the administrator *must identify himself with his administrative activity*—and thus make it his way of life when he is performing it—*he must not identify his administrative activity with the whole of his life* in such a way that his other roles are stereotyped replicas of it. Here is the real menace of ''the organization man'' or ''the other-directed man.'' This is not personal involvement in administration, but personal abandonment to administration. The line between them is very fine, but they are worlds apart both psychologically and ethically.

What are some of the specific differences? First, personal involvement in administration is characterized by both commitment to and critical objectivity about administration. The best example in contemporary life of this almost paradoxical combination is the scientific endeavor. The scientist who is not thoroughly involved in his investigations is not likely to come up with any significant results, and yet if he is unable to achieve a very real, critical objectivity with reference to the data and his methods of dealing with them, his results are equally unlikely to be significant. So it is with the administrator. He cannot be detached from his activity, and yet he must achieve some kind of detachment within it. When personal involvement is interpreted in largely emotional terms—which is a common error today—it is difficult to find a place for this detachment. The result is personal abandonment to administration, which has destructive consequences in administration itself and in the rest of the administrator's personal and social life. It is at this point that the philosophical dimension of administration becomes meaningful to the administrator himself and to his relation to his work—for philosophical thinking, much more than science, is personal and critical at one and the same time. There are no mechanical techniques or easy formulas for achieving this attitude; it must come from within the administrator's own reflective habits.

Knowing Ourselves

Second, personal involvement in administration is characterized by both ''ego-identification'' with administrative activity and a critical attitude toward oneself. The former is often put in colloquial terms, "we must give it all we have," and needs no further elucidation. The latter is much more complex, for it entails the fundamental image we have of ourselves. Psychologically, this image is the product of many forces operative in our experience, some involuntary and some voluntary. The fundamental philosophical imperative concerns the latter. To whatever extent possible, we need to know ourselves, to stand in judgment upon the inner source of our administrative activities, and to get on with our job without either too much introspective self-depreciation or too little awareness of our natural tendency *to be* the administrator rather than *to perform* our administrative activities critically and naturally. To repeat a quotation from Aiken which was used earlier in describing philosophy, "In a word, the aim of philosophy again becomes merely the Socratic aspiration toward self-knowledge, self-discipline, and self-fulfilment."[9] In this sense, the administrator is a philosopher or he is not likely to be effectively related to his job.

Withdrawing for Effectiveness

Third, personal involvement in administration is characterized by both a commitment to administration and an ability to get away from it when not engaged in it. This may not seem to be very realistic in a day when the pressures of administrative responsibility never let up. And yet it is perhaps the most realistic suggestion of all. For it is a fact of intellectual and moral experience that withdrawal is a necessary part of effectiveness in any area of human activity. Whether in his other social roles, in the family, the community, the church, and all the rest, or in the relaxation of recreation and contemplation, the administrator must make the withdrawal real or the tyranny of his job will destroy the very moral and personal qualities which ensure the success of his work.

Here "philosophy of hospital administration" merges with the "personal ethics of hospital administration." We must think in terms of both "administrator and administration" and "administrator or administration" at one and the same time. How we work them out in thought is the philosophical dimension; how we implement them in action depends, far more than our practical minds often acknowledge, upon the willingness and the seriousness with which we make that dimension real in ourselves.

[9] *Op. Cit.*

The Administrator and Policy Processes

John W. Hennessey, Jr., Ph.D.

In a hospital there is an apparent conflict surrounding policy-making represented by these three observations:

1. The legally responsible group in the hospital, charged with legislating policy, is the board of trustees; therefore these men must be the policy-makers.
2. The essential activity in the hospital is medical care for the sick, a specialty of physicians; therefore they should determine the policies of the organization.
3. The person most knowledgeable about all phases of life in the hospital, the only full-time professional with wide perspective, is the administrator; therefore he should decide policy.

The fact of multiple interest and involvement in policy-making causes the process to be complex and ambiguous. In this sense it is like policy processes in the federal government, implying a balance of contending powers. Thus the relationships among the three principal groups have a crucial effect on hospital policy.

The purpose of this article is to report one part of a study aimed at illuminating the multiple relationships which influence hospital policy-making. The part reported here singled out the administrator for special scrutiny. Other parts focused primarily on the board of trustees, the medical staff, and the processes of organizational control. The overall study took the form of case studies which evoked insights to be tested against other relevant literature. Three hospitals in the Northeast provided the research field for the group of investigators.

This examination of three administrators' special roles in policy processes can best be summarized by turning to excerpts from the data gathered by interviews and observations in the three hospitals, called Allenbury, Benton, and Cloverdale. These extracts give a suggestion of the differences and similarities among the three cases. They lead to an analysis of some of the important facets of each of the situations and an emergent definition of the central role of the administrator in policy-making.

Allenbury Hospital

Mr. James Tyler received his MBA degree from a prominent university. Since then he has held an administrative job with an urban health agency, a staff position in a national consulting firm in the hospital field, and an assistant administrator post in a metropolitan hospital. In 1960 he became administrator at Allenbury Hospital.

Six months after he arrived Mr. Tyler asked for time at a quarterly board meeting to present his thoughts for the future of the hospital. He gave the trustees an hour's presentation covering a variety of new programs for future development, including such areas as an ambulatory care unit, a rehabilitation long-term unit, and a mental health program. In Mr. Tyler's words,

> I laid out a blueprint for the future, presenting a good bit of new material. Afterward, I had a sense of disappointment or reservation about whether it had been worthwhile. In retrospect I feel it was very important . . . I worried about the board's reaction, but I think they were just overwhelmed at the possibilities. It looked like a grand design that would be too much to tackle.
>
> But they began to get a sense of vision for the future of the hospital, a sense that there was a great deal that could be done that wasn't being done. So the stage was set to bite off individual pieces of the program, realizing any piece was a small part of what they would be asked to do eventually. It established a good climate for change.
>
> I think the board felt that they would not want to dampen the enthusiasm of the new administrator. Psychologically, to some extent, they wanted to acquiesce to proposed changes. I felt this in my first month on the job when I lent my support to the innovation of an intensive-care unit, which had been under discussion for a year or more. I brought in a statement of the policies and procedures I had established when we opened such a unit in my former hospital, and fortunately the physician-chairman of the committee planning the change was willing to accept my idea. He was a man who liked to move fast after making a decision, and we had our intensive-care unit by July, 1960. I was lucky that this physician was liberal and willing to promote change. With this backing the plan was quickly accepted by the board, which had learned over a ten or 15-year period to stay out of medical matters and give fairly automatic support to matters of this kind proposed by the medical staff. Also, I made it clear the intensive-care unit was experimental and would be reviewed in six months.
>
> The intensive-care unit was highly successful, and thus it conditioned readi-

ness of both the medical staff and the board to accept future changes. Success breeds success.

Other factors encouraging change were the commitment of the president, who after all had hired me and wanted to see me succeed, and the effect left by the previous administrator. You see, my predecessor had been asked to resign because the board felt he did not show enough initiative to evaluate how the hospital was performing, to give the board data to evaluate what should be done in the future, what modifications should be made.

Broader Trustee Participation

Mr. Tyler described other influences on the development of his policies. He attributed some of the credit for change to his practice of asking a board member to sit on committees assigned to evaluate and plan particular new programs. He explained that he did this both to establish "trustee presence" (and quell "irresponsible disagreements") and to put the trustee in the role of bringing proposals for change to the board. "Administration would be working through this trustee," he explained, "to get broader trustee participation and understanding of hospital affairs. Our general philosophy would be a preference for working behind the scenes . . . to encourage others to feel . . . a part of whatever is transpiring."

Mr. Tyler believes it important for an administrator to recognize that the board *is* the policy authority. The administrator is a catalyst, a resource, an instigator, but "he deludes himself if he gets to feeling he *is* the hospital." This is not just legal or theoretical fact, it is pragmatic truth, too. Mr. Tyler continued:

On policy matters involving the utilization of facilities, it is up to me to advise the board and for them to take action. But *basic* policy is not something that gets articulated or put down. Policy is academic and meaningless anyway, unless it is followed by action. For example, when the previous director resigned and when they interviewed me, I asked a number of questions as to what they thought was the fundamental philosophy of the hospital program here. They then expressed their basic philosophy concerning growth and quality, and their specific interest in the value of such programs as the nursing school. I agreed with what they said on this, and it tipped me off that their philosophy of growth and interest was basically there.

The basic question is, "Does a board of trustees have a philosophy as to their obligation and the obligation of the hospital to the community?" If you find a board is neutral, then the administrator can bring knowledge to bear to alert them to needs and they will respond. If the board is negative to some of the modern ideas of the function of the community hospital, then an administrator can do nothing. In other words, if the philosophy is there, then it is less important to talk about the formulation and implementation of policy. If it is not there the administrator is powerless.

As it happened, I have been able to bring information to bear on the board within the general framework of their philosophy and this in turn has generated the confidence of the board in me. This doesn't mean that the board has "rubber-stamped" any of my ideas; on the contrary they have continued to exercise their strong and independent judgement. The fundamental and right decisions were there to begin with because of the board's philosophy. Fortunately, they have been supportive to me.

I know some administrators who feel that somehow their ego is undercut if they admit any feeling that the board of trustees has this essential role. I feel that to a certain extent they are ostrich-like in this viewpoint.

Working Behind the Scenes

Mr. Tyler's strategy for relating himself to the board of trustees has a counterpart in his relationship with the medical staff. He identifies what he calls "progressive elements" and works through them. He depends on doctors to influence other doctors, board members to sway other trustees. In his catalytic role, the administrator should do as little open persuading as possible, as Mr. Tyler sees it. He should not let his "ego" stand in the way of getting participation and team assistance from these other key policy groups. The administrator must work "behind the scenes" and let other people "speak the main parts."

The process of laying the groundwork for a major change is complex, Mr. Tyler reported. Each step must be thoroughly studied, many people must be involved, before any formal proposal gets to the board as a whole. At times this is "preselling" or nurturing consensus; at other times it is testing one's ideas and revising or rejecting them. One must avoid the costly mistake of getting officially turned down by the board on a major proposal.

Balance of Power

There is evidence that Mr. Tyler's reception by the medical staff was relatively favorable when he arrived in 1960, but his stock began to fall substantially after two years or so. Mr. Tyler felt this came about because the doctors became aware of a real change in the balance of power. In Mr. Tyler's own words:

I recognized that I was impatient about time, and I sometimes moved too fast. I didn't always communicate as fully as I should have, and this was one of the causes of dissension in the medical staff ranks.

At one meeting of the full medical staff in May 1962, there was a move to impeach the administrator. This was generated largely by the chief of surgery, a man who is quite a master politician and who had strong aspirations to the leadership role. He expected to inherit this leadership from the past, and he was frustrated by my attempts to perform in this role. Initially he tried to sway me to his views so that he might control me. When the chief of surgery found that controlling me was not possible and that I would operate independently, with board support, he tried to unseat me through impeachment proceedings.

The impeachment motion failed, but the medical staff did vote that there should be increased communication so that the administrator would not act on medical matters without prior consultation with the medical staff. The fact that I had gained the respect and support of the board of trustees by this time was very instrumental in causing the board to pay little attention to the fact that impeachment proceedings had been launched against me. I informed the board about the impeachment. I did not report it as a problem but almost parenthetically as a matter of information.

This storm subsided rather quickly after the impeachment failed. In an effort to rebuild a favorable climate between me and the medical staff I arranged individual meetings with each of the chiefs of service to obtain their views about the basic problems of the relationship between me and the staff and how to correct it. The conclusion of each of these interviews (which I helped to bring out by the way I led the interviews) was that the problem was a matter of communications, rather than a basic problem of different motivations or conflicting goals. These meetings were very significant because they indicated the strong concern of the administrator and his attempt with regard to soliciting medical staff views and working with the medical staff. This gave the chiefs an opportunity to express themselves.

Before I took this approach it was agreed to and supported by the chief of the medical staff.

After this I did go a bit slower and I did communicate more effectively. As a result the climate now, two years later, is better.

Joint Commission Visit

Another key development in the relationship between Mr. Tyler and his medical staff took place that same year, 1962, when the Joint Commission on Accreditation visited the hospital. The result of its report was to lower Allenbury's accreditation to one year because of imperfections in medical staff organization, the keeping of records of staff review, and other items. Mr. Tyler anticipated this negative action on the part of the Joint Commission but he took no action to prepare the medical staff before "the blow fell," for two reasons. In the first place the climate of Mr. Tyler's relationship to the medical staff was "explosive'' at that time because of the incidents reported above. In addition, Mr. Tyler perceived the president of the medical staff at that time to lack the capacity to accomplish an effective anticipation of the Joint Commission visit, because he was a man philosophically opposed to Joint Commission scrutiny in any case. Also, this physician was just about to end his final (second) year in the office of president of the medical staff, and the vice-president of the medical staff (new to the presidency) was perceived by Mr. Tyler to have the capacity to handle this situation.

One action Mr. Tyler took in anticipation of an unfavorable report from the Joint Commission was to appoint his administrative resident as a consultant to the medical staff to review matters most important to the accreditation process. Mr. Tyler saw this as a move to prepare the ground for the time when the new president of the medical staff would come into office, but he ''sold'' the idea to the medical staff primarily on the basis of its being a ''good educational experience'' for the administrative resident.

Limited Publicity

When the criticisms of the Joint Commission arrived at the hospital, the new president of the medical staff was in office, and it was through him that Mr. Tyler could communicate. Mr. Tyler's approach was one of helping to improve medical care procedures, ''not to punish or embarrass anyone.'' The problem was kept entirely within the executive committee of the board of trustees because it was felt that exposing the full contents of the accreditation report to the entire board might, by publicizing the criticisms within the community, have destructive effects on the relationships between the board and the medical staff.

Mr. Tyler reported the events subsequent to the Joint Commission's report in the following way:

> When the criticisms arrived we wanted to have the board more involved than they had ever been before in medical matters and we wanted them to express their concern more directly. This would be a good way to set a precedent for the board to delve more deeply into medical staff affairs. We also recognized that unless the board expressed concern, the president of the medical staff would not use his leadership talents to make improvements. At the same time we discerned that if the board exercised an excessively strong role, the medical staff would develop an antagonistic attitude toward the board which might be destructive, both to general relationships and to the medical staff attitude toward the Joint Commission report.

So it was agreed between me and the president of the board, before the executive committee of the board meeting, that there should be a strong expression of concern in the executive committee meeting, with the president of the medical staff present. At the same time we agreed that the executive committee would not communicate the full contents of the report to the board, for reasons I have cited earlier. The executive committee told the president of the medical staff to let the doctors know the executive committee's action and that the board would have strong interest in what the physicians subsequently did.

The administrator is a vital resource to policy processes in Allenbury Hospital because he is playing the part for which the board engaged him. He is a catalyst, a coordinator; and he contributes importantly to the development of a vision of the hospital's future. He supplies information and judgements that the board can use to evaluate the degree to which the hospital is meeting the requirements of the board's basic policy of quality. Beyond that, Mr. Tyler also initiates policy. This is important in his own concept of his responsibility, even though it may be expressed differently in the board's view of the role of the administrator.

Mr. Tyler is sensitive to the quasi-political character of the environment within which policy processes operate in his hospital. As a result he has a respect for the need to maintain a felicitous balance of power among the majority of representatives of the principal power groups: the board, the medical staff, and the administration. His strategies for information flow, the use of influence and persuasion, direct and indirect lobbying, and timing are derivatives of the political character of his situation as he perceives it.

One final observation can be made on the basis of the Allenbury case: the administrator's personality obviously plays a part in policy processes in a hospital. Mr. Tyler suggested that he would be less effective if his "ego" prevented his recognition of the proper role of the board (and the medical staff) in decision-making. He has experienced, at Allenbury Hospital, the need to be tolerant of the limitations of his own power and, beyond that, of situations wherein other people receive credit for ideas the administrator originated. Boldly stated this looks like manipulation of a sort; actually the phenomenon is a more complex administrative reality. Because of *his* unique position as the full-time "expert," the *board's* legal position as the policy body, and the *physicians'* rightful claim to a pre-eminent role in matters of patient care, the administrator must have the capacity to balance patience and humility on the one hand and confident leadership on the other.

Benton Hospital

Mr. Wood had been a private school teacher for more than seven years when he first became interested in hospital work. A friend persuaded him to assume responsibility, in 1947, for the educational programs of a 300-bed hospital in a large metropolitan area. He soon became assistant administrator as well as educational director, then left in 1950 to be administrator of a rural 60-bed hospital. Three years later he came to Benton Hospital.

When Mr. Wood was interviewed for the post of administrator at Benton Hospital he hesitated to view the opportunity favorably because he was cautioned by many people that the hospital was dominated by a powerful, active president of the board. This president had been in office since the consolidation of two hospitals in 1947. He combined an energetic interest in the hospital with an expertness and a detailed knowledge of the operation which made it impossible for him not to intrude into the proper bailiwick of the administrator. This president's regime was a felicitous one for the hospital at a crucial time in its history. Nevertheless, the strong success of the president had two negative side effects: it weakened the position of the administrator and it lessened the effective participation of other members of the executive committee and the full board.

Acceptance Terms

Mr. Wood agreed to take the administrative post at Benton after a candid discussion with the board president which resulted in the latter's assurance that he would withdraw from his dominant position in the administrative life of the institution. He carried out this agreement in a gracious way, passing the presidency on to a new person, although he continued to serve the hospital admirably at times when Mr. Wood called on him for special help.

During his twelve years as administrator of Benton Hospital, Mr. Wood has developed the reputation of a strong and effective leader. For a variety of reasons he has developed a position of direct power and influence which appears to be stronger in some ways than that occupied by the administrators of Allenbury or Cloverdale Hospitals. In part this is due to the fact that he came to Benton at a crucial time, when centralized leadership was essential, when the organization was struggling with those final aspects of the consolidation of two separate hospitals which would result in the construction of an entire new plant. The withdrawal of the dominant leadership of the former board president created a kind of executive vacuum which it was logical for Mr. Wood to fill. In addition, Mr. Wood's own charismatic qualities of leadership played no small role in his administrative success.

During the period of research Mr. Wood's principal department heads characterized him with admiration and respect. On the one hand, they reported that he is a strong, knowledgeable leader who pushes them hard in the stages of planning and policy-making, encouraging their proposals and forcing them to defend their ideas. At the same time he encourages independence of operation and "backs his department heads to the limit, right or wrong." "He is forceful and sets high standards, and essentially he is an understanding and sensitive man and inspiring to work for." One department head added her admiration of how Mr. Wood deals effectively with the large problem of managing power and emotion in a small town environment with all the pressures which can be generated in such a situation.

This positive view of Mr. Wood seemed to be shared by members of the board of trustees, and by the appointed leaders of the medical staff. On the other hand the medical staff was not unified by any means in its feelings about the administrator, and there were blocs of physicians who were negative in their appraisal.

Central Role

One result of Mr. Wood's experiences as the administrator at Benton Hospital was the development of a distinctive self-concept in his executive role. In talking about his experiences and current problems, Mr. Wood frequently used the first-person singular pronoun in describing the organization and its parts. This was in contrast to the administrators in Allenbury and Cloverdale Hospitals, who seemed consciously to avoid putting themselves in such a central role. In what seemed to be a natural way, Mr. Wood would refer to "my patients, my departments, my board, my medical staff, etc." This phenomenon is a superficial manifestation of what was evidenced by more substantial factors: such as the centrality and power of the administrative position of Mr. Wood.

An illustration of this is contained in some of Mr. Wood's comments about his hospital budget. During the 1963 budgeting year Mr. Wood suspended the budget because of the unpredictable factors involved in opening the new wing of the hospital. Although he received the approval of the board of trustees for this act, Mr. Wood's description of it showed that he looks upon the budget as his own tool and not that of the board. At the time of this decision he reported that he felt he could get along easily without a budget in the year in question. "After eight years I know the key control points and the key questions asked. I have a sufficient feel so that we can easily get along without a budget this year, waiting for the new wing to settle down."

Mr. Wood does not hold regular department head meetings. He found in his first administrative assignment that meetings of the entire department head group forced the discussion of subjects which are not the concern of the whole group. As a result meetings are held at Benton only when they are specially called.

Finally, Mr. Wood uses one member of the organization as a special confidant or sounding board, a phenomenon also reported by the administrator in Cloverdale Hospital. In Mr. Wood's words, "Various people have filled this role for me, usually a doctor. I pick a doctor who knows management's problems so that I can ask this man for his considered reaction to questions like 'Are there any traps or danger points in what I am proposing?' The man I am currently using as a sounding board is a fair, objective, clear thinker with a good mind, a man who knows the thinking and the position of various people on the staff. In my position I need somebody outside the formal authority line who is both a good listener and a knowledgeable, wise individual."

Catalyst Role

The demonstrated strength of Mr. Wood's leadership assures a heavy mutual involvement with his board of trustees, beyond what one might expect simply from the official, legal structure of the organization. Nevertheless, Mr. Wood, somewhat like Mr. Tyler of Allenbury, is careful not to be drawn into the role of final policy-maker. He sees himself as a "catalyst" (he and Mr. Tyler use the same term) or a guide; but it is the board that must take ultimate responsibility for making policy and watching the results.

If Mr. Wood finds the president of the board is heading in a direction he does not agree with, he feels no hesitation to express his view, but he does it indirectly. In his words, "I feed more information to the president and to others who will influence him. That is all I can do or should do, because he is my boss. When I go too far with him [the president], he will bluntly call me on it."

Both Mr. Wood and Mr. Tyler find it useful to work through people who can influence the person who is the real target. In a technical sense this is a skillful use of "reference group" concepts, and it flows naturally from the ambiguous policy role the administrator must play. He must influence his board without direct authority. He must let others take the credit, often, for what are essentially his ideas. The demands this makes on his personality say something about the requirements for the job and they also predict the need for compensating adjustments or reactions.

Avoiding Public Defeat

Mr. Wood voiced the sentiment that it is unwise and damaging to push a point with the board and not succeed. If "nothing succeeds like success," then nothing spoils like defeat, especially when one's position rests less on authority than on respect for one's wisdom, professional counsel, and full-time administrative experience. The administrator is the sole representative in the organization of the science of hospital management. If he is "publicly" compromised, defeated, or proved wrong, he is as vulnerable as an elected political officer. This was the belief of all three administrators.

Occasionally Mr. Wood tells the board directly, "We must have a policy in this area [such as whom to admit: alcoholics, mental cases, and others]." He sees it as part of his catalytic role to call attention to policy needs. In the realm of employee pensions, Mr. Wood suggested the need for policy for several years, then asked the president to appoint a committee of the board to study the issue. When the committee had not met, seven months later, Mr. Wood said, "I blame myself for that. I should remind the chairman and be a catalyst to get things moving."

Mr. Wood reported:

> Some of our policies came into being because of specific problems that came up. Maybe that is the primary cause for policy. As these issues become *visible* to me, I think it is my duty to carry the ball and suggest to the proper parties (medical staff or board) that we devise policy. Examples from recent years are a formulary policy, limiting the number of duplicate drug items, and the automatic stop-order on narcotics after 24 hours, because doctors were sometimes forgetting.
>
> Our policy of relating charges closely to the cost of service rendered came about as a result of Blue Cross influence. Room and board went up, ancillary charges (previously inflated in proportion) stayed the same or went down. This is an example of the influence of outside institutions on the policies of the hospital, and it is my job to bring these things to the board and get them to study and act on them.

With regard to what problems he should allow to go to the board, he stated:

> In eight years I've developed a "feel" for what I should take to the board and what I shouldn't. It was tough in the first year, but then I worked it out over time. It's a matter of give and take, trial and error. When I'm wrong, the board (president or executive committee) lets me know, and they should.

Mr. Wood spoke frequently of the difficulties of "educating" the medical staff to the policy problems of the hospital. He was not concerned with the elected officers of the staff; in fact he felt service in a position of responsibility educated a physician and made his criticisms and suggestions more realistic. The best example of an issue in which the attitude of the medical staff became a major preoccupation of the administrator concerned the nursing shortage situation which will be treated in some detail later.

Mr. Wood commented several times during the research period on his displeasure at the occasional subversion of the organization he sees practiced in the hospital by physicians. "The doctor feels easy in a one-to-one relationship," Mr. Wood put it, "and he sometimes treats a nurse, for example, as if the only thing that mattered was his particular championing of her cause. He may come to me directly and complain about a nurse's salary or something else. He freely by-passes the director of nursing service as if she didn't exist. That is quite wrong. It shows the doctor is thinking of the only organizational model he is familiar with: his own small office downtown, where he can treat problems personally."

Recounting incidents of this type, Mr. Wood spoke of the general frustration of trying to create an effective house-staff organization out of the physician group. "They are an independent bunch, not too concerned about the hospital's needs, not willing to be 'organized,' not temperamentally suited to parliamentary procedure or administrative systematization, or the fine points of management. They don't analyze organizational problems, they react to them."

One result of Mr. Wood's expressed difficulty of managing policy and administrative processes when the physicians were involved was his concern with how to educate the ("parochial") physicians. He consciously uses all opportunities to try to educate—coffee time, lunch, staff meetings. He seemed to take a more direct approach to this problem (as he perceived it), in comparison with Mr. Tyler and the administrator in Cloverdale Hospital. Once he spoke of how the program planners of Northeastern Hospital Assembly conferences (mostly administrators) often say they must have a panel on "educating the MD," but someone always "spoils the fun" by pointing out that no doctors will attend the sessions, no matter how many are invited.

Visible Leverage

One support Mr. Wood respects in his general dealings with the medical staff is the Joint Commission on Accreditation. "The Joint Commission," he said, "is one of the strongest supports a lay group could have to assure that good medicine is being practiced." He spoke of welcoming the Joint Commission because it gives him visible leverage to get some things accomplished which he and the board want the medical staff to do. This is especially true in the realm of meetings, minutes, records, and reports. There is a parallel here, with Mr. Tyler's feelings about the Joint Commission, in Allenbury Hospital.

A significant addition to Benton Hospital's plant, the west wing, was ready for opening in early 1963. Its three wards had been planned to provide enough space for needed present expansion and for future growth. Two wards were to be used immediately, with the expectation that this would reduce the patient waiting list to proper size.

Mr. Wood began to add extra nursing personnel to the payroll in September 1962, in anticipation of the needs of the west wing. It was partly the effect of this build-up that caused Mr. Wood to "suspend the budget," as noted earlier, until the income and costs of the new facility stabilized.

Mr. Wood had anticipated difficulty in providing enough nurses to staff the new wards adequately. He recommended to the board that they attempt to retain more graduates of the school of nursing by agreeing to refund tuition to any girl who stayed. He elicited the help of the local newspaper editor in publicizing the nursing shortage and emphasizing that it was a *national* shortage.

When the new wing was opened only one ward was put into service. Two RNs were lacking in the staffing of the second ward. Opening the second ward was essential to any dramatic decrease in the patient waiting list, and many complaints and suggestions were received from the medical staff. Mr. Wood followed up all responsible suggestions: "With all these multiple forces, you see, we have felt obligated to investigate, although we know from our talks with colleagues that this is an exhausted market at this stage."

Direct Confrontation

This issue seemed headed for a significant confrontation between the administrator and the medical staff. Mr. Wood was anxious about his inability to staff the new ward, as were the physicians. But he felt he had done all he could do to meet the problem and he clearly found it difficult to appreciate the growing implication of some elements of the medical staff that there were "easy solutions" to the nursing shortage.

Mr. Wood met with the executive committee of the medical staff, with the board president in attendance, prior to the medical staff meeting, and explained exactly how he felt about the nursing shortage and the "sniping" he was receiving from some doctors. He said he intended "to have a real blast tonight at the staff meeting." The president of the medical staff and the chairman of the board spoke in clear support of Mr. Wood during this meeting and the other members of the executive committee showed in one way or another that they would back up Mr. Wood in the medical staff meeting.

The meeting of the medical staff opened with a speech by the chief of staff who cited three ways to help nursing service: in connection with the timing of the doctors' rounds, the timing of the admission of patients, and the attention paid to the need to issue stop-orders on medicines.

After that Mr. Wood spoke to the medical staff, calmly, about why the new ward could not be opened, and again he listed some of the suggestions which had been put forth by physicians and logically countered each one. Finally, he said:

> There is sometimes the attitude that the director of nursing is responsible for the nursing shortage. I tell you this is a chronic problem all over the United States, and it does no good to fix the blame on some one person. I would at least hope that we had your understanding. We are all in it. We must come to a decision as to how we are going to solve the problem of staffing. Please, don't throw brickbats around.

Some members of the medical staff responded by blaming low salaries, long hours, and the inflexibility of the director of nursing. Mr. Wood again answered each comment, though somewhat more heatedly, in spite of his own opinion that it was generally unwise to take on the medical staff as a group.

Seat of Authority

As these events unfolded, it seemed clear that Mr. Wood sat alone in a central decision chair. He had the support of the chairman of the board and the president of the medical staff, but he managed this series of events almost entirely by himself. At a later meeting of the executive committee of the board of trustees, Mr. Wood again explained in detail how he viewed the problem of coping with the nursing shortage and the suggestions of the medical staff. He explained why each of the ideas proposed by doctors had flaws.

Several months later, Mr. Wood again talked to the full medical staff and explained the continued reasons why the new ward could not be opened. Several suggestions for dealing with the problem were voiced by doctors who were not present at the earlier meeting when Mr. Wood had confronted the medical staff with feeling. These suggestions were similar in nature to those which had been put forth at the earlier meeting, and this time other doctors quickly jumped on them and pronounced them "ridiculous!" After this meeting the president of the board appointed a committee, headed by Mr. Wood, to study nurses' housing as a factor in keeping nursing graduates.

By this time Mr. Wood's feelings on the nursing shortage were so strong that he had staked a considerable amount of his power and prestige on his point of view. The fact that more than six months had gone by since the new wing was ready to use, and during all this time the lack of two nurses had prevented the opening of the second ward, added to Mr. Wood's feeling about the matter.

High Housing Costs

When the Wood committee reported to the board in August, it concluded that the cost of housing was excessively high. It also stated that it had polled the students in the nursing school and found that housing was not a high motivational factor in the students' decision about staying at Benton Hospital after graduation from the school. The conclusion of the report was to ask the board to match any money voted by the medical staff for nursing school scholarships.

Subsequently the medical staff presented a strong petition to the trustees in behalf of a board policy to instruct the administration to keep the patient waiting list at a minimum level. The board debated this issue strenuously and arrived at a statement that the patient should expect Benton to provide both readily-available beds and the lowest possible costs. In this context a policy was voted, as follows:

> It will be the policy of the hospital, within the limitations of the facilities and personnel available, to staff and make available for use the number of beds necessary to meet all emergency and urgent needs and to meet elective needs

within a reasonable "waiting period." Within the context of this policy, a reasonable "waiting period" is defined as a period generally not to exceed two weeks and preferably to approach ten days. In implementing this policy, percentage of occupancy will not be a controlling factor.

The nursing shortage case shows the vital role Mr. Wood plays in implementing policy. His use of the power of his person and his office to educate and even discipline the medical staff illustrates his basic feeling that good policy will result only from the *responsible* coalition of the board, medical staff, and administrator. He was, thus, dealing not only with the nursing shortage situation but also with the quality and character of the power balance which, in the end, produces policy in the hospital. Through aggressive administration he was attempting to supply a "corrective" which will aid future policy processes.

In the nursing shortage drama, Mr. Wood used power more openly and forcefully than in any other situation observed in the research. He called on the strength of his position, developed over years of interaction and progress, to support an attack on the medical staff and a demand for its acquiescence. In retrospect it appears that the more power Mr. Wood used so openly the less he had. Through these particular tactics he aroused direct opposition. He coalesced what had been scattered, inchoate forces within the medical staff and in the end made it less possible ever again to use his own power so directly. He would have this be a caveat to his fellow administrators.

Administrator's Unique Position

The board's confidence that Mr. Wood is right and the board's willingness to sanction his use of power with respect to the medical staff were key elements in the situation. This brings into relief the inescapable responsibility of the board president and his associates on the executive committee. They may delegate to the administrator the implementation of policy but they must reserve to the board both the ultimate policy-making authority and the task of evaluating the continuing contribution of the administrator to the welfare of the institution. Mr. Wood not only understands and accepts these organizational facts, he does what he can to make it possible for the board to exercise its crucial functions, and he supplies correctives in this realm too, if he judges they are legitimate. The demands this makes on the personality, integrity, and wisdom of the hospital executive are unusual, if not unique, in organizational life.

Cloverdale Hospital

John Emory has been administrator of Cloverdale Hospital for over ten years. He is a graduate of the master's program in hospital administration of a leading university. Prior to coming to Cloverdale in 1945, he had been administrator of several larger hospitals. He has served with distinction in a number of national and regional offices in organizations in the health field. Directly under Mr. Emory is an assistant administrator, a comptroller, and 22 department heads of which five are physicians.

His department heads unanimously painted a picture of Mr. Emory as a strong, knowledgeable administrator, an equitable man, and a friendly person. They saw him as democratically inclined; he helps set the goals of departmental operation but doesn't interfere in day-to-day decisions. Many commented on the special quality of the hospital environment: "a fine spirit," "a special friendly flavor," "a true cottage-hospital feeling," "a family atmosphere." They attributed this distinctive cachet primarily to Mr. Emory, more than to any other single factor.

Closer Guidance Desired

The policy of giving department heads freedom and authority has not always worked smoothly, in the view of several department heads. The chief dietitian, for example, expressed the need for closer guidance when she found her pricing policies were not consistent with the board's perceptions. Her response was to ask for written policies for department heads. She showed some doubt as to whether policies should come from Mr. Emory or the board, partly because of the new, active role played by the budget committee of the board.

Another senior department chief said no one could have managed the development of Cloverdale Hospital as well as Mr. Emory had, and that the administrator's job is, at heart, almost an impossible one, one which puts unreasonable and conflicting demands on the personality of the incumbent. He said:

> There are severe psychological demands on the administrator. He must be a diplomat, a mediator, and yet he must take the wheel and steer the ship at critical times—he is the only one with sufficient intimate knowledge to do that. He must let others take credit and chip away at his authority in normal times, but he must not let any major decisions go counter to his best judgment. The frustrations of dealing with the board and medical staff would be difficult for anyone.

Mr. Emory copes with all this very well, partly because of his personality and partly because of experience. Nevertheless he has occasionally had to settle for the possible, the real, rather than the ideal, especially in more recent years. Part of this has to do with the board.

The board's view of Mr. Emory is conditioned by two main sets of evidence: the results of Mr. Emory's administration, in terms of hospital performance, and the participation of Mr. Emory in board and executive committee meetings. In some degree these two aspects have created different impressions.

Strong Internal Leadership

The general confidence of the board of trustees in Mr. Emory's management of Cloverdale Hospital has been expressed strongly and in a variety of ways over the years. All signs point to the vitality of Mr. Emory's internal leadership in the hospital. Strong, competent people fill the key posts under Mr. Emory, patients are lavish in their praise of the institution, and the physical plant is kept in fine condition. Cloverdale is widely known as a superior institution.

Mr. Emory's relationship with his board of trustees has been, in many ways, felicitous and productive. An example in recent years of their working effectively together can be seen in the invited intervention of the board in the budgeting process. Several years ago Mr. Emory requested that the board budget committee become more active in financial affairs because he felt a real need to improve budgeting with respect to medically-managed departments. Administrative authority had proved inadequate, for historical purposes, to handle the medically-managed departmental problem in the optimum way. A beneficial by-product of this development was that it gave the trustee budget committee an insight into hospital financing which Mr. Emory described as immensely helpful. In his words:

> This involvement of the trustee budget committee in hospital financing has resulted in a 180° turn in their perception of the basic financial processes in the organization. Now we have developed a philosophy of planning ahead and doing such things as charging and funding depreciation. I set out to accomplish one thing, to get a better entrée and understanding in radiology, pathology, and physical medicine. The operation of the budget committee resulted in turning the whole board toward a vastly superior financial policy. My only objection is that the board budget committee did not stop with the medically-managed departments but went into too much detail in other departments.

At the same time, Mr. Emory is not entirely happy with his relationship to the board of trustees. In a real sense he feels the board does not make maximum use of his professional capacities in the policy realm. Paraphrases of his testimony can make this point best.

I have been concerned about my relationship with the board of trustees. I should be serving as a policy-making consultant to them but they don't really seem to want this. I have learned all of this the hard way, through year-by-year experience. I could cite examples of trustees agreeing to a specific course of action in private consultation with me, only to flip to another position during a board meeting.

The administrator and the chairman should have a special relationship, to build a mutual trust and respect for one another's competence. If either party is insecure or unclear about what the other can contribute, the result is regrettable. On the other hand, I know from experience the board president can be almost too wise and competent. He can be so competent and so efficient that other board members don't have a full opportunity to develop. (Cf. the situation in Benton Hospital before Mr. Wood arrived.) The administrator's delight in such a situation can be short term.

It is not a good idea for the administrator to play "power games." It is a matter of moral principle with me. I feel the only legitimate way for me to influence the board is to work through the chairman, as far as direct ideas for planning or change are concerned. If the chairman keeps me sidelined on any policy issue I feel I am up against a blank wall. And other board members do not use me as productively or helpfully as they might. They will sometimes use me as a confidant, but they don't know how to use me as a consultant. This is a problem for me.

When I do not contribute my professional expertise in policy issues, I am not really earning my salary. I am performing as a high-paid clerk rather than as a full-fledged administrator of a large, complex hospital.

One result of all of this is that the trustees have overstepped their bounds occasionally. Several years ago, I think they mistakenly felt that they could somehow maintain both prices and costs at a country-town level, in spite of obvious facts contradicting this. Costs must continue to rise in the future. But because of the board's attitude few people really understand the impact of this fact in our hospital.

Here is a case where the board is talking to itself. I need to devise a way to break into this. How can I get the board to take a fresh look at these things, to forget their status and power problems and as a result use me more in policy issues?

Given his diagnosis of the situation within which he is working, Mr. Emory clearly has reasons to be cautious in most open debates in board meetings on policy issues. He has a key role to play in producing and disseminating information on the basis of which the board will act. At each board meeting, routinely, he presents data on current operations and problems. At appropriate junctures he prepares special reports on matters which require the trustees to know more about the issues than they can discover for themselves. In the meetings of various board committees, Mr. Emory can be seen informing people, expanding the area of discussion in ways which he deems necessary, and generally contributing (albeit indirectly) to the policy process. To a limited extent he works with individual board members and individual physicians, to express views of his which should play an eventual part in policy formulation. But his personal force in meetings has been consciously modified.

Smaller Policy-Making Role

The board's perception of the part Mr. Emory plays in policy determination has, however, been colored in recent years by his relatively less active role in the board and executive committee meetings in the realm of policy-making. To the outside observer, it appears that Mr. Emory has chosen to sheath his own power and delimit his direct influence on the board of trustees. To the department heads his natural way of presenting himself is seen as courtesy or civility which is a distinctive asset to the hospital, but to the board he can appear to be restraining the power of his role, permitting other forces to dominate at times.

The major cause of what appears to be deference toward the board on Mr. Emory's part comes from his view of what the board wants of him, how it wants to use him. It is also a function of Mr. Emory's basic perception of the proper role of the administrator, which he sees as that of a catalyst. He prefers to get his ideas expressed through and by board members and medical staff members. He sees his mission as getting his professional knowledge to key people, much as Mr. Tyler expressed his perception, and he does not care if his own name does not end up attached to particular ideas. "Some administrators need ego-fulfillment, but I think this can get them into considerable trouble," Mr. Emory said.

Administrator-Board Relationship

In the context of the relationship between the administrator and the board, Mr. Emory is vulnerable to some pressure or criticism from the board. For example, one member of the board budget committee said:

Does it weaken the administration's position if we interview the department heads directly and give them a hard time on costs? Maybe so. But the administration is not a particularly strong one, with respect to the doctors. He tends to get overpowered by the medical world. He is too ready to make peace when conflicts come from that direction. If management is not strong, then the board gets involved, as we do. [Mr. Emory] seems to appreciate our stepping in, because we can be a little rougher, especially regarding finances.

In line with our policy of lowest costs, we got the administration to compare our laundry, dietary, and so forth with outside trends. He should have initiated this sort of comparison, I think.[1]

In our hearings we asked for productivity increases at the maximum rate and pressed the need to inject "management ideas," to show departments where to save money. They aren't cost conscious enough. I think we ought to reorganize and have people reporting to [Mr. Emory] along different lines.

But I will admit crossing swords with medical doctors would be tough for any layman, so I'm not blaming [Mr. Emory]. I just think he needs the power of the board to get some things done.

Another senior board member explained Mr. Emory's lessened power in different terms:

The administrator does not feel we use his experience directly enough, but I think what he is forgetting is that things have changed a great deal in the past dozen years. The board is stronger, less quick to "rubber stamp" actions of the chairman, the administrator, or board committees. Also the character of the hospital has become less that of an eleemosynary institution, as it has expanded, and more business-like. These are important changes, and they demand new kinds of responses from all of us.

More than the other two hospitals, Cloverdale can reveal the impact of human elements on policy processes. Personalities, feelings, and relationships appear to be what mark Cloverdale's uniqueness. Its unique strengths reside in the experienced leadership of the chairman of the board of trustees, Mr. Emory's effective internal management and the respect in which the departmental chiefs hold him, the friendliness or family atmosphere attributed to the hospital and the reputation of the hospital for superior medical care. A weakness is evident in the particular imbalance in the complex process of role definition and utilization between Mr. Emory and the board of trustees, and the frustrated feelings this has generated.

[1]Mr. Emory later pointed out that he has continually prepared many comparisons of costs and outside trends. This appears to be a misconception on the part of the budget committee.

Need for Explicit Roles

The most important feature of the relationship between Mr. Emory and his board, especially the chairman of the board, is that there has not been an effective development of an explicit set of understandings about what roles each will play, and will expect the other to play, in policy-making processes. This has left their collaboration too much to personal factors, transmitted through a power system. To Mr. Emory the result is an unfair domination by the board, an under-utilization of his proper professional contribution, a deprivation in his role. For personal reasons he is not eager to fight this matter openly, rather it rankles as an injustice. To the board chairman, Mr. Emory's diminished role in policy processes is the result of Mr. Emory's deliberate choice. Thus, there is no mutuality to their diagnosis of the situation, and they are stuck with an impasse which cannot help but be a limitation to optimal policy-making at Cloverdale.

After an immersion in three such different hospital situations as those in this report, one develops an appreciation for diversity. No standard set of policies could sensibly be imposed on three such institutions; but each must struggle with internal problems and external determinants to develop expressions of values and hospital goals, bits of consensus which make special sense in the given environment. By the time policy is recorded and filed it has already, in many cases, performed its function. The development of policy is valuable in itself, beyond the statements it produces, because it tests and stretches the organization's vital capacities and reflects the qualitative level at which the relationships among the board, administrator, and medical staff have come into equilibrium.

The administrator is essential to policy processes because he knows more than anyone else. He is in direct charge of the hospital departments. Only he has made hospital management his life's work. Only he has direct contact with the profession of hospital administration and access to its accumulated wisdom. He is the best one to interpret the forces in the environment, to read the winds of change which always blow, and to compare the hospital today with what it might be tomorrow. He cannot do all this alone, but he is more central to these processes than anyone else, day in and day out.

Clarifying the Relationships

The conflict in the administrator's role is that he must be the key, full-time executive without legitimate power either to make policy or to govern the medical staff. He is in a unique position. The model of no other institution quite fits well enough to be instructive or helpful. The role is shaped both by factors external to the organization and by factors within it. No internal factor is more central than the relationship between the administrator and (1) the medical staff and (2) the board of trustees. Unless these relationships are defined clearly and maturely, policy formulation will be hampered by tensions, dysfunctional assumptions, and doubts. Clarifying these roles should be high on the priority list of all people concerned.

The really unique thing about the administrator's role is not so much his lay board, although influencing and educating the group with power over one's own appointment is a subtle art indeed. It is rather the nature of his interactions with the medical staff.[2] In each of the three hospitals the administrator reported that significant portions of the medical staff as a group were either irresponsible or hostile toward him.

That the individual medical practitioner should resent the intrusion of lay authority at any level lower than the board, the ultimate legal authority, is partly understandable. This condition has been exacerbated by the doctor's changed role in the hospital, too, as Robert Wilson points out.[3] The physician's historical administrative dominance has withered as a result of the explosive growth of medical science, the increase in specialization, and the increasingly complex nature of hospital organization.

Less easy to understand is the animus which occasionally appears to dominate the doctor's attitude toward administration, and his quick tendency to introduce sharply invidious distinctions between his role and the administrator's. A comment on this phenomenon was made recently by the president of a philanthropic foundation which has done much to provide scholarships in medicine. He wrote:

> This . . . brings to the fore a most curious development in medical education —the low place of the administrator in the spectrum of respect and honor. One would think that the simplest mind could understand that anything as complex as a medical school would require some direction, so that the lives and work of those who make up the school could go forward with the greatest ease, the

[2]For a parallel view see Harold L. Wilensky, "The Dynamics of Professionalism: The Case of Hospital Administration," *Hospital Administration,* Vol. 7, No. 2 (Spring, 1962), pp. 19, 21.

[3]Robert N. Wilson, "The Physician's Changing Role," *Human Organization,* Vol. 18, No. 4 (Winter, 1959–1960), pp. 177–183.

least confusion . . . ; that, to do this well, would require a modest amount of talent; that, to be successful, an administrator would naturally be a leader as well.

It seems . . . unfair to downgrade medical school administration and then complain about the quality of the leadership that results. . . .[4]

It is obvious that the hospital administrator, to be of maximum use to his organization, must have a tolerance for such attitudes as the medical staff will display from time to time. He need not be a saint, as Mr. Wood showed, but he must be strong enough to cope with what will seem to be unfair and irresponsible resistance to his influence and his ideas. If these three hospitals are good examples, he will be aided in this process by the fact that doctors in positions of official power in the hospital often change their negative attitudes under the responsibility of decision-making. He can be reassured, too, by the knowledge that some of the sharper edges of conflict can be dulled by a skillful use of timely communication, prior consultation, and some general participation in that decision-making which can be improved through such participation.

In addition, the administrator will continue to be supported, in his relations with the medical staff, by the logic of the situation. The increased specialization and heightened pace of the physician's own work will force him to leave administration to the professional. As Wilensky points out:

[One resistance to professionalization of hospital administration is that] the almost unique position of relating as manager to the most powerful profession in the world (medical doctors) intensifies the general problem of all professionalizing occupations—carving out an area of autonomous operation.

It seems possible that the continued redefinition of the physician's role may redound to the administrator's advantage: the busier the physician becomes, the less time he will have to resist the kind of program planning and evaluation administrators can do best.[5]

Policy processes will be improved as the hospital administrator and the physician develop a capacity to analyze their role conflicts, to recognize legitimate differences in perception and in power, and to develop a reasonable set of mutual expectations and sanctions about one another's role. It is clearly not enough to leave such tasks to

[4]John and Mary R. Markle Foundation (522 Fifth Avenue, New York 10036). Annual Report of the President: John M. Russell, 1962–63, pp. 10, 15.

[5]Wilensky, *op. cit.*, pp. 21, 22.

chance or to the operation of some kind of "invisible hands" moving toward an equilibrium or balance of power. These are complex organizational problems, worthy of intellectual analysis of a high order.

Policy in the three hospitals of this research was also affected directly by the relationship of the administrator and the board of trustees. This fact has been amplified several times in this report. It is a basic fact of pervasive importance.

If the hospital is increasingly one of the most complex institutions, then the demand on the administrator for expert knowledge and a diverse set of skills is obvious. Accompanying this surely is the pressure for unusual competence at the trustee level. The chairman or president, especially, must be a knowledgeable and judicious person if he is to bring out the strength of the administrator and yet reserve the right to appraise his behavior. How a hospital goes about identifying trustee talent and preparing people for the special job of president is critical to the success of the organization, and will be more important in the future. A board should have policies generating self-evaluation and self-renewal, for its long-run health and that of the hospital.

Style of the Administrator

The "proper" role of the hospital administrator in policy-making cannot be chosen from three cases or from any list of actual situations. The fact is that administrators' styles are not only a product of their personalities, skills, length of experience, and the configuration of personal needs they bring to their job, they are also a product of the situations they are in: the strength or weakness of the board, especially the president; the length of the administrator's tenure; the medical staff attitudes (and especially whether the staff is a closed or open one); the personal and professional skill of the administrator; the kinds of issues important at a particular time in the hospital; and the environmental forces at work.

One caveat in the policy realm surely is for the administrator to avoid the temptation of depreciating the role and competence of the board to a point where it becomes the handmaiden of the executive-administrator. On the other side let a board beware if it finds it is treating the administrator as a man outside the processes of policy-making.

Developing Mutual Expectations

These warnings reveal that boards and administrators need to develop clear sets of mutual expectations about their roles, and they need to share these expectations deliberately and continuously, especially with regard to policy formulation. In each of the three hospitals, there was an area of shadow within which neither the administrator nor the board could clearly discern what the several roles really were.

This shadowy area cannot be dissipated entirely, and all parties need a tolerance for gray. Role definition in hospital policy-making will not produce black and white distinctions. The important points are (1) that the area of shade is larger in the three hospitals than it need be, and (2) that when men operate on the fiction that they share clear role definitions and expectations when in fact no explicit sharing has taken place, there are bound to be distortions, frictions and inefficiencies in their working together. Thus, in a Cloverdale, two parties assume charity in roles but the administrator feels deprived of his full professional role and the president wonders what inhibits the administrator.

What the Future Holds

What the future holds for the administrative role is a fascinating subject for speculation. Perhaps the rapid growth of the entangling vine of outside constraints (governmental, economic, and medical) will begin to close in the administrator's area of discretion and make his job more programmed and routine. If so, he will not advise young men to embark on the career of hospital administration; it will lack the special verve and challenge it has today. Or perhaps the development of new kinds of public views of total human health as a national resource and the advent of centralized health centers with their advanced technologies and satellite diagnostic stations may create even more challenging jobs for "health executives" in our society.

Whatever the future may hold, today's observer cannot but be struck by the unusual complexity and challenge of the hospital administrator's job. It has no close analogue in other kinds of organizations, really, and it makes impressive demands on men who fill it. The professionalization of the role of administrator may reflect a growing anxiety that success in the future application of the health sciences to human betterment may be impaired more by inability to solve social and organizational problems than by lack of skill to meet technical medical problems. Only with a high tolerance for ambiguity, a mature response to status incongruities and a true sense of the values of his contribution to human health can the administrator derive basic satisfaction from his work. We hope one of the results of this research may be to add some incremental knowledge about hospital administration and thus contribute to these satisfactions in the long run.

The Impact of the Hospital on the Physician, the Patient, and the Community

George Rosen, M.D., Ph.D.

Illness creates dependency. The sick need not only medical treatment, but also personal care and shelter. Throughout history societies have accepted such needs as a responsibility of group life, and have created various institutions to provide the services deemed necessary. One of these institutions, the hospital, is today a cornerstone of any modern system of health care.

Arrangements to provide for the needs of the sick have always been intimately linked with the varying political, economic, social and cultural conditions that govern the life of man. Whether man lived in a city or on the land, whether he suffered scarcity or enjoyed abundance, how he saw his fellowmen and how they looked upon him, the religion he practiced and the values he prized, the learning, sciences and arts that gave shape to his society—all have affected the development of the hospital, the form it has achieved, the services which it provided, and the impact it has had on the community and on specific groups in it. To understand these facets, the hospital has to be seen therefore as an organ of society, sharing its basic characteristics, changing as the society of which it is a part is transformed, and in turn, exerting an influence on various social groups and situations.

At various periods in history, the need to care for the sick and the disabled, the needy and the dependent, has crystallized sufficiently in terms of attitude and practice so that one can speak of institutional models characteristic of certain societies. While knowledge concerning the healing shrines and the secular healing institutions of antiquity is too incomplete to be generalized, this is not the case for the medieval period.

The medieval hospital in all its varied forms was essentially an ecclesiastical institution. While the provision of medical care was one of its functions, it was created primarily on religious and spiritual premises as a philanthropic institution, an agency for poor relief. Generally speaking, the hospital was a religious house in which the nursing personnel had united as a vocational community under a religious rule.[1] The medical staff and its activities are essential to the hospital as we conceive it today. This was not the case in the medieval hospital of Europe. The presence of monastic physicians in religious houses during the early middle ages makes it probable that the sick received some medical care. From the fourteenth century on, however, secular physicians were increasingly associated with hospitals to provide care for patients.[2] However, the physician was not yet an integral member of the hospital organization and remained independent. Nevertheless, this initially loose association did provide the basis for another trend, which, from the seventeenth century on, led the medical profession increasingly to use the hospital for the study of disease and for its own practical education.

Economic, social and political changes toward the end of the medieval period led in the sixteenth century to the replacement of the medieval institution by a hospital whose goals were not religious, but primarily social.[3] That is, the hospital as it existed from the sixteenth through the eighteenth centuries was intended to help in the maintenance of social order while providing for the sick and the needy. It was an instrument of society to ameliorate suffering, to diminish poverty, to eradicate mendicity and to help maintain public order, and it remained an institution combining the care of the sick, an old age home, an almshouse, an orphanage, and in some instances serving as a guest house. In its organization and operation, the early modern hospital still retained various features from its predecessor. One of

[1]Siegfried Reicke, *Das deutsche Spital und sein Recht im Mittelalter* ("Kirchenrechtliche Abhandlungen," Stuttgart, 1932), p. 198; Leon Le Grand, *Statuts d'Hôtels-Dieu et de Léproseries: Recueil de textes du XIIe au XIVe siècles* (Paris: Alphonse Picard et Fils, 1901); Dorothy-Louise Mackay, *Les Hôpitaux et la Charité à Paris au XIIIe Siècle* (Paris: Honoré Champion, 1923), pp. 34–50; Brian Tierney, *Medieval Poor Law: A Sketch of Canonical Theory and Its Application in England* (Berkeley: University of California Press, 1959), p. 87.

[2]E. A. Hammond, "Physicians in Medieval English Religious Houses," *Bulletin of the History of Medicine*, 35:74–77 (1961); Werner Bubb, *Das Stadtarztamt zu Basel: Seine Entwicklungsgeschichte vom Jahre 1529 bis zur Gegenwart* (Zürich Dissertation, 1942), p. 11; A. F. La Cava, *Igiene e Sanità Statuti di Milano del Sec. XIV* (Milano, 1946), pp. 40, 60–61, 71.

[3]F. R. Salter (ed.), *Some Early Tracts on Poor Relief* (London: Methuen & Co., 1929); C. L. Steinbicker, *Poor Relief in the Sixteenth Century* (Washington, D.C.: Catholic University of America, 1937); Friedrich Paret, "Der Einfluss der Reformation auf die Armenpflege," *Zeitfragen des christlichen Volkslebens*, 21:46 (1896).

these was that medical care was still not the primary function of the hospital.

18th Century Development

During the eighteenth century, there developed in Great Britain and with some modifications in the United States and Canada, a pattern of hospital services which persisted until well into the twentieth century and whose influence is still evident in hospital organization in the United States.[4] Hospitals were simply institutions maintained through public funds or private charity where the indigent poor could be cared for more economically than in their own homes. Voluntary hospitals tended to take acute cases—the short-stay patients—while the chronic cases—the insane, the incurables, and those suffering from communicable diseases—went to public institutions.[5]

From the end of the eighteenth century onward, various forces and developments external to the hospital began to impinge upon it, with the result that it was eventually transformed into the institutional type characteristic of the present in economically developed countries. This type of hospital is the product of the scientific and industrial revolutions, and may be characterized as the health workshop or medical factory. Here medical care is the primary goal of the institution, and its provision is governed chiefly by scientific-technological norms and the requirements of organizational rationality and economy. We shall be concerned with the impact of this type of hospital as it developed and as it exists at present.

The Medical Market

Over the past 40 years a marked characteristic of the organized medical profession in the United States has been its generally negative

[4] Dorothy Marshall, *English People in the Eighteenth Century* (London: Longmans, Green & Co., 1956), pp. 186 ff.; B. Kirkman Gray, *A History of English Philanthropy* (London: P. S. King & Son, 1905), pp. 126–31; T. Ferguson, *The Dawn of Scottish Social Welfare* (London and Edinburgh: Thomas Nelson & Sons, 1948), pp. 255–84; K. H. Connell, *The Population of Ireland, 1750–1845* (Oxford: Clarendon Press, 1950), pp. 198–207; M. C. Buer, *Health, Wealth and Population in the Early Days of the Industrial Revolution* (London: George Routledge & Sons, 1926), pp. 257–62.

[5] Henry J. Gibson, *Dundee Royal Infirmary, 1798 to 1948: The Story of the Old Infirmary with a Short Account of More Recent Years* (Printed by William Kidd & Sons, 1948), pp. 11, 12–13; Louisa Twining, *Recollections of Workhouse Visiting and Management during Twenty-five Years* (London, 1880), p. 37; Michael M. Davis, *Cinics, Hospitals, and Health Centers* (New York, 1927), pp. 4–5; Brian Abel-Smith, *A History of the Nursing Profession* (London, 1967), pp. 2, 4.

attitude to innovation in the financing and provision of medical care. This does not mean that one should expect to find unanimity of opinion on the various measures proposed and used to pay for and to distribute organized health services. Opinions among physicians tend toward the conservative side, and change in the organization of medical care has not been welcomed by the national, state and local bodies that speak in the name of the medical profession. Change has been met most often with outright rejection or at best with grudging acceptance. Voluntary health insurance is one example, developed and spread in large measure under the threat of a compulsory national system. This kind of behavior among physicians can be seen in relation to various forms of prepaid and organized medical care: Blue Cross, Blue Shield, union health plans and centers, prepayment group practice plans, various types of hospital programs, and above all, government action in the health field. To interpret this negativism simply as a form of human perversity would be to misconstrue its meaning completely. It should be viewed, rather, as the consequence of a process extending over a period of about 100 years during which the medical profession has endeavored to maintain intact the structure of the medical market against all factors and situations that seemingly or actually threaten its integrity so as to safeguard the area of individual, private practice.

The American physician around the middle of the nineteenth century was a small entrepreneur, a member of the middle class, who shared the socio-economic attitudes and views of his middle class neighbors. According to Richard Hofstadter, "The sanctity of private property, the right of the individual to dispose of and invest it, the value of opportunity and the natural evolution of self-interest and self-assertion, within broad legal limits, into a beneficent social order have been the staple tenets of the central faith" shared by most Americans. As far as possible, it was felt, the individual should be free of governmental regulation and given full scope for individual initiative. While certain undertakings might require joint action within the community, each man was held to be entitled to carve out for himself the largest possible stake. After all, the United States was a free society in which competition was the life-blood not only of trade but of the professions as well.

The Medical Market Structure

In medicine, each man was sufficient unto himself, except as he adhered to rules of professional behavior established by his colleagues. A basic function of these rules, concerned with the behavior of medical men toward the public and to each other, was to regulate access to the medical market, that is, to patients. Acceptance of competition as natural went hand in hand with recognition of the need to deal with excessive zeal and to avoid or patch up consequent abuses. Young physicians competed with established practitioners; in the latter nineteenth century, general practitioners competed with specialists; and the entire medical profession faced the competition of irregular practitioners and outright quacks. But while the medical profession accepted the principle of competition, it also endeavored to protect and promote its economic interests.

Some limits were set on competition so as to stabilize the medical market. Thus, fee bills were adopted to regulate service charges and to discourage under bidding by rival physicians.[6] Furthermore, rules governing competition in the medical market were formulated in codes of professional ethics.[7] Most important was the Code of Ethics adopted by the organizing convention of the American Medical Association in 1847. Its stabilizing intent is clear from the prediction by Nathan Smith Davis in 1883 that it "will probably continue to be the guide of the great mass of intelligent medical men through the centuries to come."[8] Thus, the medical market was the central institution around which medical practice has been structured in the United States since the nineteenth century. In the middle of the nineteenth century, only a few hospitals existed in this country and the medical market structure took no note of them. The same was true of public health organization.

Medical Indigence and Ambulatory Care: Reaction to a Problem

Despite these efforts and intentions, however, economic, technical, scientific and social changes were already beginning to nibble at the foundations of society, and the social organization of medicine could not remain unaffected. Industrialization led to the appearance of a working class living in a congested urban environment. Lack of proper housing, poor nutrition, unhealthful occupations, and above all, the effect of periodic unemployment, combined to make the life of the worker and his family precarious. In case of illness, the services of a

[6]George Rosen, *Fees and Fee Bills: Some Economic Aspects of Medical Practice in Nineteenth Century America* (Baltimore: Johns Hopkins Press, 1946), pp. 36–90.

[7]Donald E. Konold, *A History of American Medical Ethics, 1847–1912* (Madison, Wis.: State Historical Society of Wisconsin, 1962), pp. 9–13.

[8]N. S. Davis, *Journal of the American Medical Association,* 1:57 (1883).

local practitioner might be employed, but the financial resources of these people were too slender to permit extended use of private medical care, and in numerous instances even limited use was not possible. As a result, the worker and his family turned to medical charity, that is, to dispensaries for the sick poor, to the outpatient departments of hospitals, or to physicians whose charges were low.

Dispensaries were originally set up in France and England in the seventeenth century to provide medicines and some medical advice to the needy.[9] By the middle of the nineteenth century, these establishments had become facilities where the poor could receive ambulatory medical care. This primary intent was powerfully reinforced by the interest of physicians in acquiring medical experience, and in teaching medical students at a clinic.[10] The latter element, the teaching motive, has also been a powerful factor in the development of outpatient departments in hospitals.

Practitioners generally honored the provisions of the code of ethics, which called for free service to the sick poor. Nonetheless, many insisted that the community had no right to expect free care. Moreover, often the poor patient went to a young physician just building a practice, who might take a smaller fee, and who often had difficulty in collecting fees.[11]

Dispensaries and Outpatient Departments

Dispensaries and outpatient departments began to be more widely used during the latter half of the nineteenth century as the population increased, and as scientific developments in medicine made hospitals more acceptable to the general public. This trend was intensified by periods of economic stress, immigration, and the development of specialism. The first dispensary in the United States was organized in Philadelphia in 1786. In 1800, there were three dispensaries; by 1900, there were about 100, most of them having been organized during the

[9]"The First London Dispensaries. By a Surgeon," *Fraser's Magazine,* 11:598–607 (1875); *La Vie de Théophraste Renaudot par . . .* (Paris: Gallimard, 1929); Ernest Caulfield, *The Infant Welfare Movement in the Eighteenth Century* (New York: Paul B. Hoeber, 1931), pp. 55–58, 146–76; Harvey Cushing, "Dr. Garth, the Kit-Kat Poet," *Bull. Johns Hopkins Hospital,* 17:1–17 (1906); J. J. Abraham, *Lettsom, His Life, Times, Friends and Descendants* (London, 1933), pp. 109–10.

[10]William Osler, "Remarks on the Functions of an Out-Patient Department," *British Medical Journal,* June 20, 1908, p. 1470.

[11]George Rosen, "Five Years in the Practice of a New York Physician," *New York State Medical Journal,* April 15, 1949, pp. 125–29.

second half of the century. By 1926, the number had risen to more than 5,700.[12] In 1922, according to an estimate of the American Medical Association, these facilities were giving service to almost 8,000,000 persons.[13]

The growth of dispensaries was particularly evident in some eastern cities, and it was there that the first reactions of the medical profession appeared. Beginning in the sixties, the "abuse of medical charity" and the "dispensary evil" were discussed with increasing frequency and vehemence in the medical press. As early as 1868, the *Boston Medical and Surgical Journal* commented editorially on the needless increase of free dispensary and hospital treatment, pointing out that it was a vital injury to young physicians who had to live on the small fees obtainable from "just those middling classes of the community whom the dispensary systems invites to a gratuitous treatment."[14]

The panic of 1873 and the economic distress of the subsequent years tended to intensify the problem. People found private medical care a luxury they could not afford, and sought medical attention where it was free or less expensive. At the same time, physicians used the dispensaries and outpatient departments to obtain training, to gain a reputation, and perhaps to achieve a lucrative practice.[15] Moreover, it was recognized that the profession had an excessive number of practitioners in its ranks. In part, this was due to the Civil War, and because in the following years the study of medicine remained popular since degrees were readily obtained.[16]

Disruption of the Medical Market

Thus, given a market situation in which competition was keen, any factor or element that tended to draw off consumers of medical service, that is, patients, was hotly resented. In other words, the development of the ambulatory medical care facility, the outpatient department or

[12]Davis, *op. cit.*, p. 38.

[13]Harry H. Moore, *American Medicine and the People's Health* (New York: D. Appleton & Co., 1927), p. 31.

[14]"Duties of Hospital Physicians and Surgeons," *Boston Medical and Surgical Journal,* 1 (N.S.): 399 (1868).

[15]"Administration of Medical Charities," *Boston Medical and Surgical Journal,* 97:-279 (1877); "The Abuse of Medical Institutions," *ibid.*, 97:393, 1817; Orville F. Rogers, "The Abuse of Medical Charities," *ibid.*, 97:496–500, 1877.

[16]R. H. Shryock, *Medicine and Society in America, 1660–1860* (New York: New York University Press, 1960), p. 147; *Boston Medical and Surgical Journal,* 2 (N.S.): 112 (1868); *ibid.*, 96:180–81 (1877).

the dispensary, was seen as disrupting the market structure which the medical profession was endeavoring to stabilize. Underlying all the discussion of the dispensary evil and the abuse of medical charity is the basic fact of economic competition. As one physician put the matter in 1877, free treatment of all who applied diverted "the legitimate profits of the ordinary practitioners."[17] Another practitioner emphasized that while medicine is not a trade, "it is an occupation by which men gain a livelihood, and therefore it should be conducted on strict business principles."[18]

The economic attitudes of physicians were buttressed by contemporary social thought which held that the provision of gratuitous treatment to patients who could afford to pay for care would demoralize them. As contemporary jargon put it, they would be pauperized. Furthermore, even the "worthy poor" should not get something for nothing, but should be taught to be provident. Thus, Gurteen, in his *Handbook of Charity Organization* of 1882, described the dispensary system as a "vast school of pauperism, demoralizing the poor, educating them in improvident habits, and teaching them in one of the most vital departments of life, to be thriftless and improvident."[19]

Pauperism vs. Medical Indigence

At this point it is important to note that this was not a peculiarly American phenomenon or problem. As early as 1833, the English medical periodical, the *Lancet,* carried a protest by physicians against the "indiscriminate relief of applicants at the Sheffield Dispensary." Similar instances could be cited from the succeeding decades. Actually, the basic problem was medical indigence, a fact that was recognized as early as 1846 in evidence presented to Lord Ashley's Committee on Medical Poor Relief. Testimony indicated that in terms of medical care, pauperism in the legal sense was a relatively smaller matter as compared with medical indigence. On the basis of testimony by Southwood Smith, W. P. Alison and others, the conclusion seemed inevitable "that the *preventive* should be combined with the *remedial* provision for the health of the poorer classes." To deal with the problem, a system of public dispensaries was proposed to be financed

[17]"Abuse of Medical Institutions," *Boston Medical and Surgical Journal,* 97:393 (1877).

[18]"Letter: The Abuse of Medical Charities," *Boston Medical and Surgical Journal,* 97:508–9 (1877).

[19]Gurteen, *Handbook of Charity Organization* (1882), p.99.

through public as well as private contributions. One witness recommended that "medical care and inspection should be brought as near as possible to the habitations of the poor. In towns, it must be forced upon them, both for their own benefit, and for the safety of the community."[20]

An Active Issue

Most of the medical profession, however, did not recognize the problem of medical indigence, and it was not until 1870 that it became an active issue. This was due in large measure to the fact that after the establishment of the Medical Register in England in 1858, the function of the great voluntary hospitals as schools of medicine became more important and was more clearly defined. The reputation of the hospitals was high, and the sick poor naturally flocked to their outpatient departments and wards. As the demands on the hospitals increased, the problem of ambulatory medical care became more and more acute. The number of in-patients was limited by the number of beds, but this was not the case in the outpatient department. Furthermore, as in the United States, a number of conflicting and converging interests were involved. The hospital medical staff needed suitable and interesting cases for teaching purposes; the local general practitioners depended on patients for their livelihood, and naturally looked with suspicion and hostility on the provision of free medical care to those who should be paying for it; and thirdly, there were the patients who needed medical care, social services, food or a job.

Medical Aspects of Pauperism

In 1870, the problem was raised by Fairlie Clarke in a paper, "The Medical Aspects of Pauperism," at the annual meeting of the British Medical Association. Four years later, in an article entitled "Hospital Reform," Clarke clearly defined the problem and proposed a remedy. "The proper clients for a hospital," he said, "may be easily defined in general terms. They are those who are raised above the level of pauperism but who are not able to pay even the lowest scale of medical charges. I admit that is not always easy to say in the case of a particular individual whether he does or does not belong to this section. . . . How then are we to discriminate between those who are and who are

[20]*The Health and Sickness of Town Populations . . . District Dispensaries* (1846), pp. 21, 29; *Lancet*, 1833, p. 628.

not proper subjects for gratuitous medical charity?'' Clarke proposed the appointment of a responsible person who would make such inquiries, and deal with the problems. Twenty years later, in 1895, after various discussions and trials, the first social worker was appointed at the Royal Free Hospital in London to perform this task.[21]

Another proposal to deal with this situation was to establish provident dispensaries, that is, institutions to which prospective patients would pay a small monthly sum on a regular basis for such medical needs as might arise. A number of such facilities were established in England and the United States, but they never commended themselves to those for whom they were intended. The earnings of the medically indigent were small enough, free care could be obtained in hospital clinics, especially in teaching institutions, and so little came of this idea. It does represent one of the earlier attempts to develop a method for prepayment of medical care using out-patient departments and dispensaries as a base.

Impact of the Hospital on the Medical Market

Thus, by the latter part of the nineteenth century, the hospital, chiefly through its outpatient services and related facilities, had begun to affect the medical market, the central institution around which medical practice was organized. This occurred because the hospital as an institution was the place where a number of concurrent factors converged and exerted an influence either directly or in terms of secondary effects. On the socio-economic side were such elements as urban growth, immigration, economic fluctuations, and industrialism—all leading to the appearance of a medically indigent population. These coincided with such changes on the medical side as the appearance of specialism, advances in medical knowledge and technique, a recognition of the need for better medical education, and of the possibilities inherent in hospitals for this purpose.

It was in these terms that the emergence of the modern hospital first made an impact on the medical profession, on patients and on the community. Endeavors to provide ambulatory medical care through hospital outpatient departments and dispensaries helped call attention to the problem of medical indigence, thus leading to the first steps in

[21]Fairlie Clarke, ''Hospital Reform,'' *Macmillans Magazine,* August 1874, cited in E. Moberly Bell, *The Story of Hospital Almoners* (London: Faber & Faber, 1961), pp. 21–22).

developing medical social work, and to the earliest modern prepayment schemes. At the same time, a large segment of the medical profession developed attitudes of hostility to the facilities and institutions which they viewed as unfair competitors in the medical market. To be sure, some physicians recognized that there were people who could pay for most necessities, but not for medical care. Others, however, would have agreed with a Philadelphia practitioner who wrote in 1903, "when people in this land, except recent immigrants, are so poor that they cannot pay a moderate fee to some struggling physician, their poverty is a crime deserving punishment rather than encouragement."[22]

Forerunner of Income Ceilings

From the 1880's onward, medical charity and its abuse were discussed with increasing frequency in medical circles. Indeed, the question became even more prominent in the first decades of the twentieth century. Efforts were made to reduce the economic competition of the clinics and outpatient departments by insisting that economic criteria be established to determine who could or could not pay for medical care, and that such standards were to be used by clinics. In essence, this demand was a forerunner of the income ceilings set up in prepayment plans. Indeed, in New York State the agitation was so considerable that a law was enacted in 1899 licensing dispensaries and placing them under the general supervision of the State Board of Charities. Under this law, applicants for service who falsely represented themselves as indigent could be punished, but 15 years after its enactment no violators had been prosecuted.

The ineffectiveness of these efforts was due in large measure to the fact that many physicians were more interested in using clinics for their own purposes, professional advancement, specialized training, or building a practice. The medical profession was embarrassed and hampered by the excessive number of practitioners in its ranks. In 1860, there was one practitioner to every 572 persons in the United States; by 1938, the ratio had been changed to one to 764, and this shift occurred with a growing population.

Stabilization of the Medical Market

These figures reflect developments that occurred during the period between 1910 and 1930, which made it possible for the medical profes-

[22]Matthew Woods, *Medical News,* 83:1042 (1903).

sion to stabilize the medical market for a time and to come to terms with the hospital. To many physicians it was clear that the profession could not hope to improve its position unless it restricted the number of those who aspired to enter its ranks. This became possible after 1910 when the number of medical schools was drastically reduced as a result of the long-overdue reform of medical education. From 1910 to 1930, the ratio of physicians to population declined steadily, reaching a low of 125 per 100,000 in 1930.[23] This period also saw the final acceptance of specialties by organized medicine, and the beginnings of the system of specialty boards. After 1920, the American Medical Association not only established committees that worked with groups of specialists to develop and enforce educational standards, but also insisted that physicians who secured hospital appointments and privileges belong to county medical societies. Thus, while the medical profession was raising its standards, it was also restricting entrance to its precincts, of which the hospital was becoming the most significant, and thus creating for itself what might be called a seller's market. These developments made it possible to achieve a degree of stabilization of the medical market, at the same time increasing the power of organized medicine to combat economic heresy, that is, not only clinics, but, even more significantly, proponents of prepayment medical care—especially of those forms not acceptable to the medical profession.

Again, however, this stabilized situation was short-lived. Again socio-economic and scientific-technological developments disrupted the medical market, and this time beyond any hope of a return to the status quo ante. And again the hospital has played a major role in this process. An important factor has been the change in public attitude toward hospitals. Around the turn of the century, the adoption of asepsis had so lowered operative mortality that the public began to accept hospitals as agencies of social good. It was realized that various forms of ill-health could be treated more effectively in the hospital than in the home. This trend was further strengthened and intensified by the development of laboratory techniques for diagnosis, of roentgenology, and of a variety of costly therapeutic modalities. At the same time the value of the hospital as an educational institution for physicians, medical students and nurses was also increasingly recognized. As a result, by

[23]*Annual Report, General Education Board, 1921–1922* (New York, 1923), p. 17; *ibid., 1924–1925* (New York, 1926), p. 8; Dept. H.E.W., *Health, Education and Welfare Trends* (1960), p. 44.

the early years of the twentieth century, hospitals were admitting increasing numbers of paying patients in private rooms and other accommodations set apart from those for the indigent.

With increasing complexity of medical care and increased acceptance of hospital service, there developed a need for adjunct services in addition to the usual medical and nursing care. These have involved social work, nutrition, and more complex record and business procedures. As hospitals had to accommodate more complex functions, additional personnel, facilities and equipment, their organization also grew increasingly complex and their operation more costly. These consequences, interacting with or affected by developments outside the hospital, have, in turn, led to new phenomena and situations, namely, the appearance of a new profession: hospital administration, the growth of voluntary prepayment plans for hospital expenses, an increased awareness and greater attention to the quality of hospital service and medical care, and a more prominent role of government, at all levels, in the hospital field, especially in the financing and construction of hospitals. The consequences of these developments have been to give the hospital a central role in modern medical care, and to make it responsible for complex and wide-ranging tasks. At the same time, the impact of this situation has made itself felt both within and without the hospital.

The Situation Today

Today, for example, the medical practitioner must have some hospital connection, both for his patients and himself.[24] The fledgling physician is no longer apprenticed to another physician but to a bureaucratic institution, where he serves as intern and resident. Throughout his career, hospital appointments are crucial to his practice and to his advance in some medical hierarchy. To a considerable degree, the referral mechanism is controlled by informal cliques in hospitals. At the same time, there has been an increase in the number of ancillary occupations filled by persons on a salaried basis.

[24] O. Hall, "Informal Organization of the Medical Profession," *Canadian Journal of Political and Economic Science,* 12:30–44 (1946); *idem,* "The Stages in a Medical Career," *American Journal of Sociology,* 53:327–36 (1948); *idem,* "Types of Medical Careers," *American Journal of Sociology,* 55:243–53 (1949); C. W. Mills, *White Collar: The American Middle Classes* (New York: Oxford University Press, 1951), pp. 115–21.

These trends and developments underlie in considerable measure the behavior of physicians in relation to various agencies for the organization and financing of medical care. Attitudes developed in combating dispensaries and outpatient clinics were carried over in endeavoring to deal with such arrangements as Blue Cross, Blue Shield, prepayment group practice, union-management health plans, and, above all, government action in the health field. Earlier innovations in the organization and distribution of medical care were opposed on the ground that they destroyed the personal relation between physician and patient, they decreased professional competence, they were unethical, and similar arguments that are familiar to our ears. These reactions have been adapted to the changes which the profession faces.

One major change has been the narrowing of the area of practice (the access to the medical market) of the general physician, with the result that he has been fighting back by trying to keep hospitals, specialists, and other organizations and individuals concerned with medical care from competing with him and limiting his activities in ways he considers unfair. This aim is implicit in the establishment of the Academy of General Practice, the general practice departments in hospitals, in the idea of an American Board of General Practice, and in the opposition to review and control of the quality of medical care by prepayment agencies and labor-management funds.

This situation also affects the specialist, who wishes to maintain the status quo so that his privileged position will not be altered, and he too endeavors to render ineffective any apparent or threatened competition. This is evident in the opposition to full-time salaried appointments of clinicians in hospitals and in the controversies concerning the remuneration for services of pathologists and radiologists in hospitals. In general, considerations of this kind, whether overt or covert, are involved in the insistence on free choice of physician, on fee for service practice, and in all the other battle cries that have echoed on the medical care battlefields for over four decades.

Viewed sociologically, the behavior of a large part of the medical profession represents a reaction to the forces and processes that are compelling it to come to terms with modern industrialized society. One may say that medicine is experiencing its Industrial Revolution, and despite his Luddite behavior, the medical practitioner is being brought into the "health plant," that is, the hospital and the whole complex organization for the provision of medical care, where he is being required to accept the requisite "labor discipline." This is obvious within the hospital, especially in the voluntary hospital, where the interplay of the forces discussed above has produced the most dramatic impact, and has led to painful tensions and conflicts.

Administrative Duality

The central source of this situation is to be found in the characteristic administrative structure which the voluntary hospital inherited from its eighteenth century origins in Great Britain and the United States.[25] Each voluntary hospital was an independent institution managed by its own governors or trustees, and staffed by physicians and surgeons who gave their services gratis. In return, the medical staff was enabled to use suitable and interesting cases for teaching and research. Later, as the public began to accept the advantages of hospitalization, physicians began to use the hospital for their own patients. Moreover, as scientific medicine developed and became institutionalized in the hospital, the physician became essential for its operation, while the institution became more and more indispensable for the practice of good medicine. At the same time, the physician had no administrative or financial responsibility in the hospital. This administrative duality was possible as long as most of the patients were indigent, as long as the hospital tended to remain a self-contained, relatively simple organization, and as long as the physician could use the hospital and still retain his position as an independent entrepreneur.

However, as the hospital increased in size and complexity, as the development of medicine required the use of costly equipment, as changing social and economic conditions altered the financing of hospital care and created new patterns of hospital utilization, the organizational relationships within the hospital have been disturbed and have become unstable. Its very centrality in the provision of medical care has exposed it to the influences of various forces that have been reshaping the medical market. Increasingly important in this respect are the so-called third parties, the organized consumers of medical care and their representatives. In short, the hospital having become a large-scale organization requires a more explicit organization division of labor and more efficient management. For the physician, this means an increasing accommodation to institutionalized teamwork, a prospect which is highly distasteful to many physicians. The degree of super-

[25]George Bugbee, "The Physician in the Hospital Organization," *New England Journal of Medicine* (1959), pp. 896–901.

vision will vary with the institution and the setting, but the prospect is that increased administrative rationality will characterize the emerging community hospital and related facilities, and that the practice of the physician will be under the scrutiny not only of his professional colleagues but also of others, all of whom will appraise his activities.

Indeed, the very nature of large scale organization raises problems of administrative efficiency and rationality, productivity and accountability of personnel, including physicians, nurses and others. While I have raised these issues in relation to the voluntary hospital in the United States, they are not limited to this country.[26] An increasingly complex industrial society is bringing forth hospitals appropriate to itself wherever it has developed. And this society, in turn, through its impact on healthy institutions and the healthy professions is moving them to a new stage of development.

The Changing Years

In the first place, the medical market as it existed 100 years ago no longer is a viable reality. During this period, the organized medical profession fought to defend and to retain an institutional arrangement which was to become increasingly obsolescent. Loyalty to the profession came to be defined in terms of conformity of thought regarding one major institution—fee-for-service solo-practice. As part of this endeavor, the organized medical groups (national, state, local) concentrated their energies on the repression of heresy and raised intellectual barriers against the ideas of a critical and unfriendly world. Knowledge that it was increasingly being isolated as the champion of a system that was becoming more and more irrelevant to the needs of a modern society added to the feeling of insecurity. As a result, many members of the profession took refuge in a never-never land, and insisted that others accept their view as an accurate description of existing conditions. Under economic and moral attack, they identified the security of its economic organization (medical market on a fee-for-service solo-practice arrangement) with the internal security of society itself, and sought political and ideological allies on this basis. And, finally, they set about to celebrate, glorify, and render all but sacrosanct with praise the very institution that was under attack, and that has been largely responsible for public reaction to the medical profession. The medical

[26]Charles Chilard, "L'Hôpital dans L'économie nationale: Efficacité et rendement en milieu hospitalier," *L'Hôpital et l'Aide sociale à Paris* (1961), pp. 644–67.

profession rallied to defend what has had to give way, and thus allowed its values and valid claims in numerous areas to be identified with one institution: the medical market of a simple competitive situation.

Now, in the second half of the twentieth century, this creed still prevails in many respects, but it has become increasingly nostalgic as the assumptions embedded in it have become largely irrelevant. The medical market as it is now being reorganized will take account of physicians, patients, hospitals, prepayment organizations, industry and government. Some leaders within organized medicine are becoming aware of the realities of life. Indicative is the recent statement by Dr. Leonard J. Raider, president of United Medical Service of New York, that "we are going to have to learn to put behind us our age-old fear of government participation."

Hospital: Central Element

Secondly, the hospital 100 years ago was still peripheral to the medical market but was making its influence felt. Today, the hospital is a central element in the structure of the medical market. At the same time, the very process which has changed an institution for the sick poor to a medical center for everyone has also made the hospital an object of community interest, investigation and action. For example, concern has been expressed over the lack of coordination between hospitals and other community health institutions. In part, this is related to the circumstance that those who administer hospitals still are more concerned with their individual institution rather than with community problems. For example, the doctor and the family may wish to have a patient in a hospital even when not medically necessary. This factor may concide with the desire of the hospital administration to have operating incomes increased by high occupancy. Thus, from the viewpoint of a single institution there may be apparent advantages in having more beds. However, every bed added beyond actual community needs, and every bed occupied by a patient who could be served in a lower cost facility or cared for at home, tends to raise overall medical costs as well as prepayment and insurance premiums. In turn, increased costs lead to a search for more economical and efficient use of resources. Clearly, the hospital because of its impact on the community is today integrally involved in the social reconstruction of health institutions in which we are engaged.

For this reason it is important to understand what has happened and what is happening in terms of societal structures, functions and processes. What I have endeavored to do in this broad review is to pull together some points from a number of studies that I have made. These points show:

1) That a study of the hospital as a social institution related to its societal environment provides a useful point of departure for understanding what goes on within it;
2) That such a study makes it possible to understand how this institution has undergone change in the course of time, thus throwing light on problems that seem obscure when viewed in strictly contemporary and operational terms;
3) That the internal organization of the hospital must be seen not only in formal terms, but also in terms of social attitudes, beliefs, and ideas that derive as much from experience outside the institution as from within;
4) That the hospital can thus be seen as an element in a dialectical process which therefore can never be entirely stable, and which requires the introduction, exploration and application of a broad concept of planning (national, state, local) to make sure that the hospital can provide for the needs of the community, and that the community can provide what the hospital needs to carry out is functions.

The Spontaneous Development of Informal Organization

E. Jackson Baur, Ph.D.

We are all familiar with the office "grapevine" that transmits unofficial news, with the cliques that gather at the water cooler during coffee breaks or at lunch tables, and with "empire-building" by supervisors. These are all examples of the informal side of large organizations. Although administrators everywhere have been aware of these things for a long time, their significance to the organization has not always been apparent. The event that illuminated the importance of informal groups was the accidental discovery of the human factor in industry by social scientists who studied workers at the Western Electric Company in Chicago around 1930.

The Discovery of Human Relations

A team of experts from Harvard University's Graduate School of Business Administration undertook to investigate the various environmental factors that affect the efficiency of industrial workers. They began their experiment by assigning six young women who assembled telephone relays to a separate room where they continued the same work, but under special supervisors and under conditions where their behavior could be observed and their individual work output measured. The experimenters first introduced rest pauses of differing duration and frequency; later, they varied the length of the working day and week. Throughout the two years of the experiment, the output of the girls followed a general upward trend, regardless of any particular change in rest pauses or working hours. To the surprise of the investigators, productivity did not decline when they restored the original work schedule without breaks.

Two Unanticipated Changes

After testing and rejecting explanations for this phenomenon in terms of fatigue, monotony, and wage incentives, the experimenters concluded that the true explanation lay in two unanticipated changes:

(1) the growth of cohesion and friendship among the six girls, and (2) the personal consideration and attention given them by their new supervisors. The girls themselves had been consulted and advised about the changes that were being made on the assumption that this would enlist their whole-hearted co-operation and minimize the effect of uncontrolled psychological factors. They had been set apart from the ordinary workers, observed by important visitors, and even interviewed in the superintendent's office. Their increasing productivity reflected gratifying changes in their social environment.

To learn more about the nature of these human factors within the plant, the Harvard social scientists designed another study for a group of workers. This time, however, they did not alter their working conditions or encourage them to co-operate. Instead, they merely observed and interviewed a dozen men who worked at wiring banks—parts of electrical equipment for telephone exchanges. The researchers simply wanted to find out what went on in such a group rather than to study the effects of experimental changes in working conditions.

The second study group was assigned to a special room where the facilities and procedures were identical with those of the department from which they were selected, except that a trained observer sat at a desk in the back of the room and kept a record of what occurred. An interviewer talked with the men occasionally and they were invited to talk to him privately about their work and what went on in the room whenever they felt like it. This objective study of the Bank Wiring Room uncovered some of the spontaneous relationships and informal activities that exert a strong influence on the attitudes and productivity of workers. Within this group researchers found friendship circles, leadership and distinctions of status, production standards different from those of management, techniques for disciplining, and ways of solving production problems without appealing to supervisors. In short, a complex informal system within the formal setting of the factory.

The Human Relations Movement

The implications of this research for the personnel policies of management initiated what has been called the human relations movement in business administration that has affected a revolution in personnel practices. Subsequently, further research was done on informal groups in other organizations—military units in World War II, prisons, schools, hospitals—and in each case unplanned, personal relationships were found to exert a significant influence on the functioning of the larger system.

Studies of informal activities among employees, students, prisoners, and soldiers may give a false impression that cliques are peculiar to persons in the lower ranks who traditionally resist the demands of executives, supervisors and officers. Not so. Informal practices and groups are also found among executives and professional men. In the field of journalism, for instance, newspaper publishers have been found who have unannounced policies on the selection and treatment of news that conflicts with the official code of the publishers' association. Reporters get to know what these policies are from experience and the "grapevine." In one large city, physicians were found to be unified through a complex system of formal and informal ties controlled by an inner circle which selected men for admission to practice in the area and even determined their advancement within the profession.

In all enduring large organizations there is an informal aspect. However, it is not equally developed in all organizations; there are conditions that encourage or retard its growth. An informal system tends to flourish where large numbers of persons come together in the same place, as in factories, schools, and hospitals. There is more opportunity for close personal ties when the turnover of personnel is low. Perhaps informal associations achieve their fullest development among persons who are separated from their families, who room and board as well as work together, such as college students, sailors, soldiers, and prisoners. Informal contacts at work tend to increase when the job itself requires communication and co-operation between employees rather than separate tasks focused on materials or customers. For instance, a social scientist who studied the social structure of a bank found few informal bonds among tellers, but many among employees of departments that had no contacts with customers.

Persons Who Work Together, Stay Together

However, persons who work apart from one another may associate during "breaks" or after work if they are much alike and have similar problems. Private secretaries to the executives of a large corporation were found to spend much time together. Railroad men, although they are usually dispersed when at work, get together when they are off duty. Their irregular hours of work make it difficult for them to establish durable associations with men in occupations having routine working hours. Furthermore, those who pursue a craft with strong traditions and pride in their work are inclined to recreate and socialize with others in the same trade. Printers in larger cities have formed a multitude of clubs for hobbies, sports, intellectual and political activity. Whenever persons in similar situations, and with the same status are confronted with comparable problems, they tend to find a collective solution to their individual needs.

For many persons, association with workmates on or off the job provides their most satisfying social activity. One study cited the case of an unemployed textile worker who carried her lunch to the mill every noon so she could continue to eat with the "girls." However, persons with a satisfying family life and congenial neighbors and relatives are less likely to form friendships with their workmates. This tendency was the explanation offered for the surprising discovery that British longshoremen preferred random work assignments to being reassigned with the same men. A similar attitude was found among industrial workers with strong family ties who were recent migrants from rural areas. They may also have felt different from and rebuffed by the city-bred people among whom they worked.

Large and Small Informal Groups

The informal groups we have been considering consist of a few persons who know one another intimately—the kind of small group sociologists call "primary." Also important are large groups divided by differences of religion, nationality, race, socio-economic class, sex, or age that divide the personnel of organizations in ways highly significant to the employees but unrecognized in management's formal charges. The interactions of persons different in these easily recognizable ways, but who are not friends, are governed by stereotyped preconceptions. Since they treat one another in an impersonal, categorical way rather than as unique personalities, it is convenient to refer to these large divisions simply as categories. Categories may be temporary, or peculiar to one industry or a single establishment. A unionization drive may raise issues that for a short time divide workers into bitterly hostile factions. For instance, one study disclosed that the employees of a gypsum plant were divided between the below-ground miners and the above-ground mill workers, who although drawn from the same population, saw themselves as wholly different kinds of people.

Primary Groups Are Adjustive for Individuals

Primary groups fulfill a number of significant functions for persons in large organizations. The newly hired worker often depends on the small, informal group to show him "the ropes," knowledge which supplements whatever formal training he may receive from his superior. News travels quickly via primary groups. They are the clandestine transmitters and receivers of information before it is officially released. After the news is released, they amend, amplify, and interpret it. Thus, each person gets a larger, more detailed, and meaningful—but possibly distorted and erroneous—picture of what is going on in the organization. In case of accidents or illness, members of a primary group may help one another. When some of the most dexterous workers in the Bank Wiring Room at Western Electric completed what they felt was a normal day's work, they helped slower workers. Furthermore, if a member breaks a company rule, his primary group may "cover up" for him. The group often provides acceptable ways of compensating for personal deficiences. The less competent interviewers in a state employment agency, one study revealed, used their lunch hour to cultivate friendships with their more able colleagues and thus compensated for their lower competitive position in the office.

Thus, the group protects its members from authoritative action. It provides a psychological buffer between the individual and the organization. In general, it functions as a haven from the impersonal, rationalized methods of large organizations. As such, it can be a positive aid for the adjustment of individual employees to the demands of the organization.

The Subculture of Informal Groups

Informal groups are the source of many practices and customs. They generate new words, carry out ceremonies, invent games, exert discipline, and relate people to one another. In long established industries and services, informal groups create a unique way of life—what, in the language of the social scientist, is called a "subculture."

Perhaps the most colorful trait of any trade or profession is its jargon or special language. New words are coined to refer to tools and techniques—distinctions that are meaningful only to the practitioner. The argot includes words that express subtle and significant distinctions which can thereby be communicated with greater efficiency to those who share the language. However, new synonyms are often substituted for perfectly serviceable English words, which suggests that the jargon also serves the social function of secrecy and exclusiveness. It protects the in-group's monopoly of a given field of work and it distinguishes persons "in the know" from outsiders. It serves as a "pass" for mobile members of the trade.

Small groups tend to develop a set of rituals. Newcomers, for instance, must be initiated before they are fully accepted by members. The initiation may take the form of hazing or practical jokes which test the ability of the novice to "take it." Although these tests are rarely formalized, they have some of the same functions as initiation ceremonies of fraternal orders, and the ordeals of primitive adolescence rites. The group may also observe important events in the lives of its members, such as becoming a father or having a birthday. Such transition rituals confirm the acceptance of the individual who is honored as well as strengthen the bonds among all the members. Parties, on and off the job, and picnics or excursions add to the solidarity of the work group. Subsequent reports of these events take on the character of legends, especially if there is exaggeration in the retelling that emphasizes qualities valued or respected by the members.

On the Lighter Side

Work groups often develop habitual forms of play that fill time during "breaks," in the lunch hour, or after work. For example, the men at the copy desk of a morning newspaper that was studied always concluded their night's work with a gambling game invented by one of their group. The sport of corkball was invented by workers in one St. Louis brewery to while away time during the lunch hour.

The men of the Bank Wiring Room periodically engaged in a simple game of "binging" in which one man would strike another sharply on the upper arm thereby incurring the obligation to submit to a similar blow in return. The same technique was used when one member of the group incurred the displeasure of the others, except that the blow would be harder than usual. What started as play became a technique of control, along with the more familiar devices of razzing, name calling, and slighting. For example, one of the men was derisively called by the name of a famous race horse because he persisted in working faster than the others thought appropriate.

Restriction of output has been a chronic source of frustration to foremen and supervisors. Wherever several people are employed at the same job, they tend to develop a common understanding of what constitutes a fair day's work. Needless to say, it is invariably less than what their superiors think they could do. Although the men of the Bank Wiring Room were paid according to a group incentive plan, they adhered to a norm of 2,000 connections per day. Some consistently produced a little more and others a little less, but the coercive effect of their norm was apparent from the tendency of the overproducers to report less than they made and the underproducers to report more. One man who persisted in turning out *and reporting* more than the norm was subjected to ridicule and sarcasm. Not only was this "rate buster," to use the jargon, berated, but some of the other men who occasionally lagged below an acceptable rate were vilified as "chiselers." The punishment of both kinds of transgressors is evidence that the group abided by a real standard, and restriction of output was not simply an attempt to do as little work as possible.

Informal Standards at Work

Adherence to an informal standard of production served to protect the group from management's pressure to produce. It nullified the objective of the incentive payment plan. That is "worked" for the men is evident from the favorable attitude of their supervisors who felt that they were good, dependable workers with a satisfactory record of output and efficiency. It also reduced competition among the men in the group, thereby removing one source of internal tension. In sum, restriction of production contributed to group stability by minimizing internal dissension and providing protection from outside pressure.

Job trading was another practice contrary to the rules of the company that was engaged in by the employees under observation in the Bank Wiring Room. In spite of an explicit regulation prohibiting trading—on the apparent assumption that specialization is more efficient than versatility—wiremen frequently traded jobs with soldermen. Although trades were usually arranged among the men themselves, they occasionally requested permission of their group chief, despite the fact that he was officially responsible for enforcing the very rule he helped violate. Without exception, all trades were made on the initiative of the wiremen and often reluctantly acceded to by the solderman. The significance of this sub rosa activity became apparent when it was noted that wiremen held a status in the group higher than that of soldermen. In light of the current trend in personnel practice away from overspecialization, we can surmise that informal trading was better practice than the company's official rules, at least in this particular situation.

The Informal Social Order

However, increased efficiency was certainly not the motive for trading or the reason it persisted. In addition to providing relief from the monotony of wiring, it appears to have fulfilled a need for expressing and acknowledging the superiority of wiremen over soldermen.

The status distinction between wiremen and soldermen was but one feature of the informal social order in the Bank Wiring Room. The men also divided themselves into two cliques, each including wiremen, soldermen, and inspectors. The clique of men who worked at benches near the front of the room were superior in status to the clique seated at the back of the room. Associations through play, trading, and helping one another tended to be confined to clique mates.

Rudimentary law and government, the researchers found, emerged through the acknowledged leadership of one member of the dominant clique who consistently took the initiative in emergencies. When disputants threatened to lose their tempers, he intervened and settled the quarrel. On one occasion, the group exhausted its supply of high-quality wire and the foremen would not distribute more until they had used up some that the men considered defective. At this juncture, the informal leader took matters into his own hands and obtained a supply of good wire through his connections in other departments.

From these illustrations, it is apparent that the informal work group, in a real sense, is a miniature society. It possesses in simple form all of the essential features of larger, more complex social systems. For example: (1) It has its own culture that includes a set of norms and values that fix standards of conduct for its members among themselves and with outsiders. (2) Its participants engage in a continuous process of communication and interaction facilitated by a specialized vocabulary and conventional patterns of action, ritual, and play elaborated far beyond the requirements of the job. (3) It has an internal social structure of roles and relationships divided by factional distinctions and graded into a hierarchy of ranks. (4) It is maintained by established techniques of social control that eliminate internal sources of tension by resolving conflicts and punishing offenders, and by protecting itself from threatening outside forces. (5) It possesses a conception of the whole organization and of its own place within this larger structure.

The Typical History of an Informal Group

The informal group develops slowly and the very fact that its members have been together for some period of time makes a difference in their relations with one another and with newcomers. For this, and other reasons, we can distinguish a typical sequence of stages in the histories of informal groups.

It is obvious that a pre-condition for the emergence of a group is communication among the potential members. When people come into contact with one another and interact, the conditions are ripe for a group to take form. When they interact more frequently with one another than with others—and do this repeatedly for successive days and weeks—a rudimentary group has made its appearance.

The realization of common interests tends to knit informal groups together and marks the second stage of their development. The members may do the same kind of work or different—but co-ordinated—work in the same department; the linking element is a common interest in the product manufactured or the service performed. They may have similar problems or privileges. A significant effect of common interests is that they not only draw some people together but simultaneously separate them from others with divergent or conflicting interests. Common interests at one and the same time generate a sense of likeness and of difference. The consciousness of being different from others, or having higher or lower status, of being more or less privileged, stengthens the unity of the group. The *esprit de corps* among the girls in the Relay Assembly Test Room at Western Electric, for example, was attributed in large measure to their conception of themselves as a priviliged group treated with consideration and solicitude not accorded ordinary assemblers.

Toward Group Solidarity

Curiously, low status may also generate group solidarity. In one situation that was studied, the working conditions in the anodizing department of an aircraft plant were arduous and repulsive. Uncomfortable rubber clothing and masks were necessary to protect workers from the acid; the heat and non-porous clothing caused profuse sweating. In the plant, the department was generally referred to as the "tank hole," and the men who worked there as "those dirty tank men." Perhaps in part because of their despised status, they developed strong camaraderie.

As communication continues between a small group with common interests, they gradually begin to think alike and to understand one another. They agree on what constitutes a fair day's work. They coin words with a meaning unique to the group. Stories of past exploits give them a history. They introduce games, hold parties, and invent rituals. A whole complex of social activities is elaborated that goes far beyond the requirements of the job. In short, they act together, agree on how things are to be done, and decide what is and what is not important. They adhere to prescribed patterns of conduct and believe in the same values. The sociologist would say they exhibit "consensus" and possess a subculture.

Consensus can include acceptance of differences among themselves as well as likenesses. One among them becomes the leader, another his lieutenant, another the clown, and an eccentric one perhaps the group's scapegoat. A status hierarchy becomes manifest in the consistency with which certain persons take initiative over others, and this crystallization of differentiated roles marks the third and most advanced stage of group development. With the roles and their interrelations prescribed according to an established subculture, the group acquires a degree of stability and capacity for collective action that makes it appropriate to say it has a social structure.

If the group becomes larger, lays down rules, and chooses officers, it ceases to be an informal group and becomes a club or association. Some labor unions have originated in just this way. If the original group does not become formalized, it may split into factions and divide or dissolve altogether.

To summarize, the typical evolution of an informal group includes three definite stages, each distinguished by the emergence of interaction, common interests, and structure. Each stage is marked by the addition of new features until the group is fully developed and exhibits the essential qualities of a complete social system.

Effects of Informal Groups on the Organization

What are the effects of these informal groups on large organizations? As we have previously indicated, they do not necessarily conflict with the objectives of management, as is so often assumed. In fact, the findings of considerable social research suggest that informal groups are *essential for organizational stability*. Objective studies of large organizations have shown that informal groups can strengthen employee morale, reduce absenteeism and turnover, promote harmony, and increase efficiency. These positive influences are stressed in this paper because they are often overlooked by administrators concerned over the informal group's possible negation of their attempts to effect good management.

The presence of small, spontaneous groups is one of the essential elements of morale in large organizations. Other ingredients include confidence in leadership, a reasonable expectation of continued employment, and opportunities for advancement. Morale depends upon solidarity with one's fellow workers or associates as well as upon a willingness to follow orders. Field studies of German soldiers at the close of World War II disclosed the power of primary groups to hold military units together despite fearful losses, frantic retreats, and broken communications. National Socialist political convictions contributed only slightly to the unity of the German army when compared with the solidarity motivated by dependence on primary groups for the satisfaction of fundamental personality needs. Soldiers, being cut off from families and friends, are more dependent on their comrades than workers, but the functions of primary groups in an enterprise or institution are similar if, less salient, than in an army.

Minimizing Absenteeism and Turnover

The value of informal groups in minimizing absenteeism and turnover was convincingly demonstrated by a comparison of two wartime aircraft plants in California. The causes of absences and resignations could be isolated because one plant had high and the other low turnover, yet both recruited employees from the same labor market. The firm with high turnover adhered to personnel policies that interfered with the development of spontaneous groups, while the other company made every effort to keep workers in their jobs, stabilize their relations, and create an environment favorable to the development of informal groups.

Efficiency is often increased by changes in the work assignments arranged among primary group members. They may divide work among themselves in order to increase the specialization of their tasks beyond what is prescribed in the job description. On the other hand, they may combine work by sharing and trading what is supposed to be done by separate persons. Perhaps the most common practice is the arrogation of supervisory functions, so abundantly evident in the earlier cited Bank Wiring Room, where the men set their own standard of production and developed techniques to enforce it.

Innovations in work techniques, it would seem, are accomplished more successfully when they are introduced to small groups who are given an opportunity to participate in the necessary planning for them rather than by simply telling workers to adopt new methods of doing their job. A study of operatives in a pajama factory demonstrated that the greater the amount of worker participation in adopting new techniques and adjusting rates of pay, the quicker they recovered a satisfactory level of efficiency, the lower was the rate of turnover, and the fewer expressions of hostility toward the company.

Evidence that informal groups are inevitable and that they can help attain management's objectives inescapably implies that the wisest course for administrators to follow is to encourage the development of constructive informal groups. A policy of discouraging spontaneous groups is futile and ignoring them is dangerous.

The Dynamics of Professionalism: The Case of Hospital Administration

Harold L. Wilensky, Ph.D.

There are two major ways of thinking about people at work. The first is to become immersed in the unique history, traditions, vocabulary of the group under study and thus come to appreciate its peculiarities—to learn that no one is quite like a hospital administrator, a school superintendent, a watch repairman, or service-station manager.

The second approach is comparative and sociological. It forces the observer to seek the common elements beneath the surface—to compare apparently dissimilar occupations in one time and place, to compare the same occupations across time and place, and thus come to appreciate the oneness of human nature. For instance, consider the phenomenon of output restriction. On the one hand, you have the industrial worker who goldbricks, slows down, or to be more tolerant and more accurate, regulates his workpace according to the expectations of the work group. But the output restriction of the laborer is matched by the output restriction of the doctor, who in the course of his training and his practice comes to acquire a slippery definition of "emergency"—e.g., one for patients who call in the daytime, another for patients who call at 3 a.m. on a rainy morning. The point is not that doctors are as blameworthy as laborers in regulating their workpace but that people everywhere seek some control over their jobs—and one of the main targets for control is the question of how much work will be done and how fast.

When I am tempted to treat the professions as unique in their claim to great dignity and their expression of a service ideology, and to treat the professional association as something quite different from let us say, the labor union, I take out three quotations from my file.

One concerns a Detroit garbage collector, another, a physician in 12th-century Salerno, and the third, the South African Dingaka, an association of witch doctors. Each quotation provides us with a theme for our consideration of the dynamics of professionalization.

The garbage truck driver was interviewed by the *Detroit News* upon his retirement after 31 years of collecting garbage. "I hated the job at first," he said, "But I grew to love it. I got to know my customers as well as the milkman. It's surprising how much you can find out about people by looking at their garbage cans!" Our garbage collector points up the fact that all men seek to make their work dignified, if not interesting, in their own eyes as well as the eyes of the public; the professions are not unique in this respect.

Across Time and Place

Now a comparison across time and place. An account of medicine in the middle ages quotes 12th-century essays on decorum—practical guides to the physician on how to manage the patient in such a way that threats to the doctor's authority are minimized. Here is the artful advice of an anonymous physician of the school of Salerno:[1]

> At your entrance inquire of him who greets you from what disease the sick man suffers and how his illness progresses: this is advisable in order that when you come to him you may not seem entirely uninformed as to the illness. . . . Entering the sick-room you should have neither proud nor greedy countenance; you should [make] . . . a few remarks in which you praise the neighborhood, commend the arrangements of the house, if it seems appropriate, or compliment the liberality of the family.
>
> Then turning to the patient you may ask how it goes with him, and have him put out his arm. At first there may be differences between your own state and that of the patient, either because he is excited at your arrival, or because he is worried about the size of your fee, so that you find the pulse rather confusing; therefore you should consider the pulse only after the patient has become steadier . . . observe the pulse for at least 100 beats in order to feel all its variations, and thus you will be able to satisfy the expectant bystanders with words which they are glad to hear.
>
> Next have the urine brought to you that the sick man may see you study his illnesses not only from the pulse but from the urine. When examining the urine you should observe its color, substance, quantity and content; after which you may promise the patient that with the help of God you will cure him. As you go away, however, you should say to his servants that he is in a very bad way, because if he recovers you will receive great credit and praise, and if he dies, they will remember that you despaired of his health from the beginning. Meanwhile, I urge you not to turn a lingering eye upon his wife, his daughter, or his maid servant, for this sort of thing blinds the eye of the doctor, averts the favor

[1]Quoted in David Riesman, M.D., *The Story of Medicine in the Middle Ages* (New York: Paul B. Hoeber, 1935), 40–42.

of God, and makes the doctor abhorrent to the patient and less confident in himself. Be therefore careful in speech, respectable in conduct, attentively seeking Divine aid. If the people of the house invite you to a meal, as often happens, do not seem too much gratified, and do not seek the first place at the table, although it is the custom to give this to the priest or the doctor. Do not criticize the food or drink, and when in the country do not show distaste for country food, for example, millet bread, even though you can scarcely control your stomach.

Our Salerno physician reminds us that many professions have been with us a long time and that even the established professions in the past, as now, had to make heroic efforts to sustain professional authority. This delightful man also recalls a time when the typical physician had to maintain his dignity and his control over the client without the elaborate machinery of social support we call the hospital.

My last quotation is from a *New York Times* dispatch from Pretoria, South Africa, headed "WITCH DOCTORS CONVENE!" "Once a year," the *Times* reports,

this South African capital, 36 miles south of Johannesburg, is the scene of one of the strangest conventions in the world—the meeting of the African Dingaka Association, the organization of South Africa's witch doctors. To the most recent meeting this October came 900-odd delegates, some arriving in flashy American-made automobiles, some in jalopies and some on foot. Many of the men wore the conservative gray, brown or black suit one might see on an American country doctor. The woman practitioners adorned their gaily-colored native dresses with beads and gaudy feathers. And like convention-goers anywhere, all wore delegate badges.

The delegates spent three days listening to discussions of what to do about 10,000 witch doctors practicing outside the 4,000-member association; sharing secrets and new discoveries, and watching demonstrations of new techniques.

Like any other professional organization, the Dingaka Association has standards which it insists be met. Thus, practitioners who employ such voodoo medicaments as animal bones, skins of snakes and lizards, and potions containing powdered rhinoceros horns and elephant tusks, were denounced as quacks; association members rely primarily on herbs and roots for treatment. Acceptable, however, at the convention apparently were the rolling of bones on the ground as a diagnostic aid and tribal dancing to ward off evil spirits. . . .[2]

The relevance is self-evident: all occupations wishing to exercise professional authority must find a technical basis for it, assert an exclu-

[2]*New York Times Magazine*, October 30, 1955.

sive jurisdiction, and link both skill and jurisdiction to standards of training.

With an eye to such comparisons among occupations, and across time and place, what can we say about the dynamics of professionalization?

Defining Profession

It seems wise to begin by defining profession. What is the difference between hospital administrators and garbage collectors, doctors and plumbers, that makes us speak of one as professional and deny the label to the other?

Both in the minds of the lay public and professional groups themselves the criteria of distinction seem to be two: (1) The job of the professional is *technical*. (2) The professional man adheres to a set of *professional norms*. The degree to which an occupation fits these criteria is the degree of its professionalization.[3]

A profession claims exclusive possession of competence in a specified area. This competence is "technical" because it comes from a systematic body of knowledge acquired only through long, prescribed training. The profession represents a monopoly of skill, which is linked to standards of training and which justifies a monopoly of activity in an area. It is felt that not just anyone can do the job, so the job territory is marked "off limits" to the amateur, often by law.

The basis of the claim to technical competence varies—with each profession emphasizing the distinctive features of its own background. Medicine, since its "reform" in the United States some fifty years ago, has emphasized its roots in the physical and life sciences along with high, rigorously defined and enforced standards of training designed to impart that body of knowledge. Contrast the ministry. Clearly it does not claim possession of a science-based body of knowledge. But it does stress rigorous standards of training, and its doctrines are well-codified and systematized, providing a technical base for practice.

The Norm of Selflessness

The criterion of "technical" is not enough, however. The plumber goes to a trade school, has an apprenticeship, forms an occupation

[3]The following discussion is based in part on H. L. Wilensky and C. N. Lebeaux, *Industrial Society and Social Welfare* (New York: Russell Sage Foundation, 1958), chap. xi.

association to uphold standards and regulate entry to the trade, and gets legal sanction for his practice. But the success of the claim to professional status is governed also by the degree to which the practitioners adhere to a set of moral norms that characterize the established professions. These norms dictate not only that the practitioner do *technically-competent,* high-quality work, but that he adhere to a *service ideal*—devotion to the client's interests more than personal or commercial profit should guide decisions when the two are in conflict.

Despite the temptation to adopt C. Wright Mills' cynicism,[4] the norm of selflessness is more than lip service. It is doubtless acted out in the established professions at a somewhat higher rate than in other occupations. Among the reasons: (1) The belief that the professions offer superior opportunity for service is widespread; it is one of the motives accounting for the excess of aspirants over entrance to these occupations—and there may be a self-selection of the service-motivated. (2) The client is peculiarly vulnerable; he is both in trouble and ignorant of how to help himself out of it. If he did *not* believe that the service ideal were operative, if he thought that the profit of the professional were his commanding motive, he would be forced to approach the professional the way he does a car dealer—demand a specific result in a specific time and a guarantee of restitution should mistakes be made. He would also refuse to give confidences or reveal potentially-embarrassing facts. In my opinion, the service ideal is the pivot around which the moral claim to professional status revolves—a point I shall elaborate below, when we discuss some factors promoting and impeding professionalization in the medical service occupations.[5]

[4]C. Wright Mills, *White Collar: The American Middle Classes* (New York: Oxford University Press, 1956), chap. vi.

[5]Professional norms covering client relations also dictate that the professional be *impersonal* and *objective* (limit the relationship to the technical task at hand, avoid emotional involvement) and *impartial* (do not discriminate, give equal service regardless of personal sentiment). Cf. Talcott Parsons, *The Social System* (Glencoe, Ill.: Free Press, 1951), pp. 433–39, 454 ff., and *Essays in Sociological Theory* (Glencoe, Ill.: Free Press, 1949), chap. 8. Except in degree of enforcement, however, these norms do not provide a clear demarcation between professional and non-professional occupations, for many crafts and commercial establishments foster similar work rules; such statements describe customer-clerk relations in established department stores almost as much a doctor-patient relationships. In the area of colleague relations, two norms seem especially well developed in established professions: (1) "Do what you can to maintain professional standards of work" (e.g., professionals tend to honor the technical competence of the formally qualified, avoid criticism of colleagues in public, condemn unquali-

The main rules of the professional game are usually expressed in codes of ethics, and in varying measure, acted out in the daily round of professional life.

In short, the degree of professionalization is measured not just by the degree of success in the claim to exclusive technical competence, but also by the degree of adherence to professional norms of conduct.

Becoming Professional

I want now to turn to the process by which an occupation becomes a profession.

As we survey the world of work we find an astonishing variety of occupations; the *Dictionary of Occupational Titles* lists more than 30,000. In the slaughter and meat-packing industry, for instance, you can make a living as: a gut snatcher, ear cutter, stomach washer (sometimes called belly pumper), hindlegs toenail puller, and a hundred delectable specialties. As coordinators of a more pleasing list of medical occupations (surgery, proctoscopy), hospital administrators are all familiar with the amount of specialization in the medical industry.

Occupations Seek Professional Status

It has often been said that there is a general tendency for occupations to seek professional status. The remarkable thing is that very few of the 30,000 attain it. Perhaps no more than 30 or 40 occupations are fully professionalized—an estimate that moves up or down depending upon how many of the scores of engineering and scientific specialties we include.[6] The professions of law, medicine, the ministry, and

fied practitioners, avoid too much or too little work if it lowers standards, etc.); (2) "Be aware of the limited competence of your own specialty within the profession, honor the claims of other specialties, and be ready to refer clients to a more competent colleague" (Wilensky, *op. cit.*, pp. 303–8). Both norms can be viewed as essential conditions for the maintenance of the master norm—the technical service ideal.

[6]An obvious ambiguity here is the overlap between a scientific discipline (psychology, physics) and a profession (the practice of clinical psychology, aerospace science). A science, in contrast to a profession, has no clients, except in an ultimate sense, society; and bosses, if any, are often indeterminate. The main public for the scientist is fellow-scientists, who are in a position to judge competence; the main public for the professional is clients, who usually cannot judge competence. The ambiguity arises from the fact that the scientist as teacher or employee may come to view his students or other groups as clients and reduce his sensitivity to colleagues, while the professional may have a high degree of sensitivity to his colleagues and reduce his openness to influence

university teaching have been established solidly since the late middle ages. The military, architecture, and some areas of engineering (e.g., civil engineering) were professionalized by the end of the 19th century; dentistry, certified public accounting, and several scientific and engineering fields came along more recently.

Some are still in process—social work, correctional work, veterinary medicine, perhaps city planning, and, of special interest here, various managerial jobs for non-profit organizations—school superintendents, foundation executives, administrators of social agencies and hospitals.

Those Borderline Cases

There are many borderline cases, such as school-teaching, librarianship, nursing, pharmacy, optometry. Finally, it seems certain that many occupations will assert claims to professional status and find that the claims are honored by no one but themselves. I am inclined to think that public relations, advertising, and funeral directing go here.[7]

Can a comparison of the few occupations which are clearly recognized and organized as professions tell us anything about the process of professionalization? Is there an invariant sequence of events, a path along which they have all traveled to the promised professional land?

from clients or bosses. The typical case in the professional world of the future (assuming a larger percentage of salaried professionals and more scientific practice) may combine elements from each model. At any rate, the scientist's disinterested search for truth is the functional equivalent of the professional's technical service ideal.

[7]For discussion of the forces promoting and impeding professionalization of these occupations, see M. Lieberman, *Education as a Profession* (Englewood Cliffs, N.J.: Prentice-Hall, Inc., 1956), and J. L. Colombotos, "Sources of Professionalism: A Study of High School Teachers" (unpublished doctoral dissertation, University of Michigan, 1961); W. J. Goode, "The Librarian: From Occupation to Profession?" *Library Quarterly*, XXXI (October, 1961), 306–20, and M. L. Fiske, *Book Selection and Censorship: A Study of School and Public Libraries in California* (Berkeley: University of California Press, 1958); R. W. Habenstein and E. A. Christ, *Professionalizer, Traditionalizer, and Utilizer* (Columbia, Mo.: University of Missouri, 1955), a study of general-duty nurses, and L. Reissman and J. H. Rohrer, *Change and Dilemma in the Nursing Profession* (New York: Charles Putnam's Sons, 1957); T. H. McCormack, "The Druggists' Dilemma: Problems of a Marginal Occupation," *American Journal of Sociology*, LXI (January, 1956), 308–15; L. H. Orzack and J. R. Uglum, "Sociological Perspectives of the Profession of Optometry," *American Journal of Optometry and Archives of American Academy of Optometry*, XXXV (August, 1958), 407–24; R. W. Habenstein, "The American Funeral Director" (unpublished doctoral dissertation, University of Chicago, 1954).

A "Natural History" of Professionalism

Such students of the sociology of work as Everett Hughes have pictured a "natural history" of professionalism.[8] Their studies are suggestive, but I think we may have too few detailed accounts and too little systematic comparison of the cases in hand to establish anything firm here.[9] In a general way, however, the following seem to be the necessary elements in the package, although the sequence may vary and one or another event be emphasized by one or another occupation.

1. An obvious first step is to *start doing full-time the thing that needs doing*. The sick were always nursed, but technical and organizational developments created nursing as an occupation. Hospitals have always been managed, more or less, but the development of the modern hospital created the occupation of hospital administration. At this early stage, the practitioners come, of necessity, from other occupations. As recently as 1948, for instance, a study done by The American College of Hospital Administrators of the careers of 1,000 members showed that they were recruited from 131 diverse occupational backgrounds and were greatly varied in education, age, and viewpoint.[10] Similar data have turned up for city planners.[11]

[8]For the neatest statement, see E. C. Hughes, *Men and Their Work* (Glencoe, Ill.: Free Press, 1958), pp. 133–37, on which I draw heavily. Cf. A. M. Carr-Saunders and P. A. Wilson, *The Professions* (Oxford: Clarendon Press, 1933), the classic history of professionalism in various occupations, and the work of Hughes' students, especially O. Hall, "Some Problems in the Provision of Medical Services," *Canadian Journal of Economics and Political Science,* XX (November, 1954), 456–66. Cf. T. Caplow, *The Sociology of Work* (Minneapolis: University of Minnesota Press, 1954), pp. 139–40. See also the work of R. K. Merton, W. J. Goode, and J. Huntington—e.g., R. K. Merton, "The Functions of the Prrofessional Association," *American Journal of Nursing,* LVIII (January, 1958), 50–54; Goode, *op. cit.;* and Merton, Reader, and Kendall (eds.), *The Student Physician* (Cambridge, Mass.: Harvard University Press, 1957).

[9]Among the excellent occupational histories available for such analysis is R. W. Habenstein and W. M. Lamers, *The History of American Funeral Directing* (Milwaukee, Wis.: Bulfin Printers, 1955).

[10]See *Hospital Administration: A Life's Profession* (Chicago: American College of Hospital Administrators, 1948) on the careers, and C. E. Prall, *Problems of Hospital Administration* (Chicago: Physicians' Record Co., 1948) on attitudes.

[11]A doctoral dissertation in process on the professionalization of urban planning by Harry Gold, The University of Michigan, supported by the American Institute of Planners. The recruitment base for welfare agency executives, too, was once heterogeneous: public administration, business administration, law, politics.

A Time of "Soul-Searching"

2. These early recruits *combine to form a professional association* and engage in *much soul-searching*—on whether the occupation is a profession, what the professional tasks are, how to raise the quality of recruits, and so on. At this point they may *change the name of the occupation*. In this way hospital superintendents have become hospital administrators; relief investigators, caseworkers; newspaper reporters, journalists. The change in label may function to reduce identification with the previous, less-professional occupation. Many, of course, are unsuccessful in this effort. Thus funeral directors or morticians have not escaped the public image of undertaker, and salvage consultants are, alas, still confused with junk dealers.

3. The question of training soon arises. The professional association presses for *establishment of a training school*. The early teachers, Everett Hughes suggests, are enthusiastic leaders of a movement (like municipal reform among the city managers) or protagonists of some new technique (case work among social workers), or both (probation officer is a new occupation based both on the prison reform movement and a new technique).

If these training schools do not *begin* within universities, as in the case of hospital administration, they always eventually seek *contact with universities,* and there is a steady development of standard terms of study, academic degrees, and research programs to expand the base of knowledge. A corps of people who teach rather than practice is an inevitable accompaniment. Higher standards increase length and cost of training and force earlier commitment among recruits. In the successful case, the standardized training is requisite to entering the occupation.

Defining and Re-defining

4. All this is accompanied by a *campaign to separate the sheep from the goats*. This involves further definition of essential professional tasks, the development of internal conflict among practitioners of varying background, and some competition with outsiders who do similar work.

a) Further self-conscious definition of the area of competence. It is here that a pecking order of delegation occurs: the doctor allocates much of his job to less trained nurses and laboratory and X-ray technicians; the nurses, as they seek to professionalize, allocate much of their less attractive work to practical nurses, aides, and nurse assistants; and these, in turn, allocate some of their work to ward helpers. A similar tendency exists among all professional groups in short supply—dentists, teachers, engineers, scientists, and social workers, all of whom are redefining their functions upward and at the same time are sloughing off their less-technical (or less-rewarding) tasks.

At the same time that the long process of defining and re-defining the area of competence goes on, and entry is gradually restricted to those willing to go through the prescribed training, problems of internal morale and inter-professional conflict develop.

b) The relations between the home guard who learned the hard way and are committed to the local establishment, on the one hand, and the newcomers who took the prescribed course, and are committed to practicing the work wherever it takes them (these newcomers tend to job hop a bit more in search of better working arrangement[12]) —this age-old conflict comes to a head. The newcomers see the oldtimers as a block to successful professionalization; the latter see the former as upstarts. If hiring and firing is out of the hands of the professional association, this remains a sore spot, for those who recruit take their choice and may prefer old experience to new training.

Competition from Neighboring Occupations

c) As with internal conflict, so with external relations: *hard competition with neighboring occupations seems to go with these later stages of professionalization.* All occupations in the human relations field have only tenuous claims to exclusive competence. This results not only from their newness, uncertain standards, and the embryonic state of the social and psychological sciences on which they draw, but also from the fact that the types of problems dealt with are part of everyday living. The lay public cannot recognize the need for special competence in an area where everyone is "expert."

[12]Half of the thousand hospital administrators in the association study mentioned above had made one or more moves among administrative posts within the six years prior to the study. Among labor union staff experts, men with the strongest professional commitments tend to be the most mobile. Cf. H. L. Wilensky, *Intellectuals in Labor Unions: Organizational Pressures on Professional Roles* (Glencoe, Ill.: Free Press, 1956), pp. 133 ff. This holds for nurses, too. See also Habenstein and Christ, *op. cit.*, pp. 87, 134.

The competition among clinical psychology, psychiatry and other brands of psychotherapy for the right to practice therapy is typical. But even more clearly technical occupations, like medicine, find themselves doing battle with marginal practitioners—with peaceful absorption as one outcome (osteopathy) and all-out war as another (chiropractic).

5. Somewhere along the line rules to eliminate the unqualified and unscrupulous, rules to reduce internal competition, rules to protect clients and emphasize the service ideal will be embodied in *a formal code of ethics*. This may appear at the beginning of a push for professional status (as in the case of hospital administration whose code of ethics was adopted in 1939, six years after the association was founded), or further along (as in the case of clinical psychology).

6. Finally, there will be persistent *political agitation* in order to win the *support of law* for the protection of the job territory and its sustaining code of ethics. Where the area of competence is not clearly exclusive, legal protection of the title will be the aim (certified psychologist, registered engineer); where definition of the area of competence is clearer, then mere performance of the act by someone outside the fraternity will be declared a crime (medical practices laws).

Barriers to the Professionalization of Hospital Administration

It is evident that those technical occupations which have gone through this process and which to some extent adhere to professional norms, have acquired extraordinary autonomy—the authority and freedom to regulate themselves and act within their spheres of competence. Elaborate arrangements, formal and informal, sustain this autonomy.

Now it is possible to argue that such control as these professions have exercised in the past will decline. An increasing percentage of professionals work in bureaucratic organizations (scientists, engineers, teachers, architects, even lawyers and physicians). These organizations develop their own controls; bosses, not colleagues, rule—or at minimum, power is split among managers, professional experts, and lay boards of directors.

This view that bureaucracy, or more accurately, complex organization, threatens professionalism raises some interesting questions. What is the future of professionalism? In what circumstances do strong professional commitments survive? Are professionalism and professional associations doomed?

I would like to make some brief remarks about these general questions and then consider the case of hospital administration and mention some barriers to professionalism, as well as some forces promoting it.

There is some merit to the argument that professionalism clashes with complex organizations. These service workshops acquire a life of their own and that life is not always fully described by the technical service ideal. The image of rational, technical work routines aimed solely at client welfare is difficult to sustain in many such establishments, whatever the occupation. Some hospitals are operated frankly for the profit of their owners. And in all hospitals, patients come to feel that much of what goes on is dictated by non-medical considerations—that many rules for patient management are designed for the convenience and comfort of the staff. (I do not think that everyone feels that way—only a sizable, growing, strategic minority.)

The Convenience of the Staff?

This is especially true where the disease is chronic and the stay in the hospital long. A sensitive study of TB hospitals by Julius Roth, which focuses on what is urgent to the patient, his timetable of progress, illustrates the point: Professor Roth notes that crucial decisions to discharge the patient, schedule him for surgery, promote him to a new activity classification, when made on Friday are commonly not reported to the patient until Monday. If an X-ray is defective, physicians at a discharge conference will not order another but will instead put off the decision in this case until the next routine conference. Surgery, of course, may be put off for weeks, even months, for the sake of maintaining a regular schedule for the surgeon.[13]

The difficulty of sustaining the fiction that all effort is bent toward technical service is even more apparent in the mental hospitals described by Erving Goffman in the fascinating paperback, *Asylums,* and the problems of maintaining professional status for any of the personnel are accordingly intensified.[14] It should be noted that rates of long-term disability increase as life expectancy rises. Thus, these cases of lengthy hospitalization should have increasingly-wide applicability.

All this is not to say that the hospital should be geared for full-speed production: this would mean more examinations, tests, conferences,

[13]J. Roth, *Timetable in Treatment and Everyday Life* (Indianapolis, Ind.: Bobbs-Merrill, 1962).

[14]E. Goffman, *Asylums* (New York: Doubleday-Anchor, 1961), especially "The Medical Model and Mental Hospitalization," pp. 321–86.

more irregular work (examinations and surgery would bunch up), less leisure, even less sleep, perhaps lowered staff morale and increased labor turnover. All this does imply, however, that when prison-like custodial care becomes a major institutional function, the technical service ideal will be threatened, whatever the anxious effort to preserve it.[15]

The Pre-existing Power Structure

A barrier to the professionalization of any new group in a service workshop is the pre-existing power structure. When a stranger to hospital administration first asks himself "What occupations are like this one," the answer is by no means obvious. Are hospital administrators like private welfare-agency executives? Many of the new breed of welfare administrators are social-work trained, they often confront active boards comprised of top-drawer community leaders, and they are charged with coordinating professional specialists and supervisors. But hospital administrators are rarely M.D.'s exercising authority over their former colleagues. Perhaps comparison should be made with school superintendents, men squeezed by the demands of community pressure groups, professional groups like the teachers, and the School Board. Or with city managers as they coordinate technical groups engaged in planning and relate them to elected officials and to the public.

I think that there must be one key difference, at least in degree. The welfare-agency executive, the school superintendent, the city manager —one of them faces a professional group so powerful as the physicians. The doctor is still officially a guest of the hospital, but, like the Man Who Came to Dinner and stayed for several months, he carries heavy weight and indeed, upon occasion, has full charge of the management of daily affairs. If autonomy in the technical performance of one's job is a mark of the professional, then hospital administrators, like pharmacists, must travel a rocky road. By legal and informal means medicine resists encroachment on its authority; doctors do not want administrators or any other group moving in on their territory.

[15]Even where the inside view made possible by long-term incarceration does not give the patient the impression that medical care is sometimes a subordinate aim of the hospital, the point may be dramatized in (1) the inevitable conflict between the needs of patients and the needs of teaching and research programs; and (2) the restriction of communication intrinsic to all status systems ("I'm not going to call Dr. Smith," says the nurse to the nurse's aide, as the patient gasps for breath. "It'll be my neck if nothing's wrong with her").

A Common Dilemma of Organizational Life

This fact reflects a common dilemma in organizational life: the simultaneous necessity of giving autonomy to highly-trained specialists and yet giving some occupations the authority to coordinate the specialists. Two outcomes seem typical: the layman gets control, as in teaching and librarianship; or professionals administer, as social workers in welfare agencies, clergy in churches, or professors in universities. Hospital administration may be something new: professionals and laymen together hire administrators who then must struggle for the authority to do their coordinating job.

If the hospital administrator decides to intervene in such touchy matters as the use and payment of salaried medical specialists, the control of the quality of surgery, a death from a new drug or anaesthetic, or sometimes even on more routine matters of scheduling or operations and admissions, or the use of proper techniques of sterilization, he is likely to be lectured about interferring with the "sacred doctor-patient relationship."[16]

It seems clear that hospital administration will arrive at an autonomy befitting professional status only at the expense of control now in the hands of physicians and board members who will not readily yield.[17]

We are now in a position to summarize the resistances to professionalization of hospital administration:

1. The area of competence, while requiring considerable technical knowledge, is not exclusive. The hospital administrator, like managers

[16]For detailed treatment of such matters see T. Burling, E. M. Lentz, and R. N. Wilson, *The Give and Take in Hospitals* (New York: G. P. Putnam's Sons, 1956).

[17]C. Perrow, in an analysis of patterns of hospital administration, postulates a cycle from trustee domination (when the central tasks are money-raising and community legitimation) through physician domination (when mobilization and development of medical skills and technology are crucial) to administrative domination (when the problems of coordination of interdependent personnel and facilities loom large). Perrow also describes a pattern of multiple leadership he observed in one hospital—a distribution of power such that no one of the three groups is in a position to control most of the actions of the others. "The Analysis of Goals in Complex Organizations," *American Sociological Review,* XXVI (December, 1961), 857 ff. With respect to the cycle idea, we have seen that the resistances to the third stage are strong. Multiple leadership is an attractive solution where the base of power of each party is roughly equal; indeed, the ideology of hospital administration—which accents consultative leadership and gentle persuasion—makes it doubly attractive. The instability of "collective leadership" in such places as the Kremlin, however, is suggestive (conflict seethes beneath the harmonious surface); in the long run such cases come and go.

of other types of enterprises, must be a jack of many trades—a planner of physical plant, a purchasing agent, a labor relations expert, a personnel manager, a cost accountant, not to mention public relations man.

2. The recruitment base, as in all newly emerging professions, is still quite heterogeneous. The professional association does not control entry and hence cannot fully impose its standards of training on all practitioners of the art.

3. Hospital administration is in a service workshop, which has a life of its own apart from the technical services it renders. Along with other occupations so situated, it encounters client resistance to the claim that the only interest it serves is its official one—that of the care of the sick (or in some hospitals, teaching and research).

4. The almost-unique position of relating as manager to the most powerful profession in the world intensifies the general problem of all professionalizing occupations—carving out an area of autonomous operation.

Forces Promoting Professionalization of Hospital Administration

I do not want to end on this sad note, so let me now speculate about some forces which will support the achievement of professional status among hospital administrators and perhaps bring them authority more in line with their responsibilities.

I look for a continuation of the revolution in the organization and distribution of medical care that has been going on for decades—the increased availability yet increased costs of medical care; the shift toward financing through insurance, private health and welfare funds, and taxes; continued reorganization of service, with more doctors treating ambulatory patients in the hospital, the rise of various forms of group practice, ultimately the development of regional facilities.[18] The research base for all practice, including more social-science knowledge of administration, will expand. Concepts such as preventive medicine

[18]The rationale for functional links between small, limited-facility hospitals and large medical centers located in the same service area is well documented (L. S. Rosenfeld and H. B. Makover, *The Rochester Regional Hospital Council* [Cambridge, Mass.: Harvard University Press, 1956], and Public Health Service, ''Division of Hospital and Medical Facilities,'' *Area-wide Planning for Hospitals and Related Health Facilities* [Washington, D.C.: U.S. Public Health Service, 1961]).

and rehabilitation will be put into practice more widely. In general, this adds up to a rising effective demand for service.

All of this, given the short supply of personnel and facilities, should mean a new division of labor in the hospital. The organization and training of hospital labor will become more like that of modern industry, working conditions improved, wage rates more rationalized (more related to job content). Above all, tasks at the core of existing positions at the middle and upper levels will be redistributed. Where does the hospital administrator fit into the pecking order I mentioned before—what tasks will he give away and what will he get?

Needed: Community Service Focus

It seems possible that the continued redefinition of the physician's role may redound to the administrator's advantage: the busier the physician becomes, the less time he will have to resist the kind of program planning and evaluation administrators can do best. The administrator who now finds himself completely immersed in accounting, personnel, purchasing, and housekeeping functions may delegate more of these tasks to administrative technicians and supervisors at a lower level. He can then spend more time relating the hospital to the community and developing the quality of its service. He can undertake long-range campaigns to educate his board. He can plan new programs, evaluate old ones. If statistics are available that show his hospital to be strong on such measures of performance as the per cent of operations in which normal tissue is removed, he will report such statistics to staff and board—along with the figures that show when performance is weak. If the community needs an outpatient clinic, he will devote the time to getting it underway. Administrative leadership may eventually split off from administrative routine, so that both may function better. A community service focus at the core of the administrative operation would, of course, facilitate the professionalization of the administrator.

A second tendency concerns not how work is divided up in the hospital, but how patients come to view the service they receive.

Patients Are Becoming Sophisticated

The educational level of the average patient is rising sharply and with it his sophistication about matters medical. There is some evidence that the big thing that separates the educated patient from the less educated is the former's critical attitude toward the services he is in a position to demand. A study by Eliot Freidson of patients in the upper Bronx sheds some light on this.[19] These patients had experienced three different kinds of medical care—solo private practice, a prepaid, centralized group practice in which everyday treatment was given by professional teams, and the Montefiore Medical Group under HIP which was in between these two extremes. Whatever the cost arrangements, one thing is clear: the less educated do not make trouble for the doctor, they are typically docile and appreciative and uncritical of what they get. Contrast the more educated patient: he is more likely to perceive insult from medical personnel or the self-deprecating overtones of being treated like a charity case. His stance on medical care is active and critical, not passive and accepting. And no wonder. The patient who had had a year or more of college was the one who had "shopped around" for doctors, made efforts to assess their competence, switched doctors, and so on. He is a pretty cool customer this college man—detached and demanding. He feels he is paying for a service and he wants service. If anything will reduce the uncritical acceptance of professional medical authority, the increased numbers of this type of patient will.[20]

I see this trend toward less docile patients, combined with a shortage of medical facilities, as encouraging an upgrading of hospital administrative performance. This upgrading will take several forms. The public relations sensitivity of hospital boards will rise. Just as boards of regents of universities feel themselves under increased public pressure, and transmit this pressure to university administrators who then try to cope with independent-minded faculty, so hospital boards will increasingly sustain the hand of the administration and seek some clear channel to the medical staff by which they can be both helped to do their work and held accountable for it. Board members will be more open to

[19]E. Freidson, *Patients' Views of Medical Practice* (New York: Russell Sage Foundation, 1961).

[20]It may be that the underprivileged and disorganized lower-tenth of the income-education distribution, insofar as they receive medical care, *do* give doctors trouble. Because of their involvement in what Freidson calls a "lay referral system" based on folk knowledge, because of their lack of middle-class disciplines and understandings, they may give the doctor due deference, but ignore his prescriptions. The point still holds, however: as a proportion of total patients, the less educated will give way to more critical types. Moreover, in the upper levels of the working class, labor unions and other groups plus the mass media will diffuse more information about hospitals, doctors, and medical care—acting as pressures not only toward the organization of hospital labor but also toward the reduction of docility among workers as consumers.

suggestions from the administrator when those suggestions are based on a concept of the hospital as a community service institution.

Consideration of the morale of both patient and professional will permeate decision-making. Carpeted corridors, piped-in music (hopefully without rasping loud-speakers), guides to conduct the client through the maze, shorter waiting periods all around—these will be the by-products. The bedside conversation among experts about a "negative prognosis," the assumption that the patient cannot understand the technical vocabulary—this wonderful way of treating the patient as a "non-person," in Goffman's phrase[21] —this will fade away as the patients in the beds bring a more critical attitude with them.

Meanwhile, whether the forces impeding or those fostering professionalization prevail, a shortage of hospital administrators will develop —and if this does nothing else it will eventually give them the independence and autonomy that come not from the claim to professional status, but only from attractive outside job offers.

[21]*Op. cit.*, p. 341.

The Qualities of an Administrator

Ralph N. Traxler, Jr., Ph.D.

The hospital administrator (or any administrator) has a problem of defining his job in the broadest, most conceptual terms. Unless he develops the habit of thinking of his duties as administration in the broad sense, he finds his horizons limited by the mechanistic problems of his organization. But to have this broader attitude the hospital administrator must school himself to think *first* as an administrator. It is not an easy task to do and in order to attain this broader outlook, the hospital administrator must set for himself these basic aims:

1. He must learn to outline major long-term goals and objectives of the organization, his people, and himself.
2. He must try to determine how these goals conflict and work toward reconciling conflicts.
3. He must become a part of the administrative leadership of his community. He must think of himself as a professional administrator and not as "the person who runs the hospital."

There are ways by which the hospital administrator can help himself achieve these aims—aims which, if accomplished, should do much to lift him to a professional status within his community. The key to this achievement is that he must do this job for himself. No one will help him. It will be a lonesome road full of pitfalls and discouragement.

In order to carry out these tasks, he must have fortitude. The reason is simple. While his job also requires wisdom, courage, knowledge, and moral character, the greatest demand made of the administrative person is the fortitude to stay with the job and face the day-by-day challenge of "Thinking Big" (or sometimes even "Thinking Little"). Fortitude requires the special trait of being able to make a decision and stand by it. Often, the hospital administrator finds himself bound by the tradition of his job and the many professional, semi-professional, and service groups with whom he is associated. Under the circumstances he finds it easy to assume the political pose—to become the well-liked office-holder type. His decisions seem easier, less bound with conflicts and disagreement. He then lives in a fool's paradise because everyone seems friendly, cooperative and considerate. His ''shop'' runs smoothly (he believes) and a minimum amount of change takes place to threaten his peace of mind. A more analytical look reveals the basic errors of his delusion. He has failed as an administrator by acting the jolly good fellow. He has made few (if any) decisions beyond the routine day-by-day necessary ones. On an even closer look he has given little attention to setting goals of any kind. This is the easy road because there is no need for change that might upset his tranquillity. Then, too, he has made no attempt to introduce new methods or procedures. But this is natural since he has done no goal-setting or planning. Worst of all, he has done little to establish for himself a reputation of professional leadership in the community, a leadership status that could raise him above the everyday operative levels so often associated with the basic service institutions—especially the hospital. So the administrator must have fortitude to make decisions. Unless he can make decisions, he will never attain the status of an administrator. And he will not make decisions unless he has the courage of his convictions.

The Administrator's First Task

The first task of the hospital administrator, if he intends to do a decision-making job and assume a real professional attitude, is to define goals and objectives. This entails defining goals first in very personal terms. No administrator can make the professional breakthrough without defining his personal goals. This is one of the hardest of all tasks because it means taking a long, analytical look at himself. However, until personal goals are clearly defined, there is little opportunity to look at the organizational goals objectively or to analyze the goals of people involved in the organization. Self-analysis means self-criticism.

The administrator's first task is to make a periodic self-inspection *in writing*. This, of course, is the supreme challenge because it requires truth and the strength of character willing to admit shortcomings. A clearer concept of personal goals will help the administrator develop a more objective attitude, especially needed if decision-making is to cut through the mass of personal conflicts that exist in every organization. If the administrator can get to thinking objectively about himself, he will take a long step toward thinking objectively about other problems and situations. Attaining a less personal attitude toward problem areas will help him to overcome the tendency to be the good fellow or office-holder type who fears facing the reality of everyday problems of his organization—especially the many dealing with human relations.

An Analytical Problem

Possibly the most valuable thing to emerge from an analysis of personal goals is the effect it has on one's character. For those who survive the test, a new confidence in their ability to tackle difficult situations should result. A feeling of accomplishment is the reward. First, self-examination must be done regularly—every six months to a year. Second, it should be put into concrete terms and thought of as an analytical problem. The practice of writing out the analysis has the advantage of forcing a more detailed look at personal goals. It makes the process real. And the resulting positive attitude helps develop a blueprint for action.

Self-analysis also has the advantage of presenting concrete ideas for comparison with organizational goals. Since administration requires a definite set of standards, the analysis of personal goals helps in self-development by facilitating the review of one's technical qualifications. Only by such a process can standards be established. However, this procedure can be discouraging and even frustrating. Gauging professional qualifications is a most trying task. It involves more than a mere evaluation of personal goals. It includes examining gaps in professional knowledge and drawing up a plan of action to overcome these shortcomings. Could any task require more fortitude and courage? This, nonetheless, is the true test of a professional attitude. And one of the first requisites of professionalism is establishing an attitude conducive to preparing more adequately to meet the challenges of the job as an administrator. For the hospital administrator this means a conscious effort must be made to think in terms of personal goals and qualifications. The more he practices this discipline, the easier he finds it to make decisions based on needs instead of emotion, guess work, or special favors.

A Formidable Task

Next, the administrator must take a careful look at the goals of his people. This is not easy because it requires a thorough knowledge of his associates and their objectives. There are few questions more complex than these: "What do my people want? What are their goals and objectives?" Objectivity in evaluating the goals of other people is as difficult as self-analysis. Our biases and our likes and dislikes are a snare which can entangle us in false conclusions. Again, there is the ever-present enticement of sliding into the role of office-holder when dealing with people. If the barrier can be overcome, we encounter the need for patience an integral part of the process—because of the time it will take to know the people in the organization. Since most people have some general goals, the administrator will want to examine these first. This involves understanding the person's need to satisfy his desire for security (physical and emotional), recognition from the boss and his co-workers, a sense of belonging to the group (a feeling of being needed), and the opportunity to advance in his job or profession. The hospital administrator has a particularly difficult assignment because of the highly diverse groups with whom he works—groups with many skills, goals, and professional standards. Determining with any degree of objectivity the goals of such different groups is a most formidable task. Again fortitude is required to do this task with skill.

The administration must consider very carefully how he arrives at the conclusions about other people's goals. Whenever possible he should write down all findings even though it means considerable extra work. This step will force the administrator to reach definite and concrete conclusions. The value of such an exercise is twofold. First, the information gathered may be lost if it is not recorded. Second, the practice of this kind of analysis is excellent experience. When an idea or fact is put into writing, it gives the administrator an opportunity to study his thoughts and search them for objectivity. And there is the opportunity for a second look.

Troublesome Conflicting Goals

By analyzing other people's goals, the administrator also can compare their aims with his own. This should be extremely useful in developing a better understanding of conflicts that are difficult to identify. There is no doubt that conflicting goals are the most troublesome to identify. Sometimes the organizational problems that plague the executive are really of a more personal nature. Trying to work toward understanding people's goals may give a sounder basis for judgement that forms the groundwork for the many interpersonal relations. In fact, this is the real foundation of good human relations. The administrator who takes the time to analyze conflicts between himself and his people will benefit in his future employee relations. However, since this procedure requires a good many value judgements, there is no easy road. Here, again, fortitude is a most desirable requisite. And courage of conviction is also a "must" when using value judgements. Such judgements try the patience of the administrator as much as any task in which he becomes involved. Value judgements threaten the administrator with his greatest risk—becoming an office-holder type. After all, it is a lot easier to identify goals of a positive nature than those of a purely selfish kind—or to recognize that there may be no goals at all.

With a clear understanding of his people's goals, the administrator will have available a most useful body of information to help him outline and understand organizational goals. Unfortunately, the organization is often considered in a highly impersonal manner. Yet the organization is really little more than the sum total of people and their goals. However, the goals of people can be influenced by the organization. And the organization's goals may have a definite long-range effect on the administrator. In our democratic system we put people above the organization and herein lies the main dilemma of the management man. How can he achieve long-range organizational goals unless they are in some way identified with human aspirations, fears, and hopes? This is why the student of administration is spending increasingly more time studying the behavioral and social sciences.

Since the major job of the administrator is the shaping of organizational goals and reconciling these with those of the people involved, it might help to identify goals that are universal to *all* organization. These are: (1) to maximize the use of all facilities—economic and human; (2) to work toward a common purpose; (3) to sustain a long-range growth potential; and (4) to establish a position for the organization in the community.

Human and Economic Resources

No organization can grow unless it makes maximum use of its economic and human resources. Unfortunately, the maximum use of facilities sometimes conflicts with human needs. So it is vital that the administrator consider each decision he makes in the light of these conflicts. This is why the exercise of goal-setting is such an important factor. He should make a decision even when it might be easier to do nothing. This, in general terms, means he must understand his people *and* have a knowledge of both human and economic resources. Since the conflicts between people and the utilization of facilities will always exist, the administrator must learn to recognize and accept this fact as a reality. He must learn to deal with these conflicts and work toward solutions. This is just one of the challenges of his job. If he learns to deal with them, he is an administrator. If he tries to ignore such conflicts and does nothing, he is little more than another employee. He may be called many things but he is certainly not an administrator.

And, under such circumstances, he will begin to feel the frustration of doing nothing.

The recognition of conflicts between people and the economic factors of his organization demand continuous attention to a mass of complex human problems and facilities. It is not an easy job. It takes courage combined with wisdom that evolves from an alert and creative personal attention to details of an everyday type. The administrator also must reconcile his own goals where they might clash with those of his staff members. And he may find all his goals in conflict with those of the organization.

If the administrator can achieve these ends, he approaches the satisfaction of the second universal organization goal—the achievement of a common purpose. This really means creating a team operation. No organization can sustain long-range growth potential or establish its place in the community without the common purpose objective. The very fact that organizational goals are closely related adds emphasis to the complexity of this part of the administrator's task. It is obvious that success is not going to come by any easy formula or by the median of personality tricks, or through chance or even through intelligence alone.

Long-range Objectives

Once the reconciliation of conflicting goals has helped achieve a common purpose, the long-range growth potential becomes much less of a problem to the administrator. But even the common purpose will not help achieve long-range growth unless the administrator works with long-range objectives in mind. Therefore, he must definitively spell out where he hopes the organization will be in the future. And this means the administrator must carefully consider the goals of the community. He must work to know and *understand* his community, its people, its political and economic background, its shortcomings, its strengths. This is a most tedious assignment. Patience and knowledge must be combined if his work is to be carried out with skill. Then, the administrator must educate his community to his organization's goals. The education of the people in his organization concerning community needs is equally necessary. These objectives will not be achieved easily or quickly. His frustrations and disappointments will be many and patience will be required for this part of his task. But if the complex goals and objectives of the organization are realized in *any* measure, it will happen because he has taken the time to reconcile and understand how personal and organizational goals may conflict. If he does this well, he will be accepted as a professional by people in the organization and the community.

Although "professional status" can be achieved by gaining organizational goals, there are other factors that will help earn the administrator acceptance by the community. These factors are: recognition of community goals aside from the purely organizational needs; education of employees and the general public in special problems and services of the hospital profession; and establishing the proficiency of the professional hospital administrator as an expert in administration and in health. To achieve these objectives, the hospital administrator must become a public relations specialist. The kind of public relations needed for this situation stresses education as to the requirement for attaining the goals of the organization as it serves the community. This public relations work is the process of helping people understand the relationship between the hospital and the service to be rendered to the public. It includes helping the public understand the technical problems of the health services.

The Importance of Community Affairs

If the administrator must address himself to the goals of the community, he must also learn to think of his organization in terms of these goals. He must expend considerable effort to prove to the community his ability to handle perplexing problems of all types and to handle them with the manner and confidence of the true executive. Because manner and confidence are many times more important than action, he must become active in community affairs. Such activity is time consuming and seemingly not very rewarding, but it does much to improve his manner and confidence. There is no substitute for attention to this part of the job.

The administrator must apply himself with intelligence and imagination if he expects true acceptance as a professional. The acceptance will not come easily. The job of attaining professional status involves the most complex task of gaining public confidence and reconciling professional and technical aims with the goals of the organization, the employee, and the community. Its complexity is compounded by the need to utilize public relations attitudes and, at the same time, build a strong foundation of professional attainment. All of this will demand much of the administrator's time and patience.

The hospital administrator must work to reconcile complex and conflicting goals and objectives between the organization and the community. He must work to inspire professional respect from the community and learn to live with frustration and fatigue. He must work toward better understanding of complex community problems as they affect his decisions and his employees' demands. He must never show discouragement. He must, indeed, be wise. To be wise means to search for truth. And in the classical sense this means he must become a philosopher. But the administrator's only confidence will come through his *own* search for wisdom and the development of his *own* philosophy.

Problem-oriented Administration

Warren G. Bennis, Ph.D.

During the past decade we have seen a spate of creative, artistic, and scientific novels, plays, movies, and research which reflects some of the basic problems of our society, which testifies to one of man's most central concerns: how he organizes his productive activities and how he co-ordinates these activities with his fellow men.

Such films as *Patterns* and *Executive Suite* have been seen by millions of moviegoers and television viewers; such books as *Jefferson Selleck,* a novel of life in the industrial organization, will be read by thousands; while many, many other persons will be influenced by William Whyte's provocative *The Organization Man* and C. Northcote Parkinson's entertaining *Parkinson's Law,* both of which in their way point to the foibles and folkways of human organization.

In addition, there are two journals devoted exclusively to problems of organization and administration: *Human Organization* and *Administrative Science Quarterly,* while *Human Relations* and various other social psychological journals are increasingly adding to their contributions in this area.

Among the discerning authors are Herbert Simon, Harold Leavitt, Mason Haire, Chris Argyris, Robert Weiss, and others, most of whom have published in the past two years systematic efforts at conceptualizing the basic processes of organizational behavior.

The general purpose of this paper is to explicate some of the major findings from these various sources which have implications for the administrator, particularly those within the hospital setting. (I will not, however, confine my remarks to the hospital setting.)[1] Before surveying some pertinent administrative problems, it might prove illuminating to examine the background and structure of organizations in general.

[1]In general, until very recently, most of the research conducted on organizations has been focused on the industrial organization. Fortunately, more recently, hospital organization has received considerably more attention.

The Unchallenged Organization

Our society is probably most distinguished by an amazing establishment of structures known as organizations, systems wherein individuals co-ordinate their activities in order to produce something (i.e., automobiles, research patents, cured patients, graduating students, ice-cream sodas, etc.). These organizations, for the most part, have achieved peak efficiency and productivity. As a result, they have not been challenged.[2] Through the early 1930's, organizations—particularly industrial organizations—were thought to be analogous to a machine. As Max Weber, the German sociologist responsible for the conceptualization of the formal organization, stated:

> The fully developed bureaucratic mechanism compares with other organizations exactly as does the machine with the non-mechanical modes of production. Precision, speed, unambiguity, discretion, knowledge of the files, continuity, unity, strict subordination, reduction of friction and of material—these are raised to the optimum in the structure.
>
> The rational machine eliminates from official business, love, hatred, and all purely personal irrational, and emotional elements which escape calculation.[3]

This, then, was the image that men held about the organization of work, based on the early-twentieth-century Weltanschauung of rationalism: the organization of men is rational and predictable, based on the solid knowledge of engineering, economics, and physiology. Man, it was believed, is motivated by economic gains; man will work better under certain environmental conditions; man's performance will improve if we transfer engineering principles to the human organism. In short, it was felt that man is a maximizing animal, a hedonistic calculating machine. The spokesman for this school was Frederick Taylor, a mechanical engineer and the "father" of what has been referred to as "scientific management."

The "New Look" in Organization

Since the early 1930's there has been a distinctive shift in thinking and acting about organization, crystallized in 1938 by the study of F. J. Roethlisberger and P. W. Dickson entitled, *Management and the*

[2]Perhaps with the Russians' recent scientific successes, our educational and research organizations will come under investigation for "inadequate performance."

[3]Max Weber, *Essays in Sociology,* trans. and ed. H. H. Gerth and C. W. Mills (New York: Oxford University Press, 1946).

Worker. The dominant focus of organization was transformed from a rational model free from the friction of man's emotions to a model which appears to be less determined and less fathomable. That is, the "new look" in organization took cognizance of the unanticipated consequences of organizations: workers' feelings, beliefs, attitudes, perceptions, ideas, and sentiments—exactly those elements of passion Weber believed escaped calculation. Administration began to reappraise—in part through the seminal work of several social scientists[4] —not only their neatly drawn organization chart but the workers' feelings about the structure and hierarchy. What followed was the creation of another model of organization—let us call it the "human relations model" for lack of a better title—whose major assumption was that man could be *motivated* to work more productively through the fulfilment of certain sociopsychological needs.[5] This "new look" of organizations was no less rational than the earlier machine model, except that man's motivation was a more complex and considerably more elusive concept than the machine. What accelerated the acceptance of this new model of organization is difficult to answer; undoubtedly, this group of factors contributed: union organization, World War II, prosperity, a worker shortage, and research in the social sciences.

The revolutionary nature of some of the concepts which we now take so much for granted cannot be underestimated: informal group, worker motivation, morale, group structure, valid communication, etc., are now incorporated in our organizational argot.

"Comprehensive Medicine"

In a similar way, medical practice has undergone a profound development. Since the Abraham Flexner Report in 1910, *Medical Care in the United States and Canada,* with its stress on "scientific medicine," we have seen the evolution to "comprehensive medicine." Scientific medicine involves specialization, the development of the

[4]Surprisingly enough, the major contributors to this movement were foreigners: Elton Mayo, an Australian anthropologist, who inaugurated the now classic Hawthorne Studies; J. L. Moreno, an Austrian psychiatrist, who developed psychodrama, role-playing, and sociometry; and Kurt Lewin, German psychologist, whose pioneering studies on leadership are still influencing administrative behavior.

[5]See *Journal of Social Issues,* 1948, articles by D. McGregor, "Staff Functions in Human Relations," and I. Knickerbocker, "Leadership," for best explication of this point.

hospital as the chief treatment and research institution, with its depersonalized and fractionated services as well as refined procedures, exemplifying the ideals and principles of the scientific approach to the problem of disease. The great pioneering discoveries of the nineteenth and early twentieth centuries were capable of yielding to analysis the various organs of the body. The fundamental postulate of this period was that living organisms could be understood in terms of biophysics and chemistry.

Since that time, sweeping changes have taken place in medical practice; comprehensive medicine views man not as a fragmented series of discrete organs but as a total, functioning, dynamic person interacting in an interpersonal matrix. In a sense, the organization of medicine and the organization of industry have made parallel strides in recognizing the human elements in their system and elevating this position to the same level as the technological aspects of organization.[6]

Up to this point, organizations have not been distinguished among types; such as, universities, the military, research, hospital, and industrial types. Now, while there are important distinctions to be made among these various structures, their similarities are actually more impressive. It is my contention that there are unifying concepts under which all organizations can be analyzed. No matter what the task or goal of the organization, for example, we see, in all cases, a group of people working together under some leadership, attempting to achieve some goal. The individuals who come to work for the organization bring with them some system of needs which they desire to have satisfied on the job and certain expectations about the job they are to perform. On the other hand, the organization has certain needs to be fulfilled and a set of expectations to be fulfilled by the people who work for it.

Goals: Effectiveness and Efficiency

According to industrialist Chester Barnard, who has written on the subject of management, all organizations are geared—or should be geared—to accomplish two major goals: effectiveness and efficiency. By effectiveness he meant the job of achieving the organizational goals, some output criterion. By efficiency, he meant the creation of an

[6]Some say this shift of emphasis has gone too far. They claim that preoccupation with the human factors has created "psychotherapy on the assembly line." Workers become patients and patients—particularly those in mental hospitals—become workers.

interpersonal work system which would facilitate the output goals. To oversimplify, effectiveness relates to production and technology, while efficiency concerns the internal system of worker relationships—typically conceptualized in terms of morale and satisfaction. The optimum organization is one where effectiveness and efficiency are maximized, where the workers' needs and the organizational needs are satisfied to the greatest extent. Some recent research indicates that maximizing both of these goals simultaneously is the most challenging problem facing management.[7]

To appreciate some of the distinctions between various types of organizations, I have prepared a special chart in which I have divided the field of organizations into four separate categories: organizations which are concerned with the replication of standard and uniform products; organizations which are concerned with creative problem-solving; organizations which are geared to indoctrinate; and organizations which are concerned with giving services. Figure 1 on the following page elaborates these categories.

These, of course, are "ideal types" and rarely will there be an organization that falls sharply into one of these categories. Many Habit organizations contain Problem-solving groups in the form of a research wing, and, at the same time, many Indoctrination organizations also include Problem-solving organizations. However, this crude classification system does serve to focus attention on the differences among organizations.

Now, in many ways, the hospital organization as an example of the Indoctrination type is one of the most difficult to understand and the one in which the role of administration is the most complex and tortuous. For one thing, it encompasses aspects of all the other types of organizations. It gives service to the community and to itself. The hospital, furthermore, performs some functions which we usually associate with hotels—restaurant and living problems—without enjoying any of the predictability inherent in a Hilton chain. Disease knows no holidays, and we cannot expect a certain number of patients during certain seasons.

[7]Relevant to this see D. Katz, N. Maccoby, and N. C. Morse, *Productivity, Supervision and Morale in an Office Situation* (Ann Arbor: Institute for Social Research, University of Michigan, 1950). Also R. Likert, "Developing Patterns of Management" (Ann Arbor: University of Michigan, 1955); C. Argyris, *Personality and Organization* (New York: Harper & Bros., 1957). The findings indicate that there is no simple positive correlation between morale and productivity and that in some cases these goals operate independently of each other.

Type of Organization	*Major Function*	*Examples*	*Output Criteria*
Habit	Replicating standard and uniform products	Highly mechanized factories, etc.	Number of products
Problem-solving	Creating new ideas	Research organizations; design and engineering divisions; consulting organizations, etc.	Number of ideas
Indoctrination	Changing peoples' habits, attitudes, intellect, behavior (physical and mental)	Universities, prisons, hospitals, etc.	Number of individuals ejected
Service	Distributing services either directly to consumer or to above types	Military, government, advertising, taxi companies, etc.	Number of services distributed

Figure I

Diversified Staff

In addition, hospital administration—more than any other administration with the possible exception of the university—is responsible for a tremendously diversified staff. Hospital staffs embrace a range from virtually unskilled workers to highly trained and specialized professionals. To make matters worse, many of the professionals are protected from administration's jurisdiction by the specialists' professional allegiances and outside obligations. The academic robes and mantles of these professionals create special problems for administrtion unless it is prepared to offer what we consider excessive supplications.[8] This creates further problems in that highly trained people bring to their jobs

[8]For a brilliant conceptualization of this problem see Alvin Gouldner, ''Cosmopolitans and Locals: Toward an Analysis of Latent Social Roles,'' *Administrative Science Quarterly,* December, 1957, and March, 1958.

particular values and ideals which create real problems of communication not only to administration but across disciplines such as between nurses, social workers, technicians, and physicians. And, finally, hospital administration is a relatively new profession with all the growing pains of an emerging profession. As a consequence, the administrator may be viewed by himself and others as *arrivestés* in the traditional hospital setting.

In addition to a highly trained professional staff, hospital administration has to be concerned with volunteer groups who come to the institution for a variety of motives and who cannot be controlled by the usual incentives of pay and good working conditions. Almost all activity within the hospital, furthermore, is activated by some external agent, not formally included in the organization, namely, the patient. In most organizations, activity is inaugurated by some office within the organization, and thereby control and predictability are somewhat easy to manage. But, in the hospital, an outsider activates the activity for the system.

The hospital, moreover, has to be continually vigilant; in this sense, it is a good deal like an emergency and urgency organization such as the military. But, even there, planning and prediction can go on in a smoother fashion than in the hospital. As a result of this requirement of round-the-clock responsibility, the hospital organization has to be fashioned to account for any contingency at any hour.

And, finally, the hospital value system is imbued with a non-profit motive. That is, the hospital typically is not expected by the community to earn a profit but only to offer a service. Yet there are equally strong expectations for the hospital to be run like a tight ship, with all the efficiencies which we expect from industrial organizations.

Three Major Issues

Let us now examine more closely some specific problems in organization and administration and pose some alternative resolutions for solving them. I have chosen three major issues: (1) motivation and rewards; (2) leadership; and (3) communication.

An appropriate first question is: "Why do people work?" An even more basic question is: "Why do people do anything?" I submit that people work—or perform acts—in order to satisfy needs. This, I admit, sounds at once too simple and obvious. But let us translate this into the organizational world. An individual works in order to garner the means to satisfy needs. The needs of the individual are not simple.

They are diversified, complicated, and, at times, unconscious. Superficially, what individuals seem to want are a fair salary, status and prestige, an opportunity for personal development, and a job which will enhance self-esteem. The astute, intuitive administrator knows this and, even more, appreciates the fact that needs vary between individuals; he understands, furthermore, that an individual does not have the same focal needs at all times.

Now, in an organization, the superior is the person who typically controls the rewards—or means—for the need satisfaction of the individuals. The intuitive boss knows that, if he desires certain behaviors, he must reward those behaviors. When he does, the probability of their being repeated is exceedingly good.

The "Law of Effect"

Consider how we teach our youngsters standards of conduct. We frown when they do something we regard as inappropriate, and, at times, we even punish them more severely by depriving them of some privilege. Occasionally, we show our displeasure more actively by a sound slap where it hurts. But the process is reversed when they do something we like. Then we applaud or smile or give them extra privileges and indicate in a variety of ways how pleased we are with them. Psychologists call this the "law of effect"; that is, people tend to repeat behaviors which are rewarded and tend not to repeat behaviors which are not. And, simple as it sounds, it is truly remarkable how often this principle is forgotten. Yet it is significant in order to understand how individuals behave in organizational systems.

In the organization, the superior has to know, first of all, what is truly rewarding. Second, the superior has to take active part in giving the reward. I have heard any number of individuals bemoan the fact that "no one around here ever credits you with doing a good job." The implication of this is inevitable: "Why continue to do it?" Third, the supervisor has to be able to control and manipulate the rewards. For example, I may want smaller classes for my graduate seminar, but it may very well be impossible for my department head to control the numbers of students per class.

One of the studies that my associates and I have been involved in at the Boston University Human Relations Center does, I think, shed some light on this problem.[9] For the past two years we have been

[9]W. G. Bennis, N. Berkowitz, M. Affinito, and M. Malone, "Authority, Power and the Ability To Influence," *Human Relations,* Vol. XI, No. 2 (1958).

conducting research on the role of the nurse in the Outpatient Department. The study has been sponsored by the American Nurses' Foundation, the United States Public Health Service, Division of Nursing Resources, and the Rockefeller Foundation.

What Rewards Are Really Rewards?

During the course of our interviews with nurses and their supervisors, we discovered that nurses desired certain rewards which were significantly different from those they in fact expected to get. That is, there was a strong discrepancy between rewards "hoped for" and rewards "expected." In addition, those rewards which the nurse wanted were typically not within the scope of her supervisor to control. For example, the things the nurses desired were generally intangible elements in the working situation; such as, the general hustle and bustle of the hospital environment, seeing their patients getting better, good staff relations, personal growth, etc. Typically, the supervisor thought of rewards in terms of pay and promotion. The irony, here, is that nurses' pay is fairly standard, so that pay alone does not serve as a good motivator unless it is substantially higher. And the nurse does not usually view promotion as a reward! In fact, our data and other data collected on nurses indicate that promotion may be seen as a punishment rather than a reward.[10] Nurses can usually be promoted only to an administrative or supervisory post which, some feel, takes them away from their training and disposition. Incidentally, our findings show that where nurses had a high degree of congruence between rewards "hoped for" and "expected," supervisors generally were made more effective in their leadership.[11] In one of the hospitals in our study sample, there was no commonality of rewards "hoped for" and "expected"; this was the lowest hospital in terms of leadership performance.

What can we learn from this? Well, first of all, the administrator needs to know what rewards are in fact perceived as rewards. He can

[10]See W. G. Bennis, N. Berkowitz, M. Affinito, and M. Malone, "Reference Groups and Loyalties in the Outpatient Department," *Administrative Science Quarterly,* March, 1958. See also C. Argyris, "Diagnosing Human Relations," in *Organizations: A Case Study of a Hospital* (New Haven, Conn., 1956).

[11]The proportion of nurses where there was at least one reward that was both "hoped for" and "expected" ranged from 52 per cent in one of our seven hospitals to 0 per cent in another.

do this by attempting to find out why people come to work at his institution. The hospital is a very complicated system, and individuals join it for a variety of reasons: some enjoy the prestige, others, the research opportunities; some because of a strong social conscience; others to work with important people; still others for highly personal reasons, etc. Unquestionably, many doctors work in clinics in order to facilitate their training and are not particularly concerned at this stage of their career about the financial income. Having assessed the needs of our working staff, we then have to plan the degree to which we can satisfy them. Thus the first question concerns accurate perception; the second, administrative control.[12] The third step is to indicate quite clearly that these rewards are given for specific behavior. Psychological evidence shows unequivocally that rewards which follow behavior as quickly as possible reduce any ambiguity on the part of the individual. There is nothing as eerie as being rewarded for the wrong thing or being rewarded months later for some performance which you have already decided does not bring rewards.

Another Perplexing Problem

The question of accurate perception of the reward menu of the workers is one of the most important—and neglected—problems in all types of organizations—not just hospitals.

Leadership or administrative style is a perplexing and perennial problem in organizations. For centuries man has been attempting to divine the mysteries of leadership, its conditions and its men. Are leaders born or made? Is it the situation that brings out the man or the man who creates the situation? The debate raged between Tolstoi and Carlyle, for example, for many years. Tolstoi believed that man was a pawn, swept along in some inexorable sea; that the conditions of the time produced the need for a man fortunate enough to be in a position for leadership, Stephen Vincent Benét, in one of his most clever short stories, showed how Major Louis Bonaparte died as an obscure major in the south of France at a time when there was no revolution. Carlyle took just the opposite point of view. He believed that great men, imbued with certain traits, could create the situation whereby their leadership qualities would be recognized.

[12]In our nursing study we discovered that of the eighty-eight gratifications (or rewards) nurses obtained from their jobs, none was actively under the administrative control of supervisors.

Leadership Differs with Situations

Our psychological research over the past fifty years has reflected this dispute. During the first thirty years or so of this century, most of the research conducted assumed that leadership was a property of the individual, that a limited number of people were uniquely endowed with abilities and traits which made it possible for them to become leaders. These abilities and traits were believed to be inherited rather than acquired. Examination of this literature reveals an imposing number of supposedly essential characteristics of the successful leader—over 300, in fact.[13] The trouble is that only 5 per cent of the 310 traits uncovered showed up on more that a few lists, and, consequently, the leaders studied varied enormously. Thus, while the quest for certain underlying traits which are inborn goes on, present research is looking more at the behavior of individuals in leadership situations.

The research generally indicated that leadership varies enormously from one situation to the other; that, depending on the particular situation, a leader may emerge with a given set of qualities. This point of view makes sense. It simply states that different kinds of individuals may be leaders in different situations, that leaders of the bridge clubs or the Rotary Club may behave quite differently from community and political and organizational leaders. A tycoon supervising an industrial empire may be quite inadequate in supervising his own family. What is suggested might be stated in this manner: *leadership results from a particular person satisfying organizational needs or creating conditions where these needs may be satisfied.* This sounds simple, but it has profound implications. For one thing, it indicates that leaders do not have to be born with certain mystical properties but that they are definitely trainable. And what leaders should be trained in is increased sensitivity to diagnosing and sensitivity to organizational and group needs.[14]

There is another implication of this, supported by other research: It is probably neither realistic nor practical for the officially designated leader—that is, one person—to fulfill all the needs of his group or organization. There are too many roles and functions, both of efficien-

[13]See D. McGregor, "Leaders and Management Development" (Massachusetts Institute of Technology Memo, 1958). Also C. A. Gibb, "Leadership" in *Handbook of Social Psychology*, ed. G. Lindzey (Cambridge, Mass.: Addison-Wesley Press, 1954).

[14]It is probably significant to note that the type of training which has expanded over the past ten years is the laboratory approach of the National Training Laboratory, which attempts to train individuals in diagnostic and sensitivity skills in a small-group setting.

cy and of effectiveness, that have to be played. It appears to me that the best leaders are those who capitalize on what other members of their organization can bring to bear on satisfying existing needs of the staff, without, of course, losing their own important position.[15]

Few Leaders Are Omniscient

This is easier said than done. Most bosses, unfortunately, view the distribution of responsibility as the loss of their own command and leadership. In actuality, however, it creates a more productive staff or group, inasmuch as this increased involvement creates higher motivation, usually leading to higher productivity. However, sooner or later, I believe, administrators and bosses have to realize that they cannot possibly know everything, do everything, and be omniscient—not, at any rate, in this highly compartmentalized, specialized, and fractionized organizational world. President Dwight D. Eisenhower, for example, has a much more difficult time in our highly complex government than did presidents fifty years ago.[16] And more and more he is finding it necessary to delegate responsibility, to share functions with cabinet and bureau officers. We should no longer expect our President to know everything—a view apparently held by some of our news reporters. Nor should we expect it of a president of a large industry—or of an administrator of a hospital, for that matter.

In organizations, leadership, as I have said, is a perplexing problem because the leader, informally or formally, has to satisfy the needs of the workers and the needs of the organization. This is never easy to do. It is difficult to ask a person to work week ends, to give up part of a vacation, to work for less pay than he may deserve, simply to help achieve some organizational goal. An extreme example, to illustrate, would be the military leader who has to order his men on a dangerous mission. Now, all of us at times are placed into similar positions, although lives are not usually at stake.

[15]Philip Slater has shown in his studies that the most influential member of groups is typically not the same person who is best liked. These functions are most often distributed separately to different individuals. This illuminates the point made earlier about effectiveness and efficiency functions in organizations, i.e., it may be difficult for one leader to play both functions (see P. E. Slater, "Role Differentiation in Small Groups," *American Sociological Review,* 1955, pp. 20, 300–310).

[16]See James Reston, "Dilemma of the White House Q & A," *New York Times,* Sunday Magazine Section, June 1, 1958.

Recognizable Administrative Styles

How does administration resolve these crises? I have noticed a variety of responses which I would like to share with you. Perhaps we can take a "bird walk" in which I will describe recognizable administrative styles.

The first administrative style I call the "Yellow-breasted Symbol-manipulator." (Some call him "The Benevolent Autocrat.") He believes the job is best done by the "soft sell" method, by employing sugar-coated techniques backed by a fist of iron.

"Change the symbols," he says. "Give the workers the *feeling* of participation and involvement without the real essence of responsibility. Make them feel like 'one happy family,' where everyone can realize his own goals."

Underneath this thin disguise, however, we recognize the person who maintains power and control by the use of gimmicks and devices, by attempting to ignore or distort reality by manipulation. We have all seen examples of this: the worker who is told that, were it not for his screwing in 20,000 bolts weekly into a right-rear fender, the automobile company would be helpless. The tragic aspect of the symbol-manipulator is that no one, least of all himself, really is taken in. These administrators are the ones who have probably learned that direct coercion does not get the job done but that "soft-soap" does; that, by giving the *appearance* of democracy, they can gain the support of the workers.

The next most common type of administrative stylist, seen less in this vicinity and practically extinct, unfortunately, but noted quite regularly twenty-five years ago, is the "Blue-necked hardheaded Realist." He is tough and knows it. And what is more, he lets everyone else know it. He came up the hard way, and he is certain that the way to get people to pick up their socks and work is to tell them to do it in certain positive terms. His basic assumption regarding human behavior is that people are, by nature, lazy and indolent; that they respond only to force and coercion.

The "Laissez Faire"Type

In a way, the "Blue-necked hardheaded Realist" may be a little easier to work for than "The Benevolent Autocrat," because, at least with him, you know where you stand, whereas "The Benevolent Autocrat" spends so much time manipulating that you never know quite where you are.

The third type we encounter on this bird walk of administrative behavior is quite rare and is only found in the most comfortable, overprotected kind of environment. There is no easy phrase to characterize him, but perhaps the label of "Laissez faire" would be appropriate. This person, having recently returned from a human relations workshop, is eager to convert his organization into a "leaderless group." He is quite willing to abdicate all leadership responsibility to the group, with the utopian hope that by "bouncing ideas off one another" or by "pooling ignorance" a solution can emerge. The result, all too often, is chaos. This administrator may be well intentioned, but, unfortunately, he tries to dodge responsibility through abdication of his position of leadership.

The fourth type of administrative stylist is one for whom I have great partiality. He is rare and distinguished. Peter Drucker refers to his technique as "management by objectives." Chris Argyris calls it "reality-centered leadership." This leader does not abdicate from the tough decisions of management but attempts to deal with them by exploring with his group or organization the facts at hand, involving his people directly with the solution of the problem. His style is problem-oriented leadership and relies not solely on organizational power or status but rather on situational demands. This administrator does not try to muddy the situation by making it appear what it basically is not, nor does he rely on force and coercion. Rather, he tries to mobilize his people, to activate them to explore mutually the job or problem that has to be accomplished. He does so by communicating the problem, by insisting on involvement and participation, and by jointly working on the problem. His is management by objective, not management by control.

Role Flexibility Is the Ideal

Perhaps under different conditions and with different individuals, different styles of leadership would be indicated. Some conditions force the hardheaded administrative approach; there may be others when the "laissez faire" style would be more appropriate. Similarly, certain individuals respond negatively to responsibility and would be immobilized in a "laissez faire" atmosphere; others find it challenging. "Appropriate" is the key word—appropriate to conditions and people. What is demanded of the administrator is a role flexibility that is attuned to diagnosing what particular style is appropriate.

Communication appears to be the most current and pressing problem of all. Invariably, when I talk to administrators and ask them to name their most significant problem, they shake their heads ruefully and respond, ''Communications.'' Then they look at me balefully and helplessly as if I understand only too well what they mean. Actually, however, I do not! More often than not I have discovered a ''communication problem'' means different things to different people. In short, there is a communication problem about communication!

Usually, when administrators discuss communications, they are referring to some mechanical media, such as the hospital newsletter, the bulletin board, the internal routing of messages, or interoffice communication. Now while I think these media are important—and even indispensable—I do not really believe that they are at the heart of the problem. A good example of what I mean was provided in the last presidential election. It has been generally regarded that mass media, such as television, are not so effective in influencing the voting public as a personal heart-to-heart talk culminating in a handshake. And, yet, some recent research indicates that mass media are effective where the audience *trusts* the speaker; that this could be as effective as more intimate relationships when the element of trust is present. President Eisenhower was very effective on television for precisely this reason: the people trusted him.

Communication Is Understanding

This is the important point: the basis of valid communication is people understanding each other. An organization may have the most elaborate printing equipment available—yet communications may still be subpar. This is true, I believe, because people tend to bring to a situation their biases, values, likes, dislikes, and personal wishes, which tend to distort what they see, hear, and read, no matter how well the communication is modulated in its presentation. It is on the basis of understanding these personal and interpersonal feelings that we establish good communication, even with the crudest equipment.

A good illustration of what I am referring to occurred at the Brussels Fair, where America had an exhibition. Some of our most devoted and well-meaning American critics have been disturbed by the fact that our exhibit did not communicate to the peoples of other nations.[17] They

[17]See M. Mannes, ''Our Soft-Sell at Brussels,'' *The Reporter*, May 29, 1958; also H. Taubman, ''Brussels—American Mistakes and Lessons,'' *New York Times*, Sunday Magazine Section, June 8, 1958.

claimed that the other countries presented, for a much lower cost, exhibits which communicated the essence of their peoples. The displays of Thailand, Holland, England, and Japan are examples they cited. In these critics' opinions, Saul Steinberg's cartoons used in our American display were too esoteric. Furthermore, they felt that our exhibits were underplayed, there was too much of "soft-sell," which, they believed, presented a picture of complacency rather than that of an aggressive and strong land.

Is this criticism valid? If we had presented an aggressive display, would we not then have been censored for attempting to impress peoples of other nations with our might and strength? It seems to me that at this time, when our general public relations are considered to be poorer than they have been in several years, any exhibit would have difficulty communicating. I submit this: if our relations with some nations were not suspect, if people trusted us, the Steinberg cartoons would be understood and appreciated and our exhibit would be viewed as magnificent, modest, and honest.

Barriers to Communication

The same principle holds true in organizations. Al Smith once said he could "run on a laundry ticket and win an election." If people understand us and we feel understood by others, communications are first rate, regardless of the caliber of the mechanical equipment employed to impart the messages.

What about these barriers to good interpersonal communication? This is probably one of the most complex questions we can ask. Unfortunately, time and space considerations do not permit a comprehensive answer, even if one were fully known, which it is not.

One possible approach to this question, I would like to suggest, is to look at two factors: the role of the individual role-player in the structure and the status system within the structure. With reference to the first of these factors, it is generally acknowledged that individuals perceive reality on the basis of what they bring to a situation. Hungry people tend to see derivatives of food when they perceive, and sex-starved people tend to see sexual symbols. People who have strong, negative attitudes about Negroes tend to see Negroes in a way that reinforces their suspicions.

Translated to an organizational setting, we might state that all of us bring to the organization a set of beliefs, stereotypes, if you will, that focus and at times distort reality. This is particularly striking when we observe individuals' differing views and attitudes toward authority. Some individuals, on the basis of very early experience, view all superiors as punishing ogres; others consider them bland and benign. It would appear that, no matter how the boss really acts, these attitudes persist. As a result, when the boss says, "Good morning," this is considered a threat by some; by others, a reward. These individual needs which channelize our perceptions diffuse themselves into a variety of areas—not just the superior-subordinate relationship.

The Problem of Disparate Orientation

Add this to the fact that, in general, people tend to share the same beliefs and values of people they admire. It is impossible to say whether we agree with people we like, or like people with whom we agree. (Probably both are true, but our research has not yet indicated which is causal.) But given these two facts, well supported by research, that our needs operate to form impressions of reality, and this reality is shared by people we like, then we can possibly understand why conflicts and administrative tangles develop in organizations.

From the organizational point of view, we can observe a group of statuses or positions. In the hospital organization we observe administrators, physicians, nurses, orderlies, record clerks, personnel managers, research specialists, social workers, etc. Each of these positions develops—through training and on-the-job experience—a system of values co-ordinated with the position. Many times, these value orientations are in conflict. A good deal of research, both in the military and in industry, points to the fact that the position we hold—along with our personality—determines to some degree our attitudes and perceptions.[18] Thus officers and enlisted men had widely differing attitudes about a wide range of problems—from redeployment to eating facilities. In the industrial organization, we observe disparate orientations between the research and development staffs and the line production staffs. And, in the hospital, it is not uncommon for conflict to arise because of the particular orientation of the staff member. To illustrate: the nurse in the outpatient department may be concerned mainly with racing as many patients through treatment as possible, to clear the seemingly unending lines outside her office. The physician,

[18]See S. A. Stouffer *et al.*, *The American Soldier*, Vol. I (Princeton, N. J.: Princeton University Press, 1949); also S. Lieberman, "The Effects of Changes in Roles on the Attitudes of Role Occupants," *Human Relations*, November, 1956.

on the other hand, may balk at seeing certain patients because they do not fit his present research interests.

Many times, after one has become acculturated to the characteristic behavior of some of these professional roles, a barrier of stereotypes builds up which seems almost impossible to break through. That is, one is just so sure that a nurse or physician or clinical psychologist will behave in a certain way that no one makes the effort to listen and to observe to see if they really do.

Need Better Ways to Listen and Observe

What can be done to remedy these fixed stereotypes? The cure, it is safe to say, is more difficult than the diagnosis. In general, I would suggest that we all have to learn better ways to listen and to observe, in order to gauge reality more accurately. Unfortunately, there is no short cut to this proficiency. My associates and I have been attempting to resolve this problem by setting up, within hospital and industrial organizations as well as interdisciplinary research groups, training programs to develop more realistic images of the organizational roles. We do this by meeting with such groups as surgical nurses and surgeons, for example, and discussing with them some of the problems they are exposed to on the job. What typically eventuates is that the individuals begin seeing each other in new ways—in more accurate ways—not just as other staff members who have certain duties to perform. Often, they are usually quite surprised to learn that, underneath the garment of an organizational position, there is a thoughtful human being.

I do not mean to imply that all conflict can be ameliorated or even should be. There will be situations where there is a definite conflict of interests, and, at those times, unpopular decisions will have to be made. I am suggesting, however, that many of the seemingly insoluble problems of organization can be diminished when individuals share with each other their mutual concerns and perceptions. Under such circumstances, reality, with all its antithetical harshness and tenderness, can be dealt with practically.

New Orientation to Administration

Although I have covered a wide variety of what seem like disparate topics ranging from communication to leadership, there is a point of view—an editorial position—based on objective research findings. This point of view now can be etched more completely. In all the situations I have described, organizations have been viewed in terms of how people work together, perceive each other, and interact with each other. Organization, then, can be seen as nothing more complicated or simple than people working with other people. This approach departs substantially from the doctrines associated with "scientific management" and traditional bureaucratic patterns which very rarely included man in all his humanness as an essential part of organization. Traditional organizational theory regarded man as an automaton responding to certain forces around him—usually a superior. This superior was also seen not as a person but as another automaton, usually black with power, who, by occupying a position, had certain rights and responsibilities attributed to him. This new orientation to administration that I am recommending is markedly different from the bureaucratic pattern. It entails:

1. Wide participation in decision-making rather than centralized decision-making.
2. Recognition of the face-to-face group, rather than the individual, as the basic unit of organization.
3. Mutual confidence, rather than authority, as the integrative force in organization.
4. Responsibility of the supervisor as the agent for maintaining intragroup and intergroup communication, rather than as the agent of higher authority.
5. Growth of members of the organization to greater responsibility, rather than external control of the members' performance of their tasks.[19]

In Conclusion

To conclude, I would say that I can think of no more challenging role than that of an administrator in today's complex organization. He has to be the juggler of a highly important set of functions and, most particularly, the relationship between the goals of the organization and the goals of the individuals. Fortunately, this is not a No-Man's Land, but a territory which has to be occupied more and more with competent human beings—such as modern hospital administrators.

[19]See H. A. Shepard, "Superiors and Subordinates in Research," (Massachusetts Institute of Technology Memo, 1956).

Motivation and Morale

Oswald Hall, Ph.D.

There was a book written not long ago in the general area of motivation by Vance Packard called *Hidden Persuaders* in which he alerted people about the nefarious uses to which this kind of research and this kind of science are being put. Well, I suppose this warning is appropriate. In our day and age we are peculiarly respectful of the scientist. We're almost uncertain as to whether there are any limits to what the scientist can do. When he can flip a new planet into orbit around the sun, or when he can flick on to your television screen an unseen message that sends you out to buy more popcorn that you did previously, we ask ourselves, ''Are there any limits to what the scientist can do?''

As a matter of record, in this area they've discovered a good number of what I think are interesting things: For instance, the people who sell ''soap'' have discovered that—non-rational as it may seem—people don't buy soap in order to get themselves clean; this doesn't seem to be the reason. The manufacturers discovered this in a rather interesting way: if you take the ingredients of soap and put them in a bar and offer the bar for sale, the most you can get for it is 25¢; but if you grind them up, make a liquid out of them, put them in a bottle, and call the concoction ''Beauty Cream,'' you can sell these same ingredients for $2.50!

This kind of ''news'' has led the soap manufacturers to realize that you shouldn't try to sell ''cleanliness'' to customers; that what women want when they buy a cake of soap is ''beauty.'' So you offer them this, and they buy the soap incidentally. Similarly, you don't try to sell a woman perfume; you don't tell her that she'll smell different; but you sell her ''hope.'' And you don't sell her shoes; you advertise ''lovely feet.''

To people involved in administration this kind of research deserves some serious consideration. And yet, I don't think that we should allow ourselves to be too ''impressed'' by the achievements in this area. We should keep in mind the fact that administration is only partly a science; it is an art as well. And while we admire and perhaps suspect what the scientist can do, we must realize that his contributions have a limited use, at least from this point of view of the administrator.

If we look at the success of these people in helping the advertiser, it's rather clear that the help extends only to a limited group of items; that is, it is the luxury goods, peripheral items in our standard of living, that the motivation research can help to sell in this fashion. And moreover, that even these things can be sold only under rather special conditions.

The advertisers who tried to sell the 1958 motor cars "flopped" rather badly in doing this; Americans turned around and bought a large number of small European cars. But did this mean that these great, husky egos, which American cars are supposed to symbolize, had shrivelled up in the meantime? Obviously there's much more to selling an item than simply motivating the buyer by the use of this kind of research.

You Can't Sell Social Values

And similarly, this set of techniques is useful mainly for selling inanimate objects. It doesn't work when you try to sell human objects. Actually, the people who try to sell political candidates have found that one of their tasks is to persuade the candidate to keep his mouth shut most of the time; as soon as he starts to talk he often offsets the impression that the advertiser was trying to make for him!

Clearly, the techniques of subtle persuasion won't work in areas of real social consequence. And you can appreciate this fact if you ask yourself some questions: Could an advertiser persuade the customers in our society to substitute polygamy for monogamy? Or, take another illustration: Could the advertiser persuade customers *to refrain* from buying goods; that is, to practice poverty and humility rather than to seek an improved standard of living? I doubt very much whether this could be effected by the advertiser.

Or, to get to our own interests: could the advertiser persuade workers to change their work habits? For instance, could they persuade doctors to work less? Or even to earn less? Doctors as an occupational group are extremely highly motivated. It is their tenacious motivation to carry on their work as they think it should be carried on which creates a lot of the problems for the administrator who tries to fit them into an institution like a hospital.

How Doctors Are Motivated

What accounts for this motivation in the doctor? And how can the administrator use the motivation to improve his organization? In order to understand motivation, let us see how it happens, or how it operates spontaneously in work situations. We must recognize, with respect I am certain, the formidably strong motivation of doctors in their daily work. How did this arise?

I think we can say that the motivation in doctors is inculcated in them, without the use of any formal device. No wily advertising is used to create this drive; nor is there any hidden persuasion in the background. In fact, it seems to develop so spontaneously that we're likely to assume that it's something inborn in a doctor, and that he starts out being that way.

Well, I would not accept the notion that such motivation is inborn, or that it can be achieved by cleverly controlled training devices, or by subsequent persuasion and indoctrination. Rather, I would invite you to consider the possibility that we deal here with substantial social models; with the time-tested, long-life models, on which occupations are organized.

Here I invite you then to be sociologists, and to entertain the idea that an important part of any society is a set of work images, or work models, that lie in wait for each of us when we enter the work world. Let me suggest two models which workers may use, two that are poles apart in character; both of them are relatively dramatic types:

First, let us take a pharmacist working in the hospital who has in the course of his work become a drug addict. He gets his own drugs in this fashion, gratis, and perhaps sells some to fellow addicts. This is one model. This is the model of a racket. He gets more than he seems to get, while doing less than he seems to do.

Rackets are not uncommon in our society. For the people who take them up they are, of course, undependable models; others find out about them, and the models can't stand too much publicity. Hence, rackets have a rather high death rate. However, among rackets the high death rate is off-set by an equally high birth rate. Rackets seem to be part and parcel of our kind of society.

At the opposite extreme, let me suggest the model of a "calling." Perhaps in our society, as it has been suggested, people may have become progressively materialistic, and tend to sneer at those who heed a "calling." But be this as it may, I think you will meet a good many of them. There are, I would suggest, in your own ranks many people who would not only reject any other sort of work, but feel inwardly drawn to the kind of work you do. In contrast to the racketeer, you put into your job much more than you draw out of it. Nor is this idea of a "calling" restricted to highly esteemed occupations, such as your own. Janitors and cleaning staff may pattern their work lives on such a model.

Three Types of Work Images

In your own organizations you may have few people who respond in saintly fashion to a "calling"; and you may have even fewer who practice a racket within your organization. I assume this, and proceed to call your attention to three other models which one encounters in large numbers.

Generally speaking, your work organization makes use of three distinctly different work models:

1. The first of these is simply that of a job, something a person does in order to earn a living.
2. The second is that of a *position,* which one holds within an organization.
3. And the third is that of a *profession*.

These three are sharply differentiated models, both by those inside who practice them, and those outside who take note of them. For example, a person goes and gets himself a *job*. But, he FILLS a *position*. And in contrast to these two, a person is ADMITTED into a *profession*.

These three models provide markedly varied self-images for the persons who will work within them. I would like to analyze each of the three, along seven different lines. My contention is that each of these is dramatically different from each of the others, but each is also, one might say, a model of inner consistency; therefore, it's likely to survive in the face of whatever social change goes on in the society around it.

Let me say something about each of these three work models in terms of seven points:

1. First, the way in which a person is paid for what he does;
2. Second, the way in which his duties are delegated to the person who performs those duties;
3. Third, the way in which he is trained for the job;
4. Fourth, his relation to the work organization;
5. Fifth, his orientation towards authority in the work world;
6. Sixth, the kind of work-self that arises from within this model;
7. Seventh, the kind of a social-self that a person develops from utilizing such a model.

Let me consider each, in turn.

1. As far as remuneration is concerned, the person who has a job receives a "wage" for what he does. Now a wage is specifically a *quid pro quo,* that is, the person is paid precisely in terms of the services which he provides. These services, of course, are evaluated by the person employing him. A wage earner doesn't say: "Look, I put this much energy and effort into that job, and therefore I shall be paid on that basis." He's paid in terms of the employer's notion of what services he actually contributed. This is one kind of model for remuneration.

For the person who occupies a position there is no "wage." He gets a *salary*. Not only is it larger; it's paid in different ways. Salaries are not related to the activities and services a person performs. Salaries are commensurate with the dignity of the position within the whole organization. And this is the basis on which the size of the salary can be determined.

The people in a profession, on the other hand, have an idyllic picture of themselves as "people who receive a fee." And traditionally the "fee" represents an impersonal transaction. A bill is submitted; a payment is made; and no money ever passes between the hands of the professional and the person who receives the service. This is a different model, an interesting model, on which remuneration is patterned. Should you ask how large the fee shall be, the recipient of the service has no voice in the matter; the fees are set by the fellow-members of the profession; they are set in terms of what they consider to be the dignity of their particular kind of work. And in their case, the fee is not based on the service or amount of time which the recipient received, but rather in terms of the service which the professional says he gave to them, which is a very different way of computing a fee.

2. Let us turn now to the relation of each of these kinds of workers to his duties.

The person in a job assumes that his duties will be assigned to him, by a supervisory staff, or by an administrative staff.

For the person in a position in an organization the situation is very different. He is expected to assume whatever duties and responsibilities are required to maintain that organization as a going concern. If he is filling his position he is sensitive to what the organization needs, and this sense of organizational needs prescribes what he should do in his particular position. These are very different ways of looking at duties; on the one hand, something assigned, inspected, and supervised, and on the other something which a person himself defines as being required of him for the good of the organization.

How are duties assigned in the professions? Professions are very jealous on that point. They like to specify, very narrowly, what duties they are willing to perform, and to prohibit any other group in society from performing such services. Moreover, most of the duties of the profession have a stable quality stemming from historic roots; a person comprehends his duties because a whole series of generations of preceding professionals have performed them, thus providing clear, historic models on which the activities can be based. In the course of time a profession develops an established code among its members which specifies unambiguously what they should do and what they should not do. Moreover, it specifies the proper penalties for people who transgress in either way.

Training Distinguishes Jobs

We may conclude that these are three very different ways of assigning work; that on this point these three models are highly distinct.

3. Turning to training, one can say that training for the job is a rather casual affair. It is something that requires very little time. Frequently it is a most informal matter. The worker goes to the job, watches somebody else for a day or two and "picks up the job" in this fashion; for certain kinds of work this is the essential nature of the training.

But for the person in a position within an organization, training is something which goes on within that organization as a rather diffused process. The person has to "learn the ropes," and learn his relationships to many other parts of the organization as part of learning his own place within that organization. As a consequence of this pattern of training, the person so trained is unable to transfer to other work organizations except to a limited degree. Although the training may be long and detailed, skills learned may have limited usefulness beyond the organization of which it is a part.

By contrast, the people in professions do not usually learn their work inside the institution in which they're going to work. The training of a professional takes place in specialized institutions, and, unlike training in a job, customarily is long and even prolonged. Interestingly enough, it is made of equal length for everybody who comes along; the dullest and the slickest must spend the same amount of time in getting this training into their systems. One might add that an important part of the training of a profession is of an intellectual sort; that is to say, the discipline involves him in absorbing a large range of ideas that are associated with the work.

4. The fourth line of analysis concerns the relationship of the worker to the work organization.

The person in a job has a terminable contract. Generally speaking, he's a hired hand. If there's no work, there's no job. This is the traditional relation of job-holder to job.

In work organizations those people who occupy positions develop a system of tenure. A person is entitled to his position, even if there's no work for him that day, or that week. And, in the extreme cases, even though he handles the work in a relatively incompetent fashion, he's entitled to remain within that kind of position—within limits, of course. The person who has been appointed to a position can, in a great measure, expect that there's some kind of semi-permanent, or, in many cases, genuinely permanent, tenure. This sharply differentiates the holder of a position from the person who has a job, who is hired, who can be dropped at the end of the week.

The Professional's Relationship

But what about the relationship of the professional to a work organization? This is an interesting point. Professionals like to serve in an "advisory capacity," or to occupy a "staff" position, rather than be a part of the main line of the organization. Or, if they are admitted into the organization, they tend to develop an autonomous empire of their own within the organization. For instance, the medical people who come into a manufacturing organization are likely to develop a medical service which is largely autonomous. Hence again we have a distinctive model of relating a person to the organization.

One might add here, too, that very frequently the person in a profession, who relates himself thus to an organization, has the feeling that this is the "second best" way of carrying on his work. The lawyer who moves into a business on a salary will find himself referred to by his colleagues, rather indelicately, as a "kept" lawyer. This distinction between the "free" lawyer who sells his services for a fee on the one hand, and the person who "attaches" himself by a salary, is an interesting line that we see cutting through a great range of professions in our society. This seems to indicate that working *within* an organization is considered inferior to working for fees. By contrast, for the persons who occupy positions or hold jobs there are no alternative ways of relating oneself to work.

5. What is the relationship of each of these three models to the system of authority which operates in an organization? Parenthetically, I don't see how you can run a large organization without this very interesting device—the notion of authority—by which one person willingly accedes to the demands of another, and the person who makes those demands feels no guilt about making demands upon those around them. This, I insist, is a fundamental kind of human relationship, and it seems to me an essential requirement for a large-scale organization. But how do these various kinds of workers relate to authority?

The person with a job, one might say, always works under supervision. There's always an inspector or foreman who has the right to question how he's performing. Moreover, he is expected to be deferential to persons placed over him in this fashion. And this puts him on a one-way street, so to speak. He must be deferential to those above him; but there's nobody down below him who must be deferential towards him. And this is one of the main differences between a person with a job and a person in a position. The person with a position is caught up in a chain of positions; and if he must be deferential to those above him this is nicely balanced by those below who must be deferential towards him. And there is a great deal of difference, I insist, between the kind of work model in which deference is a one-sided affair and those positions where it's mutual.

True, a person in a position cannot demand deference from a person to whom he owes deference; but there is deference built into his position which compensates for the other side of the relationship. Moreover, this deference is associated with a kind of dignity that the person is expected to enjoy and perhaps to display.

There is not much in the way of dignity that can be built into a job. But dignity can very easily be built into a position. In fact, one of the big hazards of large-scale organizations is that the people who administer them tend to become *dignitaries,* that is, they become invested with the dignity of their positions to the point where they lose concern for their daily tasks.

As for the professionals, by and large, they're not very responsive to the authority pattern of large-scale organizations because, historically, they have been self-controlling. This has been the nature of the profession, that *nobody* outside it sets up a standard for its activities, or supervises these in any fashion. Over the course of generations professions have tended to become autonomous in this sense. Where you have a true profession every man calls the other "brother," that is, they view one another as "colleagues"; they are leagued together in a coordinate fashion of equality, one to another. Therefore, they can have dignity without deference; they have need to be deferential toward no one in living up to the demands of their own particular kind of work, indeed deference to outsiders seems distasteful.

Job Identification Actually Hinders

6. We turn to the sixth of these points, the matter of the kind of work-self that a person develops by virtue of carrying on a particular kind of work. What sort of a "self" does the person on the job develop? It seems to me that it has two components. "Self" is likely to be a reflection of the group of workers within which one is cast. The identification of the job-holder is largely restricted to the fellow workers one meets daily.

Having said that I would add that, generally speaking, this identification is counter-organization; it is contrary to the goals of the organization. This seems to be a built-in characteristic of the self-definition that comes to the person who holds a job; he develops solidarity toward fellow workers, but suspicion and hostility toward those in authority over him.

For the person who holds a position, his definition of his "self" his work self, his work identification—becomes one of seeing himself as part of an organization. An executive who has worked for Ford becomes a "Ford man"; an executive who works for Sears Roebuck becomes a "Sears man." And it means that this "self" that grows up tends to see the boundaries between self and organization as very fluid. On the other hand, he does *not* characteristically develop warm relationships with those about him, because he's usually a man who's on the move; he's mobile, he's getting ahead in the world. It's dangerous for him to identify too closely with his associates, because it may hurt them and him if he moves up in such a situation. Hence, the typical occupant of a position develops relatively brittle relationships with those around him. And so he must, if he wishes to have an independent career and climb up within an organization. If he's going to be an "organization man" and advance in the organization, he cannot give too many hostages to those immediately round about him and with whom he works.

Now for the professional. What can we say about his identification? One item has been alluded to already. Professions usually have historic elements in them. They can look back a long way in time. And by being able to do so they can look back to the "saints" that arose in their work, and the "heroes" who achieved within it. Thus, the person who becomes a professional develops a "work-self," an image of himself as far as his work is concerned, that relates to the historic type.

His self-image, then, as far as his work is concerned, is both with his colleagues on the one hand, the living colleagues, and with the historic figures, saintly, heroic and otherwise, that have developed in the course of time. Moreover, he is likely to feel that the prestige of this historic—I was going to say apostolic procession, but no, it's simply an historic procession of colleagues—that this kind of prestige is highly superior to any prestige that he could borrow from any organization of which he might become a part.

7. Now for the last point: What kind of social-self springs up out of the fact of being incorporated in one or another of these work models? What kind of social justification does the person develop for the work he performs?

The person who has a job can interpret it to himself and to others in the simple terms that it permits him to survive. Perhaps that is all he asks of it: it's a decent job, it enables him to get by, and permits him to look after his family. If it has these three characteristics it offers him an acceptable social identification; it is an instrumental device for doing these other things. His social self, of course, is firmly rooted in these other things: in his family and in his standard of living. Basically, a job simply permits the person to survive.

But not so with a position. The person who fills a position may feel, usually quite legitimately, that his position is essential to the survival of the organization, that if he does *not* fulfill that position, somehow or other, the organization suffers considerably. This is a very different kind of justification from the one previously stated, and permits a very different kind of social self to be built around one's work.

Now what about the profession? The person who is part of a genuine profession will tell you that without his profession society itself could not survive! He sees his profession as being the "kingpin" around which the rest of the society is organized. The lawyer will tell you that without the majesty of the law society would come crumbling down. The doctor can give you equally convincing arguments to support his belief that the whole society is dependent upon his efforts.

Why Workers Behave Differently

The kind of social self which emanates from one's work thus varies markedly from one kind of work to another. At one level the worker can say, "I do this simply because it's important to me to survive." At another level the person says, "If I do this, this organization survives and flourishes." At still another the person says. "Unless I do my work in the way in which it's supposed to be done, society itself will crumble in some essential kind of way."

All three of these—the job, the position, the profession—are social models that are in the world around about us. We encounter them in virtually every kind of work. They represent constellations you might say, or clusters, each of which is differentiated, one from another. And each of the items in these, I would suggest, tends to support, mutually, the other items in the model. In this sense these models become consistent kinds of molds for the persons who follow them. They do something more than this: They provide for those who use them a distinctive kind of "life mold"; one's life can be organized around these models.

You might say that they also prescribe the level of effort that one is expected to make in the work world. By an interesting process, they become "internalized" by persons; once internalized they become an essential part of the personality concerned. They are the social forces of motivation.

Now what I would argue here is the proposition that *most of the work world is organized around clearly distinguishable models; and that these models are so fundamentally different, in crucial aspects, that any failure to distinguish between them can lead to grief.*

If you have concurred in this argument, I'd like to make this further proposition: that *workers in these various categories behave differently because they are enmeshed in different kinds of social structures.*

A professional doesn't act like a wage worker. Perhaps he *can't* do so; he's bound up in a different social pattern. Therefore we, as students of organization, cannot use an identical set of ideas for understanding these different social patterns. It's at this point that I have to part company with those persons who attempt to understand workers *in toto;* of the child and the man, and of the *universal* patterns that appear in *all* cases as the worker fits into an organization.

I would prefer to argue that, for administrators, the trouble with these total schemes is that, by trying to explain all cases of motivation, they do not do justice to any of the variations between kinds of situations and kinds of workers. Therefore, I would argue that, as administrators, you should take instead the model of the medical man who must develop differential diagnoses to explain the different kinds of cases. The search for a single, all-embracing, explanation for poor morale would put us where the doctors were fifty years ago when they argued whether homeopathic theories or allopathic theories provided the solution for human illness.

In conclusion, may I return to our title: "Motivation and Morale." What do we mean by "good morale"? Good morale is sometimes interpreted as an attitude towards work, a cheerful warm-hearted attitude, one that ignores the minor inconveniences of day-to-day happenings; an attitude that lets the person plow ahead with a low-pitched kind of ambition, coated with "belongingness" and "togetherness," to use William Whyte's phrase. My view of good morale would be rather different. I would say it refers to work attitudes; but those attitudes that are good for the long pull; I think it refers to the readiness to press ahead with the job, with full recognition of the inconveniences that have to be endured, of the setbacks that are going to be encountered, and of the difficulties that have to be faced. An army that has good morale can fight back even after it has suffered a defeat. In fact, an army of good morale can fight on even while it's retreating. To get a useful analysis of good morale in the group, I would say that morale for a group is on the same level as good stamina for an athlete.

Other Possibilities Not Explored

Now my argument to you would be that men and women have always, and everywhere, faced this problem of finding the means to continue working at difficult tasks. And in their effort, in their common efforts, they have discovered or hit upon a few time-tested models that operate in such a way that the work can get done. I haven't discussed all of these by any means. I've merely mentioned the person with a "calling," the person who is drawn dramatically into a work that absorbs him completely. Perhaps I should have discussed the person with a fate; the person who is driven, relentlessly, into a groove from which there's no escape. It would be revealing to explore the work world of the scientist with its distinctive obligations and rewards. And so, too, the person to whom work is a hobby; the person whose occupation is his preoccupation, and whose vocation is his avocation. These are alternative models.

In closing on a practical note, may I suggest that one obligation of the administrator's role is to sort out the various models that are operative in his own organization. Don't expect professional standards in work that can't be professionalized; don't expect people to develop responsibility to organizations if their work is sheerly a job. Don't embarrass people in positions by offering the rewards, or stigmas, attached to conventional jobs. This advice is not particularly easy to follow. Organizations are dynamic affairs, as you vividly recognize. Jobs do become transmuted into positions; and people in positions strive for professional status and professional prestige. These things do shade into each other, and sometimes shift from one category to another.

Nevertheless, I would suggest that an obstinate effort on your part to understand the images and the models that are operative in your organizations will pay at least modest dividends.